Microsoft SQL Se
Survival Guide

Tear-out Card

Built-in Functions

AGGREGATE FUNCTIONS

AVG([ALL | DISTINCT] expression)
COUNT([ALL | DISTINCT] expression)
COUNT(*)
MAX(expression)
MIN(expression)
SUM([ALL | DISTINCT] expression)

DATE FUNCTIONS

DATEADD(datepart,number,date)
DATEDIFF(datepart,number,date)
DATENAME(datepart,date)
DATEPART(datepart,date)
GETDATE( )

MATHEMATICAL FUNCTIONS

ABS(numeric_expr)
ACOS(float_expr)
ASIN(float_expr)
ATAN(float_expr)
ATN2(float_expr1,float_expr2)
CEILING(numeric_expr)
COS(float_expr)
COT(float_expr)
DEGREES(numeric_expr)
EXP(float_expr)
FLOOR(numeric_expr)
LOG(float_expr)
LOG10(float_expr)
PI( )
POWER(numeric_expr,y)
RADIANS(numeric_expr)
RAND([integer_expr])
ROUND(numeric_expr,integer_expr)
SIGN(numeric_expr)
SIN(float_expr)
SQRT(float_expr)
TAN(float_expr)

NILADIC FUNCTIONS

CURRENT_TIMESTAMP
CURRENT_USER
SESSION_USER
SYSTEM_USER
USER

STRING FUNCTIONS

+
ASCII(char_expr)
CHAR(integer_expr)
CHARINDEX('pattern', expression)
DIFFERENCE(char_expr1, char_expr2)
LOWER(char_expr)
LTRIM(char_expr)
PATINDEX('%pattern%', expression)
REPLICATE(char_expr, integer_expr)
REVERSE(char_expr)
RIGHT(char_expr, integer_expr)
RTRIM(char_expr)
SOUNDEX(char_expr)
SPACE(integer_expr)
STR(float_expr [, length [, decimal]])
STUFF(char_expr1, start, length, char_expr2)
SUBSTRING(expression, start, length)
UPPER(char_expr)

SYSTEM FUNCTIONS

COL_LENGTH('table_name', 'column_name')
COL_NAME(table_id, column_id)
DATALENGTH('expression')
DB_ID(['database_name'])
DB_NAME([database_id])
HOST_ID( )
HOST_NAME( )
IDENT_INCR('table_name')
IDENT_SEED('table_name')
INDEX_COL('table_name', index_id, key_id)
ISNULL(expression, value)
OBJECT_ID('object_name')

OBJECT_NAME(object_id)
STATS_DATE(table_id, index_id)
SUSER_ID(['login_name'])
SUSER_NAME([server_user_id])
USER_ID(['user_name'])
USER_NAME([user_id])

TEXT/IMAGE FUNCTIONS

DATALENGTH('expression')
PATINDEX('%pattern%', expression)
TEXTPTR(column_name)
TEXTVALID('table_name.column_name', text_ptr)

TYPE-CONVERSION FUNCTION

CONVERT(datatype[(length)], expression [, style])

System Stored Procedures

sp_addalias login_id, user_name

sp_addextendedproc function, dll

sp_addgroup group_name

sp_addmessage message id, severity, 'message text'
[, language [, {true | false} [, REPLACE]]]

sp_addremotelogin remote_server [, login_ID
[, remote_name]]

sp_addsegment seg_name, logicalname

sp_addserver servername [, LOCAL]

sp_addtype type_name, physical_type [, null_type]

sp_addumpdevice {'disk' | 'diskette' | 'tape'},
'logicalname','physicalname' [, [, noskip | skip [,
mediacapacity]]]

sp_adduser login_id [, user_name [, group_name]]

sp_altermessage messageid, WITH_LOG, {true | false}

sp_bindefault default_name, object_name [, future_only]

sp_bindrule rule_name, object_name [, future_only]

sp_certify_removable database_name[, AUTO]

sp_changedbowner login_id [, true]

sp_changegroup group_name, user_name

sp_configure [configuration_name [, configuration_value]]

sp_dboption [database_name, option_name, {true | false}]

sp_dbremove database[, drop_device]

sp_defaultdb login_id, default_database

sp_defaultlanguage login_id [, language]

sp_depends object_name

sp_devoption [device_name [, option_name {, true | false}
[, override]]]

sp_diskdefault database_device, {defaulton | defaultoff}

sp_dropalias login_id

sp_dropdevice logical_name [, DELFILE]

sp_dropextendedproc function_name

sp_dropgroup group_name

sp_droplanguage language [, drop_messages]

sp_droplogin login_id

sp_dropmessage [msgid [, language | 'all']]

sp_dropremotelogin remote_server [, login_name [,
remote_name]]

sp_dropsegment segment_name [, logical_name]

sp_dropserver server_name [, drop_logins]

sp_droptype type_name

sp_dropuser user_name

sp_extendsegment segment_name, logical_name

sp_help [object_name]

sp_helpconstraint table_name

sp_helpdb [database_name]

sp_helpdevice [logical_name]

sp_helpextendedproc [function_name]

sp_helpgroup [group_name]

sp_helpindex table_name

sp_helplanguage [language]

sp_helplog

sp_helpremotelogin [remote_server [, remote_name]]

sp_helpprotect Object [, user_name]

sp_helpsegment [segment_name]

sp_helpserver [server_name]

sp_helpsort

sp_helpsql ['topic']

sp_helpstartup

sp_helptext object_name

sp_helpuser [user_name]

sp_lock [spid1 [, spid2]]

sp_logdevice database_name, database_device

sp_makestartup procedure_name

sp_monitor

sp_password old_password, new_password [, login_id]

sp_placeobject segment_name, object_name

sp_processmail [@subject = subject] [[,] @file_type-
= file_type][[,] @separator = separator] [[,] @set_user =
user] [[,] @dbuse = database_name

sp_recompile table_name

sp_remoteoption [remote_server, login_name,
remote_name,- option_name, {true | false}]

sp_rename object_name, new_name [, COLUMN | INDEX]

sp_renamedb old_db_name, new_db_name

sp_serveroption [server_name, option_name, {true | false}]

sp_setlangalias language, alias

sp_spaceused [object_name] [[,] @updateusage = {true |
false}]

sp_unbindefault object_name [, futureonly]

sp_unbindrule object_name [, futureonly]

sp_unmakestartup procedure_name

sp_who [login_id | 'spid']

MICROSOFT®
SQL SERVER
DBA
SURVIVAL GUIDE

Orryn Sledge
Mark Spenik

SAMS
PUBLISHING

201 West 103rd Street
Indianapolis, Indiana 46290

Orryn's Dedication

This book is dedicated to my wife, Victoria. Thanks for being there when I needed you.

Mark's Dedication

My parents—John and Anna Jane Spenik. Thanks for being the best.

COPYRIGHT © 1996 BY SAMS PUBLISHING

TRADEMARKS

PUBLISHER AND PRESIDENT *Richard K. Swadley*

ACQUISITIONS MANAGER *Greg Wiegand*

DEVELOPMENT MANAGER *Dean Miller*

MANAGING EDITOR *Cindy Morrow*

MARKETING MANAGER *Gregg Bushyeager*

ACQUISITIONS EDITOR
Rosemarie Graham

DEVELOPMENT EDITOR
Todd Bumbalough

SOFTWARE DEVELOPMENT SPECIALIST
Steve Flatt

PRODUCTION EDITOR
Jill D. Bond

TECHNICAL REVIEWERS
Michael McGeehan
Jim Dugan
Brian Moran

EDITORIAL COORDINATOR
Bill Whitmer

TECHNICAL EDIT COORDINATOR
Lynette Quinn

FORMATTER
Frank Sinclair

EDITORIAL ASSISTANT
Sharon Cox

COVER DESIGNER
Dan Armstrong

BOOK DESIGNER
Alyssa Yesh

PRODUCTION TEAM SUPERVISOR
Brad Chinn

PAGE LAYOUT
Mary Ann Abramson,
Carol Bowers, Charlotte Clapp,
Terrie Deemer, Judy Everly,
Louisa Klucznik, Steph Mineart,
Casey Price, Andrew Stone,
Susan Van Ness, Mark Walchle,
Colleen Williams

PROOFREADING
Michael Brumitt, Michael Henry, Kevin Laseau, Paula Lowell, Nancy C. Price, Brian-Kent Proffitt, Erich J. Richter, SA Springer, Robert Wolf

INDEXER
Cheryl Dietsch

Overview

Part VI   Maintaining the Shop

Part VII   Appendixes

Contents

PART II   THE WORLD OF MICROSOFT'S SQL SERVER

3   The Evolution of SQL Server   31

4   SQL Server: The Big Picture   37

PART V   PERFORMANCE AND TUNING

Acknowledgments

MARK AND ORRYN'S ACKNOWLEDGMENTS

We would like to thank the following people for helping us put this book together. Tony Mann, for putting us in touch with the folks at Sams. Andrew Coupe of Microsoft for all of his help, knowledge, and timeliness during this project. John McVicker of Sybase, for allowing us to pick his brain. Paul Galaspie for developing the Database Estimator. Marco Dulog and Mike Dermer for their SQL Server expertise. Everyone at Keiter, Stephens Computer Services, Inc., for their SQL Server commitment. The staff at Sams who did such a great job. Jill Bond, our production editor, our tech editors, and special thanks to Rosemarie Graham and Todd Bumbalough for the feedback and help!

ORRYN'S ACKNOWLEDGMENTS

I would like to personally thank my wife Victoria for her encouragement and motivation, which helped make this book a reality (thanks for proofing all those chapters!). An extended thanks goes out to Mark Spenik for getting this book off the ground and having the confidence in me to be his co-author. This book would not be complete without thanking some of my friends who have influenced my life; Roger Forester for always making me laugh, Mike Gordon and the gang at CC Pace Systems for starting my career in the right direction by giving me my first job, and the guys at Circuit City for keeping me on my toes.

MARK'S ACKNOWLEDGMENTS

I want to thank my wife Lisa for her enduring love and support. Without her, this endeavor would not have been attempted or completed! To my brother John for getting my family involved in computer technology. The rest of my family—David, Adam, Gary, and Lisa for all the great times. The Meyer and the Rimes families for their interest and encouragement. Special thanks to those all-time greats I have worked with, whose experience and knowledge made it into this book: Cary Longest, Don Burdick, Mark Swank, Len Greenburg, and Hugh Bryant. And lastly, Orryn Sledge for jumping into this project and always surpassing my expectations!

About the Authors

Orryn Sledge is a client/server consultant in the metropolitan Pittsburgh, PA area. He specializes in developing high-performance, mission-critical systems using Microsoft SQL Server, Sybase SQL Server, PowerBuilder, Visual Basic, and Access. He has been actively involved with SQL Server consulting since 1992. In addition to SQL Server consulting, he has trained several Fortune 500 companies on SQL Server administration and development. In early 1995, he was one of the first developers in the nation to complete the Microsoft Certified Solution Developer (MCSD) program. He also is certified by Microsoft in SQL Server Administration, SQL Server Database Implementation, Windows NT, Access, Windows System Architecture I, and Windows System Architecture II. In addition to his Microsoft certifications, he is a Certified PowerBuilder Developer (CPD). Orryn can be reached via CompuServe at 102254,2430 or the Internet at 102254.2430@compuserve.com.

Mark Spenik is employed as the Manager of Client/Server technologies at Keiter, Stephen's Computer Services in Richmond, Virginia, where he spends a lot of time working with, setting up, and advising companies (ranging from small businesses to Fortune 500 companies) on Microsoft SQL Server.

Introduction

In the late 1980s and early 1990s, the Sybase RDBMS (Relation Database Management Systems) was one of the most popular and innovative RDBMS systems. RDBMS systems could be found in UNIX and Netware environments. The entry fee to purchase a RDBMS system was not within the reach of many small businesses and workgroups.

To this end, Sybase and Microsoft entered into a joint venture. Microsoft would license and sell the Sybase RDBMS system, SQL Server, under the Microsoft name on the OS/2 platform. Microsoft SQL Server for OS/2 became a good affordable workgroup RDBMS system. The product, however, was limited by OS/2 in its scalability and performance.

The relationship between Microsoft and Sybase became strained and ended around the time Microsoft announced that they had rewritten SQL Server for the Windows NT platform. The Windows NT platform is Microsoft's operating system of the future, slated to take on the UNIX and NetWare operating systems. Due to pricing and performance, Microsoft SQL Server for Windows NT quickly became one of the most popular Windows NT applications.

The split between Sybase and Microsoft is quite apparent when looking at the two SQL Server products. Microsoft SQL Server is tightly integrated into the NT operating system, and the database administration tasks are packaged into several graphical front-end tools. Administering Microsoft SQL Server for Windows NT is not the same as administering a Sybase SQL Server lacking the graphically administrating and scheduling tools.

It was about this time that I first started hearing the cries from customers and various online services for a book that specifically covered Microsoft SQL Server. Microsoft began previewing to customers and SP's the next generation of SQL Server for Windows NT that was to compete in the VLDB (Very Large Database Arena) arena against Sybase and Oracle.

The next generation of SQL Server had a brand-new graphical interface code named *starfighter*, and was designed to allow database administration in an enterprise environment. When I saw the sweeping changes being added to SQL Server, I began to realize that it was time for a book that concentrated on Microsoft SQL Server.

To make a long story short, Tony Mann, the author of *Real World Programming with Visual Basic*, put me in touch with the folks at Sams Publishing, who were introducing a brand-new series of books called the *DBA Survival Guides* that concentrated on real-world experience in managing RDBMS systems. When we saw the format for the *DBA Survival Guide* series, Orryn and I realized that this was the type of book everyone had been asking for!

THE GOALS OF THIS BOOK

Managing Microsoft SQL Server is quite different from managing several other RDBMS packages because of the graphical nature and ease of use of the overall SQL Server system. The trick in becoming a good Microsoft DBA is to become familiar with the graphical front-end, understand what happens behind the scenes (that is, what happens when you push that button), and have a good understanding of the product and your job. The goals of this book are as follows:

◆ To provide the knowledge and know-how to be an administrator of a SQL Server database

◆ To appeal to all levels of DBAs: beginner, intermediate, and experienced

◆ Offer any tips, tricks, and suggestions buried deep within the documentation

◆ Offer real-world insight and experience and to pass on any tips, tricks, or suggestions learned the hard way

◆ Provide checklists and examples for SQL Server DBA tasks

◆ Provide conventions and naming standards

◆ Provide insight into the tasks that make up a DBA

THE ORGANIZATION OF THE BOOK

The book is organized into several different sections that comprise the various jobs and tasks the DBA performs. The first section is an overall introductory section which includes the following chapters:

For DBAs that are new to the world of client/server computing, Chapter 1 provides an overview of general client/server concepts. It explains what client/server really means (all vendors seem to attach the term client/server to their product, even when it really does not meet the definition of client/server). This chapter also explains the benefits of client/server computing compared to other types of computing (mainframe, PC/File Server).

Not sure what a DBA is or the responsibilities of a DBA? Then Chapter 2 is for you.

The next section, called "The World of Microsoft's SQL Server," is a high level overview. The chapters overview are as follows:

Chapter 3 discusses enhancements made to SQL Server 6.0. Chapter 4 details how SQL Server integrates with Windows NT and also illustrates the benefits of SQL Server being tightly integrated with Windows NT, and how this integration helps differentiate the product from its competitors.

The next section is dedicated to the planning, installation, and upgrading of Microsoft SQL Server.

Chapter 5 covers the planning steps required before attempting a SQL Server upgrade or installation. Do you have all your bases covered in the event an upgrade fails? This section covers this topic and many more. Chapter 6 discusses installation and upgrade.

The largest section of the book, entitled "Database Operation," includes many of the functions that you will perform as a DBA, such as the following:

Chapter 7 provides a high-level explanation of the types of tasks that can be performed through the Enterprise Manager. Chapter 8 discusses how to manage devices.

Chapter 9 explains how to create, manage, and delete a database. This includes a discussion on how logs are an integral part of a database. DBAs new to SQL Server will not want to skip the topic entitled "The Two Most Common Database Errors." Without exception, every DBA encounters the errors discussed in this section. Knowing ahead of time how to deal with these errors will simplify a DBA's life. Chapter 10 discusses user management.

Every organization should be concerned with data security. Chapter 11 discusses in detail how to implement data security through SQL Server. Several strategies are offered to help simplify security administration while maintaining an effective security model.

Not sure what Microsoft SQL Server's replication is all about? Having trouble installing the distribution database? Not sure why a replicated database should be read-only? Find these answers and more in Chapter 12.

Curious how to use your backups? When and how often to backup? These standard questions all new DBAs are faced with. What happens if a database fails after a backup—can you provide up-to-the-minute recovery? See Chapters 13 and 14.

Can't get BCP to work? You're not alone; almost every DBA hits a snag or two when trying to work with BCP. Chapter 15 discusses in detail how BCP works and provides numerous tips and examples on how to make BCP work. Also included in this chapter are several alternatives to BCP. Having problems? You won't want to miss Chapter 16, which discusses checkups and problem detection.

What would a database book be without a section on performance and tuning?

Having performance problems with SQL Server? Look at Chapter 17. SQL Server provides numerous tools to help diagnose and isolate bottlenecks. The secret is knowing how to effectively use these tools. For example, the Performance Monitor allows you to monitor over 40 different SQL Server counters and several hundred different operating system counters. Which counters do you look at? Chapter 17 guides you in the right direction as to which Performance Monitor counters should be analyzed. Also discussed in the chapter is how to monitor user activity, a feature that has been extensively enhanced in Version 6.0.

Need to configure SQL Server? So which knobs do you turn? Check out Chapter 18. Chapter 19 provides information on database design issues. Do the indexes have you all tangled up? If so, don't miss Chapter 20.

Chapter 21 explains in an easy to understand vernacular the inner workings of SQL Server's cost based optimizer. When transactions are slow to process or you are experiencing blocking or deadlocks, you will want to refer to the tips and tricks discussed in this chapter. Knowing how to read a SHOWPLAN is a key element to diagnosing query performance problems. The hard part about reading a SHOWPLAN is knowing what to look for because a lot of cryptic information is generated. This chapter explains what to look for in the output generated by a SHOWPLAN, what the output really means, and how to improve performance based on SHOWPLAN information.

I think every DBA has seen an application that runs fine when a single user is logged into the system, but when multiple users are logged on, the system bogs down. With multi-user applications, issues such as BLOCKING and DEADLOCKS must be addressed. Chapter 22 offers solutions that can reduce the headaches associated with a multi-user system. Be sure to take a look at the section entitled "10 Tips To Help Minimize Locking and Prevent Deadlocks."

The remaining section consists of ways to automate and help you plan and schedule various DBA tasks.

Chapter 23 explains why maintenance should be periodically performed on SQL Server and the Window NT operating system. In addition to explaining why you should perform maintenance, the chapter provides step-by-step instructions on how to maintain the system.

After reading Chapter 23, you will want to automate several of the maintenance tasks discussed in the chapter. Chapter 24 explains how to automate common DBA tasks through the use of two core components of SQL Server: Task Scheduler and Alert Manager. Graphical automation and advanced features such as e-mail and pager notification are two examples of how these components can help simplify a DBA's life.

You already know that OLE is included with SQL Server, so what can you do with it? Chapter 25 walks through the construction of an application that helps simplify database administration tasks using Visual Basic.

The last part of the book is dedicated to some useful quick reference appendixes to provide you additional information.

Every DBA should understand how to use DBCC commands. Otherwise, inadequate DBCC knowledge can prolong data corruption and complicate data restoration. Be sure to look at the appendix on DBCC commands. It details each command, provides a comparison of the commands, and recommends which commands should be frequently run as part of a maintenance schedule.

True ANSI standard cursors are finally available with SQL Server 6.0. The appendix on cursors explains how to use cursors and provides examples of common DBA tasks that can take advantage of cursors.

CONVENTIONS USED IN THIS BOOK

The following conventions are used in this book:

`Computer font` indicates commands, parameters, statements, and text you see onscreen.

`Boldfaced computer` font indicates text you type.

Italics indicate new terms or items of emphasis.

Note

Notes provide information that is pertinent to the subject matter.

Tip

Tips offer useful hints and information.

Warning

Warning boxes provide cautions and consequences to particular actions.

STRANGER THAN FICTION!

Some say that truth is stranger than fiction. These boxes offer fun facts to know and tell that *are* stranger than fiction!

- Introduction to
  Client/Server
  Database Computing

- The Role of the
  Database
  Administrator

PART I

Introduction

- PC/File Server Database Computing

- The Advent of Client/ Server Database Computing

- FAT Client or FAT Server: Where to Place Business Logic

- Why RDBMS is the Standard in Client/ Server Database Computing

CHAPTER 1

Introduction to Client/ Server Database Computing

Client / server (C/S) database computing is a relatively new technology that only recently has been adapted as a system architecture for the deployment of applications. C/S database computing is the wave of the 90s and it is anticipated that C/S database computing will continue to gain popularity. To understand the reasons behind the success of C/S database computing, it helps to understand the other common types of database computing: mainframe and PC/file server.

MAINFRAME DATABASE COMPUTING

Prior to the late 80s/early 90s, *mainframe computing* was about the only choice for organizations that required heavy-duty processing and support for a large number of users. Mainframes have been in existence for over 20 years. Their longevity has led to their reliability. Support for a large number of concurrent users while maintaining a fast database retrieval time contributed to corporate acceptance of the mainframe.

Mainframe computing, also called *host-based computing*, describes the occurrence of all processing being carried out on the mainframe computer. The mainframe computer is responsible for running the Relational Database Management System (RDBMS), managing the application that is accessing the RDBMS, and handling communications between the mainframe computer and dumb terminals. A dumb terminal is about as intelligent as its name implies: a dumb terminal is limited to displaying text and accepting data from the user. The application does not run on the dumb terminal; instead, it runs on the mainframe and is echoed back to the user through the terminal (see Figure 1.1).

Figure 1.1.
Mainframe database
computing.

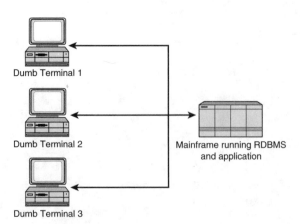

The main drawback of mainframe computing is that it is very expensive to operate. Operating a mainframe computer can run into millions of dollars. Mainframes are expensive to operate because they require specialize operational facilities, extensive support, and are not built using common computer components.

Rather than using common components, mainframes typically use hardware and software that is proprietary to the mainframe manufacture. This proprietary approach can lock a customer into a limited selection of components from one vendor.

PC/FILE SERVER DATABASE COMPUTING

PC/file server-based computing became popular in the corporate environment during the mid to late 80s. Business users began to turn to the PC as an alternative to the mainframe. Users liked the ease in which they could develop their own applications through the use of 4GL languages such as dBASE III+. These 4GL languages provided easy-to-use report writers and user-friendly programming languages.

PC/file server computing is when the PC runs both the application and the RDBMS. Users are typically connected to the file server through a LAN. The PC is responsible for RDBMS processing and the file server provides a centralized storage area for accessing shared data (see Figure 1.2).

Figure 1.2.
PC/file server database computing.

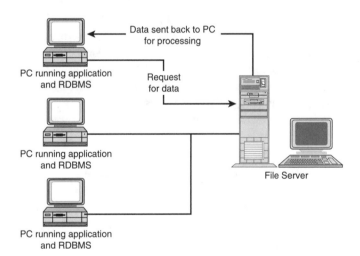

The drawback of PC-based computing is that all RDBMS processing is done on the local PC. When a query is made to the file server, the file server does not process the query. Instead, it returns the data required to process the query. For example, when a user makes a request to view all customers in the state of Virginia, the file server might return all the records in the customer table to the local PC. In turn, the local PC will have to extract the customers that live in the state of Virginia. Because the RDBMS is running on the local PC and not on the server, the file server does not have the intelligence to process a query. This can result in decreased performance and increased network bottlenecks.

PC/FILE SERVER HEADACHES

As a consultant, I am often called into projects that are running behind schedule and require additional resources. About two years ago, a mortgage banking corporation called me in to convert a mainframe application to the PC environment. The majority of the company's income is generated from the application I was converting. Not only was I converting their money maker, the system was required to be up and running within six weeks. The project manager decided that I should build the system using a popular PC/file server database product.

The application design specified a maximum of three concurrent users. Based on the type of queries that were to be performed, I felt comfortable in stating that the performance would be acceptable for the users. After rushing to meet my deadline, the system was implemented. Everything went smoothly until this company's business skyrocketed and more loans than anticipated had to be processed. Before I knew it, the number of users had increased to fifteen.

With fifteen users on the system, the network would come to a standstill. The reason that the application could bring the network to standstill is simple: in a PC/file server architecture, all database processing occurs on the local PC. Therefore, when the users would issue complicated queries to the server, the network would jam up with data being sent back to the local workstation. Often, the queries being issued from the application would require thousands of rows to be returned to the local PC.

In the PC/file server environment, this is the equivalent of calling a car dealership and asking how many blue pickup trucks they have in stock. To get the answer, the dealer drives every car to your house and you count the number of blue pickup trucks. Obviously this is not very efficient!

In the C/S database computing environment, a different approach is taken. Someone at the dealership would count the number of blue pickup trucks and pass the information back to the caller.

Eventually the system was rewritten using a C/S computing database. Performance was improved, network bottlenecks were decreased, and users were happy.

THE ADVENT OF CLIENT/SERVER DATABASE COMPUTING

C/S database computing evolved as an answer to the drawbacks of the mainframe and PC/file server. By combining the processing power of the mainframe and the flexibility and price of the PC, C/S database computing combines the best of both worlds (see Figure 1.3).

Figure 1.3.
Client/Server database
computing.

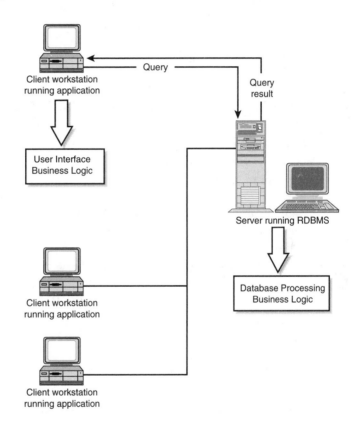

C/S database computing can be defined as the logical partitioning of the user interface, database management, and business logic between the client computer and the server computer. The network links each of these processes.

The *client computer*, also called a *workstation*, controls the user interface. It is where text and images are displayed to the user and where the user inputs data. The user interface may be text- or graphical-based.

The server computer controls database management. It is where data is stored, manipulated, and retrieved. In the C/S database environment, all database processing occurs at the server.

Business logic can be located on the server, on the client, or mixed between the two. It consist of rules and logic that govern the processing of the application.

In the typical corporate environment, the server computer is connected to multiple client computers. The server computer is a high-powered computer dedicated to running the RDBMS. The client workstations are usually PC-based. The client computer and database server communicate through a common network protocol that allows them to share information.

WHY CLIENT/SERVER DATABASE COMPUTING IS THE ANSWER

Many corporations have turned to client/server database computing as their computing answer. Following are some of the underlying reasons for its popularity:

◆ **Affordability**: C/S database computing can be less expensive than mainframe computing. The underlying reason is simple. C/S database computing is based on an open architecture. This open architecture allows for more vendors to produce competing products that drive the cost down. This is unlike mainframe-based systems, which typically use proprietary components that are available only through a single vendor. Also, C/S workstations and servers are often PC-based. PC prices have fallen dramatically over the years and this has led to reduced costs.

◆ **Speed**: The separation of processing between the client and the server reduces network bottlenecks. This allows a C/S database system to deliver mainframe performance while exceeding PC/file server performance.

◆ **Adaptability**: The C/S database computing architecture is more open than the proprietary mainframe architecture. Therefore, it is possible to build an application by selecting a RDBMS from one vendor, hardware from another vendor, and development software from yet another vendor. This allows customers to select components that best fit their needs.

◆ **Simplified Data Access**: C/S database computing makes data available to the masses. Mainframe computing was notorious for tracking huge amounts of data that could only be accessed by developers. With C/S database computing, data access is not limited to using procedural programming languages that are difficult to learn and require specialized data access knowledge. Instead, data access is provided by common software products tools that hide the complexities of data access. Word processing, spreadsheet, and reporting software are just a few of the common packages that provide simplified access to C/S data.

FAT CLIENT OR FAT SERVER: WHERE TO PLACE BUSINESS LOGIC

To this point, we have explained that with C/S database computing the user interface runs on the client computer and the RDBMS runs on the server computer. A third component in the C/S database computing environment is the placement of business logic. As mentioned previously, business logic is the rule that governs the processing of the application. Business logic can be placed on the server, on the client, or mixed between the two.

A *FAT server* is when business logic is located within the RDBMS on the server (see Figure 1.4). The client issues remote procedure calls to the server to execute the process. The advantage of a FAT server is centralized control and decreased network traffic. FAT servers are best suited for structured and consistent business logic, such as online transaction processing (OLTP). Modern RDBMS products support FAT servers through stored procedures, column rules, triggers, and other methods.

Figure 1.4.
A FAT server.

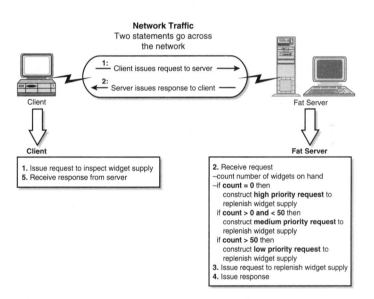

A *FAT client* is when business logic is embedded in the application at the client level (see Figure 1.5). A FAT client is more flexible than a FAT server, but also results in increased network traffic. The FAT client approach is used when business logic is loosely structured or when it is too complicated to implement at the RDBMS level. Additionally, FAT client development tools, such as 4GL languages, typically offer more robust programming features over RDBMS programming tools. Decision support and ad hoc systems often are FAT client-based.

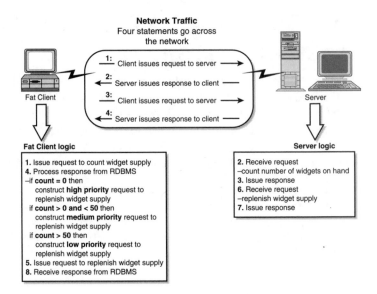

Figure 1.5.
A FAT client.

A *mixed environment* is when business logic is partitioned between the server and the client (see Figure 1.6). For practical reasons, an application may need to implement this approach. This balancing act is a common approach with C/S database computing.

Figure 1.6.
A mixed environment.

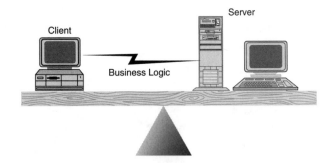

RDBMS: THE STANDARD DATABASE FOR CLIENT SERVER

RDBMS stands for *Relational Database Management System*. It has become the standard for C/S database computing. Database software vendors and corporate IS departments have rapidly adopted the RDBMS architecture. It is based on the relational model that originated in papers published by Dr. E.F. Codd in 1969. In an RDBMS, data is organized in a row/column manner and is stored in a table. Records are called rows and fields are called columns (see Figure 1.7).

Figure 1.7.
Row/column layout,
relational model.

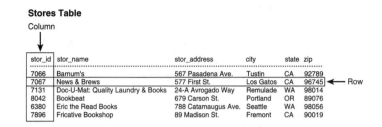

Stores Table

Column

stor_id	stor_name	stor_address	city	state	zip
7066	Barnum's	567 Pasadena Ave.	Tustin	CA	92789
7067	News & Brews	577 First St.	Los Gatos	CA	96745	← Row
7131	Doc-U-Mat: Quality Laundry & Books	24-A Avrogado Way	Remulade	WA	98014
8042	Bookbeat	679 Carson St.	Portland	OR	89076
6380	Eric the Read Books	788 Catamaugus Ave.	Seattle	WA	98056
7896	Fricative Bookshop	89 Madison St.	Fremont	CA	90019

Data is structured using relationships among data items. A relationship is a link between tables (see Figure 1.8). A relationship allows flexibility with the presentation and manipulation of data.

Figure 1.8.
Relationships among
data items, relational
model.

Stores Table

stor_id	stor_name	stor_address	city	state	zip
7066	Barnum's	567 Pasadena Ave.	Tustin	CA	92789
7067	News & Brews	577 First St.	Los Gatos	CA	96745
7131	Doc-U-Mat: Quality Laundry & Books	24-A Avrogado Way	Remulade	WA	98014
8042	Bookbeat	679 Carson St.	Portland	OR	89076
6380	Eric the Read Books	788 Catamaugus Ave.	Seattle	WA	98056
7896	Fricative Bookshop	89 Madison St.	Fremont	CA	90019

Sales Table

stor_id	ord_num	date	qty	payterms	title_id
7066	QA7442.3	Sep 13 1985 12:00AM	75	On invoice	PS2091
7067	D4482	Sep 14 1985 12:00AM	10	Net 60	PS2091
7131	N914008	Sep 14 1985 12:00AM	20	Net 30	PS2091
7131	N914014	Sep 14 1985 12:00AM	25	Net 30	MC3021
8042	423LL922	Sep 14 1985 12:00AM	15	On invoice	MC3021
8042	423LL930	Sep 14 1985 12:00AM	10	On invoice	BU1032
6380	722a	Sep 13 1985 12:00AM	3	Net 60	PS2091
6380	6871	Sep 14 1985 12:00AM	5	Net 60	BU1032
8042	P723	Mar 11 1988 12:00AM	25	Net 30	BU1111
7896	X999	Feb 21 1988 12:00AM	35	On invoice	BU2075
7896	QQ2299	Oct 28 1987 12:00AM	15	Net 60	BU7832
7896	TQ456	Dec 12 1987 12:00AM	10	Net 60	MC2222
8042	QA879.1	May 22 1987 12:00AM	30	Net 30	PC1035
7066	A2976	May 24 1987 12:00AM	50	Net 30	PC8888
7131	P3087a	May 29 1987 12:00AM	20	Net 60	PS1372
7131	P3087a	May 29 1987 12:00AM	25	Net 60	PS2106
7131	P3087a	May 29 1987 12:00AM	15	Net 60	PS3333
7131	P3087a	May 29 1987 12:00AM	25	Net 60	PS7777
7067	P2121	Jun 15 1987 12:00AM	40	Net 30	TC3218
7067	P2121	Jun 15 1987 12:00AM	20	Net 30	TC4203
7067	P2121	Jun 15 1987 12:00AM	20	Net 30	TC7777

Discounts Table

stor_id	discount
7131	6.7
8042	5.0

WHY RDBMS IS THE STANDARD IN CLIENT/ SERVER DATABASE COMPUTING

The RDBMS has become the standard in client/server database computing for the following reasons:

- **Data Integrity**: The primary goal of the relational model is *data integrity*. Data integrity prevents incorrect or invalid data from being stored. With an RDBMS, it can be implemented at the server level rather than the application level. This approach offers a significant advantage: centralized control. When data integrity is changed at the RDBMS level, it will automatically be represented at the application level. This ensures consistency and alleviates the need to modify application logic. For example, a data integrity constraint states that the ship_to_state for a customer's order must be a valid two-digit state code. Whenever ship_to_state data is entered or updated, it is checked against a list of valid state codes. If an invalid state code is entered, the RDBMS prevents the data from being saved.

- **Structured Query Language** (SQL, pronounced "sequel"): The SQL language was developed by IBM during the mid-1970s. The SQL language provides a common method for accessing and manipulating data in a relational database. This common language has been adapted by RDBMS vendors as an industry standard. The standardization of SQL allows someone to move to new RDBMS without having to learn a new data access language.

- **Flexibility**: Modifications can be made to the structure of the database without having to recompile or shut down and restart the database. New tables can be created on-the-fly and existing tables can be modified without affecting the operation of the RDBMS.

- **Efficient Data Storage**: Through a process called *normalization* (see chapter 19 for more information), redundant data is reduced. Normalization is a primary concept of the relational model.

- **Security**: Data security can be implemented at the RDBMS level rather than the application level. Like data integrity, this approach offers the advantage of centralized control at the database level as opposed to the application level.

WHO ARE THE POPULAR RDBMS VENDORS?

The number of RDBMS vendors has increased over the years as C/S has grown in popularity. Although each vendor's database product stems from the relational model, each vendor has taken a different approach to implementing it. These differences, combined with price, performance, supported operating systems, and a host of other items, make choosing the right RDBMS a difficult choice. Following is brief summary of popular RDBMS vendors.

Vendor: Microsoft
Product: SQL Server
The SQL Server product was originally developed by Sybase in the mid 1980s. Microsoft partnered with Sybase, and in 1988 they released SQL Server for OS/2. In 1993, Microsoft shipped the NT version of SQL Server. In 1994, Microsoft and Sybase ended their partnership. Microsoft's SQL Server has grown to be a huge success in the RDBMS market. Microsoft has been successful in combining performance, support for multiple platforms, and ease-of-use. When SQL Server shipped in 1993, it set a new price/performance TPC benchmark. Since then, it has continued to be a leader in the price/performance benchmark. Support for multiple platforms is accomplished through Microsoft's NT operating system, which runs on Intel, RISC, and other chip sets. Ease-of-use is accomplished through SQL Server's graphical management tools.

Vendor: Computer Associates
Product: INGRES
The INGRES database software was one of the original RDBMS products to be offered. INGRES supports the OS/2, UNIX, and VAX/VMS platforms. They were the first company to provide cost-based optimization, which has become an industry standard. Distributed processing support is available as an INGRES add-on product.

Vendor: IBM
Product: DB2
DB2 is IBM's mainframe relational database that offers impressive processing power. DB2's support for massive databases and a large number of current users gained it corporate acceptance during the 1980s. IBM is the original developer of the relational model and SQL.

Vendor: Gupta Technologies
Product: SQL Base
Gupta introduced SQL Base for the PC/DOS platform in 1986. Since then, Gupta has added support for the OS/2, Novell NLM, and UNIX platforms. Price, fully scrollable cursors, and declarative referential integrity help differentiate SQL Base from its competitors.

Vendor: INFORMIX Software
Product: INFORMIX OnLine
INFORMIX Software was the first vendor to release a UNIX RDBMS. Although available on other operating systems, INFORMIX for UNIX is the

company's most popular offering. INFORMIX offers high performance transaction processing, advanced security, and distributed processing capabilities.

Vendor: Oracle
Product: Oracle
Oracle is one of the largest and most popular vendors in the RDBMS industry. They have the honor of being the first company to offer an RDBMS for commercial usage. Oracle's portability to practically every major hardware and operating system platform is impressive. This means that Oracle code written on a VAX/VMS platform will can be easily ported to run on a Macintosh platform. Currently, Oracle supports over 80 different hardware platforms.

Vendor: Sybase
Product: SQL Server
Sybase originally released SQL Server in the mid-1980s. Sybase's SQL Server is designed to run on UNIX, Novell NLM, NT, and VMS platforms. Sybase has proven its innovativeness by being the one of the first companies to offer features such as triggers and symmetrical multiprocessing support. UNIX is Sybase's predominate platform. Reliability, performance, and scalability have enabled Sybase's to become one of the most respected RDBMS vendors in the industry.

Vendor: XDB Systems
Product: XDB-Server
XDB-Server's strength lies in its 100 percent–DB2 compatibility. Developers can downsize to XDB-Server from IBM's DB2 or can upsize from XDB-Server to DB2. In addition to full DB2 support, the product also offers SQL/DS and ANSI level 2 compatibility. XDB-Server is available for DOS, OS/2, and Novell versions.

THE EVOLUTION OF THE CORPORATE SYSTEM: ENTERPRISE NETWORK

An *enterprise network* links multiple information servers that can be accessed and managed from a centralized source (see Figure 1.9). In the 1980s and 1990s, distributed computing grew in popularity. Distributed computing physical moved computer systems closer to the source of the information. In doing so, distributed systems became more geographically disperse over their mainframe counterparts.

Figure 1.9.
Enterprise network.

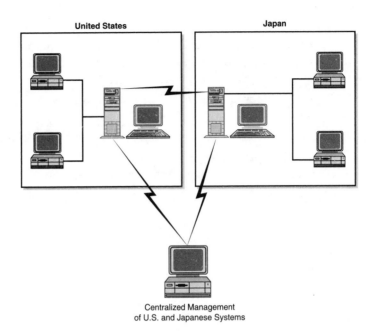

With distributed computing comes decentralized control and with decentralized control comes increased difficulty in managing and accessing data among distributed systems. To solve this problem, tools, such as SQL Server's Enterprise Manager, have been developed to help manage the enterprise network.

SUMMARY

In this chapter, you learned about the following:

◆ C/S database computing evolved as an answer to the drawbacks of the mainframe and PC/file server.

◆ C/S database computing partitions the user interface, database management, and business logic between the client computer and the server computer. The network links each of these processes.

◆ The client computer controls the user interface. The server computer controls database management. Business logic can be located on the server, on the client, or mixed between the two.

◆ Advantages of C/S database computing include affordability, speed, adaptability, and simplified data access.

◆ A FAT server is when business logic is located within the RDBMS on the server and a FAT client is when business logic is embedded in the application at the client level.

◆ An RDBMS is the standard database in the C/S environment. With an RDBMS, data is organized in a row/column manner and is stored in a table. Records are called rows and fields are called columns. Data is structured using relationships among data items.

◆ Advantages of an RDBMS include data integrity, SQL, flexibility, efficient data storage, and security.

◆ Multiple vendors offer powerful and robust RDBMS products.

◆ An enterprise network links multiple information servers that can be accessed and managed from a centralized source.

The next chapter discusses the role of the database administrator in regard to RDBMS computing.

CHAPTER 2

The Role of the Database
Administrator

In Chapter 1, you read about the new world of Client/Server computing and the different RDBMS systems. What about the people that manage and maintain these systems? Let's examine a small Client/Server network with 2 servers: a file/print server and a database server with 15 client workstations that access the two servers.

In this chapter, you will learn about the different jobs and responsibilities required to maintain a Client/Server network. Begin by examining the type of tasks that are required to maintain the Client/Server network shown in Figure 2.1.

Figure 2.1.
Small client server
network.

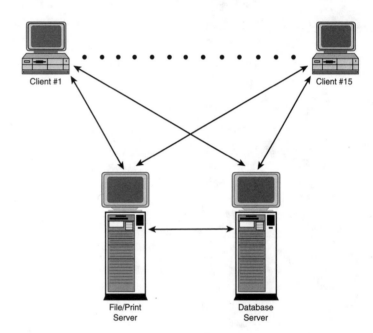

Client #1

Client #15

File/Print
Server

Database
Server

HARDWARE

Figure 2.1 shows a total of 15 client machines and 2 servers. Someone needs to be responsible for maintaining the physical machines to ensure they are continually running. This person is responsible for routine maintenance and upgrades such as adding more disk space or memory.

NETWORK

The 15 client machines communicate with the 2 servers via the *network*. The network consists of the hardware and software that ties all the machines together such as the cabling, routers, repeaters, and network protocols (TCP/IP, Named Pipes, SPX/IPX and so on). Again, someone has to take responsibility to make sure the network stays up and running. If the network goes down, none of the machines can talk to each other!

OPERATING SYSTEMS

All machines, clients and servers, utilize some sort of *operating system*. Because this is a book on NT SQL Server, you can safely assume that the servers in Figure 2.1 are running Microsoft Windows NT and the clients are running Microsoft Windows or Microsoft Windows NT Workstation. Each client and server machine needs to be properly configured and set up.

FILE/PRINT SERVER

The *file/print server* needs general maintenance, backups, and upgrades to protect against the loss of data. Someone needs to be responsible for adding user accounts and installing new applications and maintaining the stability of the file/print servers. After all, if the file and print server go down, users will not be able to perform their jobs.

DATABASE SERVER

The *database server* requirements are similar to that of the file and print server. The difference is the administration occurs with the RDBMS package. The database server needs to be set up and tuned correctly to produce the best performance. Above all, the data in the databases needs to be protected, and in the case of data loss, the data needs to be restored. Someone also has to manage the users' access and security on the database server.

SO WHO DOES WHAT?

You may be thinking to yourself, "For such a small Client/Server network, there seems to be a lot of different jobs and responsibilities to keep the whole network up and running." Imagine a Client/Server network 10 to 100 times the size of the relatively small network we are using in this example! So who is responsible for which task? Someone has to be responsible for the many different tasks required to maintain the network. The answer to who does what can become quite complex because the size of an organization and the size of the Client/Server network will dictate who does what. In some organizations, a single individual may wear many different hats. In other organizations, an individual may need to be more specialized. The following sections examine some of the general job titles and the responsibilities that accompany each position.

PC AND TECH SUPPORT

The PC and tech support group is responsible for maintaining and setting up the hardware on the different client machines and sometimes, the server machines. If more disk space or memory needs to be added, the PC and tech support group is called in.

NETWORK ADMINISTRATOR

The network administrator is responsible for maintaining the network. A network administrator makes sure all the hardware components are working correctly and the networking software is set up correctly. In many cases, the network administrator is responsible for maintaining the network operating system.

SYSTEM ADMINISTRATOR

The system administrator is responsible for maintaining the many different servers in the organization. The responsibilities include backup and recovery, maintaining user access and security, scheduling task and batch runs, and upgrading and maintaining the operating system.

DATABASE ADMINISTRATOR

Simply put, someone once told me, the database administrator (DBA for short) is responsible for the data! Well, there is a lot more to being a DBA than just being responsible for the data and that is what you will concentrate on for the rest of the chapter!

Note

You may notice that in many cases there is a fine line separating job responsibilities, where one job starts and ends, such as the possible overlap of the network administrator and the system administrator. Most organizations, based on their size, will divide the work accordingly, but one of the most important things to remember is that it takes a team effort to keep a Client/Server network healthy. Cooperation among the different individuals is a must!

WHAT IS A DATABASE ADMINISTRATOR?

A *database administrator* is in a very general sense the individual who is responsible for maintaining the RDBMS system, in this book, Microsoft SQL Server. The DBA has many different responsibilities, but the overall goal of the DBA is to keep up the server at all times and to provide users access to the information required when they need it. The DBA makes sure the database is protected and that any chance of possible data loss is minimized.

WHO ARE THE DBAS?

Who are the DBAs and how do you become one? A DBA could be someone who, from the start, has concentrated in the area of database design and administration. A DBA could be a programmer who, by default or by volunteering, took over the responsibility of maintaining a SQL Server during project development and enjoyed the job so much he or she switched. A DBA could be a system administrator who was given the added responsibility of maintaining SQL Server. To start on your journey to become a Microsoft SQL Server DBA you will need the following:

◆ A good understanding of Microsoft Windows NT

◆ Knowledge of Structured Query Language (SQL)

◆ Sound database design

◆ Knowledge about Microsoft SQL Server

Tip

If you are part of a technical team looking for a Microsoft SQL Server DBA, do yourself a favor and volunteer. It is a great job and good DBAs are in demand!

DBA RESPONSIBILITIES

Let's examine some of the responsibilities of the database administrator and how they translate to Microsoft SQL Server tasks.

INSTALLING AND UPGRADING A SQL SERVER

The DBA is responsible for installing SQL Server or upgrading an existing SQL Server. In the case of upgrading SQL Server, the DBA is responsible for making sure that if the upgrade is not successful, the SQL Server can be rolled back to a prior release until the upgrade issues can be resolved.

MONITORING THE DATABASE SERVER'S HEALTH AND TUNING ACCORDINGLY

Monitoring the health of the database server means making sure the following is done:

◆ The server is running with optimal performance.

◆ The server is properly configured with the correct amount of memory and set with the proper configuration parameters.

◆ The error log or event log is monitored for database errors.

◆ Databases have routine maintenance performed on them and that the overall system is having periodic maintenance performed by the system administrator.

PROPER UTILIZATION OF STORAGE

Maintaining the proper utilization of storage means making sure databases and transaction logs are created correctly, monitoring space requirements, and adding new storage space when required.

BACKUP AND RECOVERY

Backup and recovery are the most critical tasks a DBA has and include the following:

◆ Establishing standards and schedules for database backups

◆ Developing recovery procedures for each database

◆ Making sure the backup schedules meet the recovery procedure

MANAGE DATABASE USERS AND SECURITY

The DBA is responsible for setting up the user's database server login ids and determining the proper security level for each user. Within each database, the DBA is responsible for assigning permissions to the various database objects such as tables, views, and stored procedures.

WORK WITH DEVELOPERS

It is important for the DBA to work closely with development teams to assist in overall database design, such as creating normalized databases, helping developers tune queries, assign proper indexes, and aid them in creating triggers and stored procedures.

Tip

In many places I have been, all too often the DBAs were content to sit back and watch developers go off and make bad design and SQL Server decisions. I have also seen situations where the DBA wanted to be involved and management prevented it because it was not the DBA's "job." Don't be underutilized. If you are in this situation, show them this tip! Remember to take an active role in new project development. The entire team will benefit from your insight and knowledge!

ESTABLISH AND ENFORCE STANDARDS

Establish naming conventions and standards for your SQL Server and databases and make sure everyone sticks to them!

DATA TRANSFER

The DBA is responsible for importing and exporting data to and from SQL Server. In the current downsizing trend and the coexistence of Client/Server systems with mainframe systems, importing data from the mainframe to SQL Server is a common occurrence.

REPLICATION

SQL Server Version 6.0 has added a new requirement and responsibility for the DBA: setting up and maintaining data replication throughout the workplace. Replication is a tremendous feature that will play a big part in many organizations.

TOOLS AND SCHEDULING

The database administrator is responsible for setting up and scheduling various events using Windows NT and SQL Server to aid in performing many of the tasks defined previously, such as backups and replication.

24 HOUR ACCESS

Although you may say to yourself, "No way!", the database server must stay up and the databases must always be protected and online. Be prepared to perform some maintenance features and upgrades after hours. If the database server should go down, be ready to get the server up and running. After all that's your job!

CONSTANT LEARNING

To be a good DBA, you must continue to study and practice your mission critical procedures, such as testing your backups by recovering to a test database. In this business, things change very fast so you must continue learning about SQL Server, available Client/Servers, and database design tools. It is a never-ending process.

LEARNING THE TRICKS OF THE TRADE

Now that you understand the different responsibilities of a DBA, how can you learn the tricks of the trade? Well, you are off to a good start by reading this book! Now examine some other ways to learn the tricks of the trade.

CLASSES AND TRAINING

Taking a Microsoft certified SQL Server training class is a very good way to get started. Find a class that gives you hands-on classroom training. The class will introduce you to many of the concepts and procedures required to maintain SQL Server. To find out about authorized Microsoft SQL Server training centers near you, call 1-800-SOL-PROV and ask for information on Microsoft Solution Provider Authorized Technical Education Centers. On CompuServe, GO MECFORUM.

Tip

If you go to class, make sure when you return that you start practicing immediately what you learned in class. Most classes are three to five days; in order to retain the information, you must start practicing and using it immediately!

ON THE JOB

Learning to be a DBA occurs on the job, and for many that is where they learned. On-the-job training can be difficult when you are the only one learning the system that no one else knows! You may have the luxury of having a seasoned DBA walk teach you the ropes. Ultimately, on-the-job training is where we all learn.

Tip

Practice, practice, practice. Constantly practice different procedures and tasks, such as backup and recovery or importing data on a non-production server. When the day comes to perform the task, you will be well prepared.

MICROSOFT TECHNET, MICROSOFT DEVELOPER'S NETWORK, AND ONLINE SERVICES

Take advantage of the vast knowledge base of articles Microsoft makes available on the TechNet and Developer's Network CDs. Many times, you can simply solve a problem by searching the two CDs for the problem and possible resolution. Use online services that have a Microsoft SQL Server forum. On the forum, you can post problems and get help from other DBAs or you can scan through the various messages posted and learn how to solve problems you have not yet experienced. The CompuServe SQL Server forum is GO MSSQL. Microsoft's Web page for SQL Server is http://www.Microsoft.com/SQL. You can learn more about Microsoft TechNet by calling 1-800-344-2121, Internet at technet@microsoft.com or on CompuServe, GO TECHNET.

MAGAZINES AND BOOKS

Subscribe to various database magazines that will keep you abreast of topics, such as the latest database design and development tools, relational database concepts, and SQL Server. Also search the book store for books on database design and SQL Server (like this book). Pinnacle publishing publishes a magazine called the *Microsoft SQL Server Professional* and they can be reached at CompuServe 76064,51, the Internet at 1119390@mcimail.com or by fax at 1-206-251-5057.

CERTIFICATION

Microsoft offers product certification for SQL Server database administration and SQL Server database implementation. It is strongly encouraged that you take the test to become certified. Certification does not replace experience and training but it will help point out possible weakness in your understanding of SQL Server and give you credibility that you understand the concepts and procedures to maintain SQL Server. To find out more about Microsoft certification on CompuServe, GO MECFORUM or on the Internet at http://www.Microsoft.com. You also can call 1-800-636-7544, and ask for "Certification Roadmap."

HOW THE DBA INTERACTS WITH OTHER TEAM MEMBERS

Now that you have decided to become a DBA, how will you interact with other team members such as the system administrator, network administrator, developers, and users? As stated earlier, many times these relationships are hard to determine because each organization will have people filling one to many different roles. Based on earlier job descriptions, however, quickly examine the type of interaction to expect.

SYSTEM ADMINISTRATOR AND NETWORK ADMINISTRATOR

A DBA's interaction with the network administrator is more along the lines of "What type of network protocols can I use? What network address or port number should I use for the server?" If users are complaining about query times and SQL Server is executing the queries very fast, the two of you may examine possible networking problems.

The interaction with the system administrator and the DBA is much tighter. The system administrator will be responsible for tuning the Windows NT server on which your SQL Server runs. The system administrator will be responsible for adding the hard drives and storage space required for you to create database devices. If you choose to use integrated user security with SQL Server, then you must work with the system administrator to set up the correct NT user accounts and groups. The different types of backup and recovery procedures for the NT Server and the SQL Server should be worked out by both parties because in some cases, the system administrator may need to restore a system drive that contains a database.

DEVELOPERS

The interaction with developers is where I have seen the greatest difference in an organization's definition of a DBA. In some organizations, the DBA works very closely with the developers, and in other organizations the DBAs work very little with the developers and are stuck maintaining the developer's systems and designs without any input. It is my humble opinion and belief that the DBA should work very closely with the developers; after all, the DBA will be the one maintaining the database side of the application and, in many cases, has the most experience in relational database design and tuning. The DBA should design, aid, or review any and all database designs for the organization. The DBA should also provide assistance in helping the developers select proper indexes, optimize queries and stored procedures, as well as being a bundle of information to provide the developers with answers to questions that will come up during development.

USERS

In most organizations the DBA's interaction with the users of the system is limited to user account maintenance, security, and database recovery requirements.

SUMMARY

In summary, the role of the database administrator is a very important role in an organization. The job can be challenging and exciting. If you are a DBA or want to be a DBA, remember that it is important to constantly study SQL Server and database tools. Become certified and practice your backup and recovery procedures. The following is a quick list of the many duties and responsibilities of a DBA:

- Installing and upgrading SQL Server
- Monitoring the database server's health and tuning accordingly
- Proper utilization of storage
- Backup and recovery
- Manage database users and security
- Establish and enforce standards

◆ Perform data transfer
◆ Set up and maintain data replication
◆ Provide tools
◆ Set up server scheduling
◆ 24 hour access
◆ Work with development teams
◆ Learn!

PART II

The World of Microsoft's SQL Server

- What's New in Version 6.0

_____

CHAPTER 3

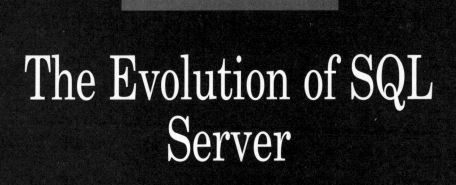

The Evolution of SQL Server

In 1988, Microsoft released its first version of SQL Server. It was designed for the OS/2 platform and was jointly developed by Microsoft and Sybase. During the early 1990s Microsoft began to develop a new version of SQL Server for the NT platform. While it was under development, Microsoft decided that SQL Server should be tightly coupled with the NT operating system. In 1992, Microsoft assumed core responsibility for the future of SQL Server for NT. In 1993, Windows NT 3.1 and SQL Server 4.2 for NT were released. Combining a high-performance database with an easy-to-use interface proved to be very successful. Microsoft quickly became the second most popular vendor of high-end relational database software. In 1994, Microsoft and Sybase formally ended their partnership. In 1995, Microsoft released version 6.0 of SQL Server.

WHAT'S NEW IN VERSION 6.0

Microsoft made significant changes to SQL Server in Version 6.0. Many of these changes were in response to the complaint that Version 4.2x was better suited to handle the needs of a department rather than an enterprise. Version 6.0 meets the demanding requirements of an enterprise and also includes several other features that help differentiate it from its peers.

ENTERPRISE MANAGER

The Enterprise Manager combines the functionality of Version 4.2x's Object Manager and SQL Administrator into a single easy-to-use interface. From the Enterprise Manager, you can administer multiple servers, configure data replication, and develop databases.

Tip

> In addition to managing SQL Server 6.0, you can manage SQL Server 4.2x from the Enterprise Manager. To do this, you must first run from your 4.2x version of SQL Server the SQLOLE42.SQL script that came with Version 6.0.

DATA REPLICATION

Prior to Version 6.0, if you wanted replication you had to buy a replication product or build your own replication services. Neither alternative was very appealing. Data replication products are expensive to purchase and building your own replication service can be complex and time-consuming. Fortunately, SQL Server 6.0 provides a robust replication component that can meet the needs of an enterprise. The uses for replication are endless. Data warehousing, distributed processing, and end-user reporting are just a few examples of how SQL Server's data replication component can be utilized.

SQL EXECUTIVE

SQL Executive helps automate many of the routine tasks a DBA must perform. Event scheduling, alert notification, replication management, and task management are some of the functions that SQL Executive provides.

Note

SQL Executive replaces Version 4.2x's SQL Monitor.

OLE AUTOMATION

Distributed Management Objects (SQL-DMO) allow developers to tap into the power of SQL Server through the ease of OLE automation. Developers can use Visual Basic, Excel, and other products that support the VBA programming language to build custom administration scripts. These objects simplify the process of creating management scripts by allowing programs to interface with SQL Server through objects, methods, and properties.

PARALLEL DATA SCANNING AND READ AHEAD MANAGER

Through parallel data scanning and read ahead algorithms, Version 6.0 has significantly improved performance. Certain types of queries execute 400 percent faster over Version 4.2x.

MULTITHREADED KERNEL

Version 6.0 features a redesigned kernel that results in improved transaction performance and scalability. Previous versions of SQL Server were unable to effectively scale beyond two or three processors. Version 6.0 is better suited to take advantage of multiple processors.

OPTIMIZER IMPROVEMENTS

Version 6.0's optimizer has been significantly improved. The likelihood of a proper query execution plan has increased through better index utilization and improved subquery support.

Also new with Version 6.0 are optimizer hints. Now you can explicitly force the optimizer into choosing an index. Prior to Version 6.0, developers would sometimes have to use nonstandard techniques to force the optimizer into choosing an appropriate index.

HIGH PERFORMANCE BACKUP AND RESTORATION

Version 6.0 uses parallel optimization techniques to minimize backup and restoration times. These techniques allow very large databases to be backed up and restored in a reasonable amount of time.

VERY LARGE DATABASE (VLDB) SUPPORT

Previous versions of SQL Server had a practical size limitation of 50 to 60GB. Version 6.0 can effectively support databases in excess of 100GB. SQL Server uses parallel optimization techniques to maximize performance. This enables SQL Server to post significant performance gains over previous versions.

DATATYPES

The following three datatypes have been added to Version 6.0:

- ◆ Decimal
- ◆ Numeric
- ◆ Double-precision

Additionally, an *identity* property has been added. It is a value that is automatically incremented when a new record is inserted into a table. You can have only one identity column per table.

Note

Version 6.0 is ANSI SQL 92–compliant.

DATA INTEGRITY

Several new data constraints have been added to Version 6.0. These constraints relieve the developer from having to code data integrity scripts. Constraints are defined with the CREATE TABLE and ALTER TABLE statements. See Table 3.1 for a comparison of data constraints.

CHECK CONSTRAINT

The CHECK constraint limits the range of data values that a column can contain. The CHECK constraint can be created at the table or column level.

DEFAULT CONSTRAINT

A DEFAULT constraint automatically enters a default value into the column when a value is not specified. The DEFAULT constraint can be created at the table or column level.

FOREIGN KEY CONSTRAINT

The FOREIGN KEY constraint enforces foreign key relationships. It is used with the REFERENCE and PRIMARY KEY constraints.

PRIMARY KEY CONSTRAINT

The PRIMARY KEY constraint uniquely identifies a primary key and enforces referential integrity. The column it references must contain unique data values and cannot be NULL. It is used with the REFERENCE and FOREIGN KEY constraints.

REFERENCE CONSTRAINT

The REFERENCE constraint is used to enforce referential integrity in conjunction with the PRIMARY KEY and FOREIGN KEY constraints.

UNIQUE CONSTRAINT

The UNIQUE constraint prevents duplicate data values. This constraint is similar to the PRIMARY KEY constraint, except that it allows NULLs.

Note

Prior to Version 6.0, referential integrity (RI) could only be enforced through the use of triggers. This meant having to build extensive code to enforce RI. Now with Version 6.0 you can use the REFERENCE, PRIMARY KEY, and FOREIGN KEY constraints to enforce RI. However, triggers must still be used to perform cascading updates and deletes.

3

THE EVOLUTION OF SQL SERVER

TABLE 3.1. COMPARISON OF DATA CONSTRAINTS.

Version 6.0	Prior Versions
CHECK	CREATE trigger or rule
DEFAULT	CREATE default
FOREIGN KEY	CREATE trigger, sp_foreignkey
PRIMARY KEYREATE	UNIQUE index, sp_primarykey
REFERENCE	CREATE trigger
UNIQUE	CREATE UNIQUE index

Warning

The system procedures sp_primarykey and sp_foreignkey are strictly for documenting primary keys and foreign keys. They *do not* enforce data integrity! Seldom will you need to use these system procedures.

CURSORS

ANSI-SQL cursors and engine-based cursors are new with Version 6.0. In previous version of SQL Server, cursors could only be created by using DB-LIB or ODBC API calls. SQL Server's cursors are fully scrollable and permit data modifications. ANSI cursors, which are row-oriented, are preferred to engine-based cursors which are set oriented.

SUMMARY

As this chapter illustrates, SQL Server Version 6.0 offers significant improvements and enhancements over prior versions. These changes will be discussed throughout this book.

CHAPTER 4

SQL Server: The Big Picture

SQL Server is a high-performance relational database system that is tightly integrated with the Windows NT operating system. This allows SQL Server to take advantage of the features provided by the Windows NT operating system. This makes SQL Server an excellent choice for meeting the challenging needs of today's complex client/server systems.

ARCHITECTURE

SQL Server's integration with the Windows NT operating system provides the following important features:

◆ Symmetric multiprocessing (SMP)
◆ Portability
◆ Network independence
◆ Reliability

SYMMETRIC MULTIPROCESSING (SMP)

SMP allows SQL Server to increase performance through the use of additional processors. SQL Server uses a single process and multiple threads in conjunction with NT's scheduler. This allows Windows NT to balance workloads across multiple processors. All this occurs without user interaction. This relieves administrators from the complexities of managing multiple processors.

PORTABILITY

SQL Server can run on the different hardware platforms because Windows NT is a portable operating system. Currently, Windows NT supports the Intel platform, various RISC machines, and several other hardware platforms.

NETWORK INDEPENDENCE

The Windows NT operating system supports several different types of network protocols. This level of support extends to the client-side connectivity of SQL Server. This allows you to choose the network protocol that best fits your present needs and future needs. TCP/IP, IPX/SPX, named pipes, and Banyan Vines are currently supported.

RELIABILITY

Windows NT provides crash protection, memory management, preemptive scheduling, and remote management. These types of features enable you keep SQL Server up and running 24 hours a day, 7 days a week.

NT INTEGRATION

SQL Server is designed to take advantage of the NT operating system. This means that several common NT components provide additional functionality to SQL Server.

CONTROL PANEL

SQL Server (MSSQLServer) and SQL Executive (SQLExecutive) are defined as services in the NT control panel (see Figure 4.1). This allows you to start, stop, and monitor the status of SQL Server and SQL Executive.

Figure 4.1.
Integration with NT
Control Panel.

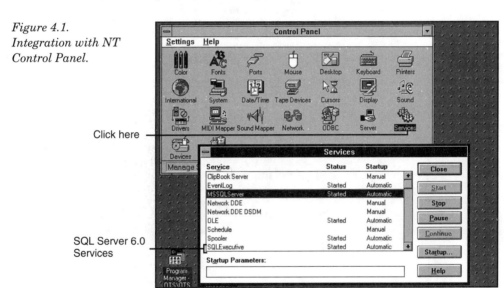

Click here

SQL Server 6.0
Services

> ## Note
>
> Version 4.2*x* of SQL Server uses different service names. They are *SQLServer* and *SQLMonitor*. In Version 6.0, SQLServer became MSSQLServer and SQLMonitor was replaced by SQLExecutive.

EVENT VIEWER

The *Event Viewer* allows administrators to view and track errors when starting and stopping SQL Server along with any unexpected connection problems (see Figure 4.2). SQL Server logs the following types of messages to the Event Viewer: Information, Error, and Warnings.

Figure 4.2.
Event Viewer.

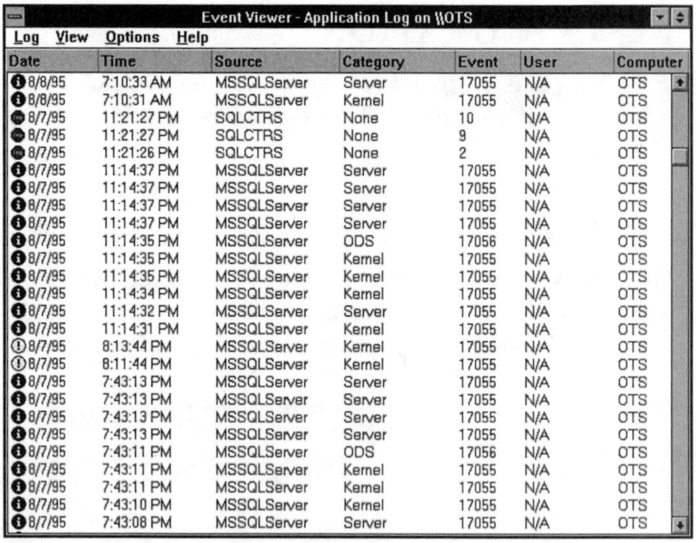

Event Viewer - Application Log on \\OTS

Log View Options Help

Date	Time	Source	Category	Event	User	Computer
8/8/95	7:10:33 AM	MSSQLServer	Server	17055	N/A	OTS
8/8/95	7:10:31 AM	MSSQLServer	Kernel	17055	N/A	OTS
8/7/95	11:21:27 PM	SQLCTRS	None	10	N/A	OTS
8/7/95	11:21:27 PM	SQLCTRS	None	9	N/A	OTS
8/7/95	11:21:26 PM	SQLCTRS	None	2	N/A	OTS
8/7/95	11:14:37 PM	MSSQLServer	Server	17055	N/A	OTS
8/7/95	11:14:37 PM	MSSQLServer	Server	17055	N/A	OTS
8/7/95	11:14:37 PM	MSSQLServer	Server	17055	N/A	OTS
8/7/95	11:14:37 PM	MSSQLServer	Server	17055	N/A	OTS
8/7/95	11:14:35 PM	MSSQLServer	ODS	17056	N/A	OTS
8/7/95	11:14:35 PM	MSSQLServer	Kernel	17055	N/A	OTS
8/7/95	11:14:35 PM	MSSQLServer	Kernel	17055	N/A	OTS
8/7/95	11:14:34 PM	MSSQLServer	Kernel	17055	N/A	OTS
8/7/95	11:14:32 PM	MSSQLServer	Server	17055	N/A	OTS
8/7/95	11:14:31 PM	MSSQLServer	Kernel	17055	N/A	OTS
8/7/95	8:13:44 PM	MSSQLServer	Kernel	17055	N/A	OTS
8/7/95	8:11:44 PM	MSSQLServer	Kernel	17055	N/A	OTS
8/7/95	7:43:13 PM	MSSQLServer	Server	17055	N/A	OTS
8/7/95	7:43:13 PM	MSSQLServer	Server	17055	N/A	OTS
8/7/95	7:43:13 PM	MSSQLServer	Server	17055	N/A	OTS
8/7/95	7:43:13 PM	MSSQLServer	Server	17055	N/A	OTS
8/7/95	7:43:11 PM	MSSQLServer	ODS	17056	N/A	OTS
8/7/95	7:43:11 PM	MSSQLServer	Kernel	17055	N/A	OTS
8/7/95	7:43:11 PM	MSSQLServer	Kernel	17055	N/A	OTS
8/7/95	7:43:10 PM	MSSQLServer	Kernel	17055	N/A	OTS
8/7/95	7:43:08 PM	MSSQLServer	Server	17055	N/A	OTS

Tip

In the Event Viewer, you can control the size of the event log. To control its size, select the Log Settings option from the Log menu. This will open the Event Log Settings dialog box. From this dialog box, you can specify a maximum log size and overwrite behavior.

From within SQL Server you can write your own messages to the event log. Use the extended stored procedure `xp_logevent`, as in the following:

```
xp_logevent error_number, message, [severity]
```

REGISTRY

Windows NT configuration information is stored in a database called the *registry*. To view and edit the registry, run REGEDT32.EXE (see Figure 4.3). Normally the registry is automatically maintained by your software. You should only change information in the registry when it is absolutely necessary. Otherwise, you may inadvertently introduce errors into your software and operating system.

Following is the key to SQL Server 6.0:

```
HKEY_LOCAL_MACHINE

 \SOFTWARE

 \Microsoft

 \MSSQLServer
```

Figure 4.3.
Registry.

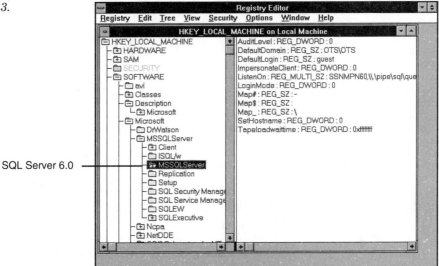

Note

If you want to view registry information about SQL Server 6.0, be sure to look at the MSSQLServer section and NOT SQLServer. SQLServer is Version 4.*x*.

NT USER ACCOUNTS

Through *integrated security*, SQL Server can utilize Windows NT user accounts and passwords (see Figure 4.4). This means that a single user account can be used to control access to NT and SQL Server. This significantly reduces account maintenance, eliminates duplication, and simplifies login procedures.

For more information on user accounts, see Chapter 10.

Figure 4.4.
NT user accounts.

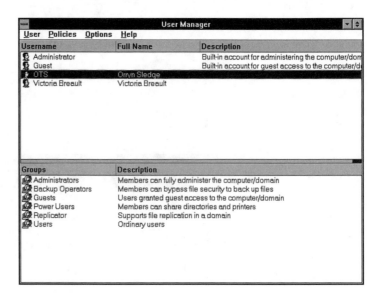

PERFORMANCE MONITOR

The *Performance Monitor* provides graphical statistics about the performance of SQL Server and Windows NT (see Figure 4.5). For more information on using the Performance Monitor, see Chapter 17.

Figure 4.5.
Performance Monitor.

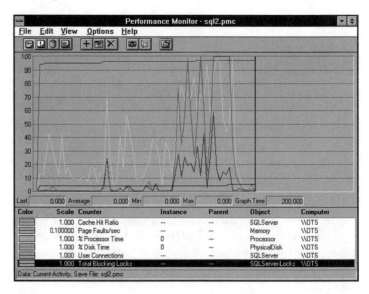

You also can define alerts in the Performance Monitor. Alerts enable you to track and monitor the frequency of an event (see Figure 4.6).

Figure 4.6.
Alerts.

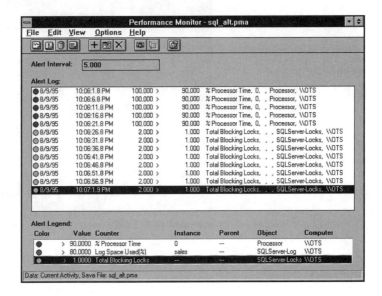

VISUAL ADMINISTRATION TOOLS

A primary goal of SQL Server for NT was to provide administrators with easy to use graphical administration tools. The ease with which someone can administer SQL Server for NT is testimony to the success of Microsoft's development efforts. This is quite a different philosophy from SQL Server's competitors. The majority of their products are not intuitive and are command-line based.

The following tools allow you to easily set up, administer, and interact with SQL Server.

SQL SERVER SETUP

Through SQL Server Setup, you can perform the following functions (see Figure 4.7):

◆ Set up SQL Server

◆ Configure an existing SQL Server installation

◆ Rebuild the master database

◆ Remove SQL Server

Figure 4.7.
SQL Server Setup.

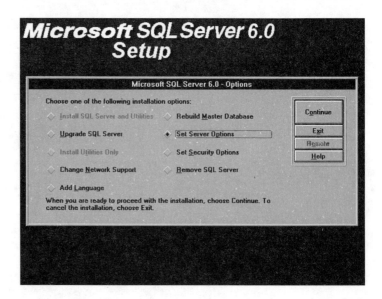

SQL SERVICE MANAGER

 From the SQL Service Manager you can start, stop, and pause SQL Server and SQL Executive (see Figure 4.8).

Tip

What is the purpose of the yellow stop light in the SQL Service Manager? This a commonly asked question. The reason it exists is to pause the server. By pausing the server, you can prevent users from logging into SQL Server while still keeping it up and running. This makes the feature useful when you want to halt users from making new connections but allow existing connections to continue processing.

Note

In addition to Service Manager, SQL Server can be started through Services on the Control Panel or from the command line by using the command NET START MSSQLSERVER.

Figure 4.8.
SQL Service Manager.

ISQL/w

ISQL/w is the Windows-based version of ISQL (see Figure 4.9). Generally it is used by developers and end-users that need to execute SQL statements. It does not provide graphical administration (use the Enterprise Manager for graphical administration).

Figure 4.9.
ISQL/w.

Through ISQL/w you can perform the following functions:

◆ Execute SQL statements

◆ Analyze query plans

◆ Display query statistics

SQL SECURITY MANAGER

 SQL Security Manager allows you to graphically manage how Windows NT users interact with SQL Server (see Figure 4.10).

Figure 4.10.
SQL Security Manager.

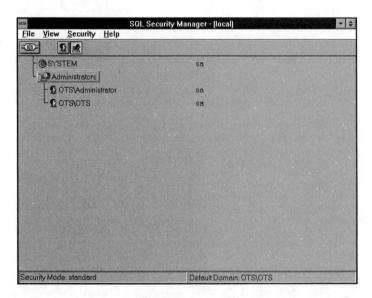

Note

You must be running integrated or mixed security to take advantage of SQL Security Manager. There is no benefit from the Security Manager if you are using standard security.

From the Security Manager you can perform the following functions:

♦ Manage security

♦ Grant and revoke privileges to Windows NT groups

♦ Search account information

SQL ENTERPRISE MANAGER

 As an administrator, you will probably spend the majority of your time interacting with SQL Server through the SQL Enterprise Manager. This is where you can administer multiple database servers through a single interface.

Through the Enterprise Manager you can perform the following functions (see Figure 4.11):

- ◆ Manage backups
- ◆ Manage databases
- ◆ Manage devices
- ◆ Manage logins and permissions
- ◆ Manage replication
- ◆ Manage tables, views, stored procedures, triggers, indexes, rules, defaults, and user-defined datatypes
- ◆ Schedule tasks
- ◆ Drag-and-drop objects from one server to another or within a server
- ◆ Generate SQL scripts

Figure 4.11.
SQL Enterprise Manager.

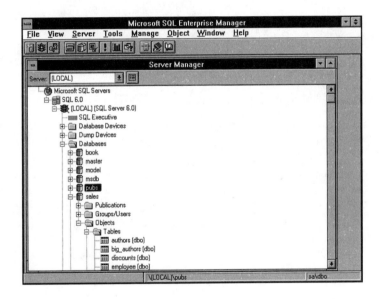

SQL CLIENT CONFIGURATION UTILITY

From the SQL Client Configuration Utility you can perform the following functions (see Figure 4.12):

- ◆ Determine DB-Library version information
- ◆ Configure client-side connections

Figure 4.12.
SQL Client Configura-
tion Utility.

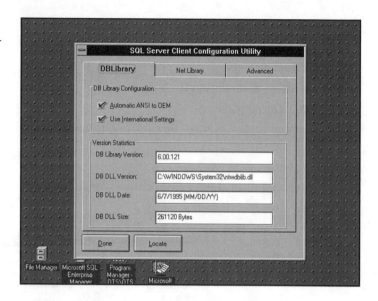

SQL TRANSFER MANAGER

From the SQL *Transfer Manager*, you can transfer an entire database between
different servers or you can transfer individual database objects, user information,
and data between servers (see Figure 4.13). The Transfer Manager can transfer
objects between different platforms and different network protocols.

Figure 4.13.
SQL Transfer
Manager.

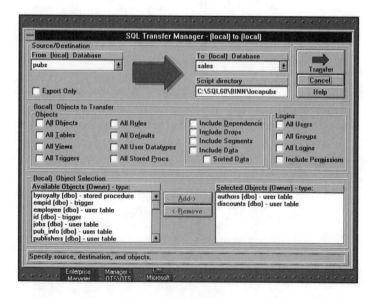

NON-VISUAL ADMINISTRATION TOOLS/ COMMAND LINE TOOLS

A DBA will probably spend the majority of his or her time using the visual administration tools included with SQL Server. However, there are two non-visual administration tools that a DBA may also use: BCP and ISQL.

BCP and ISQL are two non-visual tools that you can also use.

BCP

BCP stands for *Bulk Copy Program*. It is a command-line utility that enables you to import and export data to and from SQL Server. The advantage of BCP is that it is fast. Users new to SQL Server are often amazed at how fast it operates. The drawback of BCP is that it can be difficult to use.

By default, BCP.EXE is installed in the sql60\binn directory. For more information on BCP, see Chapter 15.

Following is the syntax for BCP:

```
bcp [[database_name.]owner.]table_name {in | out} datafile
[/m maxerrors] [/f formatfile] [/e errfile]
[/F firstrow] [/L lastrow] [/b batchsize]
[/n] [/c] [/E]
[/t field_term] [/r row_term]
[/i inputfile] [/o outputfile]
/U login_id [/P password] [/S servername] [/v] [/a packet_size]
```

Tip

BCP switches are case-sensitive.

ISQL

ISQL is a command-line utility used for executing queries and administering SQL Server. With the advent of graphical administration tools for SQL Server, the importance of ISQL has diminished. Most people prefer to perform day-to-day administration from the Enterprise Manager instead of using ISQL.

Its minimal overhead, however, makes it useful for processing non-interactive routines, such as nightly batch jobs.

By default, ISQL.EXE is installed in the sql60\binn directory.

Following is the syntax for ISQL:

```
isql /U login_id [/e] [/E] [/p] [/n] [/d dbname] [/q "query"] [/Q "query"]
[/c cmdend] [/h headers] [/w columnwidth] [/s colseparator]
[/t timeout] [/m errorlevel] [/L] [/?] [/r {0 ¦ 1}]
[/H wksta_name] [/P password]
[/S servername] [/i inputfile] [/o outputfile] [/a packet_size]
```

Tip

ISQL switches are case-sensitive.

Common SQL Server Objects

SQL Server uses the term *object* to describe a database component. Common database objects include tables, rules, defaults, user-defined datatypes, views, triggers, and stored procedures.

Note

Do not be misled by the term object. SQL Server is not an object-oriented database.

Tables

A *table* is used to store data. It is organized in a row/column manner (see Figure 4.14). You can retrieve, modify, and remove data from a table by using the SQL language.

Figure 4.14.
Table example.

stor_id	stor_name	stor_address	city	state	zip	last_update
7066	Barnum's	567 Pasadena Ave.	Tustin	CA	92789	8/1/1995 4:25 PM
7067	News & Brews	577 First St.	Los Gatos	CA	96745	8/15/1995 3:00 PM
7131	Doc-U-Mat	24-A Avrogado Way	Remulade	WA	98014	3/11/1995 1:00 PM
8042	Bookbeat	679 Carson St.	Portland	CA	89076	4/25/1995 3:00 PM

Rules

A *rule* is used to enforce a data constraint (see Figure 4.15). Rules are column specific and cannot perform table lookups. Generally, rules are used to enforce simple business constraints.

Figure 4.15.
Rule example.

stor_id	stor_name	stor_address	city	state	zip	last_update
7066	Barnum's	567 Pasadena Ave.	Tustin	CA	92789	8/1/1995 4:25 PM
7067	News & Brews	577 First St.	Los Gatos	CA	96745	8/15/1995 3:00 PM
7131	Doc-U-Mat	24-A Avrogado Way	Remulade	WA	98014	3/11/1995 1:00 PM
8042	Bookbeat	679 Carson St.	Portland	CA	89076	4/25/1995 3:00 PM

Business Rule: All store ids must be between 1 and 9999.

SQL Server Translation: CREATE RULE stor_id_rule AS
@stor_id > = 1 AND @stor_id < = 9999

sp_bindrule stor_id_rule, 'stores. stor_id'

Note

In SQL Server 6.0, an alternative to creating a rule is to use the CHECK constraint. Another alternative to creating a rule is to use a trigger.

DEFAULTS

Defaults are used to populate a column with a default value when a value is not supplied (see Figure 4.16).

Figure 4.16.
Default example.

stor_id	stor_name	stor_address	city	state	zip	last_update
7066	Barnum's	567 Pasadena Ave.	Tustin	CA	92789	8/1/1995 4:25 PM
7067	News & Brews	577 First St.	Los Gatos	CA	96745	8/15/1995 3:00 PM
7131	Doc-U-Mat	24-A Avrogado Way	Remulade	WA	98014	3/11/1995 1:00 PM
8042	Bookbeat	679 Carson St.	Portland	CA	89076	4/25/1995 3:00 PM
8100	Johnston	**unknown**	Fairfax	VA	23294	8/1/1995 1:00 PM

stor_name
Barnum's
News & Brews
Doc-U-Mat
Bookbeat
Johnston

Business Rule: If store address is not known when adding a new record, enter "unknown."

SQL Server Translation: CREATE DEFAULT stor_address_default AS
'unknown'

sp_bindefault stor_address_default, 'stores. stor_address'

Note

In SQL Server 6.0, an alternative to creating a default is to use the DEFAULT constraint.

USER-DEFINED DATATYPES

With a *user-defined datatype* you can create a custom reusable datatype based on an existing SQL Server datatype (see Figure 4.17). By using user-defined datatypes, you can ensure datatype consistency.

Figure 4.17.
A user-defined
datatype example.

stor_id	stor_name	stor_address	city	state	zip	last_update
7066	Barnum's	567 Pasadena Ave.	Tustin	CA	92789	8/1/1995 4:25 PM
7067	News & Brews	577 First St.	Los Gatos	CA	96745	8/15/1995 3:00 PM
7131	Doc-U-Mat	24-A Avrogado Way	Remulade	WA	98014	3/11/1995 1:00 PM
8042	Bookbeat	679 Carson St.	Portland	CA	89076	4/25/1995 3:00 PM

stor_name
Barnum's
News & Brews
Doc-U-Mat
Bookbeat
Johnston

Business Rule: Store id is an integer and can not be null.

SQL Server Translation: sp_addtype stor_id_data type, 'integer,' 'null'

CREATE TABLE stores (stor_id stor_id_datatype,
stor_name char (35),

VIEWS

A *view* is a virtual table that looks and feels like a real table. Views limit the amount of data a user can see and modify. Views may be used to control user access to data and to simplify data presentation (see Figure 4.18).

Figure 4.18.
A view example.

stor_id	stor_name	stor_address	city	state	zip	last_update
7066	Barnum's	567 Pasadena Ave.	Tustin	CA	92789	8/1/1995 4:25 PM
7067	News & Brews	577 First St.	Los Gatos	CA	96745	8/15/1995 3:00 PM
7131	Doc-U-Mat	24-A Avrogado Way	Remulade	WA	98014	3/11/1995 1:00 PM
8042	Bookbeat	679 Carson St.	Portland	CA	89076	4/25/1995 3:00 PM
8100	Johnston	unknown	Fairfax	VA	23294	

Business Rule: End-users can only see the stor_name column

SQL Server Translation: CREATE VIEW end_user_view AS
SELECT stor_name
FROM stores

SELECT * FROM end_user_view

stor_name
Barnum's
News & Brews
Doc-U-Mat
Bookbeat
Johnston

Output from view

TRIGGERS

A trigger is a user-defined collection of Transact-SQL that is automatically executed when an INSERT, DELETE, or UPDATE is performed (see Figure 4.19). Triggers are flexible and powerful. This makes them useful for enforcing business rules, referential integrity, and data integrity. Triggers can be column, row, or table specific.

Note

Prior to Version 6.0, SQL Server triggers had to be used to enforce referential integrity. New with Version 6.0 is capability +0 create declarative referential integrity by using the FOREIGN KEY, PRIMARY KEY, and REFERENCE statements. Triggers must still be used to cascade table changes.

Figure 4.19.
A trigger example.

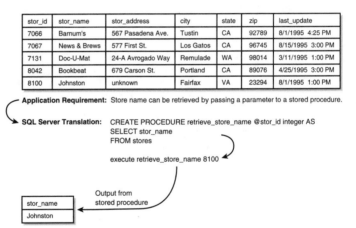

stor_id	stor_name	stor_address	city	state	zip	last_update
7066	Barnum's	567 Pasadena Ave.	Tustin	CA	92789	8/1/1995 4:25 PM
7067	News & Brews	577 First St.	Los Gatos	CA	96745	8/15/1995 3:00 PM
7131	Doc-U-Mat	24-A Avrogado Way	Remulade	WA	98014	3/11/1995 1:00 PM
8042	Bookbeat	679 Carson St.	Portland	CA	89076	4/25/1995 3:00 PM
8100	Johnston	unknown	Fairfax	VA	23294	8/1/1995 1:00 PM

stor_name
Barnum's
News & Brews
Doc-U-Mat
Bookbeat
Johnston

Application Requirement: Every time a record is modified, update the last_update column to reflect the date and time of the modification.

SQL Server Translation:
CREATE TRIGGER stores_trigger ON dbo.stores
FOR INSERT, UPDATE
AS
UPDATE stores
SET last_update = GETDATE()
FROM stores, inserted
WHERE stores.stor_id = inserted.stor_id

This trigger automatically enters the date and the time of the last modification to the record.

STORED PROCEDURES

A stored procedure is a compiled SQL program (see Figure 4.20). Within a stored procedure you can perform conditional execution, declare variables, pass parameters, and perform other programming tasks.

Figure 4.20.
Stored procedure example.

stor_id	stor_name	stor_address	city	state	zip	last_update
7066	Barnum's	567 Pasadena Ave.	Tustin	CA	92789	8/1/1995 4:25 PM
7067	News & Brews	577 First St.	Los Gatos	CA	96745	8/15/1995 3:00 PM
7131	Doc-U-Mat	24-A Avrogado Way	Remulade	WA	98014	3/11/1995 1:00 PM
8042	Bookbeat	679 Carson St.	Portland	CA	89076	4/25/1995 3:00 PM
8100	Johnston	unknown	Fairfax	VA	23294	8/1/1995 1:00 PM

Application Requirement: Store name can be retrieved by passing a parameter to a stored procedure.

SQL Server Translation:
CREATE PROCEDURE retrieve_store_name @stor_id integer AS
SELECT stor_name
FROM stores

execute retrieve_store_name 8100

Output from stored procedure

stor_name
Johnston

SUMMARY

SQL Server delivers performance and ease of use. This is accomplished through the tight integration of SQL Server and Windows NT.

The next chapter discusses how to prepare for the installation SQL Server.

- Planning an Installation or Upgrade

- Installing or Upgrading

PART III

Planning and Installing/ Upgrading the SQL Server

- Developing an
  Installation Strategy
  and Plan

- Developing an
  Upgrade Strategy
  and Plan

CHAPTER 5

Planning an Installation
or Upgrade

In this chapter, you will develop plans and strategies to help you correctly install or upgrade the SQL Server. Why bother with a planning stage? Why not just skip right to the installation or upgrade? SQL Server installation and upgrading is a simple process, but by planning ahead you can make the correct decisions prior to installation that effect the performance and operation of SQL Server. In the case of an upgrade, you can never have too many plans to limit server downtime and protect your database in case of problems encountered during an upgrade. Start by examining installation strategies and plans.

DEVELOPING AN INSTALLATION STRATEGY AND PLAN

Developing an installation plan starts with the requirements of your business or users, includes the selection and purchase of the hardware, and then making decisions for specific SQL Server options. You begin the process of collecting user and system requirements. Then you will examine possible hardware configurations and SQL Server options. Lastly, you will create a checklist to use during system installation.

STEP 1: DETERMINING SYSTEM AND USER REQUIREMENTS

How do you determine the hardware system requirements and user requirements for SQL Server? How else? Ask questions and do some homework. Start with the user requirements or business requirements. Based on the requirements of the users or business, you will determine the size and type of hardware system you need to meet the requirements. Start with the following questions:

◆ What is the purpose or goal of the system?
◆ What are the database requirements?
◆ What are the user or business requirements?
◆ How much money will it cost?

Note

One decision you won't have to make is the operating system to use. Microsoft SQL Server 6.0 is only supported on Windows NT Server and Windows NT Workstation. If you have decided to use Microsoft SQL Server, then the operating system war is already over!

The following sections expand on each of the preceding questions to help you determine the type of system you need.

WHAT IS THE PURPOSE OR GOAL OF THE SYSTEM?

The first questions you might ask yourself are, "What is the system for?" "Is the system for a single department with 10 users or for a very large database system with several hundred users?" In most cases, a system supporting more users will require more memory, disk space, and processing power. Is the system a dedicated SQL Server system or are there other services like file and printing services? Is the system replacing another system as a result of downsizing or right-sizing? In the case of replacing an existing system, you have a lot information available to you such as the current load on the system and the current systems shortcomings. Is the system a production system or a development/test system? You probably want more fault tolerance and a more storage capability on a production server as opposed to a development server.

WHAT ARE THE DATABASE REQUIREMENTS?

What are the database requirements for the system? Will the SQL Server primarily support decision support systems or transaction systems? How heavy is the expected transaction load? If the system is transaction-driven, try to determine the number of expected transactions per day and how the transactions are processed. For example, is the server idle for eight hours and then all the transactions processed during a window of a few hours, or are the transactions processed evenly throughout the day? What is the expected size of the database? Are the databases current databases in use being moved to SQL Server due to downsizing or right-sizing? If so, you should be able to obtain information, such as current database size, expected database size, and the transaction load of the system from the current system.

Tip

> If you have the means, dedicate a machine for SQL Server. Then you can tune the hardware to give the best SQL Server performance.

WHAT ARE THE USER OR BUSINESS REQUIREMENTS?

It is always important to know the requirements and expectations of the individuals who use the SQL Server. What type or query response time do the users expect? How many users will be logged on to SQL Server at one time? What are the backup and storage requirements of the users or business?

HOW MUCH MONEY WILL IT COST?

Maybe this question should be listed first! In the real world, many times the driving factor behind the system you need and the system you get is the amount of money you have available to spend on the system. Enough said!

STEP 2: SELECT THE RIGHT PLATFORM

After you obtain the answers and information to the questions from Step 1, you are ready to select the hardware platform for your SQL Server. For this discussion the hardware is broken down into three areas:

◆ Hardware (includes the processor(s) and peripherals)

◆ Memory

◆ Disk Drives

Examine each area and the type of decisions you need to make for each area.

HARDWARE

When deciding the type of hardware platform to use, the first and last place to check is the Windows NT Hardware Compatibility List to make sure that the brand and model of the machine you are considering is on the list. If the brand and model you are interested in is not on the compatibility list, download the latest list from an electronic bulletin board. If the machine is still not listed, check with the manufacturer.

Tip

Save yourself a lot of problems and potential headaches. Only use machines that have been approved for Microsoft Windows NT. Although you may get other machines working, I have seen the difficulty involved and the potential to not get the machine up and running when using non-approved platforms and configurations.

Currently, Windows NT is supported on the following microprocessors:

◆ Digital Alpha AXP

◆ Intel 32 bit x86 (486, Pentium, and so on)

◆ MIPS

◆ PowerPC

> *Note*
>
> Remember to check the compatibility list, as support for new systems is an ongoing process.

So how do you determine the correct hardware platform for your business or organization? Start with cost and examine hardware platforms that are within your budget's range. There is no point wasting your time researching hardware platforms you can't afford.

The next step is to use the information you gathered earlier, such as the expected number of transactions during a given time period, and talk to the hardware manufacturers or integrators to see whether the platform you are considering can meet your goals and requirements. Check for SQL Server benchmarks on the particular platform and ask to speak to other clients currently using the platform. Consider other factors, such as manufacturer reliability, service, and maintenance. These three factors are extremely important if the machine runs into a hardware problem and you are faced with downtime. Consider expandability; for example, will you require multiple processors in the future and if so, can the current platform be expanded to accept more processors?

DO I NEED SMP (SYMMETRIC MULTIPLE PROCESSORS)?

Windows NT 3.51 currently supports up to four processors out of the box that SQL Server can take advantage of without any special add-ons or configuration. In theory, a perfect scalable SMP machine would scale 100 percent, meaning that if your SQL Server performed 20 transactions per second, then adding a second processor would increase the number of transactions per second to 40. The scalability of systems will vary widely and can range from near 100 percent to below 60 percent. Check with the manufacturer.

What does it mean to you and SQL Server? If you are performing heavy transaction database processing, then you can expect your transaction performance to increase with the scalability of the system. So, if you perform 10 transactions per second and add a second processor on a system that provides 80 percent scalability, then expect roughly 18 transactions per second. SMP works very well for transaction-based systems.

What if you do primarily decision-support (such as database queries)? Adding a second processor may not be the best way to improve your system performance. In decision-support systems, the queries are I/O-bound not processor-bound, so adding additional processors will not provide the same substantial performance gain found with transaction based systems.

MEMORY

A common theme you will see throughout this book is give SQL Server enough memory! Not because SQL Server is an inefficient memory hog, but because SQL Server uses memory very intelligently. Extra memory can provide you with some very cost-effective performance enhancements. The minimum memory requirement for an Intel-based Windows NT Server with SQL Server is 16MB; RISC machines like the ALPHA AXP and the MIPS require slightly more. If you want to use replication, the minimum requirement jumps up to 32MB of memory with at least 16MB assigned to SQL Server.

Tip

Although a Windows NT server with 16MB is the minimum requirement, I would recommend starting with 32MB, allocating 16MB for Windows NT, 16MB for SQL Server, and then tuning up from there.

The setup program will allocate up to but not exceed 8MB of memory to SQL Server. Once SQL Server is up and running, you can increase the amount of memory allocated to SQL Server. So how does SQL Server get memory? When SQL Server starts, the operating system obtains the SQL Server configured amount of memory. Memory is allocated for the SQL Server executable code, static memory, data structures, and miscellaneous overhead. SQL Server divides the remaining memory into the procedure cache and data cache (discussed in detail in Chapter 18).

Tip

When SQL Server starts, it requests the amount of memory in the configuration parameter. The operating system then allocates as much physical memory as possible to SQL Server and if needed, uses virtual memory to meet the memory configuration requirement. Avoid setting the option higher than the amount of physical memory available. Using virtual memory can slow performance. Never set the memory parameter to high; if SQL Server cannot get the required amount of memory from physical and virtual memory, the server will not start.

In later chapters, you will learn how to correctly tune your server with the correct amount of memory. So for installation, how much memory should you use? Microsoft has published the following suggestions that are rough estimates for SQL Server and Windows NT memory configurations. These figures are from the SQL Server books online documentation:

Machine memory (MB)	Approximate SQL Server memory allocation (MB)
16	4
24	8
32	16
48	28
64	40
128	100
256	216
512	464

Another published formula, published in the *Configuration & Tuning of Microsoft SQL Server for Windows NT on Compaq Servers*, Feb. 1994, by Database Engineering, Compaq Computer Corporation, suggests the following formula to use as a rough estimate for memory allocation:

```
SQL Server Memory = 5MB for Kernel and Data Structures
          + (2% Total Data and Index Space) + (50 KB * Number of Users)
```

Regardless of the amount of memory you start with, once SQL Server is up and running, you can monitor SQL Server to more accurately determine your memory requirements.

DISK DRIVES

One of the most important system decisions you will make is the type of disk drives you select. Selecting the proper disk system has a big impact on the overall performance of the SQL Server system and the type of data fault tolerance used to protect the databases.

Before you get into the specifics, you want to select fast disk drives and smart controller cards to take advantage of Windows NT multitasking and asynchronous read ahead features. When buying disk drives for a database server, consider using more physical drives rather than one large physical drive. This allows you to spread your databases and transaction logs over several different physical devices. If you are considering buying a 2GB hard drive, for example, reconsider and purchase two 1GB hard drives or four 500MB hard drives.

Tip

The new Asynchronous Read-Ahead Technology introduced in SQL Server 6.0 is only beneficial with multiple disk configurations!

Just as important as the speed of your hard disk system is the fault tolerance offered in modern disk drive systems. You want the best protection for your databases with optimum performance. One option available to you is the use of *RAID* (Redundant Array of Inexpensive Disks) disk drive configurations. RAID disk configurations use several disk drives to build a single logical striped drive. Logically, a striped drive is a single drive, but the logical drive physically spans many different disk drives. Striping the drives allows files and devices to span multiple physical devices. By spreading the data over several physical drives, RAID configurations offer excellent performance. Another benefit of RAID configurations is fault tolerance and recovery. A RAID 5 configuration can lose a single disk drive and recover all the data on the lost drive. When a new drive is added, the RAID configuration rebuilds the lost drive on the new drive. A RAID 5 system offers you good protection and performance for your databases. RAID configurations can be hardware-based solutions or software-based solutions using Windows NT. Hardware-based RAID solutions are typically faster than software-based RAID solutions.

File System

Should you use NTFS (New Technology File System) or FAT (File Allocation Table)? From a performance standpoint, it does not really matter. The performance difference between the two file systems is negligible. In general, NTFS performs faster in read operations, and FAT performs faster in write operations. With the NTFS file system, you can take advantage of Windows NT security. If you are required to have a dual boot computer, then use a FAT partition.

Tip

I typically recommend NTFS to take advantage of NT security and auditing features.

The Right Platform

What is the right platform for SQL Server? The best system you can afford that will do the SQL Server processing you require! A good configuration for a SQL Server system is shown in Figure 5.1. A computer configured with one to many processors, starting with 32MB of memory. Use a RAID 5 stripe set disk configuration for the databases and the operating system and SQL Server on a non-striped drive. How could this system be enhanced? Add additional stripe sets or more memory. Additional stripe sets will give you additional logical drives so that you can place a table on one logical drive and the index on another. For the memory requirements, monitor your SQL Server and determine the correct amount of memory for your Server. After all, SQL Server can run with as little as 4MB of memory and as much as 2 GB of memory.

Figure 5.1.
SQL Server hardware
configuration.

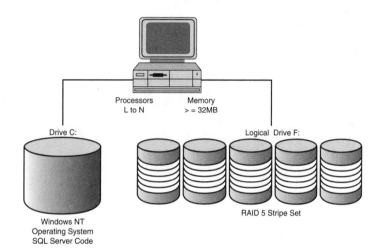

STEP 3: ANSWERING REQUIRED QUESTIONS AND WHY THEY ARE IMPORTANT

When you begin a new SQL Server installation, you will be asked several questions, such as your name, company name, and the type of license agreements for the SQL Server. You should be able to answer these questions with no problem, but you will be asked to answer other questions that affect SQL Server performance, maintenance, and behavior. Examine the following installation topics in more detail to help you make the correct choices for your SQL Server:

- ◆ Master Device
- ◆ Character Set
- ◆ Sort Order
- ◆ Network
- ◆ SQL Server Executive Account

THE MASTER DEVICE

During installation, you will be asked to give the drive, path, and filename of the master device. The master device is the most important database device and is described in more detail in Chapter 8. The master device contains the master database that houses all the SQL Server information required to manage and maintain the server's databases, users, and devices (basically all the information required to maintain and run SQL Server). The master device also contains the model and tempdb databases, as well as the optional pubs database. The default name for the master device is master.dat and the default path is the drive and root directory selected for the SQL Server installed in the directory \DATA. The default/minimum size for the master device is 25MB.

Tip

The default size for SQL Server 4.21 is 15MB.

25MB is the minimum installation size for the master device in Version 6.0. You should use a size of 35- to 40MB to give you room for expansion. A larger master device size will give you more room to create SQL Server objects and will enable you to expand the temporary database (tempdb) beyond the default of 2MB (if tempdb is not placed in RAM).

CHARACTER SET

The *character set* is the set of valid characters in your SQL Server database. A character set consists of 256 upper- and lowercase numbers, symbols, and letters with, the first 128 characters in a character set being the same for all the different character sets.

Note

If you plan to use SQL Server replication, you must select the same character set for all the SQL Server's participating in replication.

The following are the character sets you can choose from at installation time:

Code page 850 (Multilingual)   Code page 850 includes all the characters for North American, South American, and European countries.

Note

Code page 850 is the default character set for SQL Server 4.21 installations.

ISO 8859-1 (Latin 1 or ANSI)   This character set is compatible with the ANSI characters used by Microsoft Windows NT and Microsoft Windows.

Note

ISO 8859-1 is the default sort order for SQL Server Version 6.0.

Code Page 437 (US English)   The common character set used in the United States. Code Page 437 also contains many graphical characters that are typically not stored in databases.

Warning

Deciding on the correct character set is important because the character set cannot be changed easily! Changing the character set requires rebuilding and reloading all of your databases!

SORT ORDER

The sort order you select for your SQL Server determines how the data is presented in response to SQL queries that use the GROUP BY, ORDER BY, and DISTINCT clauses and how certain queries are resolved, such as those involving WHERE clauses. For example, if you choose a sort order that is case sensitive and you have a table called MyTable, then the query to select all the rows from MyTable must have the following format:

```
Select * from MyTable
```

If the sort order selected is case insensitive, then the preceding query could be written in the following manners:

```
Select * from MyTable
```

```
Select * from mytable
```

```
Select * from MYTABLE
```

SQL Server offers many different sort orders that each have their own set of rules. Next, examine briefly some of the possible sort orders choices.

DICTIONARY ORDER, CASE-INSENSITIVE

Dictionary order means the characters, when sorted, appear in the order you find them in a dictionary. Dictionary order, case-insensitive uses the following rules to compare characters:

◆ Upper- and lowercase characters are treated as the same.

◆ Characters with diacritical marks are treated as different characters.

Note

> Dictionary order, case-insensitive is the default sort order for SQL Server 6.0.

BINARY SORT ORDER

The *binary sort* order uses numeric values to collate the data. Each charter is compared to its numeric representation of 0 to 255. Data will not always come back in dictionary order; for example, UUU will return before aaa in ascending order.

DICTIONARY ORDER, CASE-SENSITIVE

Case-sensitive, dictionary order uses the following rules:

◆ Upper- and lowercase characters are not treated the same.

◆ Characters with diacritical marks are treated as different characters.

Tip

> If you have two servers available and you want to change the sort order or character set, use the Transfer Manager to rebuild the database and transfer the data.

The sort order affects the speed and performance of SQL Server. Binary sort order is the fastest of the sort orders, with the other sort orders being in a range of 20 to 35 percent slower than the binary sort order. The default sort order dictionary order, case-insensitive is about 20 percent slower than the binary sort order.

Warning

> Selecting the correct sort order is important because, like the character set, changing the sort order requires rebuilding your databases and reloading the data.

Tip

> If you have several SQL Servers in your organization, you should use the same character set and sort order for each of the servers, especially if you want to share databases using the DUMP and LOAD commands. You can't load a database that was dumped with a different character set and sort order.

NETWORK

Because SQL Server supports many different network options simultaneously, clients running TCP/IP can connect to SQL Server along with clients using IPX/SPX all at the same time! SQL Server installs different network libraries during installation to handle network communication with other servers and client workstations. SQL Server always installs the named-pipes protocol. You have the option during installation (and after) to install one or more network libraries. Keep in mind the type of network support you select determines the security mode you can use for SQL Server. Before you examine the network libraries available to you, look at the three different security modes (for detailed information, see Chapter 10):

- Standard
- Integrated
- Mixed

STANDARD SECURITY

An individual logging on to SQL Server supplies a user name and a password that is validated by SQL Server via a system table. Standard security works over all network configurations.

INTEGRATED SECURITY

Integrated security takes advantage of Windows NT user security and account mechanisms. Integrated security can be implemented over the following network protocols: *named-pipes protocol* or *multi-protocol*.

MIXED SECURITY

Users using trusted connections (named-pipes or multi-protocol) can log on using integrated security or users from trusted or non-trusted connections can log on using standard security.

Now look at the network options available for SQL Server 6.0.

NAMED-PIPES

Named-pipes are the default protocol installed with SQL Server. Named-pipes allow for interprocess communication locally or over networks and is used in NT networks using the NetBUI protocol.

MULTI-PROTOCOL

Multi-protocol is new for SQL Server Version 6.0. The multi-protocol uses Windows NT Remote Procedure Call (RPC) mechanisms for communication and requires no setup parameters. Multi-protocol currently supports IPX/SPX and TCP/IP, enabling users of those protocols to take advantage of SQL Server integrated security features.

Note

Prior to SQL Server 6.0, Integrated Security was only supported by named-pipes protocol.

NWLINK IPX/SPX

IPX/SPX is the familiar network protocol used for Novell networks and is the default network protocol with Windows NT 3.5x Servers. If you select NWLink IPX/SPX during installation, you will be prompted for the Novell Bindery service name to register SQL Server.

TCP/IP

TCP/IP is a popular communications protocol used in many UNIX networks. If you select TCP/IP, you will be asked to provide a TCP/IP port number for SQL Server to listen on for client connections. The default port number and the official Internet Assigned Number Authority socket number for Microsoft SQL Server is 1433.

BANYAN VINES

Banyan Vines is another popular PC-based network system. Support for Banyan Vines is only included on Intel-based SQL Server systems. If you install Banyan Vines, you will prompted for a valid street talk name that must first be created using the Vines program MSERVICE.

APPLETALK ADSP

AppleTalk ADSP allows Apple Macintosh clients to connect to SQL Server using AppleTalk. If you select AppleTalk, you will be prompted for the AppleTalk service object name.

DECNET

Decnet is a popular network protocol found on many digital networks running VMS and pathworks. If you select Decnet, you will be prompted for a Decnet object ID.

Note

For performance, the named-piped protocol is the fastest of the net-work protocols. Running TCP/IP and IPX/SPX is faster than using the multi-protocol but limits your security mode options.

SQL Executive User Account

The *SQL Executive* is new for SQL Server 6.0. The SQL Executive is a new service that is responsible for managing SQL Server tasks, such as replication, events, alerts, and task scheduling. During system installation and upgrade, you will be required to assign an NT system user account for the SQL Executive. You can use the local system account, in which case you do not need to create a new NT user account. However, if the SQL Executive needs to access files on other servers, such as a Novell Netware server or Microsoft Lan Manager, which do not allow a local NT system account to access them, you will need to create a Windows NT user account for the SQL Executive.

Step 4: SQL Server Installation

The next step is to skip to the next chapter and begin the installation process. Use the following worksheet to help you prepare for the installation and then later, as a reference:

```
SQL Server Installation WorkSheet
                                 Installation Date:
                                 Installed By:
Name:
Company:
Product ID:
# of Client Licenses:
SQL Server Installation Path:
Master Device Path:
Master Device Size:
Character Set:
Sort Order:
Network Support
_X_ Named Pipes          ___ TCP/IP          ___ DecNet
___ NWLink IPX/SPX       ___ Banyan Vines    ___ Apple Talk ADSP
Auto Start SQL Server at Boot Time
Yes    No
Auto Start SQL Executive at Boot Time
Yes    No
SQL Executive Log On Account
Start the SQL Server Installation
```

DEVELOPING AN UPGRADE STRATEGY AND PLAN

The plan and strategy for an upgrade is different from a new installation. You already have decided on a platform and are currently running SQL Server. You may have very many large production databases and hundreds of users that depend on the databases, or small development databases with a few users. In many ways, upgrading an existing SQL Server is more critical than installing a new SQL Server. The existing SQL Server contains data being used and depended upon by your organization.

Now you know why it is important to develop a plan that will enable you to upgrade to the new release and in the event the upgrade is not successful, will allow you to return the system to its pre-upgrade state.

Note

Never underestimate the difficulty of an upgrade. Remember Mark and Orryn's first rule of upgrading: expect something to go wrong and if it does, make sure you can get the system back and running to its prior state. Creating a upgrade plan is essential. I was once involved with what was to be a simple upgrade for a banking organization that gave a six-hour window to get their high-powered multi-processor SQL Server upgraded from SQL Server 4.21 to SQL Server 4.21a. No problem, right? After all, the upgrade was not even a major revision number just a revision letter, nothing could go wrong...NOT! Five hours later, when the SQL Server was still not working correctly and tech support was trying to resolve the problem, we opted to restore the system to the pre-upgrade state. Once the SQL Server was restored, it did not work either! It appears that the problem had to do with the SQL Server registry entries. This was not a problem because our upgrade plan called for backing up the system registry. Once the registry was restored, the SQL Server was up and running with no problems, and the upgrade was pushed off to another day, awaiting information from tech support.

The moral of this story is never underestimate the potential problems that may be encountered during an upgrade, and be overly cautious. It's better to have to many files backed up and ready to restore than not enough!

Once you perform a SQL Server 6.0 upgrade on a 4.2*x* database, there is no turning back! The upgrade process to 6.0 makes modification to the databases such as new system tables and datatypes that are not supported in SQL Server 4.2*x*.

Note

Upgrades of SQL Server 1.*x* are not supported with SQL Server 6.0. OS/2 SQL Server version 4.2*x* systems can be upgraded, but you must first upgrade the operating system to Windows NT 3.51.

When upgrading an existing 4.21 SQL Server to SQL Server 6.0, you have two options available:

◆ Upgrade the existing SQL Server
◆ Install a new SQL Server and migrate the databases to the new server

UPGRADE THE EXISTING SQL SERVER

Upgrading SQL Server 4.2*x* is performed by running the Setup program and selecting the Upgrade SQL Server option. The upgrade option installs the new SQL Server software and upgrades the databases with new system tables and datatypes.

Before running a SQL Server upgrade you must make sure that you have adequate disk space. Upgrading SQL Server requires 45MB of free disk space. The master database must have at least 7MB of free space. If the master database does not have at least 7MB free, the Setup program will alter the master database and increase the size of the database. SQL Server 6.0 added several new keywords and follows ANSI-92 standards. Prior to upgrading a SQL Server 4.2*x* to 6.0, run the utility program CHKUPG. CHKUPG checks to make sure the database status is fine, that all required comments are in the SQL Server system table syscomments and checks for keyword conflicts in your databases.

Tip

Fix them now or fix them later! Keyword conflicts found in your databases will not prevent the successful upgrade of SQL Server from 4.2*x* to 6.0. However, you will need to make the corrections on SQL Server and your applications that reference the keywords before or after the upgrade.

The syntax for the CHKUPG utility is as follows:

```
CHKUPG /Usa /Ppassword /Sservername /ofilename
```

Where `password` is the password for the `sa` user, `servername` is the SQL Server being upgraded, and `filename` is the output file to print the CKKUPG report. The filename parameter must be fully qualified with drive, path, and filename. The following is a sample output from the CHKUPG utility:

```
==================================================================
Database:  master
    Status: 8
        (No problem)
    Missing objects in Syscomments
        None
    Keyword conflicts
        Column name: MSscheduled_backups.DAY [SQL-92 keyword]
==================================================================
Database: pubs
    Status: 0
        (No problem)
    Missing objects in Syscomments
        None
    Keyword conflicts
        Column name: sales.DATE [SQL-92 keyword]
```

If you have problems with `syscomments` entries, drop and re-create the objects. Databases with the `read only` option set to `True` will need the `read only` option set to `False`.

Tip

A full list of the new keywords and future keywords can be found in the SQL Server documentation. The following keywords have given me trouble during several upgrades: `CURRENT_TIME`, `CURRENT_USER`, `KEY`, `CURRENT_DATE`, and `USER`.

Warning

After an upgrade, be prepared to rewrite and recompile some stored procedures. SQL Server is now SQL ANSI-92 compliant. You may get the error message after upgrading when trying to execute a stored procedure `You must drop and re-create the stored procedure <stored procedure name>`. What's the problem? Transact SQL treatment of some subqueries and SQL statements such as `GROUP BY` were not ANSI-92 compliant. When you upgrade and try to execute these stored procedures that break ANSI-92 SQL rules, you will get the preceding error message. For example, the following pubs database query works and can be compiled as a stored procedure with SQL Server version 4.2*x*:

```
Select au_id, au_lname
```

```
From Authors

Group By (au_id)
```

With SQL Server 6.0 you will get an error. To correct the SQL statement with SQL Server 6.0, change the query to the following:

```
Select au_id, au_lname

from authors

Group By (au_id), (au_lname)
```

The CHKUPG utility does not report ANSI-92 SQL violations in stored procedures.

Upgrade Plan

Before you begin to upgrade an existing SQL Server installation, it is important to create an upgrade plan. The following section(s) provide you with an example of an upgrade plan to upgrade an existing SQL Server 4.2*x* installation to SQL Server 6.0.

1. **Determine whether you have the required disk space.**

   Make sure you have the required 45MB of disk space to upgrade you existing SQL Server.

2. **Run the CHKUPG Utility.**

   Run the CHKUPG utility and review the output report. Correct any errors, such as keyword conflicts, reported by the utility. Repeat step 2 until errors are no longer reported.

3. **Estimate downtime and schedule upgrade with users.**

   Estimate the amount of time you expect the upgrade to take. Remember that the larger the database, the longer the upgrade will take. Don't forget to give yourself time to perform any necessary backups before the upgrade begins, time to test the upgraded server, and time to handle any possible problems including going back to the 4.2*x* installation, if necessary. Once you have determined the amount of time required to perform the upgrade, schedule a date to perform the upgrade with your users. If you have a Microsoft Technical Support contract, notify Tech Support of your upgrade plans and check for any last minute instructions or known problems.

On the day of the upgrade perform the following:

1. **Back up all databases.**

   Perform SQL Server backups on the databases, including the master database. If possible, shutdown the SQL Server and use the Windows NT backup facilities to back up the SQL Server directories, including all the SQL Server devices for possible restoration.

2. **Back up the NT registry.**

   Back up the NT system registry again, in case you need to restore the system to the SQL Server 4.2x installation.

3. **Turn off read-only on databases.**

   For any databases that have the read only option set to TRUE, use sp_dboption to set the read only option to FALSE. The CHKUPG utility will report any databases in read only mode.

4. **Make sure no SQL Server applications are executing.**

   Before upgrading the SQL Server, ensure that no users are using SQL Server.

5. **Upgrade the Server.**

   Run the Setup program and select the Upgrade SQL Server option.

Fall Back Plan

A SQL Server upgrade is a straightforward process, but because you are usually dealing with valuable data and systems that can only be down for a limited amount of time, upgrades should be treated with extreme caution and care. Just as important as a good upgrade plan is a good fall back plan in case the upgrade does not go as smoothly as planned. Here are some suggestions on how to protect yourself. Above all, make sure that you have the backups (tapes, and so on) to return your SQL Server to the before upgrade state if necessary.

Warning

Always make sure you have a valid backup of the Windows NT system registry before starting any backup!

Suggestion 1: Complete System Backup Recovery Plan

If possible, shutdown the SQL Server before the upgrade and perform a backup of the SQL Server directories and all of the data devices. You need to shutdown SQL Server to back up files that the SQL Server is using, such as devices. If the upgrade fails for some reason, you can restore the SQL Server directories, devices, and the NT registry, returning your system to its prior setup.

Suggestion 2: Complete Database Backups—Reinstalling 4.2x

Perform SQL Server database backups on the databases, including the master. Make sure you have all the valid SQL Server configuration information such as the server name, character set, sort order, network configuration, device and database layouts. If you cannot get the SQL Server 6.0 upgrade to work correctly, having the database dumps and the required SQL Server information enables you to reinstall 4.2x and reload your databases if necessary.

Suggestion 3: Complete System Backup and Database Backups

Perform Suggestions 1 and 2. You can never be to careful!

The bottom line is that the information and data completely recover your system if the upgrade fails. Play it safe. Have a backup plan to use if the backup plan fails!

Upgrade Checklist

The following checklist can be used to help you prepare for a SQL Server upgrade. Check off each item on the list as they are completed. Perform each step in order from top to bottom.

___ Free Disk Space (> 45MB)

___ Run CHKUPG Utility

    ___ syscomments Errors Corrected

    ___ Read Only Databases set to False

    ___ Keyword Conflicts Resolved

Estimated Down Time:_____hours

___ Alert Users

___ Fall Back Recovery Plan in Place

___ Fall Back Recovery Plan in Place in Case Fall Back Plan Fails

___ SQL Server Backup of ALL Databases

___ SQL Server Backup of Master Database

___ Backup of Windows NT System Registry

___ Operating System Backup of SQL Server directories and files including devices.

___ Make sure no users are on the system.

___ Make sure no applications are using the SQL Server

___ Start the SQL Server Upgrade

INSTALLING A NEW SERVER AND MIGRATING THE DATABASES

This option is not actually upgrading an existing system but is mentioned for two reasons. The first reason is that SQL Server 6.0 can be installed alongside a SQL Server 4.2x SQL Server on the same machine. SQL Server 6.0 uses a different directory structure and registry entries than the existing SQL Server 4.2x. You can run the two SQL Servers simultaneously and migrate the databases from the SQL Server 4.2x to the new SQL Server 6.0. This enables you to test each database with SQL Server 6.0 and migrate all the databases without worrying about unexpected problems because you will have the 4.2x installation still operating and functional. This option is not for everyone because it requires enough disk space and memory to support both SQL Servers and your existing databases. The second case is mentioned for the situation in which an existing SQL Server's machine is being upgraded to a new machine. In this scenario, you can install SQL Server on the new machine and migrate the existing databases from the old machine. If you decide to use either method, first run the CHKUPG utility to check for any SQL Server 6.0 violations. Then back up the data as you would for a normal upgrade and follow the installation procedure for a new SQL Server. Use the Transfer Manager to transfer the databases and data or the DUMP and LOAD commands.

Tip

When installing alongside a SQL Server 4.2x installation, remember to change the named-pipe name used for the SQL Server 6.0 installation; otherwise, the SQL Server 6.0 will not run correctly. The named-pipe used by SQL Server 6.0 and SQL Server 4.2 is the same `\\.\pipe\sql\query`. To change the named-pipe name for SQL Server 6.0, use the Setup program and select the Change Network option. Make sure the Named-Pipe option is checked and click the OK button. A dialog box displaying the default named-pipe appears. Change the name of the named-pipe and click the Continue button. You can also use the registry editor, `regedt32`, although this method is not recommended.

Summary

Hopefully, this chapter has helped you prepare for a SQL Server upgrade or installation. In the next chapter you will walk through the installation and upgrade process.

CHAPTER 6

Installing or Upgrading

In this chapter, you will walk through the actual installation and upgrade of SQL Server, as well as the installation of software for the client PCs. Take a look at what the SQL Server installation program actually loads on your computer. The following are the directories created from the SQL Server root directory during installation:

◆ BIN: Windows- and DOS-based client executables and DLLs

◆ BINN: SQL Server NT server and client executable files as well as online help files

◆ CHARSETS: Character sets and sort order files

◆ DATA: SQL Server devices

◆ DLL: Dynamic Link Library files

◆ INSTALL: Installation scripts and output files

◆ LOG: Error log files

◆ REPLDATA: Distribution databases' working directory

◆ SAMPLE: Sample files

The following services are installed:

◆ MSSQLServer—SQL Server

◆ SQLExecutive—SQL Executive

The following utilities are installed:

◆ SQL Setup: Enables you to configure some SQL Server startup parameters, network support, and remove SQL Server after installation

◆ SQL Service Manager: Used to start and stop SQL Server

◆ ISQL/W: Utility to issue SQL queries

◆ SQL Security Manager: Used to set up integrated security

◆ SQL Enterprise Manager: Primary tool used to manage SQL Server and SQL Server objects

◆ SQL Client Configuration Utility: Utility to set up SQL Server connection information and check versions of DB-library installed

◆ SQL Transfer Manager: Allows for transfer of data and database between two SQL Servers

◆ BCP: Bulk Copy Utility to import and export flat files with SQL Server

INSTALLING SQL SERVER

Before installing SQL Server, make sure that you have read through the documentation that ships with SQL Server 6.0 regarding installation and that your system meets the minimum requirements. To help you with your installation, use the following worksheet.

SQL SERVER INSTALLATION WORKSHEET

Check off the following items as you complete or verify them:

Hardware and PC Setup:

____ Computer is Alpha AXP, MIPS, or INTEL (32-bit x86) or is on the Windows NT Hardware Compatibility List

____ Memory: 16MB for non-distribution server, 32MB for distribution server

____ Operating System: Windows NT 3.5 or greater

____ Free Disk Space > 60MB

File System ____ FAT

____ NTFS

NT Server Name:

SQL Server Options (Check or fill in)

User Name:_____Company Name:_____Product ID:_____

SQL Server Root Directory:_____

Master Device Location and filename: _____

Master Device Size (Min: 25): _____

Selected Character Set:

____ ISO 8859-1 (Default)   ___ Code Page 850   ___ Code Page 437
(Multilingual)   (US English)

(If you are planning to use replication, the character sets of all participating servers must match.)

Selected Sort Order:

Network Protocols:

____ Named Pipes (Default)   ____ Multi-Protocol

____ NWLink IPX/SPX   ____ TCP/IP Sockets

____ Banyan VINES   ____ AppleTalk ADSP

____ DECnet

Books Online Installed: ____ Yes ____ No

Auto-Start Options: ____ SQL Server

____ SQL Executive

continues

Licensing Mode:

SQL Executive User Account: _____

Tip

One of the problems that occurs quite often on new SQL Server installations is trying to install SQL Server with a user account that does not have the correct NT permissions to create new directories and files. If you get the error message `Can't create directory`, make sure you are using an account with the correct privileges. Try creating the directory with File Manager. If you have the correct privileges you will be able do so; otherwise, use an account that has the correct permissions.

STEP 1: RUNNING SETUP

Installing SQL Server requires running the Setup program, located on the SQL Server 6.0 CD. The CD contains several directories, including different directories for each of the currently supported microprocessors. Following are those directories:

◆ \I386 for Intel machines

◆ \ALPHA for Digital Alpha AXP machines

◆ \MIPS for Mips processors

Select the correct directory for the processor you are using and run the Setup program. The window displayed in Figure 6.1 appears.

Figure 6.1.
SQL Server Setup
window.

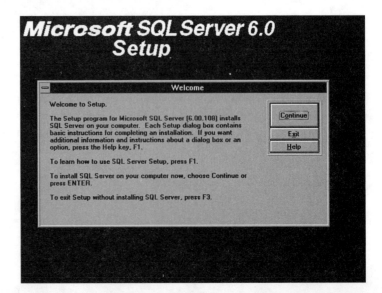

STEP 2: NAME AND ORGANIZATION

Click the Continue button. The Name and Organization dialog box appears (see Figure 6.2).

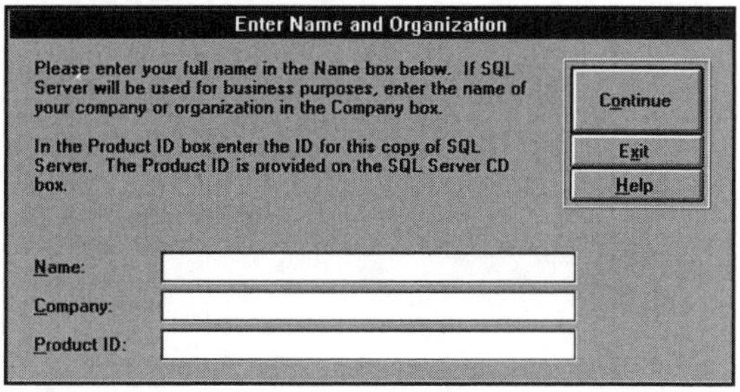

Figure 6.2.
Name and Organiza-
tion dialog box.

Fill in your name, organization, and product id and click the Continue button. Another dialog box will appear, prompting you to verify that the information you just entered is correct. If the name, organization, and product id are correct, click the Continue button. The SQL Server 6.0 Options dialog box appears (see Figure 6.3).

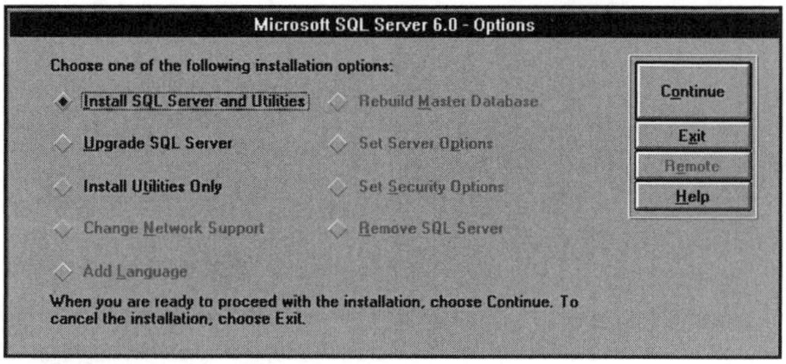

Figure 6.3.
SQL Server 6.0 Options
dialog box.

STEP 3: LICENSING MODE

Make sure the Install SQL Server and Utilities checkbox is checked in the SQL Server 6.0 Options dialog box. Click the Continue button. The Choose Licensing Mode dialog box appears (see Figure 6.4). Select the correct licensing mode for the SQL Server you have purchased and click the Continue button. When the licensing verification dialog box appears, read the agreement, check the verification checkbox, and click the OK button.

6

INSTALLING OR UPGRADING

Figure 6.4.
SQL Server Licensing
Mode dialog box.

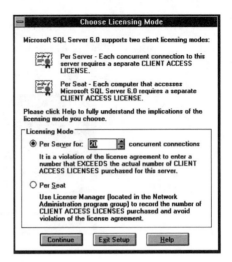

STEP 4: INSTALLATION PATH

The SQL Server Installation Path dialog box, shown in Figure 6.5, appears. Select the correct drive and path for the SQL Server installation and click the Continue button.

Figure 6.5.
SQL Server Installation
Path dialog box.

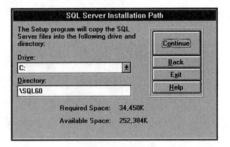

STEP 5: MASTER DEVICE

The SQL Server Master Device Creation dialog box, shown in Figure 6.6, appears. Select the correct drive, path, filename, and size for the master device and click the Continue button.

Figure 6.6.
SQL Server Master
Device Creation
dialog box.

Tip

The minimum default size is 25MB. I recommend making the master device at least 35MB to allow for expansion and a larger temporary database. I also recommend using the default filename, master.dat, since it has become a standard and makes for easy reference when looking at documents or talking to tech support.

STEP 6: BOOKS ONLINE

The SQL Server Books Online dialog box appears (see Figure 6.7). Select one of the following checkboxes:

- ◆ Install on Hard Disk
- ◆ Install to Run from CD
- ◆ Do not Install

Click the Continue button.

Figure 6.7.
SQL Server Books
Online dialog box.

> ### Tip
>
> I recommend installing Books Online. The space requirements are about 15MB, but it is space well spent. The documentation is very good and has search and find features that help you quickly track down specific topics and problems.

STEP 7: INSTALLATION OPTIONS

The Installation Options dialog box appears (see Figure 6.8). Use this dialog box to change the default character set, sort order, or add additional network support. To change the character set, click the Sets button. The Select Character Set dialog box appears (see Figure 6.9). To change the character set, select a character set from the list and click the OK button.

Figure 6.8.
Installation Options
dialog box.

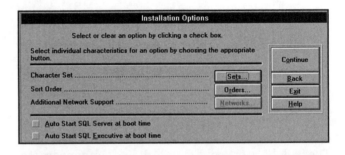

Figure 6.9.
Select Character Set
dialog box.

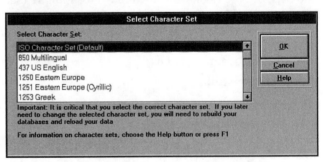

To change the sort order, click the Orders button. The Select Sort Order dialog box appears (see Figure 6.10).

Select the new sort order and click the OK button. To add additional network support, click the Networks button. To start SQL Server and the SQL Executive as an NT service when the NT server is booted, check the proper checkbox options (refer to Figure 6.8). After you make your selections, click the Continue button.

Figure 6.10.
Select Sort Order
dialog box.

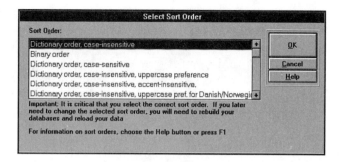

Tip

If you are setting up the NT server to be a dedicated SQL Server system, check the Auto Start SQL Server at boot time and Auto Start SQL Executive at boot time checkboxes. If the NT server goes down momentarily due to a power outage, SQL Server will start automatically when the NT server reboots (if SQL Server and SQL Executive are NT services).

STEP 8: SET UP SQL EXECUTIVE USER ACCOUNT

The next step is to assign an NT user account to the SQL Executive service using the SQL Executive Log On Account dialog box (see Figure 6.11). If you created a special account for the Executive Service, then enter the account name, password, and password confirmation. To use the local system account instead, check the appropriate checkbox. When you have made your choice, click the Continue button.

Figure 6.11.
SQL Executive Log On
Account dialog box.

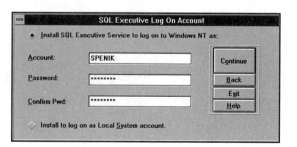

STEP 9: WAIT AND WATCH

Step 9 is the "wait-and-watch" step or the "go-do-something-else" step. The Setup program will begin to create the SQL Server directories and load the appropriate files (see Figure 6.12).

Figure 6.12.
SQL Server Setup
copying files.

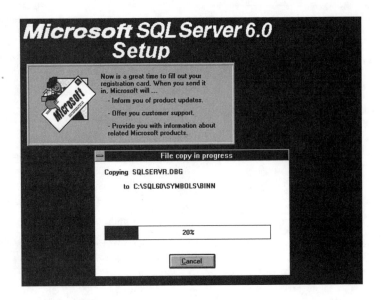

Once the file copy is complete, SQL Server will begin to create the master device (see Figure 6.13).

Figure 6.13.
SQL Setup creating
master device.

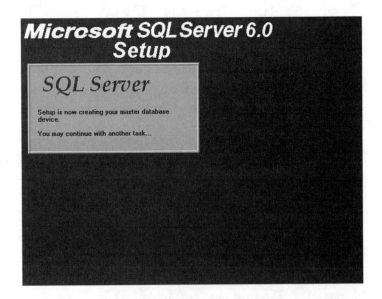

The other devices and databases are created, the registry is updated, and when the Setup program is complete, the SQL Server Completion dialog box appears (see Figure 6.14). In order to use SQL Server, you must reboot the server.

Congratulations—the SQL Server installation is complete!

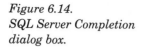

Figure 6.14.
SQL Server Completion
dialog box.

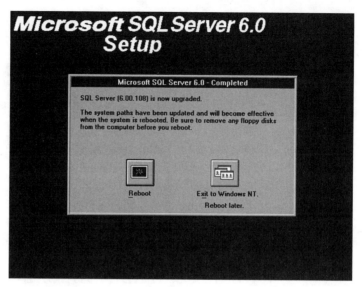

UPGRADING SQL SERVER

The upgrade procedure is very similar to the installation procedure, except that a few questions are skipped because the server is already running. Before starting the upgrade, make sure that you have performed all the items on the upgrade checklist described in Chapter 5. As a reminder, make sure you have done the following:

◆ Performed database backups

◆ Backed up SQL Server files, devices, and directories

◆ Backed up the NT registry

◆ Run CHKUPG.EXE

Now you can get started and perform the upgrade!

STEP 1: RUNNING SETUP

Upgrading SQL Server requires running the Setup program located on the SQL Server 6.0 CD. The CD contains several directories, including directories for each of the currently supported microprocessors. The directories are as follows:

◆ \I386 for Intel machines

◆ \ALPHA for Digital Alpha AXP machines

◆ \MIPS for Mips processors

Select the correct directory for the processor you are using and run the Setup program. When the SQL Server Welcome dialog box appears, click the Continue button. The SQL Server Already Installed dialog box appears (see Figure 6.15). Click Continue.

Figure 6.15.
SQL Server Already
Installed dialog box.

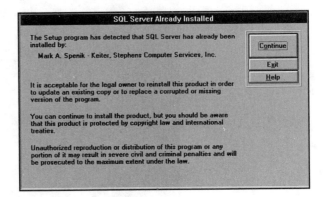

STEP 2: CHECK UPGRADE CHECKBOX

Make sure the Upgrade SQL Server checkbox is checked in the SQL Server 6.0 Options dialog box and click the Continue button (see Figure 6.16).

Figure 6.16.
SQL Server 6.0
Options dialog box.

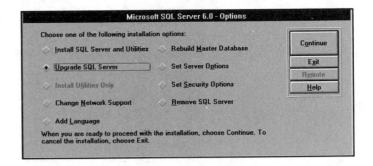

STEP 3: NAME, ORGANIZATION, AND LICENSING MODE

The Name and Organization dialog box appears with the current name and organization filled in from the previous SQL Server (refer to Figure 6.2). Fill in the product id and click the Continue button. Another dialog box will appear, prompting you to verify that the information you just entered is correct. If the name, organization, and product id are correct, click the Continue button. The Choose Licensing Mode dialog box appears (refer to Figure 6.4). Select the correct licensing mode for the SQL Server you have purchased and click the Continue button. When the licensing verification dialog box appears, read the agreement, check the verification checkbox, and click the OK button.

STEP 4: CONTINUE OR EXIT UPGRADE

The SQL Server Upgrade dialog box appears (see Figure 6.17). To stop the upgrade, click the Exit button. To continue the upgrade, click the Resume button.

Figure 6.17.
Upgrade SQL Server
dialog box.

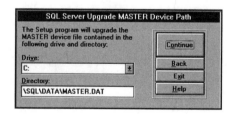

STEP 5: INSTALLATION PATH

The SQL Server Installation Path dialog box appears (refer to Figure 6.5). The current path and drive for the existing SQL Server are the defaults. To change them, select the correct drive and path for the SQL Server installation and click the Continue button.

STEP 6: UPGRADE MASTER DEVICE

The SQL Server Upgrade Master Device Path dialog box appears (see Figure 6.18). The drive and path must point to the master device being upgraded to SQL Server 6.0. If the drive and path displayed are invalid, select the correct drive, path, and filename and click the Continue button.

Figure 6.18.
SQL Server Upgrade
Master Device Path
dialog box.

STEP 7: BOOKS ONLINE

The SQL Server Books Online dialog box appears (refer to Figure 6.7). Select one of the following checkboxes:

- ◆ Install on Hard Disk
- ◆ Install to Run from CD
- ◆ Do not Install

Click the Continue button.

6

INSTALLING OR UPGRADING

STEP 8: EXECUTIVE SERVICE USER ACCOUNT

The SA Password dialog box appears (see Figure 6.19). Enter the SA password and confirmation password and click the Continue button. The SQL Executive Log On Account dialog box appears (refer to Figure 6.11). If you created a special account for the Executive Service, then enter the account name, password, and password confirmation. If you want to use the local system account instead, check the appropriate checkbox. When you have made your choice, click the Continue button (refer to Figure 6.11).

Figure 6.19.
SA Password
dialog box.

SA Password

Please enter and confirm the SA password that the upgrade will use to log in to the SQL Server.

SA Password: [   ]

Confirm Password: [   ]

To enter a different SA password, use the BACKSPACE key to delete characters, and then type the password you want the Setup program to use when upgrading.

Continue
Back
Exit
Help

STEP 9: WAIT AND WATCH

You will be prompted by the Upgrade SQL Server dialog box (see Figure 6.20). To continue the SQL Server upgrade, click the Resume button. To halt the upgrade, click the Exit button. If you click the Resume button, you will enter a waiting period while the SQL Server 4.2*x* installation is upgraded to SQL Server 6.0. When the upgrade is complete, the Microsoft SQL Server 6.0 - Completed dialog box appears (see Figure 6.21). To run SQL Server 6.0, you must reboot the server.

Figure 6.20.
Upgrade SQL Server
dialog box.

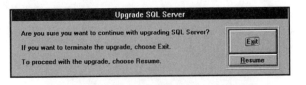

Upgrade SQL Server

Are you sure you want to continue with upgrading SQL Server?

If you want to terminate the upgrade, choose Exit.

To proceed with the upgrade, choose Resume.

Exit
Resume

Figure 6.21.
Microsoft SQL
Server 6.0 - Completed
dialog box.

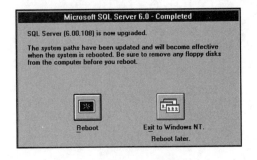

Microsoft SQL Server 6.0 - Completed

SQL Server (6.00.108) is now upgraded.

The system paths have been updated and will become effective when the system is rebooted. Be sure to remove any floppy disks from the computer before you reboot.

Reboot

Exit to Windows NT.
Reboot later.

STARTING AND STOPPING SQL SERVER

If you checked the auto boot options for SQL Server and the SQL Executive, then the two services will automatically be started when the NT server reboots. The easiest way to start, stop, pause, or check the status of SQL Server and SQL Executive is the *SQL Service Manager* (see Figure 6.22).

Figure 6.22.
SQL Service Manager.

The SQL Server Manager is located in Microsoft SQL Server 6.0 program group created during the installation or upgrade. To start the SQL Server Manager, double-click on the icon and the SQL Service Manager appears (refer to Figure 6.22). If SQL Server is running, the stoplight will be green. If the service is stopped, the stoplight is red. To start the server, double-click on the light by the Start/Continue button.

To stop SQL Server, double-click on the light next to the label Stop. To pause SQL Server, double-click the light next to the Pause label. Pausing SQL Server does not halt queries in process but prevents new users from logging into SQL Server. When SQL Server is paused, users currently logged into SQL Server can continue to work as normal.

Controlling the SQL Executive is the same as SQL Server, except that you cannot pause the SQL Executive. To perform stop, start, and status checks on SQL Executive, use the drop-down list box labeled Services and select SQL Executive instead of MSSQLServer.

You can also start SQL Server and SQL Executive from the Windows NT Services dialog box located in the Windows NT Control Panel. If you want to set up SQL Server and SQL Executive to start when the NT server is rebooted, use the Services dialog box in the Control Panel or the SQL Setup program to set the auto boot options (see Figure 6.23).

6

INSTALLING OR UPGRADING

Note

The service name for Microsoft SQL Server has changed. In previous versions, the name used for the service was *SQLServer*. With SQL Server 6.0, the name is *MSSQLServer*.

REMOVING SQL SERVER

If you need to remove a SQL Server installation, do not delete the SQL Server directories. Run the Setup program and select the Remove SQL Server option from the SQL Server Setup window (see Figure 6.23).

Figure 6.23.
SQL Server Setup
Options dialog box.

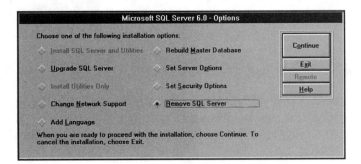

If you select the remove files option, the Setup program will clear the SQL Server entries from the system registry and will remove all the SQL Server files installed; otherwise, only the registry is cleared. If you select remove files, you will have to manually delete a few files used by the setup program when the SQL Server removal is complete. Remove the leftover files by removing the SQL Server home directory, which also is left over after a file removal.

INSTALLING CLIENT TOOLS

SQL Server provides several different tools that allow computers acting as clients to connect to SQL Server. The following are the current 32-bit operating systems supported by the SQL Server client tools:

◆ Microsoft Windows NT Server, Version 3.51

◆ Microsoft Windows NT Workstation, Version 3.51

◆ Microsoft Windows 95

If you are using one of the 32-bit operating systems just listed, you can install the following tools:

- **ISQL/W**: Utility to issue SQL queries
- **SQL Security Manager**: Used to setup integrated security
- **SQL Enterprise Manager**: Primary tool used to manage SQL Server and SQL Server objects
- **SQL Client Configuration Utility**: Utility to set up SQL Server connection information and checks versions of DB-library installed
- **BCP**: Bulk Copy Utility to import and export flat files with SQL Server

The following 16-bit operating systems are supported:

- Windows 3.1 and Windows 3.11 (Workgroups)
- MS-DOS

The tools available for Windows 3.1 and Windows 3.11 are as follows:

- **ISQL/W**: Utility to issue SQL queries
- **SQL Client Configuration Utility**: Utility to set up SQL Server connection information and checks versions of DB-library installed
- **BCP**: Bulk Copy Utility to import and export flat files with SQL Server

The tools available for MS-DOS are as follows:

- **ISQL**: Utility to issue SQL queries
- **BCP**: Bulk Copy Utility to import and export flat files with SQL Server

Note

You can use the SQL Administrator and SQL Object Manager client tools installed with SQL Server 4.2x on 32-bit and 16-bit clients. For 32-bit clients, I recommend using the new 32-bit tools, such as the SQL Server Enterprise Manager, rather than the SQL Server 4.2x tools.

To use SQL Administrator and SQL Object Manager, you need to install the following scripts on the Version 6.0 SQL Server, located on the SQL Server root directory \INSTALL:

- ADMIN60.SQL for the SQL Server Administrator
- OBJECT60.SQL for the Object Manager

Be careful if you install SQL Server 6.0 utilities on the same machine as SQL Server 4.2x utilities. When I installed the 6.0 utilities, my 4.2x utilities would no longer connect to my 4.2x servers. It turned out that the 4.2x utilities were using the newer 6.0 DB-libraries and network libraries, and were unable to properly connect. Once I removed the 6.0 DLLs from my path and started using the older DLLs, I was able to use the 4.2x client tools to connect with the 4.2x servers again.

Let's walk through a SQL Server client utilities installation from Windows 95!

Note

The BCP utility is a MS DOS-based utility for all client utility versions.

STEP 1: RUN SETUP

Installing SQL Server utilities on 32-bit operating systems requires running the Setup program located on the SQL Server 6.0 CD. The CD contains several directories, including directories for each of the currently supported microprocessors the directories:

- ◆ \I386 for Intel machines
- ◆ \ALPHA for Digital Aplha AXP machines
- ◆ \MIPS for Mips processors

Note

For 16-bit operating systems, run Setup from the correct processor directory under the directory \CLIENT\WIN16 for Windows 3.1 and Windows 3.11. For MS-DOS the directory is \CLIENT\MSDOS.

Select the correct directory for the processor you are using and run the Setup program. The Welcome dialog box appears (see Figure 6.24). To install the client utilities, click the Continue button.

Figure 6.24.
Welcome dialog box.

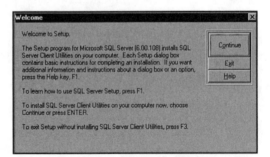

STEP 2: INSTALL CLIENT UTILITIES

The next dialog box that appears is Install/Remove Client Utilities (see Figure 6.25).

Figure 6.25.
Install/Remove Client
Utilities dialog box.

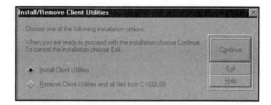

To continue the installation, check the Install Client Utilities checkbox and click the Continue button.

Note

To remove the client utilities, check the Remove Client Utilities and files checkbox and then click the Continue button.

STEP 3: SELECT UTILITIES

The Install Client Utilities dialog box appears (see Figure 6.26). Use the drive combo box to select the correct drive and enter a directory in the directory text box (the default directory is \SQL60). All the utilities checkboxes will be checked in the Utilities to be installed frame. If you do not want a utility installed, uncheck the appropriate checkbox. When you have made all of your utility selections, click the Continue button.

Figure 6.26.
Install Client Utilities
dialog box.

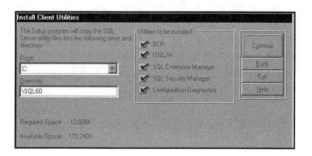

The utilities will begin to load on your computer. When the utilities are loaded, a completion dialog box will appear and the client utility installation is complete. Reboot the computer and you are ready to test the utilities. Figure 6.27 shows the Windows 95 program group created by the utilities setup program. The SQL Server utilities installation is complete!

Figure 6.27.
Windows 95 SQL
Server 6.0 Utilities
program group.

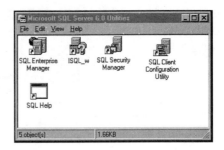

CONFIGURING CLIENTS

Now that you have the client utilities installed, you are ready to connect to SQL Server. SQL Server clients establish connections with SQL Server over named-pipes using dynamic server names. SQL Server clients can connect over named-pipes or any of the Microsoft-supplied protocols, including TCP/IP sockets and IPX/SPX.

You typically can connect to SQL Server from a client utility without any special configuration. When using ISQL/W or the SQL Enterprise Manager, click the List Servers drop-down list box to get a list of the active SQL Servers.

Tip

If you are trying to connect to SQL Server on a local machine, leave the Server name blank.

To connect to a SQL Server that is using a different network protocol or listening on an alternate named-pipe, you can set up an entry for the SQL Server using the Client Configuration Utility with the Advanced tab selected (see Figure 6.28).

To add a new client configuration, select a server or enter the server name in the Server combo box (see Figure 6.28). Select the network used to communicate with the server in the DLL Name list box. The DLL name refers to the network library that provides the communication between SQL Server and the client. Selecting the network will assign the correct DLL to the server entry. The network DLLs for each operating system are listed in Table 6.1.

Figure 6.28.
The Advanced tab in
the SQL Server Client
Configuration Utilities
dialog box.

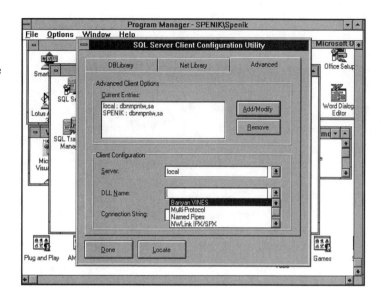

TABLE 6.1. SQL SERVER NET-LIBRARIES.

Network	Windows NT DLL	Windows 3.1 and 3.11 DLL	MS-DOS TSR
Named-Pipes	DBNMPNTW	DBNMP3	DBNMPIPE.EXE
NWLink IPX/SPX	DBMSSPXN	DBMSSPX3	DBMSSPX.EXE
Banyan VINES	DBMSVINN	DBMSVIN3	DBMSVINE.EXE
TCP/IP Sockets	DBMSSOCN	DBMSSOC3	None
Multi-Protocol	DBMSRPCN	DBMSRPC3	None

Add the proper connection string information in the Connection String text box. For example, if the network is TCP/IP and the address of the server is 200.12.20.123 and the SQL Server port is 1433, in the Connection String box add the following:

```
200.12.20.123,1433
```

Click the Add button on the Client Configuration Utilities dialog box. The server name is now available for the SQL Server client utilities.

WHAT ABOUT ODBC?

If you are trying to connect to SQL Server using the Open Database Connectivity standard (ODBC), remember that the Client Configuration Utility does not set up ODBC data sources for applications, such as Microsoft Access or PowerBuilder. You must run the ODBC setup program that ships with the applications or the operating system.

Remember, before you can connect to SQL Server from a ODBC client tool or application, you must install the instcat.sql script file, located on the SQL Server root directory. If you do not load the script file on SQL Server, you will not be able to connect to SQL Server. The resulting error messages will not tell you the instcat.sql file has not been installed. More than likely, you will get error messages that say `Improper ODBC setup` or `Unable to connect to SQL Server`.

INSTALLATION AND UPGRADE TROUBLESHOOTING

As stated earlier, the installation and upgrade process for SQL Server is fairly straightforward; however, even in the most straightforward operations, problems can and do occur. Hopefully, you will be provided with error messages that will pinpoint your problem. In some cases, you will have to do some debugging and observation to determine what has gone wrong. And in the worst cases, you may find yourself on the telephone with tech support trying to determine the problem.

Some of the common errors encountered during an installation or upgrade are improper Windows NT permissions or insufficient disk space. If you receive an error message telling you that you can't create a directory or file, then you probably have a permissions problem. Switch to an account with the correct permissions. If the installation fails, check your disk space to make sure you have enough free space to install SQL Server.

Typical problems encountered during an upgrade, other than disk space and permissions, are trying to upgrade a suspect (corrupted) database or a database with read-only flag set. Use the CHKUPG utility and make sure that you resolve any suspect database problems and reset the read-only database options to FALSE before upgrading.

So what can you do if you have completed an installation or upgrade and your SQL Server does not work? You have to start debugging and try to determine the problem. The best place to start is the SQL Server error log.

ERROR LOG AND WINDOWS NT APPLICATION LOG

The error log, located on the SQL Server root directory in the directory \LOG, is a text file used to log audit and error information for SQL Server.

The Windows NT application log is a Windows NT system log used by applications and Windows NT to log audit and error information. The Windows NT application log contains the same information as the SQL Server error log, except that only SQL Server writes to the error log but any Windows NT application can write to the application log. You can configure SQL Server to write to both logs, the default, or either log.

Tip

When trying to read consecutive error or audit messages, I find using the SQL Server error log easier to view than the Windows NT application log; however, one benefit of the Windows NT application log is error messages are highlighted with a stopsign icon and are easy to find.

Following is an example of a SQL Server error log entry during system startup:

```
95/07/12 09:20:13.24 kernel    Microsoft SQL Server 6.0 - 6.00.108 (Intel X86)
    May 8 1995 07:41:02
    Copyright (c) 1988-1995 Microsoft Corporation
95/07/12 09:20:13.33 kernel    Copyright (C) 1988-1994 Microsoft Corporation.
95/07/12 09:20:13.33 kernel    All rights reserved.
95/07/12 09:20:13.33 kernel    Logging SQL Server messages in file
    'C:\SQL\LOG\ERRORLOG'
95/07/12 09:20:13.40 kernel    initconfig: number of user connections limited to
    10
95/07/12 09:20:13.40 kernel    SQL Server is starting at priority class 'normal'
    with dataserver serialization turned on.
95/07/12 09:20:13.82 kernel    initializing virtual device 0,
    C:\SQL\DATA\MASTER.DAT
95/07/12 09:20:13.87 kernel    Opening Master Database ...
95/07/12 09:20:14.26 spid1     Loading SQL Server's default sort order and charac-
    ter set
95/07/12 09:20:14.34 spid1     Recovering Database 'master'
95/07/12 09:20:14.39 spid1     Recovery dbid 1 ckpt (6453,14) oldest tran=(6453,13)
95/07/12 09:20:14.41 spid1     1 transactions rolled forward
95/07/12 09:20:14.65 spid1     Activating disk 'MSDBData'
95/07/12 09:20:14.65 kernel    initializing virtual device 255,
    C:\SQL\DATA\MSDB.DAT
95/07/12 09:20:14.65 spid1     Activating disk 'MSDBLog'
95/07/12 09:20:14.66 kernel    initializing virtual device 254,
    C:\SQL\DATA\MSDBLOG.DAT
```

```
95/07/12 09:20:14.68 spid1      server name is 'SPENIK'
95/07/12 09:20:14.75 spid1      Recovering database 'model'
95/07/12 09:20:14.78 spid1      Recovery dbid 3 ckpt (328,25)
95/07/12 09:20:14.91 spid1      Clearing temp db
95/07/12 09:20:17.64 kernel     Read Ahead Manager started.
95/07/12 09:20:17.65 kernel     Using 'SQLEVN60.DLL' version '6.00.000'.
95/07/12 09:20:17.87 kernel     Using 'OPENDS60.DLL' version '6.00.01.02'.
95/07/12 09:20:18.13 kernel     Using 'NTWDBLIB.DLL' version '6.00.108'.
95/07/12 09:20:18.19 ods        Using 'SSNMPN60.DLL' version '6.3.0.0' to listen on
                                '\\.\pipe\sql\query'.
95/07/12 09:20:19.82 spid10     Recovering database 'pubs'
95/07/12 09:20:19.83 spid11     Recovering database 'msdb'
95/07/12 09:20:19.84 spid10     Recovery dbid 4 ckpt (514,10)
95/07/12 09:20:19.85 spid11     Recovery dbid 5 ckpt (1287,13) oldest tran=(1287,12)
95/07/12 09:20:19.86 spid11     1 transactions rolled forward in dbid 5.
95/07/12 09:20:20.43 spid1      Recovery complete.
95/07/12 09:20:20.49 spid1      SQL Server's default sort order is:
95/07/12 09:20:20.49 spid1      'bin_cp850' (ID = 40)
95/07/12 09:20:20.49 spid1      on top of default character set:
95/07/12 09:20:20.49 spid1      'cp850' (ID = 2)
```

You can view the error log using any text file editor, such as Windows Notepad or SQL Server Enterprise Manager. You can view the Windows NT application log using the Windows NT Event Viewer (see Figure 6.29).

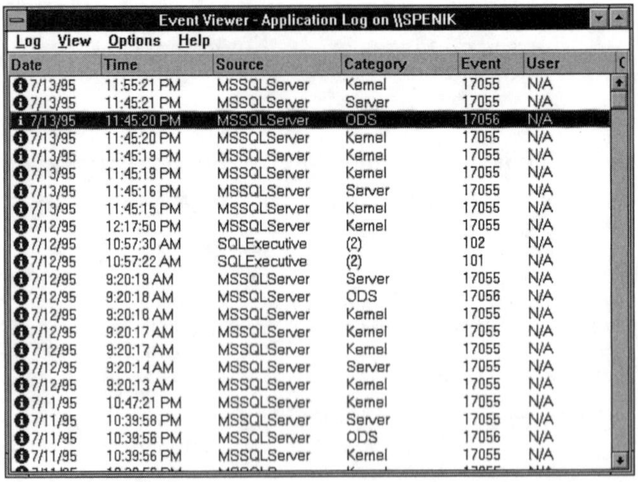

Figure 6.29.
Windows NT
application log.

Scan through the error log or application log and look for possible error messages. SQL Server saves the previous six error log files named as follows:

ERRORLOG.*X*

where *x* is 1 through 6, and the current error log is ERRORLOG.

Another possible place to find error messages is to check the \INSTALL directory on the SQL Server root directory. Each installation script file writes to an output file with a .OUT extension. To find the last script that was executed, enter the following on a DOS command line from the \INSTALL directory:

```
dir *.out /od
```

The last file displayed is the last script to execute. Check the .OUT file for possible errors.

STARTING SQL SERVER FROM THE COMMAND LINE

If you are having trouble starting SQL Server after an installation or upgrade from the Windows NT Service Manager or the SQL Server Service Manager, you should try starting SQL Server from the command line. Starting SQL Server from the command line is a great way to debug because the messages usually logged to the error log or Windows NT application log are displayed directly in the DOS command window. To start SQL Server from the command line, enter the following:

```
sqlservr <command line options>
```

Not all the command line options are discussed here, but read on to find out about a few of the important options you can use to help you get your SQL Server debugged, up, and running.

-D

The -d option specifies the path and filename of the master device.

-C

-c starts SQL Server independent of the Windows NT Service Control Manager.

Tip

The -c option is supposed to quicken SQL Server startup time by bypassing the Windows NT Service Control Manager. If you are having problems starting SQL Server, include the -c option to help further isolate the problem. I was working with one upgraded SQL Server installation where the NT Service Control Manager kept shutting down SQL Server every time it started. By specifying the -c option, we were able to get the server up and running and correct the problem. The only drawback is that you will not be able to stop the SQL Server with any of the conventional methods, such as the SQL

Server Service Manager. SQL Server can be halted by logging off
Windows NT or pressing Ctrl+C in the DOS command window running SQL Server. When you press Ctrl+C, you will be prompted with a
message asking if you would like to shut down the server. Select Y to
shut down the server.

-M

-m enables you to start SQL Server in single user mode, which means only one user
can log into SQL Server. Use the -m option when restoring databases or trying to fix
suspect or corrupted databases.

-F

You decide to push the limits of your system's capabilities and you place tempdb in
RAM, not really understanding where the RAM is coming from for the temporary
database. You restart SQL Server and you get an error trying to open the tempdb
database because you don't have enough physical or virtual memory on your
machine to create tempdb in RAM and run SQL Server! Problem sound familiar?
How do you correct this problem? Use the -f startup option!

The -f option enables you to start SQL Server in a minimal configuration. Use the
-f option only when SQL Server will not start because of a configuration parameter,
such as placing a 40MB tempdb in RAM when only 20MB of RAM is available.

The following is an example of how to start SQL Server from the command line using
some the preceding options:

```
sqlservr -c -dc:\sql\data\master.dat -f
```

SUMMARY

You now have completed the chapters on installing and upgrading SQL Server. The
remaining chapters in the book teach you how to perform database administration
task, such as database backups, SQL Server tuning and configuration, and many
other tasks!

- Managing the Enterprise

- Managing Devices

- Managing Databases

- User Management

- Managing SQL Server Security

- Replication

- Backups

- Recovery

- Importing and Exporting Data

- Database Checkup and Problem Detection

PART IV

Database Operation

CHAPTER 7

Managing the Enterprise

SQL Server 6.0 greatly simplifies database management through its Enterprise Manager. The Enterprise Manager combines the features found in version 4.2*x*'s Object Manager and SQL Administrator. Now from a single interface a DBA can concurrently administer multiple servers without the burden of having to use multiple administration products.

STARTING THE ENTERPRISE MANAGER

To start the Enterprise Manager, double-click on the SQL Enterprise Manager icon in the Microsoft SQL Server 6.0 (Common) group (see Figure 7.1).

Figure 7.1.
SQL Enterprise
Manager icon.

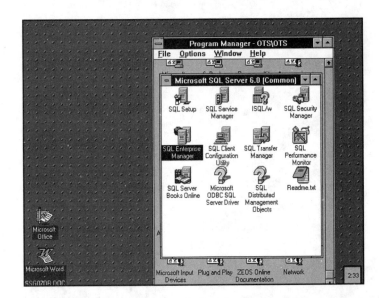

Note

Due to its 32-bit architecture, Enterprise Manager can only be run from Windows NT or Windows 95. It *cannot* be run from Windows 3.1.

NAVIGATION

Due to its graphical interface, the Enterprise Manager minimizes the number of commands required to administer a server. Following are common methods of navigation in the Enterprise Manager:

◆ Menu items
◆ Double-click

◆ Right mouse click

◆ Drop and drag

REGISTERING A SERVER

The first time you start the Enterprise Manager, you will be prompted to register a server. When you register a server, you are providing the Enterprise Manager with a logical name and user login to connect to the SQL Server database engine.

The following steps explain how to register a server (see Figure 7.2):

1. From the Register Server dialog box, enter the name of the server to register.
2. Select the type of login to use: trusted or standard. Trusted security offers the advantage of only having to maintain a Windows NT login account and password. With standard security, you must maintain a network account plus a SQL Server account and password.

   If using Standard Security, enter the login id and password.

Note

To use trusted security, SQL Server must be installed with Windows NT Integrated security or Mixed security.

3. Select a server group or create a new server group.
4. Click on the Register button to register the server with the Enterprise Manager.

Figure 7.2.
Registering a server.

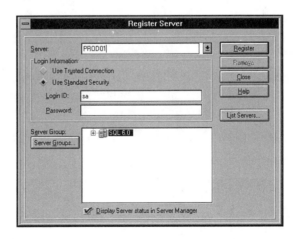

Note

The Enterprise Manager can be used to administer a 4.2*x* version of SQL Server. Run the script SQLOLE42.SQL. This script can be found in the install subdirectory of SQL Server (for example, `c:/sql60/install/sqlole42.sql`).

CONNECTING TO A SERVER

Once inside the Enterprise Manager, click on plus (+) sign to connect to a server. If a connection is successfully made, the connected symbol will appear next to the server status icon (see Figure 7.3).

Figure 7.3.
Successful server
connection.

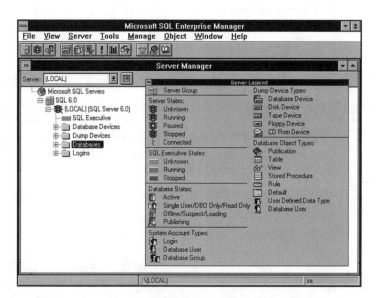

Note

If you are unable to establish a connection to SQL Server from the Enterprise Manager, check that the MS SQL Server service is currently running.

DISCONNECTING FROM A SERVER

To disconnect from a server, select the server, and then right mouse click. From the right mouse menu, select Disconnect.

> **Note**
>
> You will automatically be disconnected from SQL Server when you close the Enterprise Manager.

COMMON TASKS

This section provides a brief description on how to perform common administration tasks from the Enterprise Manager. Many of these tasks are explained in greater detail in other sections of this book.

EXECUTE AND ANALYZE QUERIES

To execute and analyze queries, select a server and click on the Query Analyzer toolbar button (see Figure 7.4). This will take you to the Query dialog box (see Figure 7.5). From this dialog box, you can issue Transact SQL statements, view results, and analyze query performance and optimization plans.

Figure 7.4.
Query Analyzer
toolbar button.

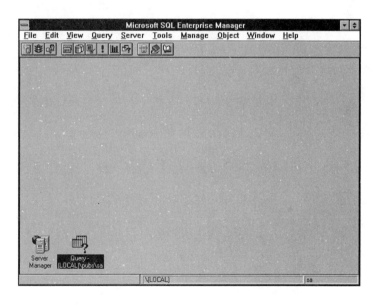

Figure 7.5.
Query dialog box.

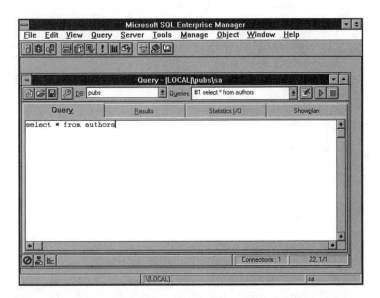

Tip

From the Query dialog box you can concurrently run multiple SQL statements against the server. Click on the New Query toolbar button in the Query dialog box. This will open a new connection to SQL Server that can be used to issue a new query while still maintaining previous connections. This enables you to switch connections while queries are being processed. Because the processing takes place on the server and not on the client, your machine is free to continue with other tasks. Queries that are being processed will have a globe next to the query number (see Figure 7.6).

Tip

From the Query dialog box, you can run an individual Transact SQL statement by highlighting just the text and clicking on the Execute Query toolbar button (see Figure 7.7).

Figure 7.6.
Query processing
example.

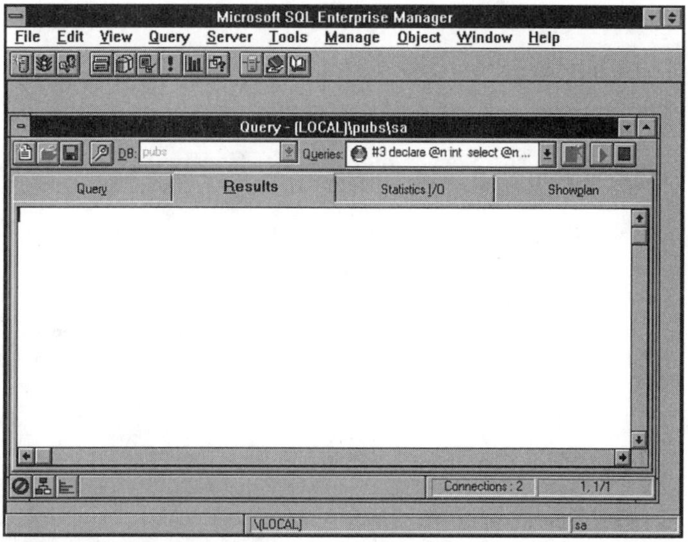

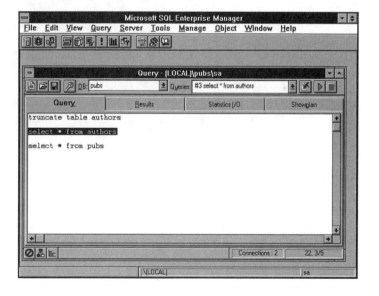

Figure 7.7.
Executing high-
lighted text.

MANAGE SERVER CONFIGURATIONS

The following steps explain how to configure a server:

1. Select a server to configure.
2. From the Server menu select Configurations. The Server Configurations/
   Options dialog box appears (Figure 7.8). From this dialog box you can
   configure server level options, security, and view SQL Server build information.

Figure 7.8.
Server configuration.

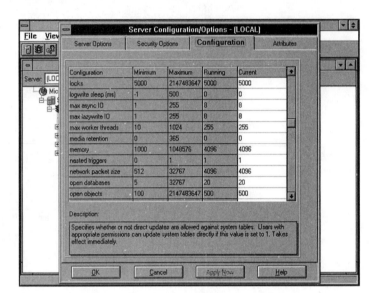

MANAGE DEVICES

Perform the following steps to create, manage, and delete devices:

1. Select the server in which you want to manage a device.
2. Open the Database Devices folder by clicking on the (+) sign. To manage an
   individual device, right mouse click over the appropriate device. To manage
   multiple devices, right mouse click on the Databases Devices folder.
3. From the right mouse menu, select Edit. The Manage Database Devices
   dialog box will appear (see Figure 7.9).
4. Double-click on a device to open the Edit Database Devices dialog box (see
   Figure 7.10). From this dialog box you can edit an existing device.

Figure 7.9.
Manage database
devices.

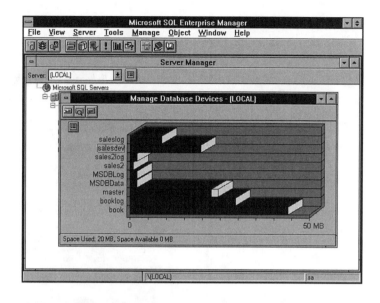

Figure 7.10.
Edit database devices.

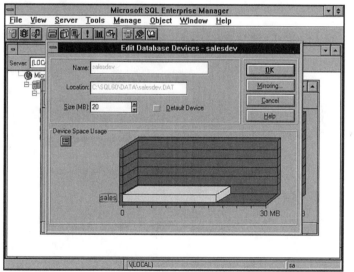

MANAGING DATABASES

The following steps explain how to create, manage, and drop a database:

1. Select the server in which you want to manage a database.

2. Click on the Databases folder. From this folder you can create a new database, edit an existing database, or drop a database. Right mouse click on the appropriate object to activate the corresponding database menu.

3. To manage multiple databases, right mouse click on the Databases folder. From the right mouse menu select Edit. This displays the Manage Database dialog box (see Figure 7.11). Double-click on a database to open the Edit Database dialog box (see Figure 7.12). From this dialog box you can edit an existing database.

Figure 7.11.
Managing a database.

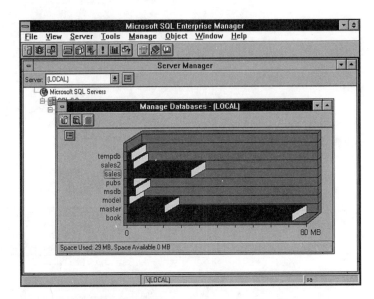

Figure 7.12.
Editing a database.

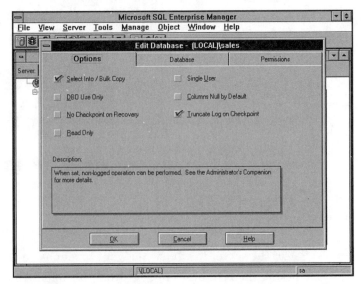

MANAGING DATABASE OBJECTS

The following steps explain how to create, manage, and drop database objects, such as tables, indexes, triggers, views, stored procedures, rules, defaults, and user-defined datatypes:

1. Select the server in which you want to manage a database object.

2. Open the Database folder by clicking on the (+) sign. Open the database that contains the objects you want to work with by clicking on the (+) sign next to the corresponding database.

3. Open the Objects folder by clicking on the (+) sign. From this folder, you can manage tables, views, stored procedures, rules, defaults, and user defined datatypes (see Figure 7.13). For example, to manage a table, click on the (+) next to the Tables folder. From the Tables folder, double-click on a table. This will open the Manage Tables dialog box. From this dialog box, you can alter an existing table or create a new table (see Figure 7.14).

Figure 7.13.
Managing database objects.

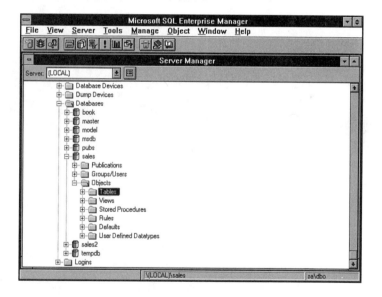

You can also manage object permissions by clicking the right button on the appropriate object and selecting the Permission menu option. This displays the Object Permissions dialog box (see Figure 7.15).

Figure 7.14.
Managing tables.

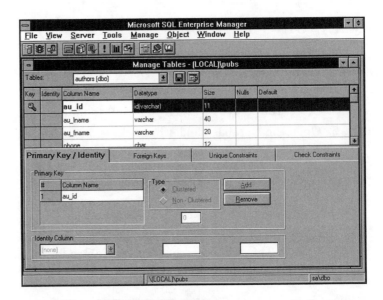

Figure 7.15.
Object permissions.

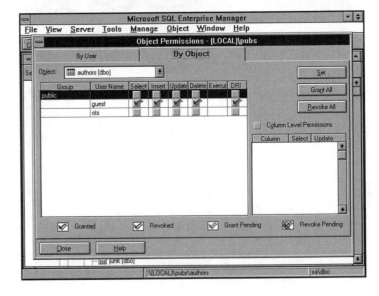

MANAGE LOGINS

Perform the following steps to manage logins.

1. Select the server in which you want to manage logins.
2. Click on the Manage Logins toolbar button in the Enterprise Manager window (see Figure 7.16). The Manage Logins dialog box will appear.

From this dialog box, you can add, edit, and drop server logins (see Figure 7.17). You can also control a user's database access and default database from the Database Access section of the dialog box.

Figure 7.16.
Manage Logins toolbar button.

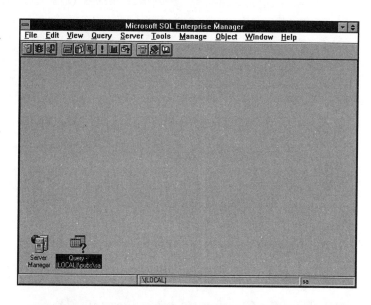

Figure 7.17.
Managing logins.

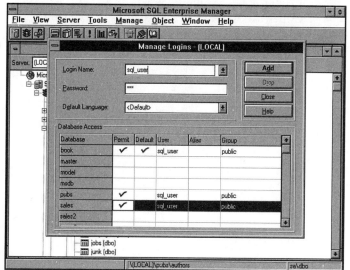

GENERATING SQL SCRIPTS

From the Enterprise Manager you can generate SQL scripts that contain the data definition language used to create an object in a database. This enables you to reverse engineer existing objects.

Tip

An easy way to add or drop a column from a table is to generate the corresponding SQL scripts, modify the script, and then re-create the object from the modified script.

SQL Scripts are useful for performing keyword searches. Suppose that you want to determine how many tables have the column au_id varchar(11). An easy way to determine this is to generate the data definition language for all the tables in the database and then search with a text editor for the au_id column.

Perform the following steps to generate SQL scripts:

1. Select the server and database from which you want to generate a SQL script.

2. From the Object menu, select Generate SQL Scripts. This displays the Generate SQL Scripts dialog box. From this dialog box you can generate the appropriate SQL syntax (see Figure 7.18).

Figure 7.18. Generating SQL scripts.

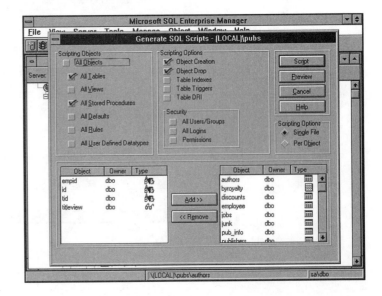

MANAGING BACKUPS AND RESTORATION

SQL Server provides a robust backup and restoration component that enables you to tailor your backup strategy in order to maximize data recovery. Perform the following steps to manage backups:

1. Select the server and database you want to backup/restore.
2. From the Tools menu, select Backup/Restore. This displays the Database Backup Restore dialog box. From this dialog box you can back up and restore databases (see Figure 7.19).

Tip

Use the Enterprise Manager's Task Scheduler to schedule backups on a recurring basis.

Figure 7.19.
Database
backup / restore.

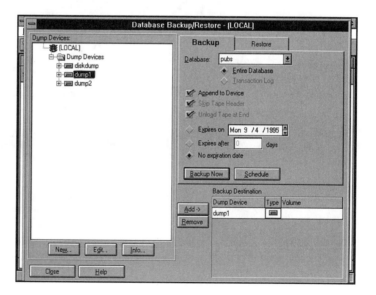

SCHEDULING TASKS

The Task Scheduler can automatically execute a task at a preset time interval. Databases dumps, transaction log dumps, and DBCC commands are just a few types of administrative tasks that can be automated with Task Scheduler. To manage scheduled tasks, follow these steps:

1. Click on the Task Scheduling toolbar button (see Figure 7.20). This displays the Task Scheduling dialog box (see Figure 7.21).

2. From this dialog box you can add, edit, and delete a task. You can also view currently running tasks.

Figure 7.20.
Task Scheduling
toolbar button.

Task Scheduling
button

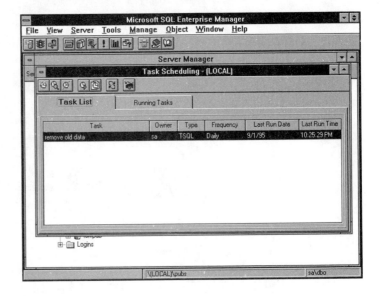

Figure 7.21.
Task Scheduling.

MANAGING ALERTS

The Enterprise Manager provides a built-in Alert Manager that enables you to define various types of alerts. When these alerts are activated, the Alert Manager can automatically notify an operator through e-mail or a pager. This allows for a more proactive approach to database administration. To manage alerts, follow these steps:

1. Click on the Manage Alerts toolbar button (see Figure 7.22). This displays the Manage Alerts dialog box (see Figure 7.23).

Figure 7.22.
Manage Alerts
toolbar button.

Manage Alerts
button

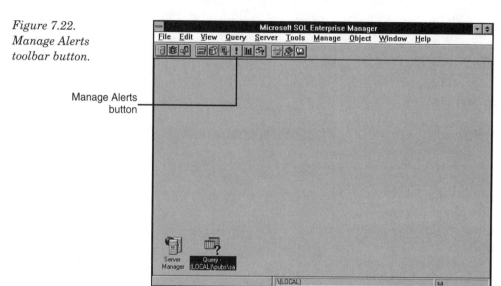

Figure 7.23.
Manage Alerts
dialog box.

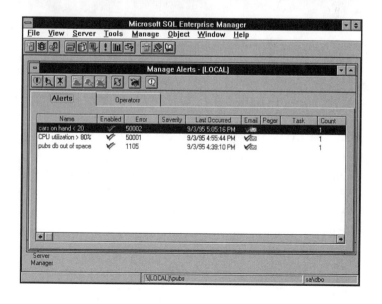

7

MANAGING THE ENTERPRISE

2. From the Manage Alert dialog box you can add, edit, and delete alerts. You can define operators for e-mail and pager notification.

MANAGING REPLICATION

SQL Server provides a graphical replication model that uses a publisher/subscriber metaphor that simplifies replication initialization and management.

Replication management is comprised of three components: Replication Topology, Replication - Manage Publications, and Replication - Manage Subscriptions.

To manage each of these components, click on the corresponding toolbar button (see Figures 7.24, 7.25, and 7.26).

Figure 7.24.
Replication Topology
toolbar button.

Replication
Topology button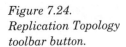

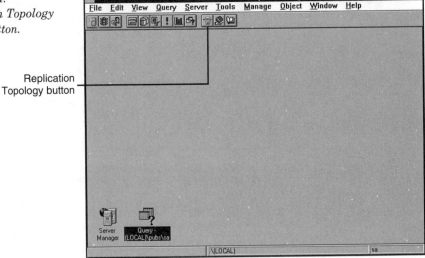

MONITORING USER ACTIVITY

With SQL Server 6.0 you can easily monitor user activity. This can help an administrator pinpoint query problems and isolate bottlenecks. Also from the User Activity dialog box you can kill a process and send an e-mail to a user.

To monitor user activity, click on the Current Activity toolbar button (see Figure 7.27). This will take you to the Current Activity dialog box (see Figure 7.28). From this dialog box you can view and terminate different processes.

Figure 7.25.
Replication–Manage
Publications toolbar
button.

Replication-Manage
Publications button

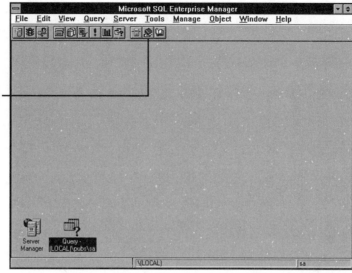

Figure 7.26.
Replication–Manage
Subscriptions toolbar
button.

Replication-Manage
Subscriptions button

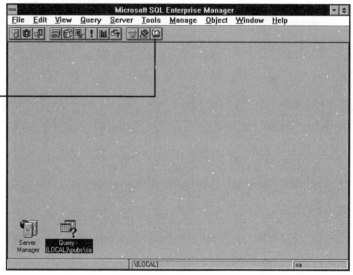

7

MANAGING THE ENTERPRISE

Figure 7.27.
Current Activity toolbar
button.

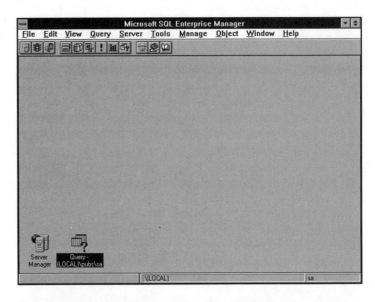

Figure 7.28.
Current Activity
window.

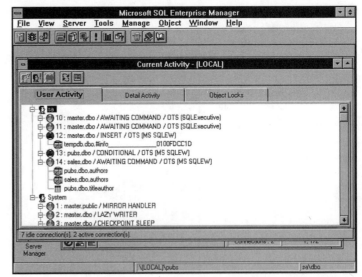

SUMMARY

As you can see, the graphical interface provided by the Enterprise Manager simplifies the tasks required to manage SQL Server. However, to manage a production environment, a DBA must know more than how to right mouse click on an object. A DBA must be knowledgeable on the various components of SQL Server and how they interact. With that in mind, the next chapter starts by discussing one of the most fundamental components of SQL Server: devices.

CHAPTER 8

Managing Devices

In this chapter, you will examine SQL Server devices. You will learn the difference between a data device and a dump device and how to create, delete, use, and maintain SQL Server devices.

WHAT IS A DEVICE?

A very general definition of a Microsoft SQL Server device is a storage area from which SQL Server can read and write. Devices are used for database storage, transaction log storage, database backups, and database recovery. Figure 8.1 depicts several examples of SQL Server devices.

Figure 8.1.
Examples of SQL
Server devices.

8 mm tape

Floppy disk

Master
Dat.

Hard disk file

DIFFERENT TYPES OF DEVICES

Not only can a device be represented by different physical objects such as a floppy disk or hard drive, but devices come in two types: database devices and dump devices.

DATABASE DEVICES

A *database device* is a disk file used to store databases and transaction logs. Creating a database device requires pre-allocating storage space for later use. A database device can be larger or smaller than the database or transaction log you allocate to the device because databases and transaction logs can span multiple devices. When SQL Server is first installed, three database devices are created in the \SQL60\DATA directory: MASTER.DAT, MSDBDATA.DAT, and MSDBLOG.DAT.

THE MASTER DEVICE

MASTER.DAT is the master database device and is the most important SQL Server device. The master device stores the master, model, tempdb, and pubs database, which are described in detail in Chapter 9. What is important to know is the master database, stored on the master device, contains all the SQL Server information required to manage and maintain the server's databases, users, and devices (basically all the information required to maintain and run SQL Server). If the master device becomes corrupted, all databases will be unusable until the master device can be restored!

Warning

Never use the master device for any database allocation, except for the default databases installed on the master device during SQL Server setup. Even though SQL Server allows you to allocate space on the master device for other databases, don't do it! The master device should be used only for its intended purpose—to store the master, model, and temdb databases! Following this advice will save you many headaches if you have to recover the master device.

The minimum master device size required to install SQL Server 6.0 is 25MB.

THE SCHEDULER DATABASE AND LOG

MSDBDATA.DAT is the database device created at installation time to store the msdb database used by the SQL Executive for scheduling information. The device MSDBLOG is used to store the transaction log for the msdb database. The default device sizes used during setup are 2MB for MSDBDATA.DAT and 2MB for MSDBLOG.DAT.

Note

MSDBDATA.DAT and MSDBLOG.DAT are new for Version 6.0 and do not exist in previous versions. Also, the SQL Server documentation incorrectly states the size of MSDBLOG.DAT is 1 MB; however, installation allocates 2MB to MSDBLOG.DAT.

DUMP DEVICES

Dump devices are used to back up and restore databases and transaction logs. When a dump device is allocated, unlike a database device, no storage space is pre-allocated. Dump devices can be tapes, floppy disks, disk files, or named-pipes.

Note

Named-pipe dump devices are new for Version 6.0. A named-pipe dump device is not created like other dump devices, but is a parameter used in the DUMP and LOAD commands. For more information, see Chapters 13 and 14.

8

Three dump devices are created during SQL Server installation: DISKDUMP, DISKETTEDUMPA, and DISKETTEDUMPB. DISKETTEDUMPA and DISKETTEDUMPB are dump devices for the A: and B: floppy drives on the machine SQL Server is running. The DISKDUMP device is a special dump device referred to as the NULL dump device because the dump device represents no physical media, only thin air!

Tip

DISKDUMP (NULL dump device) can be very helpful during database application development. Use DISKDUMP to clear out databases and transaction logs when developers are filling the databases and logs with test data that does not need to be backed up.

CREATING A DATABASE DEVICE

Now that you have an understanding of the different types of devices, you can create a database device. From the SQL Server Manager, perform the following steps:

1. Select the server on which to create the device.

2. Click the Manage Device button on the SQL Manager toolbar. The screen shown in Figure 8.2 will appear.

Figure 8.2.
The Manage Database Devices dialog box.

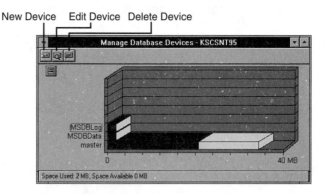

3. Click the New Device button and the New Database Device dialog box, shown in Figure 8.3, will appear.

Figure 8.3.
Creating a device
example in the New
Database Device
dialog box.

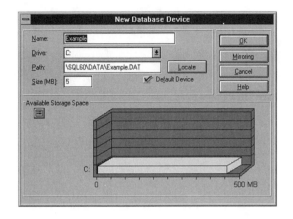

Examine the different parameters in the New Database Device dialog box (refer to Figure 8.3).

Name: The name field specifies the logical name that will be given to the device. The logical name is used to manage the device in SQL Server. The maximum size of the name field is 30 characters.

Tip

Choose meaningful names for your devices. Specify the database you plan to store on the device in the device name. If the device will be used for a transaction log, then include log in the name. This will help you remember what the device is for. As an example, think of the device names given the default devices like MSDBData for the msdb database and MSDBLOG for the msdb database transaction log.

Drive: The drive box is used to select the disk drive the device is to be created on.

Note

A database device can only be created on a local disk drive and cannot be created on an attached network drive.

Path: The path is the directory where the device will be created. The default path is \SQL60\DATA.

Size: Enter the device size in megabytes. The minimum device size is 1MB with no practical maximum size.

8

Default Device: Check the checkbox to add the device to the pool of default devices.

4. Add the necessary parameters to create the device. Figure 8.3 shows the New Database Device dialog box with the required parameters filled in to create a SQL Server device called Example.

5. To add the new device, click OK.

Figure 8.3 shows the addition of a 5 MB device named Example that is created in the default directory \SQL60\Data on the C: drive. So what happens when the device Example is created with the SQL Server Manager? The SQL Server Manager performs a command called DISK INIT. The DISK INIT command creates a 5MB initialized file EXAMPLE.DAT, located in C:\SQL60\DATA and adds a new entry in the system table sysdevices located in the master database.

Note

Creating a device in SQL Server 6.0 is much faster than in previous versions. Version 6.0 does not zero out each page of the device, thus taking advantage of the fact that a DOS FAT file or NTFS file is already initialized with zeroes. Previous versions of SQL Server zero out each page, so creating a large device with older versions takes several minutes.

The DISK INIT command can also be issued from a ISQL prompt and has the following format:

```
DISK INIT
NAME = logical_name,
PHYSNAME = physical_name,
VDEVNO = virtual_device_number,
SIZE = number_of_2K_blocks
[, VSTART = virtual_address]
```

NAME is the logical name of the device and is the same as the name field shown in Figure 8.3.

PHYSNAME is the physical location and filename of the database device (that is, the path and filename).

VDEVNO is a number between 1–255, assigned to the new device. The number 0 is reserved for the master device. VDEVNO uniquely identifies a device. The number, once used for a device, cannot be used again until the device is dropped.

SIZE is the size of the device to create. Unlike the SQL Server Manager, the size represented in DISK INIT is in 2K pages (2048 bytes). 1MB is equal to 512 2K pages.

VSTART is an optional parameter that represents the starting offset in 2K blocks in the device file. The value is 0 and should only be modified if instructed to do so.

CREATING A DUMP DEVICE

To create a dump device from the SQL Server Manager, select the server to add the dump device and then perform the following steps:

1. Select the Dump Devices folder and click the right mouse button. A pop-up menu will appear.

2. Select New Dump Device from the pop-up menu to display the Create Dump Device dialog box (see Figure 8.4).

Figure 8.4.
Create Dump Device
dialog box.

Examine the different parameters in the Create Dump Device dialog box (refer to Figure 8.4).

Device Name: The SQL Server logical name for the dump device. The rules and limitations for Device Name for a dump device are the same as for database devices.

Device Path: Only applies if the dump device being created is a hard disk file. Device Path is the path and filename of the hard disk.

Tip

The Device Path for a dump device can be located on a network drive.

Type: Select either Disk or Tape. If you select Tape, you can also select or clear the Skip Headers checkbox. Skip Headers determines whether SQL Server will search for ANSI labels that may be on a tape before a backup is performed.

Note

No file size is required for a disk type dump device. If you use disk dump devices, make sure you have enough storage to dump the object. For example, if you have 20 MB free on a hard drive for a disk dump

8

> device called MYDBDUMP, and you want to back up a full 150 MB transaction log, you cannot use MYDBDUMP because you do not have enough space.

3. Enter the required information in Figure 8.4, as described in the following options, and then click the Add button to add the dump device.

Adding a dump device with SQL Server Manager is the same as executing the stored procedure sp_addumpdevice, which has the following parameters:

```
sp_addumpdevice Type, 'Logical_Name',
'Physical_Name'
[,@devstatus = {noskip ¦ skip}]
```

The Type parameter specifies the type of device and can be 'disk', 'diskette', or 'tape'. Logical Name is the logical name of the dump device. Physical Name is the physical path and name of the dump device.

Set @devstatus to skip or noskip. These parameters determine whether SQL Server will try to read ANSI labels before performing a backup.

Note

> In older versions of SQL Server (pre-4.21), sp_addumpdevice included parameters called cntrltype and media_capacity. These parameters were never used in NT versions of SQL Server, so are not included.

When a dump device is added, SQL Server makes an entry in the sysdevices table (the same table used for database devices).

Warning

> Always back up the master database after adding any devices.

SYBASE BEWARE!

Microsoft has taken care of the most common problem (besides syntax problems) that I have encountered during device creation—running out of configured devices. In Version 6.0, the configuration parameter devices no longer exists. You now have access to all possible devices, 1–255. Previous versions of SQL Server have a configuration parameter called devices, which is the maximum number of devices that can be configured or the maximum device number allowed . The initial setting for devices in previous versions is 10, which means you can have up to 10 devices, device numbers (VDEVNO) 1-9. What about device number 10? Device numbers are zero-based. Remember that the device number 0 is reserved for the master device. When the device limit is exceeded, you will not be able to add any more devices until you reconfigure the SQL Server using the stored procedure, sp_configure. The zero-based numbering and the error message(s) seem to be very confusing to beginning administrators who often call and say SQL Server will not let them add another device. However, with Version 6.0, this is no longer a problem.

Figure 8.5 shows the system table sysdevices after the device Example has been added.

Figure 8.5.
System table,
sysdevices.

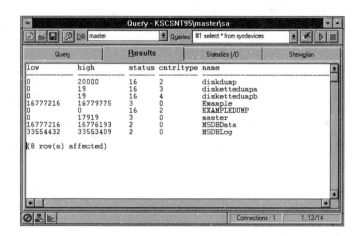

VIEWING DEVICE INFORMATION

Device information can be viewed in several different ways. To see the current devices installed on a server, use the Server Manager window to select a server and then click on the database device folder. Dump devices can be viewed in the same manner.

Figure 8.6 shows a view of database devices and dump devices using the SQL Manager. To see more detailed information, click the Manage Devices button on the Enterprise Manager toolbar.

Figure 8.6.
SQL Manager database
and dump devices.

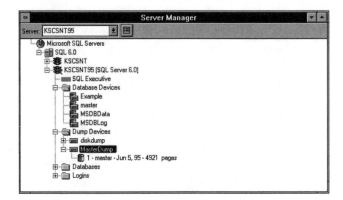

Figure 8.7 shows the detailed database window. Each bar graph represents a database device. The graph shows the amount of space used on each device and the space available.

Figure 8.7.
Detailed Database
Device window.

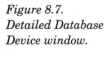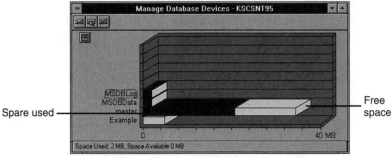

The stored procedure `sp_helpdevice` can be used to display device information from the ISQL command line and has the following syntax:

```
sp_helpdevice [device_name]
```

device name is the logical name of the device on which you want information. If the parameter is omitted, all the devices in the `sysdevices` table will be listed.

REMOVING A DEVICE

Now that you can add and view devices you have created, how do you get rid of them? Removing a database or a dump device in SQL Server terms is called *dropping* a device. When a device is dropped, the row containing the dropped device is removed from the system table `sysdevices`. The logical name and device number (VDEVNO) can then be reused. Before you can reuse the physical name of the device, you first must delete the file. When a database device is dropped, the actual physical file created for the device is not removed. To remove the file and regain the space, you must delete the file using the NT File Manager or the DOS DEL command to delete the file. Once the file is deleted, you can then reuse the physical name.

Warning

For versions of SQL Server earlier than Version 6.0, you must shut down SQL Server after a device is dropped before the physical file can be removed.

Database and dump devices can be dropped with the stored procedure sp_dropdevice. The syntax for sp_dropdevice is as follows:

```
sp_dropdevice device name
```

Where *device name* is the logical name of the device to drop.

To drop a database using the SQL Server Manager, access the Manage Database Device dialog box. Select the device by clicking on it and then click the Delete Device button that was shown in Figure 8.2. Before the device is dropped, a confirmation box will appear to prevent accidental deletions.

Warning

When a device is dropped, any databases or transaction logs using the device will also be dropped. SQL Server will display a warning message that lists any database(s) and transaction log(s) currently using the device. If you decide to continue the operation, the databases or transaction logs on the device will be dropped and then the device will be dropped.

To delete a dump device using the SQL Server Manager, click on the server on which the device resides. Click on the dump device folder and select the dump device to delete. Click the Delete button or click the right mouse button to display a pop-up menu. Choose Delete from the pop-up menu. A confirmation dialog box will reappear to prevent accidental deletions.

EXPANDING A DATABASE DEVICE

Once a database device is created, the size of the device cannot be decreased, but it can be increased. To increase the database device size with the SQL Server Manager, double-click on a device displayed in the device folder (see Figure 8.8).

Figure 8.8.
Edit Database Devices
dialog box.

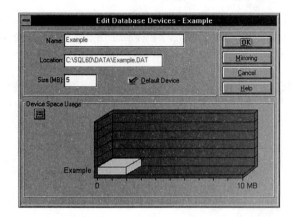

To increase the size of the device, change the Size parameter to the new device size and click OK.

Warning

The drive(s) the device resides on must have available free space greater than or equal to the amount the device is to be increased by.

The corresponding command to increase disk space is the DISK RESIZE command, which has the following syntax:

```
DISK RESIZE
NAME = 'logical device name',
SIZE = device final size
```

NAME is the logical device name of the device to expand.

SIZE is the size of the database device after the device is expanded. The size is specified in 2K pages. Remember, 512 pages equals 1MB.

DEFAULT DEVICE POOL

SQL Server maintains a pool of database devices that will be used if a database is created without specifying a device. Devices in the pool are referred to as *default devices*. The default device pool can consist of one or many database devices. SQL Server allocates the default space one device at a time, going in alphabetical order. When a default device runs out of space, SQL Server will use the next default device available. A database device can be designated as a default device during device creation using the SQL Server Manager by checking the default database device checkbox in the Create Database Device dialog box or after the device has been created by checking the device checkbox in the Edit Database Device dialog box (refer to Figure 8.8). The database device can be removed from the default database pool by unchecking the Default Device checkbox in either dialog box.

Warning

At installation, the SQL Server master device is placed in the default disk pool. Remove the master device from the pool immediately so that a database or transaction log is not accidentally placed on the master device.

The stored procedure used to add and remove devices from the default device pool is `sp_diskdefault`. Following is the syntax for `sp_diskdefault`:

```
sp_diskdefault device name, defaulton ¦ defaultoff
```

Where `device name` is the logical device name for the device, and `defaulton` or `defaultoff` are the flags used to add or remove the device from the default device pool. `defaulton` adds the device and `defaultoff` removes the device.

DISK STRIPING

In an earlier chapter, SQL Server disk configurations were briefly covered, so now we are going to expand on some of the points mentioned earlier and see how they relate to SQL Server devices and performance. In SQL Server or almost any database server, one of the most likely bottlenecks is disk I/O from clients reading and writing from different tables or different databases simultaneously.

Suppose that you have a PC configured as a server, with a fast processor and a large amount of memory, but you bought a single 2GB hard drive, with a single disk controller to store all your database information. Because you only have one disk drive, any devices created will physically reside on the single hard drive. What happens when users start inserting and retrieving data simultaneously? SQL Server has more than enough memory and the processor is fast enough to handle the request, but what about the single disk drive and disk controller? A bottleneck will quickly form as I/O requests queue up to the single disk. An old SQL Server trick, dating back to the days of Sybase, has been to use a smart disk controller card or disk array, rather than a single 2GB hard drive, or four 512MB hard drives. Devices can then be created on different physical hard drives, enabling you to spread databases and transaction logs on to different physical devices. This is a better solution than a single hard drive but it still has some deficiencies. Databases and transaction logs could be placed on different physical devices, improving transaction processing. Databases can be spread over multiple SQL Server devices, thus different physical

8

devices, but the hot data everyone is after may be on a single drive causing disk I/O bottlenecks. Smart SQL Server DBAs would take advantage of segments (see Chapter 9). The NT operating system and new advanced hardware systems have created better solutions: hardware or software disk striping.

Figure 8.9 is a conceptual diagram of disk striping for a drive labeled J:. The J: drive looks like a single physical drive to the SQL Server DBA creating devices. Logically a striped drive is a single drive, but physically the logical drive spans many different disk drives. A striped disk is made up of a special file system called a striped set. All the disks in the disk array that make up the logical drive are part of the striped set. Data on each of the drives is divided into equal blocks and is spread over all the drives. By spreading the files system over several disk drives, disk I/O performance is improved because the disk I/O is spread over multiple drives. The balancing of the I/O is transparent to the DBA, who no longer has to worry about spreading out file I/O. Disk striping is also referred to as *RAID 0* (Redundant Array of Inexpensive Disks). RAID 0 is the fastest RAID configuration. The 0 is the level of fault tolerance, measured in levels 0–5, with 0 providing no fault tolerance. If a single disk fails in a RAID 0 system, none of the data in the stripe set can be accessed. Windows NT provides software-level disk striping. Disk striping can also be handled by special hardware disk arrays.

Figure 8.9.
Disk striping.

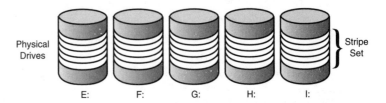

Note

Hardware-based disk striping (RAID configurations) will outperform Windows NT disk striping. NT's implementation is done via software implementation and thus requires using processor system resources. The disadvantage to hardware solutions is cost. RAID systems can be quite expensive, depending on the level of fault tolerance.

A RAID 0 system has 0 fault tolerance and the entire file system can be rendered useless if a single drive fails. RAID 1 is also known as disk mirroring. In a RAID 1 configuration, data written to a primary disk is also written to a mirror disk. RAID 2 uses disk striping along with error correction. RAID 3 and RAID 4 also use disk striping and error correction and vary in the degree of effectiveness and disk space requirements. A RAID 5 system has the maximum fault tolerance. A single disk can fail and the system will continue to function. A backup drive can be placed in the disk array and the lost device will be re-created on the new drive by the RAID system. RAID 5 technology can be implemented using Windows NT disk striping with parity or as a hardware-based solution.

MIRRORING A DEVICE

SQL Server provides a method of redundancy to protect against a device failure called *device mirroring*. When a SQL Server device is mirrored, a duplicate copy of the device is maintained. If either device becomes corrupted, the uncorrupted device takes over SQL Server operations to provide uninterrupted processing.

Figure 8.10 shows a mirrored device. NT SQL Server mirrors a drive using *serial writes*. A serial write is when information is written to the primary device first. When the I/O operation is complete, the information is then written to the secondary device.

Figure 8.10.
Device mirror.

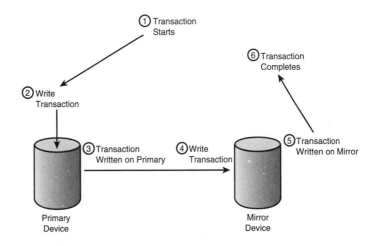

Note

Non-Windows NT SQL Servers can perform non-serial writes to mirror devices, writing to both devices simultaneously or performing serial writes. Windows NT SQL Server mirroring always performs serial writes.

If an error occurs while writing to either of the mirrored devices, the bad device becomes unmirrored and the uncorrupted device takes over as the primary device, protecting your server from downtime due to a lost device.

8

Remember that devices are mirrored, not databases! If you want to mirror a database, you must mirror all the devices that make up the database.

To mirror a device use the SQL Manager, select the server and device to mirror, and perform the following steps:

1. Access the Edit Database Devices dialog box (refer to Figure 8.8).
2. Click the Mirroring button. The Database Device Mirroring - Example dialog box will appear (see Figure 8.11).

Figure 8.11.
Database Device
Mirroring - Example
dialog box.

3. Use the default mirror device name in the Mirror Name text box or modify it to change the location or filename of the mirrored device.
4. Click the Mirror button. The device will be mirrored.

Tip

Mirroring a device requires SQL Server to create the mirror device, which will use the same name as the device being mirrored but with a .mir file extension. Once the mirror device is created, used pages from the primary device are copied to the new mirror device. Large databases can take a while to mirror.

The SQL Server command to mirror a device is the DISK MIRROR command, which has the following syntax:

```
DISK MIRROR
NAME='logical device name',
MIRROR = 'mirror device physical name',
[,WRITES=SERIAL ¦ NOSERIAL]
```

NAME is the SQL Server logical device name of the device to be mirrored.

MIRROR is the location and filename of the mirrored device.

WRITES SERIAL or NOSERIAL is not required and is provided for SQL Server compatibility on non-Windows NT platforms.

Tip

If the master device is mirrored and fails, the mirror device will take over and operation will continue uninterrupted. If the SQL Server is later halted and restarted, the server will fail due to a bad master device. To prevent this failure at startup, use the SQL Server Setup utility to add the following startup parameter to the server:

`-rphysical mirror device path and name`

The `-r` startup option tells SQL Server at startup to use the mirrored device when the primary device fails.

When a device is mirrored, the `sysdevices` table is modified. The physical name of the mirrored device is placed in the `mirrorname` column and the `status` column is modified to indicate mirroring has been turned on.

UNMIRRORING AND REMIRRORING DEVICES

Unmirroring a device halts SQL Server from performing writes to the mirrored device. Unmirroring is performed automatically by SQL Server when an I/O error occurs on the primary or mirrored device.

Tip

Devices can be mirrored and unmirrored without shutting down SQL Server.

A DBA can also unmirror a device using the SQL Server manager. To unmirror a drive, select the server and the device you want to unmirror and perform the following steps:

1. Display the Edit Database Devices dialog box.
2. Click the Mirroring button. The Unmirror Device - Example dialog box will appear (see Figure 8.12).

Figure 8.12.
Unmirror Device -
Example dialog box.

3. Select one of the options shown in Figure 8.12, and click OK.

The checkbox options in Figure 8.12 enable you to perform the following unmirroring options:

Switch to Mirror Device - Retain: Makes the mirrored device the primary device but keeps the original device. Use this option if you want to temporarily turn off mirroring but plan to remirror later.

Switch to Mirror Device - Replace: Replaces the primary device with the mirrored device.

Turn Off Mirroring - Retain Mirror Device: Pauses SQL Server mirroring. Use this option if you plan to remirror to the same device later.

Turn Off Mirroring - Remove Mirror Device: Stops mirroring on the selected device, clears the status bits, and sets the mirrorname column in sysdevices to NULL.

Note

Removing a mirrored device does not remove the operating system file. Use the Windows NT File manager or the DOS DEL command to remove the physical mirrored file.

The SQL command to unmirror a disk is the DISK UNMIRROR command, which has the following syntax:

```
DISK UNMIRROR
NAME = 'logical name'
[, SIDE = PRIMARY ¦ SECONDARY]
[, MODE = RETAIN ¦ REMOVE]
```

NAME is the SQL Server logical device name to unmirror.

SIDE specifies the device to disable the primary or the secondary.

MODE, the default mode, is to retain the mirror device entry in the sysdevices table. The REMOVE flag clears mirror information in the sysdevices table.

If mirroring has been paused or halted due to device failure, mirroring can be turned on by remirroring the device. To remirror a device with SQL Server Manager, select the server and the device to remirror and perform the following:

1. Display the Edit Database Devices dialog box.
2. Click the Mirroring button to display the Re-Mirror Device - Example dialog box (see Figure 8.13).
3. Click the Re-Mirror button. The device will be remirrored.

Figure 8.13.
Re-Mirror Device -
Example dialog box.

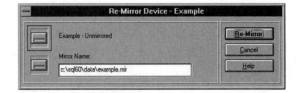

The command to remirror a device is DISK REMIRROR, which has the following syntax:

```
DISK REMIRROR
NAME = 'logical name'
```

NAME is the logical name of the SQL Server device to remirror.

DEVICE MIRRORING STRATEGIES

To mirror or not to mirror: that is the question. In the olden days, mirroring a device was the best protective measure available for ensuring nonstop SQL Server operation. Today, other options such as RAID 5 hardware configurations and NT software-based RAID exist, and in most cases may be a better recovery strategy for your system. However, if you decide to use SQL Server mirroring, then develop a strategy that will be cost effective for your organization and will provide acceptable downtime in case of a recovery. The following are suggested mirroring strategies:

◆ Always mirror the master device.

◆ Mirror transaction logs of production databases.

◆ To prevent downtime with a database, all devices that make up the database must be mirrored or you have a potential to be down.

Device mirroring provides a level of protection against data corruption. The price you pay for device mirroring is more disk space and added overhead by requiring the server to perform more disk I/O.

CONSIDERATIONS AND STRATEGIES WHEN CREATING A DATABASE DEVICE

When creating SQL Server database devices, you need to take into consideration the following:

◆ What purpose will the device serve?

◆ How large should the device be?

◆ Which drive will the device be located on?

8

MANAGING DEVICES

◆ How to name the device

◆ How will the device be recovered if an error occurs?

Many decisions made about a database device will be dependent on the hardware configuration and the database that will reside on the device. Let's examine these considerations and possible strategies to implement.

WHAT PURPOSE WILL THE DEVICE SERVE?

Before creating a database device, determine the purpose that the device will serve. Will the device be used for transaction logs, database storage, or both?

I like to create a separate device for each transaction log. Doing so allows more efficient disk allocation since databases have different sizes and backup requirements. If you decide to mirror some production transaction logs but not all of them, you can select only the transaction log devices that need mirrored. I do not like to create a single device for all transaction logs. SQL Server maintains an I/O queue for each device. Placing all the database transaction logs on a single device also places all requests on a single device I/O queue. So, placing each transaction log on its own device limits the overall requests to the device I/O queue. Another advantage of a single device per transaction log is device failure. If a single database device with a transaction log fails, you will lose access to only one database. If a device with several transaction logs fails, you lose access to many databases.

Databases can be placed on several devices or span multiple devices. One of the deciding factors should be the physical disk layout. If the disk drives are striped or have a RAID configuration or a single disk drive, you will not have to concern yourself with balancing the database across different physical devices. Unlike transaction logs, I will share database devices for small databases (< 200MB).

It is a good practice not to mix database and transaction logs on the same device.

HOW LARGE SHOULD THE DEVICE BE?

Transaction logs and database sizing will be covered in detail in Chapter 9; however, let's examine the size issue as it relates to devices.

Recommended transaction log sizes are 10 to 25 percent of the size of the database. These percentages are just a starting point. Take into consideration the frequency of transaction log dumps and the number of transactions. A transaction-intensive database that will have the log dumped every 15 minutes will require a smaller transaction than the same database being dumped daily.

For database devices, I tend to shy away from creating devices larger than 1GB. If the device fails, it is much faster to recover smaller devices than larger devices.

The drawback is that many different devices are harder to manage than a single large device. It is a good idea to come up with a standard size for database devices. For a large database, create database devices anywhere from 512MB to 1GB, and 256MB for smaller databases.

WHICH DRIVE WILL THE DEVICE BE LOCATED ON?

The correct drive to select for a device typically depends on available space and whether disk striping or a RAID configuration is being used.

HOW DO I NAME THE DEVICE?

Establish consistent naming conventions for devices and logs. Include the word LOG for transaction log devices and the word DATA or DB for database devices. For dump devices, include the word DUMP. If the device belongs to a single database, use the name of the database. For example, a transaction log and database device for the pubs database would be PUBSLOG, PUBSDB, or PUBSDATA.

HOW WILL THE DEVICE BE RECOVERED IF AN ERROR OCCURS?

Take precautions to protect against data loss by using device mirroring, NT disk mirroring, or RAID configurations. It is important when you create a device to make sure you have a hardware or software plan that will allow you to recover the device if lost, and in an acceptable amount of time, especially the master device.

BETWEEN THE LINES

Following are some of the important tips and tricks to read between the lines for devices:

- ◆ Devices can be used to store databases and transaction logs or for backup and restore purposes.
- ◆ The master device is the most important device! Protect it at *all cost*!
- ◆ The minimum master device size in Version 6.0 is 25MB.
- ◆ Use DISKDUMP (NULL) device to clear out transaction logs or databases in a development environment where saving the data is not critical.
- ◆ Use naming conventions for devices.
- ◆ The devices configuration parameter no longer exists in Version 6.0!
- ◆ Always delete the physical file after a device is dropped. You do not need to shut down the server in Version 6.0 (older versions require shutting down the server to release the file).

- ◆ Devices can be expanded but not shrunk.
- ◆ Mirroring a device does not use up a VDEVNO or add a new entry to sysdevices. It only updates a current entry.
- ◆ RAID software and hardware solutions may provide better device protection then SQL Server mirroring.
- ◆ Back up the master database after any devices changes are made.

SUMMARY

You now should have a good understanding of SQL Server devices and how to create them, modify them, and remove them. It is also very important to realize the need to protect the devices (in case of failure) and the different options available to you, such as mirroring or RAID configurations. In the next chapter, you learn how to assign databases to the devices you have created and examine in more detail the placement of databases and transaction logs on devices.

CHAPTER 9

Managing Databases

It is important to understand how to manage a database in SQL Server. Every object and its corresponding data revolves around the database. If a database isn't properly managed, it may result in system downtime, countless headaches, and loss of data.

DATABASE PRIMER

This section discusses the fundamental terminology and concepts necessary to manage a SQL Server database.

WHAT IS A DATABASE?

A *database* is a organized collection of data (see Figure 9.1). This collection of data is logically structured and systematically maintained. SQL Server extends the concept of a database by allowing you to create and store other types of objects, such as stored procedures, triggers, views, and other objects that interact with your data.

Figure 9.1.
A database.

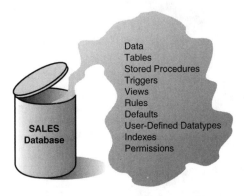

Data
Tables
Stored Procedures
Triggers
Views
Rules
Defaults
User-Defined Datatypes
Indexes
Permissions

SALES
Database

WHAT IS THE TRANSACTION LOG?

The *transaction log* is a history of data modifications to a database (see Figure 9.2). Whenever you create a database, SQL Server automatically creates a corresponding database transaction log. SQL Server utilizes the transaction log to assure transaction completeness and to incrementally restore data changes (see Chapter 13 for more information on restoring the transaction log).

The capability to guarantee transaction completeness helps separate SQL Server from lessor RDBMS software. To the world of SQL Server, virtually every data modification must have a starting point and an ending point. If the ending point isn't reached, SQL Server will automatically reverse any changes that were made. For example, suppose that the power to the server goes out at the midway point of a process that is deleting all rows from a table. When SQL Server is restarted, it will automatically restore all rows that had been deleted, thus returning the table to its original state before the delete process was run. Through the use of the transaction log, SQL Server is able to guarantee that all the work was done or none of the work was done.

Figure 9.2.
A transaction.

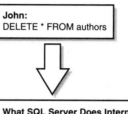

John:
DELETE * FROM authors

What SQL Server Does Internally When It Receives A Data Modification Statement
1. Marks the beginning of the data modifications.
2. Logs the deletion of each record to the transaction log.
3. Marks the ending of data modifications.
4. Once SQL Server reaches this point it will remove the records flagged for deletion from the author's table. If the server was to abort processing it will undo each change to the author's table.

SQL Server automatically uses a *write ahead* type of transaction log. This means changes to the database will first be written to the transaction log and next to the database. Examples of database changes that are written to the transaction log include data modified through the UPDATE, INSERT, and DELETE SQL commands; any type of object creation; and any security changes.

SQL Server will automatically mark the starting point and ending point whenever you execute a command that performs data modifications. For greater control, you can define the starting point and ending point for a group of data modifications. This often is used when more than one set of data modifications will occur within a unit of work.

For example, if a user transfers $1,000 from checking to savings, you can use a user-defined transaction to ensure that the checking account was debited and the savings account was credited. If the transaction did not complete, the checking and saving accounts will return to their original state before the transaction began.

To specify the beginning of a user-defined transaction, use the following:

```
BEGIN TRANsaction [transaction_name]
```

To specify the ending of a user-defined transaction, use the following:

```
COMMIT TRANsaction [transaction_name]
```

To rollback any changes made within a user-defined transaction, use the following:

```
ROLLBACK TRANsaction [transaction_name ¦ savepoint_name]
```

The transaction log is a table within the database, named `syslogs`. The `syslogs` table has two columns: `xactid` (binary) and `op` (tinyint). The data contained in the `xactid` column is useless to look at because it is in a binary format. Only SQL Server can understand the contents of the transaction log.

> ### Note
>
> No, you cannot disable the transaction log! This question is commonly asked when the log is not part of someone's backup strategy. Consequently, many people would rather not deal with periodically dumping the transaction log. Unfortunately, you can't avoid having transactions written to the log. But you can have the transaction log truncated automatically in SQL Server; set the database option `Truncate Log On Checkpoint = TRUE` (see the topic "Setting Database Options" in this chapter for more information about `Truncate Log On Checkpoint`).

HOW DATABASES AND DEVICES INTERACT

Every database in SQL Server must use at least one device. Whenever you create a database, you are dedicating a predefined amount of device space to the database. Depending on your needs, you can create your entire database on one device or multiple devices (see Figure 9.3).

Figure 9.3.
The way in which
databases and devices
interact.

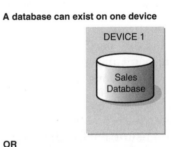

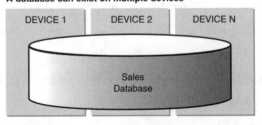

ESTIMATING THE SIZE OF A DATABASE

When you create a database, you must specify how much space to allocate to it. Other than "guesstimating," the second easiest way to estimate database size is to use the database estimator spreadsheet included on the CD.

ESTIMATING THE SIZE OF THE TRANSACTION LOG

A good starting point to estimating the size of the transaction log is to take the database size and multiple it by a factor of 10 percent to 25 percent. Whether you should use 10 percent or 25 percent, or some other factor, will depend on the frequency between transaction log dumps and the average size of your transactions. With SQL Server, you can easily increase the size of your transaction log but you *cannot* easily decrease it.

DATABASE PRE-FLIGHT CHECKLIST

Before you create a database, review the following checklist:

◆ Does the database device already exist? If not, you need to create the device before continuing.

◆ Did you decide whether you should use one device or multiple devices for the database?

◆ Did you decide whether the transaction log will be on the same device as the database or a separate device?

◆ Did you estimate the size of the database?

◆ Did you estimate the size of the transaction log?

DATABASE POST-FLIGHT CHECKLIST

After you create a database, review the following checklist:

◆ Do you need to set any database options?

◆ Did you dump the master database?

◆ Did you document the configuration of the database (use the output from `sp_helpdb` to document the database)?

DATABASE BASICS

This section provides step-by-step instruction on how to manage a database.

CREATING A DATABASE

Before you can create tables and start to manage your data, you must create a database. The following steps explain how to create a new database:

1. From within Enterprise Manager, go to the Server Manager dialog box and select a server.

2. From the toolbar, click on the Manage Databases button. The Manage Databases dialog box will appear.

3. Click on the New Database toolbar button. The New Database dialog box will appear (see Figure 9.4).

4. Enter a name for the database.

Note

Database names can be up to 30 characters and must conform to valid SQL Server naming conventions.

Be consistent when naming a database. Use all upper- or lowercase characters. Database names are case sensitive. Don't forget that you often may need to type the database name in a SQL statement—this may make you think twice about using all 32 characters! Try to make the name meaningful and relatively short.

5. Select a Data Device. This is the device on which the database will reside.

Warning

Do not put the database on the master device! This will cause a major headache if you ever have to recover the master device.

6. Enter the size of the database (in MB). The size will automatically default to the amount of available space on the selected device. You can override the default size but it cannot be larger than the amount of available space on the selected device. If the device does not have enough free space for the database, you must increase the size of the device before proceeding (refer to Chapter 8 for more information on increasing the size of a device).

Note

The minimum size of a database is 1MB. Prior to SQL Server 6.0, the minimum size was 2MB. The maximum size of a database is 1TB.

Tip

Don't worry if you allocate too little or too much space to your database. You can go back and change the size of the database after it is created.

7. Select a log device. Although it usually isn't recommended, you may set this option to None if you want to place the log on the same device as the database.

Warning

Always select a separate log device when creating production databases. This improves performance and allows the log to be backed up. If you do not place the log on a separate device, you will be unable to dump the transaction log.

8. If you selected a log device in step 7, enter the size of the log (in MB). The size will automatically default to the amount of available space on the selected device. You may override the default size but it cannot be larger than the amount of available space on the selected device. If the device does not have enough free space for the log, you must increase the size of the device before proceeding.

Warning

Do *not* select the Create for Load option. This option is only used when restoring a database from a backup (see Chapter 14 for more information on restoring a database). It is never used when creating a new database.

9. Choose OK to create the database (see Figure 9.4).

Tip

Always backup the master database after you create a new database. This will make it easier to recover your database should the master database become damaged.

Figure 9.4.
Creating a new
database.

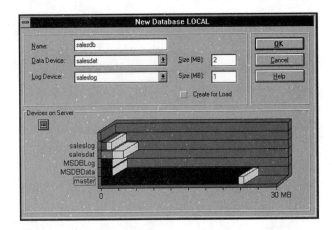

Note

The SA is the only user that can create a database, unless the statement permission is granted to another user (see Chapter 11 for more information on managing statement permissions).

You can use the following Transact SQL Command to create a database:

```
CREATE DATABASE database_name
[ON {DEFAULT ¦ database_device} [= size]
[, database_device [= size]]...]
[LOG ON database_device [= size]
[, database_device [= size]]...]
[FOR LOAD]
```

VIEWING INFORMATION ABOUT A DATABASE

After you create a database, you will periodically need to view information about it. The following steps explain how to view information about a specific database:

1. From within Enterprise Manager go to the Server Manager window, open the databases folder, and double-click on a database. The Edit Database dialog box will appear (see Figure 9.5).

2. From the Edit Database dialog box, you can view information about a database, setting database options, and setting statement permissions (see Chapter 11 for more information about statement permissions).

You can use the following Transact SQL command to view information about a database:

```
sp_helpdb [dbname]
```

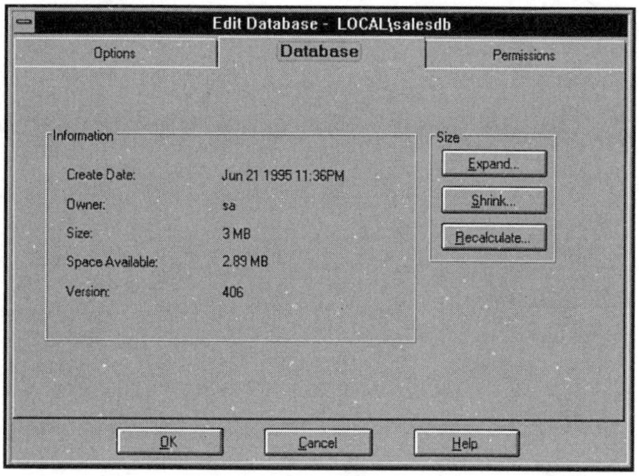

Figure 9.5.
Viewing information
about a database.

DATABASE SIZE AND AVAILABLE SPACE

The following steps explain how to determine a database's size and the amount of
remaining space in the database:

1. From within Enterprise Manager, access the Server Manager dialog box
   and select a server.

2. From the toolbar, click on the Manage Databases button. The Manage
   Databases dialog box will appear. From the Manage Databases dialog box,
   you can view in megabytes the amount of space allocated to a database,
   how much space is in use, and how much space remains. Double-click on a
   database for additional information. This displays the Edit Database dialog
   box (see Figure 9.6).

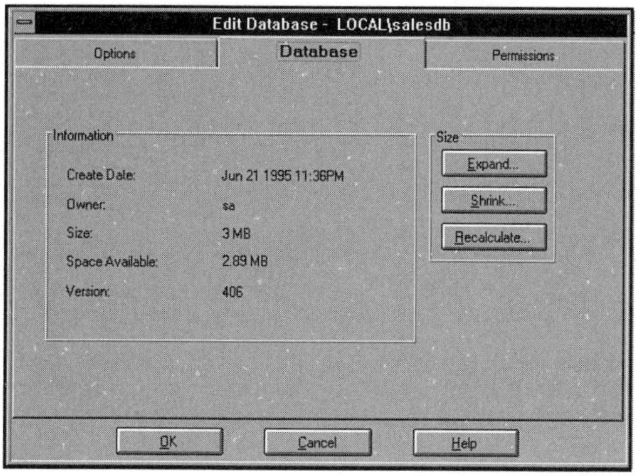

Figure 9.6.
Database size and
available space.

Tip

When you use Enterprise Manager to look at the size of database, you must remember that is reporting log size plus database size. For example, assume that the sales database has a 2MB data device and a 1MB log device. When you go to the Manage Databases dialog box, it will report the database size as 3MB. Don't let this mislead you! You only have 2MB for data storage.

The way in which available space is reported by the Enterprise Manager is the same. After creating the sales database with a 2MB data device and 1MB log device, the Enterprise Manager will report 2.89MB available space. This 2.89MB represents data plus log space available, not actual data space!

You can use the following Transact SQL command to determine database size:

```
sp_helpdb [dbname]
```

SETTING DATABASE OPTIONS

Each database in SQL Server has its own database options. The following steps explain how to set database options.

1. From within Enterprise Manager, access the Server Manager dialog box, open the databases folder, and double-click on a database. This displays the Edit Database dialog box.

2. From the Edit Database dialog box, select the Options Tab (see Figure 9.7).

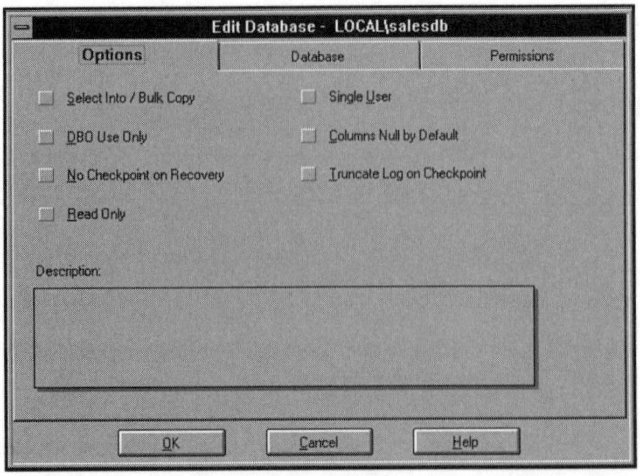

Figure 9.7.
Setting database
options on the
Options tab.

3. Check off the options you want selected.

4. Click on OK to save your changes.

Tip

When changing database options, your changes will take effect immediately. You do not need to restart the server for the option to take effect.

Use the following information to help assist in deciding how to set each database option.

SELECT INTO / BULK COPY

Default setting: FALSE

The underlying consideration as to how to set this option depends on how you are handling the backup of the transaction log. Use the following information to help determine how you should set this option.

Set this option = FALSE if you are you are DEPENDENT upon the transaction log for recovery (see Chapter 14 for more information on database recovery). This setting is typically used for production databases. When this option = FALSE, you cannot perform the following operations: Select Into, fast BCP, and Writetext.

Set this option = TRUE if you are you are NOT DEPENDENT upon the transaction log for recovery. This setting is typical for development databases and non-mission critical databases. By setting this option = TRUE you can perform the following operations:

◆ Select Into a destination table: the Into portion of the SQL statement will create a copy of the source's table structure and will populate the newly created table with data returned from the SQL statement.

Note

If Select Into / Bulk Copy = FALSE, you will get the following error message when you use the Select [column_list] Into [destination_table] statement.

Msg 268, Level 16, State 2
You can't run SELECT INTO in this database. Please check with the Database Owner.

◆ Fast BCP: BCP will run significantly faster when this option = TRUE. This is because the fast mode of BCP bypasses the transaction log. Fast BCP will only work on a table that does not have an index or a trigger (see Chapter 15 for more information about using BCP).

> ### Tip
>
> For those shops that use the transaction log for database recovery, you can temporarily set this option = FALSE, run a nonlogged operation (such as Select .. Into or fast-mode BCP), reset the option = TRUE, and dump the database. You must dump the database before you resume dumping the log. If you do not dump the database after performing a nonlogged operation, the next time you try to dump the transaction log you will receive an error message.

◆ Writetext statement: You can use this statement to perform nonlogged updating of text or image fields.

DBO USE ONLY

Default setting: FALSE

When this option = TRUE, only the Database Owner (DBO) can access the database. Use this option if you want to keep everyone but the DBO and SA out of the database.

NO CHECKPOINT ON RECOVERY

Default setting: FALSE

This option controls the issuance of a checkpoint record to the log after the database has been recovered. In SQL Server terminology, the word *recovered* means the database was successfully loaded during the startup of SQL Server. Typically you will leave this setting = FALSE unless you are dumping the log to a standby server. If you are dumping the log to a standby server, you will want to set this option = TRUE on the standby server's database. This will allow you to dump the log from the primary server and apply the log to the standby server.

READ ONLY

Default setting: FALSE

When this option = TRUE, the contents of the database can be viewed but not modified.

SINGLE USER

Default setting: FALSE

When this option = TRUE, only one user at a time (including SA) can be in the database.

COLUMNS NULL BY DEFAULT

Default setting: FALSE

This option determines whether a column will be defined as NULL or NOT NULL when it is created. This option is implemented for ANSI compatibility.

The following example illustrates how this command works.

Example A:

```
Columns Null By Default = FALSE

CREATE TABLE sales (sales_id int)
```

Result: The column sales_id will be defined as NOT NULL.

Example B:

```
Columns Null By Default = TRUE

CREATE TABLE sales (sales_id int)
```

Result: The column sales_id will be defined as NULL.

Note

> Explicitly specifying a column as NULL or NOT NULL within the CREATE TABLE command will override the Columns Null By Default option.

TRUNCATE LOG ON CHECKPOINT

Default setting: FALSE

When this option = TRUE, the transaction log is automatically truncated when a CHECKPOINT is issued by the system. (A CHECKPOINT is issued by the system about once every minute.)

Set this option = FALSE if you use the transaction log as part of your backup recovery process.

Note

> If you try to dump the transaction log when option = TRUE you will receive an error.

Set this option = TRUE if you are not concerned about using the transaction log as part of your backup recovery process. This option is useful for development databases or non-mission-critical databases. When you set this option = TRUE, you significantly lessen the chance of the transaction log running out of space.

SETTING OTHER DATABASE OPTIONS

There a three additional databases options that are not accessible through the Edit Database dialog box. You can use sp_dboption command to change any database option.

Note

The offline, published, and subscribed database options are new to SQL Server 6.0.

You can use the following Transact SQL command to set database options:

```
sp_dboption [dbname, optname, {TRUE ¦ FALSE}]
```

OFFLINE

Default setting: FALSE

When this option = TRUE, the database is taken offline from the system. It will not be recovered during system startup and will remain inaccessible until it is placed online.

Set this option = FALSE unless you are working with a removable media database.

PUBLISHED

Default setting: FALSE

When this setting = TRUE it permits the database to be published for replication. It does not perform the replication, it only allows it to be replicated.

When this setting = FALSE, it prevents the database from being published.

Set this option = FALSE unless you want this to be a published database.

SUBSCRIBED

Default setting: FALSE

When this setting = TRUE, it permits the database to be subscribed for replication. It does not perform the subscription, it only allows it to be subscribed to.

When this setting = FALSE, it prevents the database from being subscribed.

Set this option = FALSE unless you want this to be a subscribed database.

EXPANDING THE DATABASE

You can easily expand the size of database after it has been created. SQL Server offers two approaches to increasing the size of a database. Before proceeding, you should review which approach best suits your needs.

APPROACH 1: USE THE CURRENTLY ASSIGNED DEVICE

Allocate more space to the database by using more space on the device currently in use by the database (see Figure 9.8). The existing device must have sufficient space to accommodate the increase in database size (refer to Chapter 8 for more information on managing devices).

Tip

To determine which device(s) are in use by a database, use `sp_help`.

`sp_helpdb [dbname]`

Figure 9.8.
Approach 1: Expanding
the database.

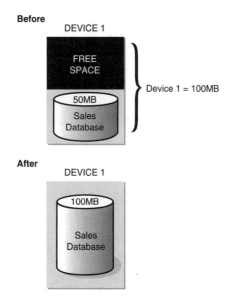

APPROACH 2: USE ANOTHER DEVICE

Assign another device to the database (see Figure 9.9). This allows the database to grow in size by spanning multiple devices. The device must exist already and it must have sufficient space to accommodate the increase in database size.

Figure 9.9.
Approach 2: Expanding
the database.

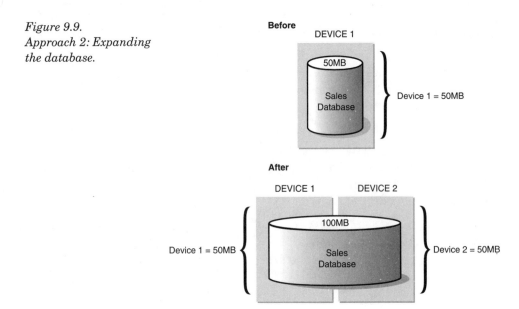

The following steps explain how to increase the size of a database.

1. From within Enterprise Manager, access the Server Manager dialog box and select a server.

2. From the toolbar click on the Manage Databases button, which displays the Manage Databases dialog box. Double-click on a database. This displays the Edit Database dialog box.

3. From the Edit Database dialog box, select the Database tab. Click on the Expand button.

4. Select a Data Device.

5. In the Size edit area, enter the amount of additional space you want allocated to the database (see Figure 9.10).

Warning

Do use the master device to gain additional database space! This will cause a major headache if you ever have to recover the master device.

6. Click on OK to save your changes.

Note

You can increase the size of a database up to a maximum of 32 times.

Tip

Always back up the master database after you increase the size of a database. This will make it easier to recover your database should the master database become damaged.

Figure 9.10.
The Expand Database
dialog box.

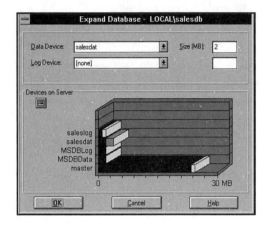

You can use the following Transact SQL command to expand a database:

```
ALTER DATABASE database_name
[ON {DEFAULT ¦ database_device} [= size]
[, database_device [= size]]...]
[FOR LOAD]
```

EXPANDING THE DATABASE LOG

You can easily expand the size of the database log after it has been created. The concept behind expanding the database log is the same as expanding the database.

The following steps explain how to increase the size of the database log.

1. From within Enterprise Manager, access the Server Manager dialog box and select a server.

2. From the toolbar click, on the Manage Databases button, which displays the Manage Databases dialog box. Double-click on a database. This displays the Edit Database dialog box.

3. From the Edit Database dialog box, select the Database tab. Click on the Expand button.

4. Select a log device.

5. In the Size edit area, enter the amount of additional space you want allocated to the database log (see Figure 9.11).

Warning

Do use the master device to gain additional database log space! This will cause a major headache if you ever have to recover the master device.

6. Click on OK to save your changes.

Tip

Always back up the master database after you increase the size of a database. This will make it easier to recover your database should the master database become damaged.

Figure 9.11.
Expanding the
database log.

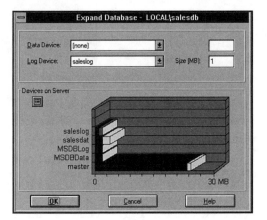

You can use the following Transact SQL command to expand the database log:

```
ALTER DATABASE database_name
[ON {DEFAULT ¦ database_device} [= size]
[, database_device [= size]]...]
[FOR LOAD]
```

SHRINKING A DATABASE

The following steps explain how to decrease the size of a database:

1. From within Enterprise Manager, access the Server Manager dialog box and select a server.

2. From the toolbar click on the Manage Databases button, which displays the Manage Databases dialog box. Double-click on a database. This displays the Edit Database dialog box.

3. From the Edit Database dialog box, select the Database tab. Click on the Shrink button.

4. Enter the new database size in megabytes (see Figure 9.12).

Figure 9.12.
Shrinking a database
using the Database tab
in the Edit Database
dialog box.

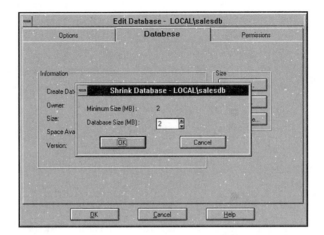

Note

You cannot make the database smaller than the amount space currently occupied by data and objects. (See the topic "Database Size And Available Space" for more information on database size). Also, you can only decrease the size of the database. You cannot decrease the size of the database's log.

Tip

Always back up the master database after you create a new database. This will make it easier to recover your database should the master database become damaged.

Use the following Transact SQL command to shrink a database.

```
dbcc shrinkdb (database_name [,new_size [[,'MASTEROVERRIDE']]])
```

Note

The capability to shrink a database is new to SQL Server 6.0.

RENAMING A DATABASE

You can rename any database after it has been created. Only the SA can rename a database. Following are steps to rename a database.

1. Set the database you are going to rename to Single User mode. (See the topic "How to Set Database Options" for more information about single user mode.)

2. From within the Enterprise Manager, access the Query dialog box and select the Query tab.

3. Enter the following syntax:

   ```
   sp_renamedb oldname, newname
   ```

4. Run the query.

5. Reset the database to multi-user mode.

Warning

When renaming a database, watch out for SQL statements that explicitly reference the database name; for example, SELECT * FROM *pubs*..authors. If you rename the pubs database to pub_db, you will need to change the statement to SELECT * FROM pubs_db..authors. Some common areas to look for database references are views, stored procedures, triggers, BCP scripts, and SQL embedded in applications.

DROPPING (OR DELETING) A DATABASE

When you drop a database, you are physically removing the database from the device(s) it resides on and you are destroying all objects contained within the database. Any device space allocated to the database will be reclaimed. Only the SA or database owner can drop a database. The following steps explain how to drop a database.

1. From within Enterprise Manager, access the Server Manager dialog box, select a server, and open the Databases folder. Click the right mouse button on the database in which you want to drop (see Figure 9.13).

2. At the prompt, click on the Yes button to delete the database.

You can use the following Transact SQL command to shrink a database:

```
DROP DATABASE database_name [, database_name...]
```

or

```
sp_dbremove database[,dropdev]
```

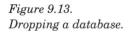

Figure 9.13.
Dropping a database.

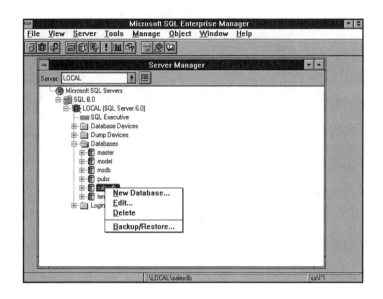

Tip

Always back up the master database after you create a new database. This will make it easier to recover your database should the master database become damaged.

New to SQL Server 6.0 is the capability to drop a damaged database with the DROP DATABASE command. Prior to 6.0, you could only use the DBCC DBREPAIR (*database_name*, DROPDB) command. You can also use sp_dbremove to drop a database. (sp_dbremove is new to Version 6.0).

TWO MOST COMMON DATABASE ERRORS

Without a doubt, you will encounter the following errors when you work with SQL Server:

◆ **The database log ran out of space**. Following is a typical error message:

```
Msg 1105, Level 17, State 2
Can't allocate space for object 'Syslogs' in database '[dbname]' because the
'logsegment' segment is full. If you ran out of space in Syslogs, dump the
transaction log. Otherwise, use ALTER DATABASE or sp_extendsegment to in-
crease the size of the segment.
```

◆ **The database ran out of space**. Following is a typical error message:

```
Msg 1105, Level 17, State 1
Can't allocate space for object '[object name]' in database '[database name]'
```

```
because the 'default' segment is full. If you ran out of space in Syslogs,
dump the transaction log. Otherwise, use ALTER DATABASE or sp_extendsegment
to increase the size of the segment.
```

DBAs new to SQL Server frequently get confused as to why they are getting these error messages. The source of confusion stems from the fact that you must preallocate space to the database and database log. If you do not allocate sufficient space, you'll get these error messages. Remember, the amount of remaining database space and log space has nothing to do with the amount of space left on your hard drive! Remaining database and log space is based on the amount of unused space allocated to the database or log.

The following sections explain in greater detail what each error means and how best to correct the error.

THE DATABASE LOG RAN OUT OF SPACE

Whenever you fill up the transaction log, you will get the following error message:

```
Msg 1105, Level 17, State 2
Can't allocate space for object 'Syslogs' in database '[dbname]' because the
'logsegment' segment is full. If you ran out of space in Syslogs, dump the transac-
tion log. Otherwise, use ALTER DATABASE or sp_extendsegment to increase the size of
the segment.
```

To resolve the error you must dump the log or increase the size of the log before continuing. (See the "How To Expand the Database Log" section for more information on increasing the size of the database log).

To help avoid this error, you can perform one of the following:

◆ Increase the size of the log until the problem goes away. This is the simplest solution but it may not be the most effective solution If you do not properly manage your transactions, you can fill up the transaction log regardless of how space has been allocated to it.

◆ Increase the frequency of the log dump. This may reduce the frequency of the error or prevent it from occurring.

◆ Set the database option Truncate Log On Checkpoint to TRUE. Only use this option if you are not backing up the transaction log—this option *is not* recommended for production databases!

◆ Use a non-logged command to perform the equivalent SQL command. Non-logged operations are not written to the transaction log; therefore, you invalidate the effectiveness of backing up your transaction log after you perform a non-logged operation. For mission-critical data, you should dump your database after you perform a non-logged command.

The following are non-logged commands that can be substituted for SQL commands.

SQL command:

```
DELETE FROM [tablename]
```

Non-logged command equivalent:

```
TRUNCATE TABLE [tablename]
```

Notes:

Use TRUNCATE TABLE [tablename] to remove all rows from the table. Because this is a non-logged operation, it will run much faster than the DELETE command. This command will only work when you what to delete all rows in a table—you cannot specify a WHERE clause.

SQL command:

```
INSERT INTO [tablename] SELECT * FROM [tablename]
```

Non-logged command equivalent:

```
BCP
```

Notes:

Rather than using an INSERT statement, try using BCP. Use BCP to export the data out of a table and into another table.

THE DATABASE RAN OUT OF SPACE

Whenever you deplete the available database space, you will get this error message.

```
Msg 1105, Level 17, State 1
Can't allocate space for object '[object name]' in database '[database name]'
because the 'default' segment is full. If you ran out of space in Syslogs, dump the
transaction log. Otherwise, use ALTER DATABASE or sp_extendsegment to increase the
size of the segment.
```

To resolve this error you must increase the size of database or reduce the amount of space used by existing objects. (See the section, "How to Expand the Database," for more information on increasing the size of the database.)

Use the following suggestions to help avoid this error in the future.

◆ Ward off this problem before it happens. You should frequently review your production databases for space allocation problems. (See the section, "Database Size and Available Space," for more information about space allocation.)

◆ Always leave yourself more space in the database than you expect to use (at least 25 percent more space than deemed necessary). This will give you room to work when you need to copy data and tables.

BEYOND THE BASICS

This section of the chapter lists helpful tips and tricks that can help improve the management of databases. These tips can help simplify database maintenance and improve database recoverability.

TIP 1: PLACE THE TRANSACTION LOG ON A SEPARATE DEVICE

Always place the transaction log on a separate device. By segregating the transaction log and database onto separate devices, you will gain the following benefits.

◆ You can dump the transaction log to a backup device. Only when the transaction log is on a separate device can you back up the transaction log to a backup device. This is the best way to recovery your data from a database failure.

◆ Improve database performance. By placing the transaction log on a separate device, the contention for page space will be reduced, thus improving performance.

◆ You reduce the likelihood of a damaged database and damaged transaction log. By splitting the database and transaction log you are will be using two devices instead of one device. This helps diffuse the risk of a damaged device.

◆ You can control the amount of space allocated to the database transaction log. When the database and transaction log are on the same device, you cannot control the size of the log. This may result in the log eating up space that you thought would be allocated to your data.

TIP 2: DOCUMENT THE DATABASE

Always document the configuration of the database after it has been modified. This is in addition to dumping the master database. The easiest way to document the configuration of a database is to use the `sp_helpdb` command. I recommend saving the output from the command to a text file (preferably somewhere other than the server's hard drive).

TIP 3: TAKE ADVANTAGE OF THE MODEL DATABASE

Use the model database to simplify object creation. The model database allows you to define a template for the creation of new databases. When you create a new database, SQL Server will copy the contents of the model database into the newly created database. This makes a handy mechanism for copying frequently used database options and objects into a new database. Anything that you want automatically copied into a new database should be placed in the model.

Note

The model database is automatically created when you install SQL Server. It cannot be deleted.

Changes to the model database will not impact existing databases. It is only used when creating new databases.

Following are common types of objects and settings that can be stored in the model database.

◆ Frequently used user-defined datatypes, rules, and defaults

◆ Database options. Any database option you set in the model database will be copied into a new database. For example, if you always set the Select Into / Bulk Copy option = TRUE, go ahead and set it in the model database.

◆ Any tables, views, or stored procedures that you always add to a new database can be placed in the model database.

◆ Database size. If you expand the model database (default size is 1MB), it will become the minimum size for any new databases.

Warning

Watch out when increasing the size of the model database. The new size will become the minimum size for all new databases. Whenever SQL Server creates a new database, it copies the contents of the model database into the new database. Therefore, the new database cannot be smaller in size than the model database.

SEGMENTS

Segments allows you to gain performance by placing frequently accessed tables and indexes on their own devices (see Figure 9.14). The use of segments is an old trick that DBAs used to improve read/write access to frequently used tables. For segments to be effective, they must have their own physical disk controller.

Figure 9.14.
Segments.

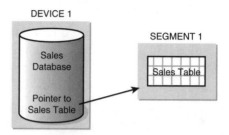

> ## Tip
>
> Before going to the trouble of using segments, you should explore using Windows NT–based alternatives. Very few SQL Server for NT installations use segments because they can be tedious to implement, difficult to maintain, and can complicate database recovery.
>
> Windows NT offers easier to use alternatives, such as Windows NT stripe sets (RAID 0–striping and RAID 5–striping with parity) and hardware disk arrays (refer to Chapter 8 for more information on striped sets and hardware disk arrays). Window NT striping performs as well as segments and is much easier to implement and maintain.

CREATING A SEGMENT

Use the `sp_addsegment` command to create a segment, as in the following:

```
sp_addsegment segname, logical_name
```

`segname` is the name you are going to assign to the segment.

`logical_name` is the name of the device that you are going to use for the segment. (The device must already exist. See Chapter 8 for more information on creating devices.)

To create a segment named `seg_sales` and use `device1`, use the following command:

```
sp_addsegment seg_sales, device1
```

> ## Note
>
> Each database in SQL Server can have up to 32 segments.

CREATING A TABLE ON A SEGMENT

Use the `CREATE TABLE` command with the `ON segment_name` option to create a table on a segment, as in the following.

```
CREATE TABLE [database.[owner].]table_name
({col_name column_properties [constraint [constraint [... constraint]]]
¦ [[,] constraint]}
[[,] {next_col_name ¦ next_constraint}...]
)
ON [segment_name]
```

To create the sales table on the seg_sales segment, use the following command:

```
CREATE TABLE sales
(sales_id integer,
sales_amount money)
ON seg_sales
```

CREATING AN INDEX ON A SEGMENT

Use the CREATE INDEX command with the ON *segment_name* option to create an index on a segment, as in the following:

```
CREATE [UNIQUE] [CLUSTERED ¦ NONCLUSTERED] INDEX index_name
ON [[database.]owner.]table_name (column_name [, column_name]...)
[WITH
[FILLFACTOR = x]
[[,] IGNORE_DUP_KEY]
[[,] {SORTED_DATA ¦ SORTED_DATA_REORG}]
[[,] {IGNORE_DUP_ROW ¦ ALLOW_DUP_ROW}]]
ON [segment_name]
```

For example, to create a clustered index on the seg_sales segment for the sales table, use the following command:

```
CREATE CLUSTERED INDEX sales_id_idx
ON sales(sales_id)
ON seg_sales
```

INCREASING THE SIZE OF A SEGMENT

Use the sp_extendsegment command to increase the size of a segment, as in the following:

```
sp_extendsegment segname, logical_name
```

For example, to extend the seg_sales segment to device2, use the following command:

```
sp_extendsegment seg_sales, device2
```

VIEWING INFORMATION ABOUT A SEGMENT

Use sp_helpsegment to list information about a particular segment or all the segments in a database, as in the following:

```
sp_helpsegment [segname]
```

For example, to view information about the `seg_sales` segment, use the following command:

```
sp_helpsegment seg_sales
```

Use `sp_helpdb` to view which segments are in use for a particular database, as in the following:

```
sp_helpdb [dbname]
```

To view segment information within the sales database, use the following command:

```
sp_helpdb sales
```

DROPPING A SEGMENT

Use the `sp_dropsegment` command to drop a segment.

```
sp_dropsegment segname
```

Note

You cannot use the `sp_dropsegment` command if an object resides on the segment you are trying to drop. You must drop the object before dropping the segment.

For example, to drop the `seg_sales` segment, use the following command:

```
sp_dropsegment seg_sales
```

DATABASE REMOVABLE MEDIA

New to SQL Server 6.0 is the capability to create database removable media. This enables you to distribute databases on media such as CD-ROM, floppy drives, WORM drives, or optical drives. You can also create new databases from removable media.

Note

The database-removable feature provides new possibilities for archiving and distributing databases.

CREATING A REMOVABLE DATABASE MEDIA

Use the `sp_create_removable` command to create a removable database, as in the following:

```
sp_create_removable dbname, syslogical, 'sysphysical', syssize,
loglogical, 'logphysical', logsize, datalogical1, 'dataphysical1', datasize1
[... , datalogical16, 'dataphysical16', datasize16]
```

For example, to create a 4MB sales database for distribution on removable media, with a 2MB device for the system catalog, and a 2MB device for the transaction log, use the following command:

```
sp_create_removable sales, salessys, 'c:\sql60\data\salessys.dat',2,
saleslog,'c:\sql60\data\saleslog.dat',2,
salesdat,'c:\sql60\data\salesdat.dat',4
```

STRANGER THAN FICTION!

The syntax for the `sp_create_removable` example in the SQL Server documentation is incorrect.

Incorrect Syntax:

```
sp_create_removable inventory, invsys, 'c:\sql60\data\invsys.dat, 2',
invlog,'c:\sql60\data\invlog.dat',4
invdata,'c:\sql60\data\invdata.dat',10,
```

Correct Syntax:

```
sp_create_removable inventory, invsys, 'c:\sql60\data\invsys.dat',2,
invlog,'c:\sql60\data\invlog.dat',4,
invdata,'c:\sql60\data\invdata.dat',10
```

CERTIFYING A DATABASE FOR REMOVABLE DISTRIBUTION

When you are ready to distribute the database, use the `sp_certify_removable` command. It will take the database offline, thus making it available for distribution, as in the following:

```
sp_certify_removable dbname[, AUTO]
```

The optional AUTO parameter will automatically drop all database users and transfer ownership of the database to the SA.

To certify the sales database for distribution, use the following command:

```
sp_certify_removable sales, AUTO
```

Tip

Be sure to record the information returned from the
`sp_certify_removable` procedure. Whenever you distribute a removable
database, you should include the output from the `sp_certify_removable`
command. This information will be needed by anyone who plans to
install the database.

The following is sample output from the `sp_certify_removable`
command:

```
DBCC execution completed. If DBCC printed error messages, see your System
Administrator.
DBCC execution completed. If DBCC printed error messages, see your System
Administrator.
DBCC execution completed. If DBCC printed error messages, see your System
Administrator.
File: 'c:\sql60\data\saleslog.dat' closed.
Device dropped.
The following devices are ready for removal. Please note this info. for
use when installing on a remote system:

Device name  Device type   Sequence   Device     Physical
                                       frag.      file name
                                       used by
                                       database
-------------------------------------------------------------------------
salessys     System + Log  1          2MB        c:\sql60\data\salessys.dat
salesdat     Data          2          4MB        c:\sql60\data\salesdat.dat

Database is now offline
Closing device 'salesdat' and marking it 'deferred'.
Device option set.
Closing device 'salessys' and marking it 'deferred'.
Device option set.
```

INSTALLING AND ACTIVATING A REMOVABLE MEDIA DATABASE

When you are ready to install a removable media database, use the `sp_dbinstall`
command. This command copies the system tables and transaction log from the
removable media to the hard drive and optionally copy the data device to the hard
drive, as in the following:

```
sp_dbinstall database,logical_dev_name,'physical_dev_name',size,
'devtype'[,'location']
```

To install the SYSTEM catalog tables and transaction log from the removable media,
use the following syntax:

```
sp_dbinstall sales,salessys,'e:\salessys.dat',2,
'SYSTEM','c:\sql60\data\salessys.dat'
```

To install the DATA tables from the removable media, use the following syntax:

```
sp_dbinstall sales,salesdat,'e:\salesdat.dat',4,
'DATA','c:\sql60\data\salesdat.dat'
```

Note

sp_dbinstall is run for each database device. For this example, the sales database used two devices: a system plus a log device and a data device. To install the entire database to the server's hard drive, run the sp_dbinstall option twice—once with the devtype parameter = SYSTEM and once with the devtype parameter = DATA.

After the database has been successfully installed, you must set it online. To place a database online, use sp_dboption with the offline parameter, as in the following:

```
sp_dboption dbname, offline, {TRUE ¦ FALSE}
```

For example, to bring the sales database online, use the following syntax:

```
sp_dboption sales, offline, FALSE
```

Note

Combining the offline and FALSE parameters brings a database online. To take the database offline, use the offline and TRUE parameters.

DELETING A DATABASE INSTALLED FROM REMOVABLE MEDIA

Use the sp_dbremove command to delete a database installed from removable media, as in the following:

```
sp_dbremove database[,dropdev]
```

Note

The optional parameter dropdev will drop any devices used by the removable database media. It does not delete the actual device from the hard drive.

Following is an example:

```
sp_dbremove sales, dropdev
```

BETWEEN THE LINES

Following are some of the important tips and tricks to read between the lines for managing databases:

- ◆ Use the Enterprise Manager or Transact SQL commands to manage databases. For ease-of-use, the Enterprise Manager is generally preferred over Transact SQL commands.

- ◆ Every database in SQL Server has a transaction log.

- ◆ SQL Server utilizes the transaction log to ensure transaction completeness and to incrementally restore data changes

- ◆ Virtually all changes to the database will first be written to the transaction log and next to the database.

- ◆ Every database in SQL Server must use at least one device.

- ◆ The SA is the only user that can create a database unless the statement permission is granted to another user.

- ◆ Watch out for the Select Into / Bulk Copy and Truncate Log On Checkpoint database options. When these options = TRUE, they can adversely affect your backup strategy.

- ◆ Use the sp_help command to document important database information.

- ◆ You can expand or shrink the size of a database.

- ◆ You can only expand the size of the transaction log—it cannot be shrunk.

- ◆ Always place the transaction log on a separate device.

- ◆ Use the model database to simplify object creation.

- ◆ Use NT stripe sets or hardware disk arrays before going to the trouble of using segments.

- ◆ New to SQL Server 6.0 is the capability to create database removable media.

SUMMARY

Basic database management techniques combined with supplemental tips provide you with the skill set to intelligently manage a database. Remember, intelligent database management is the key to keeping your database up and running. In the next chapter, you will learn how to perform user management.

CHAPTER 10

User Management

In this chapter, you will examine how to manage user login ids and database users. A *login id* is the name that allows an individual to access SQL Server. For example, sa is the system administrator user login id. A database user name allows an individual access to a specific database on SQL Server.

Note

A user login id versus a database user name can become confusing. Remember that adding a login allows an individual to log into the server; it does not allow the individual access to databases except for the login id's default database. A database user name does not allow an individual access to SQL Server, but is assigned to the login id to provide access to a specific database. The login id and the database user name can be the same, and in many cases are.

LOGIN ID

A login id (name) allows a user to login to SQL Server. When SQL Server is first installed, the server adds the following SQL Server login ids.

SA

The sa login id is the login id of the SQL Server system administrator. The sa user has permissions to do anything and everything on the server, from creating users and devices to backing up and restoring databases.

Warning

Protect the sa login id. The sa account should only be used by the Database Administrator! Do not allow developers and users access to SQL Server via the sa login id!

PROBE

The probe login id is used only in standard mode for some SQL Server administrative applications, such as the performance monitor to connect to SQL Server. In integrated security mode, the sa login id is used.

If your server has been set up to support replication, one or both of the following login ids will be installed.

REPL_PUBLISHER

The `repl_publisher` login id is set up if the server has been configured to handle subscription replication services.

REPL_SUBSCRIBER

`repl_subscriber` login id is created if the server is set up as a publication server for replication.

Warning

Do not use the `probe`, `repl_publisher`, or `repl_subscriber` login ids for user logins to SQL Server. These login ids are reserved for SQL Server applications.

TYPES OF SECURITY MODES

The type of security mode selected determines how SQL Server login ids are created and maintained. SQL Server supports three different security modes:

- ◆ Standard
- ◆ Integrated
- ◆ Mixed

The security mode is selected during SQL Server installation but can be modified at any time. One limiting factor to the security mode selected is the type of network protocol you will be using (refer to Chapter 5 for more details). Now look at the different security modes and how they relate to user management.

STANDARD SECURITY

Standard security is the standard SQL Server login facility inherited from Sybase 4.*x* systems and implemented in the Microsoft OS/2 versions of SQL Server. An individual logging on to SQL Server must supply a user name and a password that are validated by SQL Server via a system table. Standard security works over all network configurations.

INTEGRATED SECURITY

Integrated security takes advantage of Windows NT–user security and account mechanisms. SQL Server user management integrates directly with the NT operating system. Users with a valid Windows NT account can log onto SQL Server

10

without supplying a user name and password once the user account has been granted access to SQL Server. Integrated security can be implemented over the following network protocols: named-pipes protocol or multi-protocol.

Tip

Prior to NT SQL Server 6.0, only named-pipes supported integrated security.

MIXED SECURITY

Mixed security is the best of both worlds or, should I say, a combination of the integrated and security modes. Users using trusted connections (named-pipes or multi-protocol) can log in using integrated security, or users from trusted or non-trusted connections can log in using standard security.

Study Figure 10.1 to get a better idea of the different type of security modes and the options available.

Figure 10.1.
Security modes.

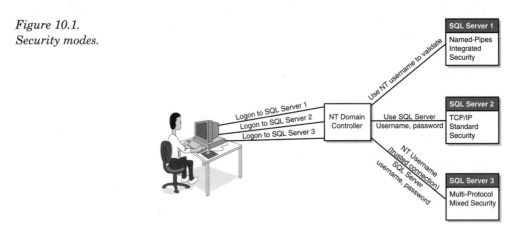

LOGINS USING STANDARD SECURITY

The standard security access mode dates back to the days of Sybase and the Microsoft pre-NT SQL Server. In standard security mode, a login id is added to SQL Server for a user. The user must then use the login id name and password to log in-to the server. The login id does not tie into the NT user name and password scheme. Standard logins are used for standard and mixed security modes.

Tip

Understanding how the standard security mode works makes using integrated security logins easier to understand.

To add a user login for standard security, perform the following steps using the SQL Server Enterprise Manager:

1. Select the server on which to add the login.
2. Click the Manage Logins button on the SQL Manager toolbar to display the Manage Logins dialog box (see Figure 10.2).

Figure 10.2.
Manage Logins
dialog box.

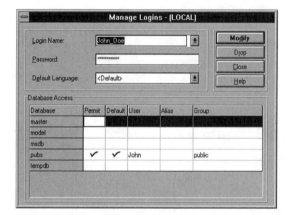

3. Add the necessary parameters to create the new login. Figure 10.2 shows the Manage Login dialog box with the required parameters to create a SQL Server login id called John_Doe.
4. To add the new login id, click the Add button. A dialog box will prompt you to verify the login id password. Enter the password for verification and click the OK button.

Following are the different parameters in the Manage Logins dialog box, shown in Figure 10.2:

Login Name: The login name is the login id used to log into the server. The login name must conform to the SQL Server identifiers standards. Briefly stated, the name can be from 1–30 characters in length and the first character must begin with a letter or number. No embedded spaces are allowed in the name.

Password: The password is the string required to log into the SQL Server. NULL password is the default.

Warning

SQL Server 6.0 encrypts the password. Previous versions of SQL Server did not encrypt the password, so on previous versions of SQL Server, the sa user can read user passwords by performing a `select * from syslogins`.

Default Language: The language used when the user logs into the server. The default is the default language set up on the server. Only languages installed on the server will appear as options.

Database Access: The database access grid allows you to assign a login id to multiple databases quickly.

Note

Always assign a login id to a default database; otherwise, the user will be in the master database when they log in.

WHAT HAPPENS WHEN A LOGIN ID IS ADDED?

When a new login id is added to SQL Server, an entry is placed in the syslogins table. Figure 10.3 shows a query displaying several columns from syslogins. The column suid stands for the *Server User Id*. The suid is a unique number used throughout SQL Server to identify a login id. When assigning a suid, SQL Server will use the lowest suid available (a possible hole is left when a login id is removed), or if no numbers are available, the suid number is incremented by one and assigned as the new suid for the login id.

Figure 10.3.
Query dialog box from
syslogins.

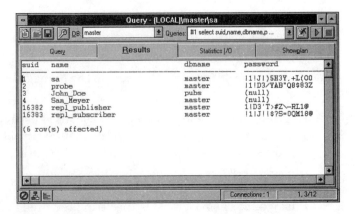

Tip

> The suid, not the name of the login id, is used internally by SQL
> Server to uniquely identify a login id. The system stored procedures
> use the login name as parameters and the SQL Enterprise Manager
> displays the login name.

The command to add a login is the system stored procedure sp_addlogin, which has
the following syntax:

```
sp_login loginame [, password [, default database [, default language]]]
```

Using Groups

Groups are used in SQL Server to simplify assigning security and permissions to
database objects like tables and stored procedures by logically grouping users
together. A group name can be whatever name you like, as long as the name follows
the rules for SQL Server identifiers. You can create groups to represent your
business groups. For example, a software development company may have groups
for developers, testers, and analysts. SQL Server installs a single default group
called public on every database when the database is created.

Tip

> Groups are created for a database, not for the entire server. If you end
> up adding the same groups to every database, then create the groups
> in the model database. When a new database is created, the new
> groups will be included in the new database.

Creating a Group

To create a group, perform the following steps using the SQL Server Enterprise
Manager:

1. Select the server and database to create the group.
2. From the Manage menu on the Enterprise Manager menu bar, select the
   Groups option to display the Manage Groups dialog box (see Figure 10.4).

Figure 10.4.
Manage Groups
dialog box.

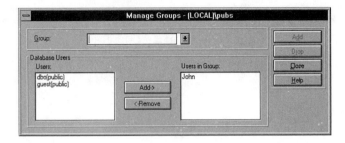

3. Add the group name in the group combo box shown in Figure 10.4.

4. Use the Add-> button to add users to the group.

5. Click the Add button to add the new group.

Warning

A user can belong to only one user-defined group at a time and the system group `public`. A user always belongs to the group `public` and cannot be removed from the `public` group. The one group limitation is a design limitation because groups are stored in a column of the user in the `sysusers` table. Beware: If you add a user that belongs to a group to another group with the SQL Server Enterprise Manager, the user will be removed from the first group and placed in the new group. SQL Server Enterprise Manager does not warn you that the user has been removed from the previous group.

When a group is added to a database, a new entry for the group is made in the system table called `sysusers`, covered in more detail in a later section. The system stored procedure to add a group is called `sp_addgroup`, which has the following syntax:

`sp_addgroup` *groupname*

The system stored procedure to change a user's group is `sp_changegroup`, which has the following syntax:

`sp_chagegroup` *groupname*, *username*

MANAGING LOGINS USING INTEGRATED SECURITY

Integrated security allows SQL Server to share the same user name and password used for Windows NT and allows the user to bypass the SQL Server login process. Some of the benefits of integrated security are that the user no longer has to remember a separate password and user name, and when the password changes in NT, the user does not have to change the password in SQL Server!

How does integrated security work? When a user logs into Windows NT and accesses a SQL Server, and is set up with integrated or mixed security over a trusted connection, the standard SQL Server login process is bypassed. SQL Server obtains the user and password information via the user's NT network security attributes, which are established when the user logs into Windows NT. Using integrated security allows you to take advantage of Windows NT features such as password aging and login auditing.

Tip

You can set up more than one sa user account with integrated security. All members of the Windows NT Admin group have sa privileges on SQL Server in integrated security mode.

Integrated security requires more NT hands-on experience or working closely with the NT system administrator when setting up user accounts and groups. Integrated security requires a few more steps than standard security, but offers many benefits. Setting up integrated security requires performing the following steps:

1. The SQL Server must be running a network protocol that supports trusted connections. In Version 6.0, named-pipes and multi-protocol can be used. In version 4.21 and 4.21a, only named-pipes are supported. If you are not running these protocols, you cannot use integrated security.

2. The server is properly configured.

3. Once all the security options are set up on SQL Server, the next step is to create the Windows NT–user accounts and Windows NT groups. NT users and groups are created using the NT User Manager.

Note

Windows NT groups are not the same as SQL Server groups, although the SQL Security Manger will create a SQL Server group for you from a Windows NT Group.

4. To add the Windows NT users and groups to SQL Server, use the SQL Security Manager.

Integrated or mixed security setup is complete! The following sections cover steps 2 and 4 in more detail.

CONFIGURING THE SERVER FOR INTEGRATED AND MIXED SECURITY

To set up the server for integrated or mixed security mode requires configuring the server. Take a look at the Security Options tab of the Server Configuration Options dialog box (see Figure 10.5).

Figure 10.5.
The Security Options
tab in the SQL Server
Configuration Options
dialog box.

Login Security Mode: To use integrated security, you must check the Windows NT Integrated or Mixed box under the Login Security Mode panel.

Note

Only the sa can change the security mode of the server.

Default Login: The NT user name that is used as a default for users logging into SQL Server without a valid login id to match their NT login name.

Tip

NT users must be in the same group as the DEFAULT user in order to use the default login; otherwise, access will be denied when they attempt to connect to the SQL Server.

Default Domain: Set this option to the NT domain you are a member of or the server name of the computer if you are not a member of a NT domain.

Set Hostname to UserName: Checking this option shows the user's network name when issuing the stored procedure sp_who.

Audit Level—Successful Login and Failed Login: Check either option to monitor successful and unsuccessful user logins. The audit messages are logged in the SQL Server error log and the Windows NT event log.

Mappings: The mapping characters replace valid NT account characters, such as the domain separator \, that are illegal identifier characters in SQL Server, with valid SQL Server characters.

Tip

If you are going to use integrated security, simplify your life and come up with a user naming convention that uses valid SQL Server characters. This will prevent possible account conversion problems.

The Apply Now button is new in Version 6.0. Selecting Apply Now changes the security mode without requiring you to restart the server, which is required in older versions.

THE SQL SECURITY MANAGER

The SQL Security Manager is a separate application and not part of the SQL Enterprise Manager. The SQL Security Manger is located in the Microsoft SQL Server 6.0 program group.

Note

Only the sa or a member of the sa group can log into SQL Server using the SQL Security Manager.

Using the SQL Security Manger, shown in Figure 10.6, is similar to using the SQL Enterprise Manger. You can view the Windows NT users and groups that currently have access to SQL Server by using the View option from the SQL Security Manager menu. Two types of privileges are available from the View option: sa and User. All Windows NT administrators will have sa privileges with SQL Server. All other users added through the SQL Security Manager belong to the User privilege group.

Figure 10.6.
SQL Security Manager.

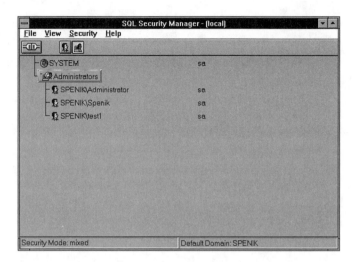

ADDING GROUPS (USERS) WITH THE SQL SECURITY MANAGER

When using the SQL Security Manager, you cannot select individual Windows NT users to add—instead, Windows NT groups are added. Adding the group adds all the users in the group to SQL Server. To add a group with user permissions, perform the following from the SQL Security Manager:

1. From the menu, select View.

2. Select User privilege.

3. Select the Security menu item, and then select Grant New to display the Grant User Privilege dialog box.

4. Select the group to add to SQL Server from the Grant Privilege panel in the Grant User Privilege dialog box shown in Figure 10.7 The Show checkbox is used to display Local or Default NT groups.

5. Check the Add Login Id for group members checkbox. If the box is checked, a SQL Server login id is created for each user in the group. If the box is not checked, the default user setup during security configuration is used.

6. Check the Add user to Database option to select a default database for each user.

7. Click the Grant button to transfer the selected Windows NT group to SQL Server. A dialog box appears showing the status of the accounts transferred, such as the login ids, database users, groups, and errors that occurred during the transfer.

Figure 10.7.
Grant User Privilege
dialog box.

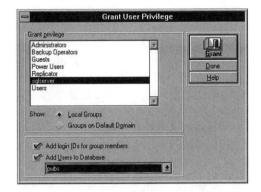

Tip

Most errors will occur due to invalid characters in the user name or group.

What happened? If the Add Login Id for group members box was checked, the SQL Security Manager uses the Windows NT group and user account information to create SQL Server login ids for each user in the selected NT group. The selected NT group and user names are added to the selected SQL Server default database. Removing the users from SQL Server is just as easy. Use the SQL Security Manager and rather than selecting the Grant New option under the Security menu, select Revoke. The `Revoke` command will remove all of the users' login ids and the group from SQL Server. The system commands used to add and revoke users for integrated security are the extended stored procedures `xp_grantlogin` and `xp_revokelogin`. For more detail on the two commands and extended stored procedures, see Appendix B.

DATABASE USERS

Once you have created a login id for a user, you grant the login id access to various databases by creating a database user for the login id. A database user must be added and associated to the login id in every database the login id has access to, with the exception of databases with the user guest and the use of aliases.

Note

When you create a login name, you automatically add the user to a database by selecting a default database for the user.

ADDING A USER TO A DATABASE

Adding a user to a database associates the login id with the user name and enables the login id to access the database. There are several ways to add a user to a database. A login id can be added to one or more databases when the login id is created using the grid in the Manage Login dialog box. To add the user to a database, check the database in the grid. When the login id is added, the login id and user name will be added to each database checked. To add a user to a database using the Manage User dialog box, perform the following steps using SQL Server Enterprise Manager:

1. Select the server and database for the new user.
2. Select the Manage menu from the Enterprise manager menu bar.
3. Select Users to display the Manage Users dialog box (see Figure 10.8).

Figure 10.8.
Manage Users
dialog box.

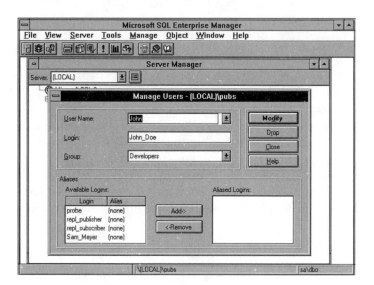

4. Add the necessary parameters to create the new user. Figure 10.8 shows the Manage User dialog box with the required parameters to create a SQL Server pubs database user named John with the login id John_Doe and is a member of the group Developers.
5. To add the new user to the database, click the Add button. A dialog box will prompt you to verify the login id password. Enter the password for verification and click the OK button.

Following are the different parameters in the Manage User dialog box that was shown in Figure 10.8.

User Name: The name of the user while he or she is in the database. The user name can be the same as the login name for the selected login id or it can be different. The size and format of the user name conform to the same rules as the login name when creating a login id.

Login: Drop-down list box of the possible login ids to associate with the database user.

Group: Group the user will belong to (the default is public).

The system stored procedure to add a new user to a database is sp_adduser, which has the following syntax:

```
sp_adduser login_id [, username [, groupname]]
```

When a new user is added to a database using the SQL Enterprise Manager or sp_adduser, an entry for the user is made in the sysusers table of the database to which the user was added. Figure 10.9 shows a select * from sysusers table. The column uid stands for *User Identifier* and is a unique number within the database to represent the user. Notice in Figure 10.9 that the uid of the group Developers is 16384, which is the starting uid for groups. A group's uid will be greater than or equal to 16384, except for public, which always has a uid of 0. gid stands for *Group Identifier* and represents the group to which the user belongs. Notice in Figure 10.9 that John has a gid of 16384, which corresponds to the uid 16384 of the group Developers. Figure 10.10 shows the relationship between the suid in syslogins and sysusers.

Figure 10.9.
SQL Query of the
sysusers table.

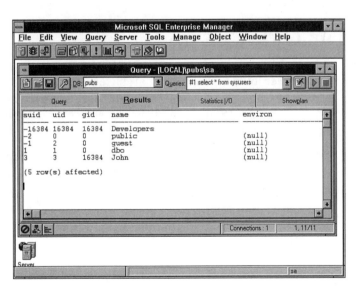

10

USER MANAGEMENT

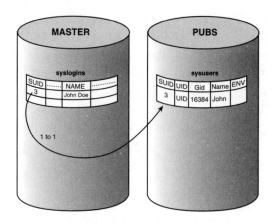

Figure 10.10.
Relationship between
syslogins and
sysusers.

REMOVING A USER FROM A DATABASE

To remove a user from a database, use the Manage Users dialog box that was shown in Figure 10.8. Select the user to remove and click the Drop button. You will be prompted by a confirmation dialog box. Click the OK button and the user is dropped from the database. The row in the sysusers table for the user is deleted. The corresponding system stored procedure to drop a user from a database is sp_dropuser, which has the following syntax:

```
sp_dropuser User_Name
```

THE GUEST USER

A special user name, guest, can be added to a database to allow anyone with a valid SQL Server login access to the database and is a member of the group public. Once a guest user has been added to a database, any individual, regardless of security mode, with a valid SQL Server login can access the database as the guest user. A guest user works as follows:

1. SQL Server checks to see whether the login id has a valid user name or alias assigned. If so, grant the user access to the database as the user name or an alias: if not, go to step 2.

2. Checks to see whether a guest user name exists. If so, the login id is granted access to the database as guest. If the guest account does not exist, then access is denied to the database.

Note

The guest user always has a uid = 2.

A guest user is added to the master database and the pubs database when the system is installed. SQL Server Version 6.0 prevents you from dropping the guest user from the master database. This is to protect you from accidentally dropping the guest user account from the master database. If guest was removed from the master database, only the sa user could login to SQL Server! When users log into SQL Server, they have access to the master database as the guest user. (Don't worry, the guest user has very few permissions in the master database.)

USING ALIASES

What is an alias? An *alias* enables you to assign more than one login id to a specific user name in a database. For example, suppose that you are running a bank and you have a database called BIG_BUCKS. You have a user name in the BIG_BUCKS database called banker. You also have three other SQL Server login ids, banker1, banker2, and banker3, which perform the same function as the user banker. So instead of adding each login id to the database, you alias the three users to the database user banker (see Figure 10.11).

Figure 10.11.
An alias example.

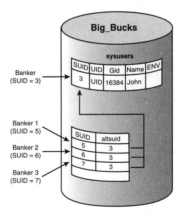

In the database BIG_BUCKS, shown in Figure 10.11, a single entry is placed in the sysusers table for the user banker. When the three other users are aliased to the user banker, an entry is made in the database system table sysalternates for each login id aliased. When one of the alias users tries to access the database, the table sysusers is scanned for the suid of the user. When the suid is not found, the sysalternates table is checked. If suid is found, then the column altsuid in sysalternates is used to search the sysusers table for the correct uid.

Aliases are typically used to assign more than one login id as the DBO (database owner).

Note

The DBO can only be assigned to a single login id. Using an alias is the only way to allow multiple logins to be DBOs.

Tip

If you use the DUMP and LOAD commands to move a database to a new server, the sysusers table travels with the database. The suids in the new server may not correctly match the suids in the database to the proper users. You can use aliases to remap object permissions in the moved database.

ADDING AN ALIAS

Alias users can be assigned in several different ways. To add an alias from the Manage Logins dialog box, follow these steps:

1. In the Database Access grid of the Manage Logins dialog box, check the database to alias the login id.

2. Click the pull-down list in the alias column and select the user name to alias (see Figure 10.12).

Figure 10.12.
Adding an alias using
Database Access grid in
the Manage Logins
dialog box.

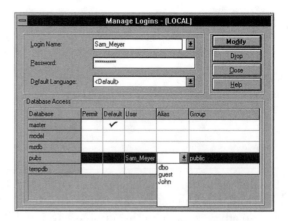

3. Click the Modify button for existing login ids or the Add button when adding a login id.

To add an alias using the Manage Users dialog box, follow these steps:

1. Select the server, database, and user to which you want to alias other users.

2. Copy the login ids to alias using the Add-> button (see Figure 10.13).

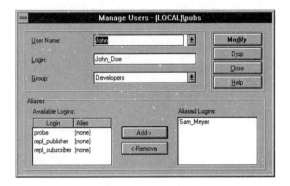

Figure 10.13.
Adding an alias using
the Manage Users
dialog box.

3. Click the Modify button for existing users or the Add button for a new user.

The system stored procedure to add aliases is `sp_addalias`, which has the following syntax:

```
sp_addalias login_id, user_name_in_database
```

Warning

Be careful when dropping a user from a database that is being used as an alias for other login ids. When the user name is dropped from the database, the alias users lose access to the database.

VIEWING LOGIN ID, DATABASE USER, AND GROUP INFORMATION

Login id, database user, and group information can be viewed in several different ways. To see the current login ids on a server, use the SQL Manager and select the server, and then click on the Logins folder. The user logins for the server are displayed as shown in Figure 10.14.

To see the current groups and users in a database, select the database and then click on the Groups/Users folder; a list of the database's groups is displayed. Click on the groups to show the users in each group. Figure 10.15 shows a listing of groups and users at the lowest level (users).

Figure 10.14.
SQL Enterprise
Manager Logins folder.

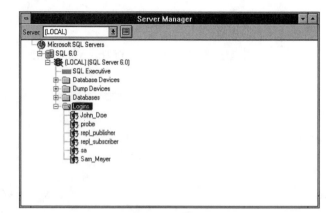

Tip

To see detailed user information, double-click on the folder to display the Manage User Dialog dialog box shown in Figure 10.8.

Figure 10.15.
SQL Enterprise
Manager Groups / Users
folder.

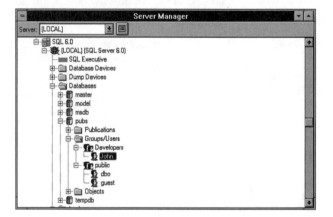

To see more detailed information for login ids, use the Manage Login Id dialog box (refer to Figure 10.2). For more detailed group information use the Manage Groups dialog box (refer to Figure 10.4). Information on database users or aliases is in the Manage User dialog box (refer to Figure 10.8).

The stored procedure `sp_helpuser` displays user information for a specific user or all users in a database and has the following syntax:

```
sp_helpuser [user_name]
```

MODIFYING AND REMOVING LOGIN IDS

Once you have created a login id, you can easily perform the following tasks:

◆ Change the password

◆ Add the login id to a new database

◆ Remove the login id from a database

◆ Alias the login id to add a user in a database

To perform maintenance tasks requires using the Manage Logins dialog box (see Figure 10.16). You have learned how to add user names to a database and use aliases. Now you see how to change a password and drop a login id.

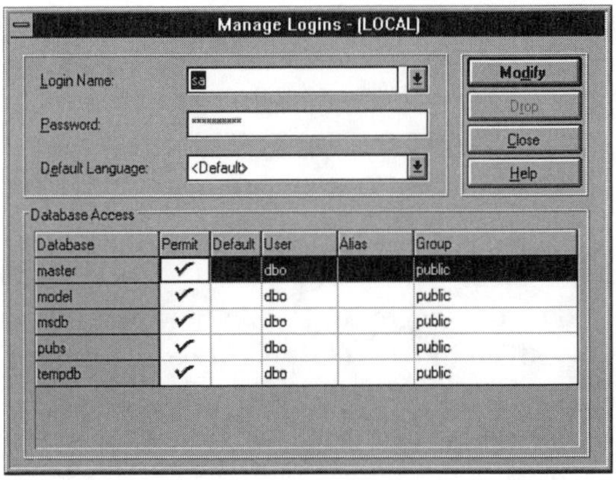

Figure 10.16.
Manage Logins
dialog box.

CHANGE THE PASSWORD

To change the password for a login id, select the login id you want to change with the Login Name drop-down list box. Enter the new password in the Password text box and click the Modify button. You will prompted by the Confirm Password dialog box (see Figure 10.17).

Figure 10.17.
The Confirm Password
dialog box.

Enter the new password and click the OK button. The password has been changed.

The system stored procedure to change the password is sp_password, which has the following syntax:

```
sp_password old_password, new_password [, login_id]
```

Note

Users are allowed to change their own passwords, but only the SA can change another user's password.

Warning

I cannot begin to tell you how many *secure environments* I have walked into and logged into their secure SQL Server as the SA, using the NULL password! As stated in Chapter 6, always give the SA a password! The environment is not secure when everyone who has ever used Microsoft SQL Server or Sybase SQL Server knows your sa password. If you are using integrated security, you do not need to give sa a password, but under standard and mixed security, *please do*! And one last thing—don't forget the sa password. If you do, you will have to reinstall SQL Server!

REMOVING A LOGIN ID

To remove a login id, select the login id you want to delete with the Login Name drop-down list box that was shown in Figure 10.16, and click the Drop button. When you are prompted by the confirmation dialog box, click the OK button and the login id is dropped.

Tip

Before you can drop a login id with SQL Enterprise Manager, you must first drop and re-create any user-owned objects in the databases using another login id. When a login id is dropped using the SQL Enterprise Manager, the login id is removed from any databases it was explicitly granted access.

The system-stored procedure to drop a login is `sp_droplogin`, which has the following syntax:

```
sp_droplogin Logon_name
```

Warning

Never use `sp_droplogin`. Always use the SQL Enterprise Manager to drop user logins, for two reasons:

1. `sp_droplogin` does not check to see whether you have removed the user from all the databases. Because `sp_droplogin` does not check, you can drop a login id from the system and leave a `sysusers` entry in another database. When the `suid` is reused later, the new user will automatically be able to access any database left over from the previous login id that used the same `suid`.

2. `sp_droplogin` does not check to see if the login id being dropped owns any database objects. Since `sp_droplogin` does not check for database objects it is possible to leave, database objects, such as tables and stored procedures that have no owner. Even worse, they will be owned by the next login id added!

SUGGESTED USER ACCOUNT MANAGEMENT STRATEGIES

Now that you know all about user management, what about some of the important maintenance and implementation issues, such as when to use integrated security or standard? What about user naming conventions and when should you use aliases? The following sections answers these questions as well as present some suggested strategies to follow for user account management.

10

USER MANAGEMENT

WHEN TO USE WHICH SECURITY MODE

If your organization is part of an NT domain or your users log into a single NT server, consider using integrated security if you are running the proper network protocols. Your users will appreciate a single login name and password, and you can take advantage of login auditing. The downside is that anyone who is a Windows NT system administrator can get SQL Server administrator privileges. If you want to take advantage of SQL Server replication, then you must be set up with integrated or mixed security. Last, but not least, if you are not using the network protocols multi-protocol or named-pipes, then you must use standard security.

LOGIN NAMES

Come up with a standard convention for your login names, whether it is the user's first and last name, such as John_Doe, or an abbreviation, such as JohnD. Just be consistent.

DATABASE USER NAMES

It is helpful that SQL Server allows you to have a different user name than the login id in a database. However, I find it is easier to manage by keeping the two names the same.

GROUPS

Groups are very important to object security. Create groups that make sense. Grouping users by business function is a very good approach.

ALIASES

There are two cases in which I would recommend using aliases.

First, when you have a development database and you want all the objects created by the DBO, alias the login ids to the DBO in the database.

Second, if you plan to share a database with another SQL Server using DUMP and LOAD commands, the login ids (suid) for the two SQL Servers may not be the same. Since the sysusers table travels with the database, when using DUMP and LOAD, the DBA for the second server can have a difficult task of properly mapping his or her users' suid to those in the moved database. So, if you plan to share a database in this manner, set up user accounts on the first database as if they were groups (login ids of developer and tester, for example) and then all the users who are developers alias to the developer login id. When you move the database, the second DBA can drop the improper aliases (the sysalternates table also travels) and then correctly alias the logins.

The following is a simple checklist to use to help set up integrated security:

___ Running trusted connection protocol (named-pipes or multi-protocol).

___ Configure SQL Server with integrated or mixed security. Add default user and map characters if necessary.

___ Create a Windows NT local or domain group for SQL Server using the *NT User Manager*.

___ Add local Windows NT users and assign them to the new SQL Server group.

___ Use the SQL Security Manager to create groups and login ids on SQL Server.

BETWEEN THE LINES

The following are some of the important tips and tricks to read between the lines for user management:

◆ A login id gives a user access to SQL Server.

◆ A database user name gives a SQL Server login access to the database.

◆ SQL Server for NT supports three security modes: standard, integrated, and mixed. The security mode influences the way user logins are added and maintained.

◆ SQL Server 6.0 encrypts passwords stored in syslogins.

◆ Create groups that match your business and place the users in the groups accordingly. You will use groups to set up security in the database.

◆ A user always belongs to the system group public and can belong to a single user defined group.

◆ If you use integrated security mode, choose Windows NT user account names that only use valid SQL Server characters to simplify adding users to SQL Server.

◆ Always assign a default database to a login id so the master database is not the default!

◆ If you plan to share a database with another server using DUMP and LOAD commands, then add the minimum number of login ids to the database and use aliases.

◆ Always use the SQL Enterprise Manager to drop login accounts!

◆ Always give sa a password! Otherwise, I may be in your system someday!

◆ Do *not* forget the password for sa. Doing so will result in having to reinstall SQL Server!

SUMMARY

You now should have a good understanding of user management in SQL Server and of how and when to use the different security modes. In the next section, you will learn about database object permissions and how to assign them to users and groups.

CHAPTER 11

Managing SQL Server Security

SQL Server provides built-in security and data protection. Its security features are trustworthy and relatively easy to administer. By taking advantage of SQL Server's security features, you can create a secure database that prevents unauthorized access and allows data modification to occur in a controlled and orderly manner.

LEVELS OF SECURITY

The term *security* is a broad term that carries a different meaning depending on how it is applied. It can be applied to the following levels (see Figure 11.1):

◆ **Operating System**: To connect to the server, a user typically must go through some type of operating system login routine that validates system access.

◆ **SQL Server**: To connect to SQL Server, the user must have a valid SQL server user login (refer to Chapter 10 for more information about user logins).

◆ **Database**: To access a database within SQL Server, the user must have been granted permission to the database (refer to Chapter 10 for more information about permitting access to a database).

◆ **Object** (table, view, or stored procedure): To access an object within a database, the user must be granted permission to the object.

When dealing with security, you will spend the majority of your time working at the database and object level. Therefore, the remainder of this chapter will concentrate on database and object security.

Figure 11.1.
Four levels of security.

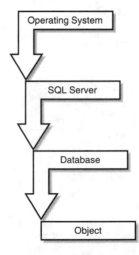

SECURITY HIERARCHY

SQL Server's security mechanism is hierarchical-based. Within the hierarchy exists four types of users: SA, database owners, database object owners, and other users of the database (see Figure 11.2).

Figure 11.2.
Security hierarchy.

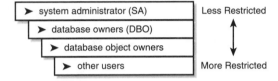

SYSTEM ADMINISTRATOR (SA)

The system administrator, or SA, is "the almighty one" that has unrestricted access to SQL Server. Any SQL Server statement or command can be executed by the SA. The SA can also grant permissions to other users.

DATABASE OWNERS (DBO)

The database owner (DBO) is the user who created the database or has had ownership assigned to him or her. The DBO has complete access to all objects within his or her database and has the capability to assign object permissions to other users.

Tip

To determine the owner of a database, use sp_helpdb or double-click on the database from the Enterprise Manager (refer to Chapter 9 for more information on managing databases).

DATABASE OBJECT OWNERS

The person that creates the database object is considered the owner of the object and is called the *database object owner*. With SQL Server it is assumed that if you have the necessary permission to create the object, then you are automatically given all permissions to it (SELECT, UPDATE, INSERT, DELETE, REFERENCE, and EXECUTE). With the exception of the Database Object Owner and SA, no one else can access an object until the appropriate permission is granted.

Tip

Use sp_help to determine the owner of an object within a database.

There is not a command in SQL Server to transfer ownership of an object within the database. To get around this limitation, the SA or *existing* Database Object Owner must drop the object and the *new* Database Object Owner must re-create the object.

To simplify object access, the DBO should create all objects within the database. This will automatically make the DBO the Database Object Owner.

OTHER USERS

Other users must be granted object permissions (SELECT, UPDATE, INSERT, DELETE, REFERENCE, and EXECUTE) to operate within the database. You can also grant statement permissions to other users so that they can create and drop objects within the database.

PERMISSIONS

A *permission* allows someone to do something within a database. There are two types of permissions: *object* and *statement*. As a DBA, you will probably spend more time with object permissions. Object permissions control who can access and manipulate data in tables and views and who can run stored procedures. Statement permissions control who can drop and create objects within a database.

SQL Server uses the terminology *grant* and *revoke* to manage permissions.

◆ GRANT: When you GRANT a permission to an object, you are allowing someone to perform an action against the object (for example, SELECT, UPDATE, INSERT, DELETE, EXECUTE). When you GRANT permission to a statement, you are allowing someone to run the statement (for example, CREATE TABLE).

◆ REVOKE: When you REVOKE a permission from an object, you are preventing someone from performing an action against the object (for example, SELECT, UPDATE, INSERT, DELETE, EXECUTE). When you REVOKE permission from a statement, you are taking away a user's capability to run the statement (for example, CREATE TABLE).

OBJECT PERMISSIONS

Object permissions control access to objects within SQL Server. You can grant and revoke permissions to tables, table columns, views, and stored procedures through the Enterprise Manager or through system procedures. When a user wants to perform an action against an object, he or she must have the appropriate permission. For example, when a user wants to SELECT * FROM table1, he or she must have SELECT permission for the table. Table 11.1 summarizes the different types of object permissions.

TABLE 11.1. SUMMARY OF OBJECT PERMISSIONS.

Object Type	Possible Actions
table	SELECT, UPDATE, DELETE, INSERT, REFERENCE
column	SELECT, UPDATE
view	SELECT, UPDATE, INSERT, DELETE
stored procedure	EXECUTE

GRANTING OBJECT PERMISSIONS

Perform the following steps to grant object permissions:

1. From within Enterprise Manager, access the Server Manager dialog box, select a server, open Databases folder, select a database, and select the Objects folder.
2. From the Object menu select Permissions.
3. Select the By Object tab or By User tab. The By Object tab allows you to select an object and manage each user's permissions to the object. The By User tab allows you to select a user or group and manage the user's or group's permissions to several objects.
4. If you selected the By Object Tab:

   From the Object list select an object (table, view, or stored procedure). This is the object you will be working with. After you have selected the appropriate object, a list of groups and users will be displayed along with the corresponding permissions to the object (see Figure 11.3).

   If you selected the By User Tab:

   From the User/Group list select a user or group to work with. After you select the user or group to work with, a list of objects and their corresponding permissions will be displayed (see Figure 11.4).
5. If you selected the By Object Tab:

   To Grant All Permissions to all users and groups click on the Grant All button.

If you selected the By User Tab:

To Grant All Permissions to all objects click on the Grant All button.

Figure 11.3.
Granting object
permissions using the
Object Permissions
dialog box.

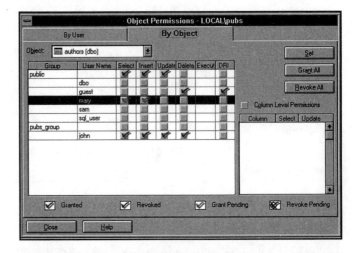

Figure 11.4.
Granting object
permissions by user.

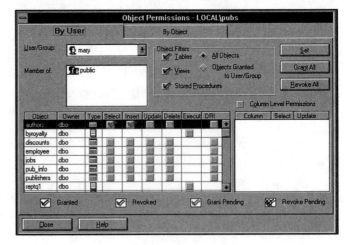

6. For either the By Object Tab or By User Tab:

   To Grant individual permissions to a group or user, select the appropriate row and click on the appropriate check box.

7. For either the By Object Tab or By User Tab:

   To Grant Column Level Permissions to a table or view click on Column Level Permissions and click on the appropriate check box.

8. Click on the Set button to commit any changes that have been made.

> ## STRANGER THAN FICTION!
>
> In Chapter 9 of the *SQL Server's Administrator Companion* manual, it incorrectly states that you should perform the following steps to manage object permissions by group or user.
>
> "From the Server Manager window, select a server, open its Databases folder, and select a database."
>
> If you follow these steps, you will be managing statement permissions rather than object permissions!
>
> The text should say:
>
> From the Server Manager window, select a server, open its Databases folder, select a database, *and select the Objects folder*.

REVOKING OBJECT PERMISSIONS

Perform the following steps to revoke object permissions:

1. From within Enterprise Manager access the Server Manager dialog box, select a server, open Databases folder, select a database, and select the Objects folder.

2. From the Object menu select Permissions.

3. Select By Object tab or By User tab. The By Object tab enables you to select an object and manage each user's permissions to the object. The By User tab enables you to select a user or group and manage the user's or group's permissions to several objects.

4. If you selected the By Object Tab:

   From the Object list select an object (table, view, or stored procedure). This is the object you will be working with. After you have selected the appropriate object, a list of groups and users will be displayed along with the corresponding permissions to the object (see Figure 11.5).

   If you selected the By User Tab:

   From the User/Group list select a user or group to work with. After you have selected the user or group to work, a list of objects and their corresponding permissions will be displayed (see Figure 11.6).

5. If you selected the By Object Tab:

   To revoke all permissions to all users and groups click on the Revoke All button.

   If you selected the By User Tab:

   To revoke all permissions to all objects click on the Revoke All button.

11

MANAGING SQL SERVER SECURITY

Figure 11.5.
Revoking object
permissions by object.

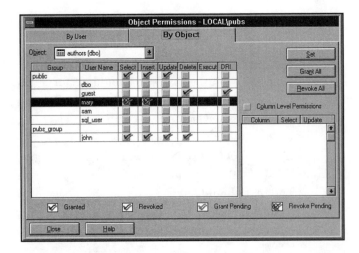

Figure 11.6.
Revoking object
permissions by user.

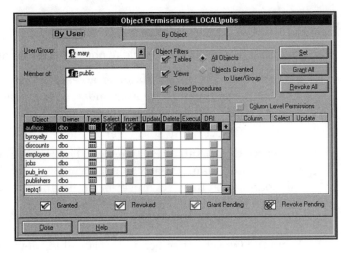

6. For either the By Object Tab or By User Tab:

   To revoke individual permissions to an object, select the appropriate row and click on the appropriate check box.

7. For either the By Object Tab or By User Tab:

   To revoke column level permissions to a table or view, click on Column Level Permissions and click on the appropriate check box.

8. Click on the Set button to commit any changes that have been made.

TIPS FOR MANAGING OBJECT PERMISSIONS

Use the following tips to help manage object permissions:

◆ When an object (table, view, stored procedure) is first created, only the creator of the object or the SA can access and manipulate the object. Object permissions must be assigned to users so that they can access the object.

◆ Object and statement permissions take effect immediately. Unlike other systems, a user does not have to log out and log back into SQL Server for the change to take effect.

◆ Permissions are object specific, not database specific; therefore, each object (tables, view, or stored procedure) must be assigned the appropriate permission.

◆ By default, SA automatically has all permissions for all objects; therefore, you do not need to assign permissions to the SA.

◆ With the Enterprise Manager you can limit the type of object to be displayed for an individual user or group by checking the appropriate choice in the Objects Filters area of the dialog box. For example, to look at only table permissions assigned to the public group, check off the Table option in Object Filters and deselect the other options (see Figure 11.7). To look at only stored procedure permissions, check off the Stored Procedures option in Object Filters and deselect the other options (see Figure 11.8).

Figure 11.7.
Viewing permissions
through object filters
(table filter).

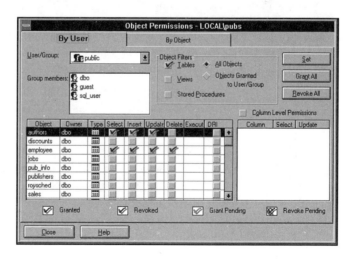

11

MANAGING SQL SERVER SECURITY

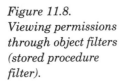

Figure 11.8.
Viewing permissions
through object filters
(stored procedure
filter).

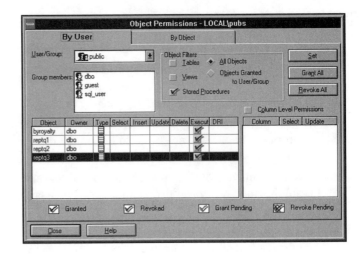

◆ If you are logged in as the SA or the database owner you can use SETUSER to impersonate another user within the system. This is an easy way to test changes without having to log out and log back in. Also you do not need to know the user's password that you are trying to impersonate. Look at the following syntax:

```
SETUSER ['username' [WITH NORESET]]
```

If the WITH NORESET parameter *was not* specified, you can issue the SETUSER statement without any parameters to revert back to the profile of the logged in user. If the WITH NORESET parameter *was* specified, you can reopen the database (USE *database_name*) to revert back to the profile of the logged in user.

If you forget who you are impersonating, you can use the user_name() function to determine active user profile, as in the following syntax.

```
SELECT user_name()
```

◆ Be sure to save an object's permissions before you drop and re-create a table, view, or stored procedure! All permissions to the object will be removed when it is dropped. SQL Server will not prompt you to save permissions to the object! An easy way to save the permissions to an object is to select the object from the Enterprise Manager and from the Object menu select Generate SQL Scripts. From the Generate SQL Scripts dialog box, click on the permissions checkbox and generate the script. After you re-create the object, you can apply the script to restore permissions.

Understanding the Importance of Permission Order

When assigning and revoking permissions, it is important to keep in mind the order in which the assignment occurs. The order in which permissions are assigned will determine a user's access to an object. If the order of permission assignment isn't properly followed, it may lead to undesirable results. Consider the following examples.

Example A:

1. Grant the SELECT permission to the authors table for Joe.
2. Revoke the SELECT permission to the authors table from the public group (by default, Joe is a member of the public group).

When Joe tries to issue a SELECT against table A, he will be denied access. This is because the SELECT permission was revoked from the public group *after* the SELECT permissions was granted to Joe.

Example B:

1. Revoke the SELECT permission to the authors table from the public group.
2. Grant the SELECT permission to the authors table for Joe.

When Joe tries to issue a SELECT against table A, he will be granted access. This is because Joe was granted the SELECT permission *after* the SELECT permission was revoked from the public group.

As you can see, the order of permission assignment can impact the actions a user can perform to an object. An easy way to understand this concept is to remember the saying *"Last In—Wins!"*

Corresponding Transact SQL Commands to Manage Object Permissions

The following command syntax can also be used to manage object permissions.

To add object permissions:

```
GRANT {ALL | permission_list}
ON {table_name [(column_list)] | view_name [(column_list)] |
stored_procedure_name | extended_stored_procedure_name}
TO {PUBLIC | name_list}
```

To remove object permissions:

```
REVOKE {ALL | permission_list}
ON {table_name [(column_list)] | view_name [(column_list)] |
stored_procedure_name | extended_stored_procedure_name}
FROM {PUBLIC | name_list}
```

To view permissions by object or by user:

```
sp_helprotect objectname [, username]
```

STATEMENT PERMISSIONS

Statement permissions control who can drop and create objects within a database. Only the SA or DBO can administer statement permissions. I advise prudence in granting access to statement permissions, such as CREATE DATABASE, DUMP DATABASE, and DUMP TRANSACTION. Usually it is better to let the SA or DBO manage these statements. The following is a list of statement permissions that can be granted or revoked.

- ◆ CREATE DATABASE: Creates a database. This can only be granted by the SA and only to users in the master database
- ◆ CREATE DEFAULT: Creates a default value for a table column.
- ◆ CREATE PROCEDURE: Creates a stored procedure.
- ◆ CREATE RULE: Creates a table column rule.
- ◆ CREATE TABLE: Creates a table.
- ◆ CREATE VIEW: Creates a view.
- ◆ DUMP DATABASE: Dumps the database (backup database) to a dump device.
- ◆ DUMP TRANSACTION: Dumps the transaction log (backup transaction log or clear the transaction log) to a dump device.

Tip

Watch out for objects that have been created by someone other than the DBO. This can cause grief when the DBO tries to access or manipulate the object.

GRANTING STATEMENT PERMISSIONS

Perform the following steps to grant statement permissions:

1. From within Enterprise Manager access the Server Manager dialog box, select a server, and double-click on a database.
2. Select the Permissions tab. Existing permissions are indicated with a checkmark (see Figure 11.9).
3. Click on the appropriate user and statement permission until a green check appears in the checkbox.

Note

The CREATE DB permission can only be granted by the SA and only to users in the master database.

Figure 11.9.
Granting statement
permissions.

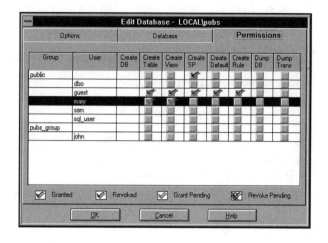

4. Click on OK to commit any changes that have been made.

REVOKING STATEMENT PERMISSIONS

1. From within Enterprise Manager access the Server Manager dialog box, select a server, and double-click on a database.
2. Select the Permissions tab. Existing permissions are indicated with a checkmark (see Figure 11.10).

Figure 11.10.
Revoking statement
permissions.

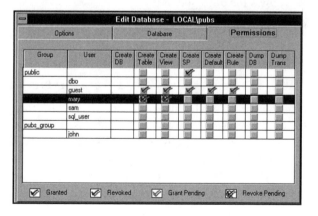

3. Click on the appropriate user and statement permission until a red circle and slash appears in the checkbox.
4. Click on OK to commit any changes that have been made.

CORRESPONDING TRANSACT SQL COMMANDS TO MANAGE STATEMENT PERMISSIONS

The following command syntax can also be used to manage statement permissions.

To add statement permissions:

```
GRANT {ALL | statement_list}
TO {PUBLIC | name_list}
```

To remove statement permissions:

```
REVOKE {ALL | statement_list}
FROM {PUBLIC | name_list}
```

To view statement permissions by user or group:

```
sp_helprotect username
```

BEYOND SECURITY BASICS: SUGGESTED STRATEGIES

In addition to object and statement permissions, you can combine different components within SQL Server to help ease administration and provide improved security. The following is a list of suggested security strategies.

◆ Group-based security management

◆ Views for data security

◆ Stored procedures for data security

◆ Triggers for audit trails

GROUP-BASED SECURITY MANAGEMENT

In the corporate environment, users often work in groups and these groups require similar permissions to the database. Whenever multiple users require similar permissions, you should use group-based security. With group-based security, you will reduce the number of GRANT and REVOKE statements that must be maintained (refer to Chapter 10 for more information on the creation and management of groups).

Before going headfirst into group-based security management, you should keep in mind the following points:

◆ A user can belong to only one user-defined group per database plus the public group (a user automatically becomes part of the public group when he or she is permitted access to the database). From a maintenance standpoint, this limitation may result in a less than optimal security strategy.

You might need to assign a user to a user-defined group that gives him or her the majority of his or her permissions and then grant the user additional individual permissions.

◆ When everyone in a database needs the same permission to the same object, use the public group. When you grant or revoke a permission to the public group, everyone will feel the effect. This is often any easy way to streamline security administration.

◆ When a user is assigned to a group other than the public group, it appears that the user is no longer a member of the public group. Don't worry—the user is still a member of the public group! Any permissions assigned to the public group will impact all users within the database.

VIEWS FOR DATA SECURITY

Views help control data security for the following reasons:

◆ A view can limit the amount of data a user can see and modify. To the user, a view looks and acts like a real table, even though he or she may be working with a subset of the data. Behind the scenes, a view is a virtual table that defines the presentation and manipulation of the actual table(s).

◆ A user only needs permissions to the view, not the table(s) that make up the view.

USING VIEWS FOR COLUMN LEVEL SECURITY

Often a view is used when a user needs access to a table but for security reasons you want to restrict access to certain columns (such as salary data) within the table. Through a view, access to sensitive data can easily be restricted.

Syntax:

```
CREATE VIEW [owner.]view_name
[(column_name [, column_name]...)]
[WITH ENCRYPTION]
AS select_statement [WITH CHECK OPTION]
```

For example, to prohibit access to the employee_ssn, salary, last_updated_by, and last_update_datetime columns in the employee table (see Figure 11.11), use the following syntax:

```
CREATE VIEW  employee_view AS
SELECT name, address, city, state, zip
FROM employee
```

Figure 11.11.
Employee table schema.

```
employee_ssn char (9)
name char (35)
address char (35)
city char (35)
state char (35)
zip char (35)
salary money
last_updated_by char (50)
last_update_datetime datetime
```

When the user issues `SELECT * FROM employee_view`, he or she will only get back the following columns:

```
name
address
city
state
zip
```

To users, the view looks like a real table except that they never see the `employee_ssn`, `salary`, `last_updated_by`, and `last_update_datetime` columns. If they can't see it, they can't modify it!

USING VIEWS FOR ROW AND COLUMN LEVEL SECURITY

A simple way to implement row level security is to add a `WHERE` clause in the `CREATE VIEW` statement. For example, use the following syntax to create a view that limits column and row access:

```
CREATE VIEW  employee_view_by_state AS
SELECT name, address, city, state, zip
FROM employee
WHERE state = 'VA' OR state = 'MA'
```

When users issue

```
SELECT * FROM employee_view_by_state
```

they will only see employees that have a state code of VA or MA.

Tip

To further ensure data security and to prevent keying errors, you can add the `WITH CHECK OPTION` to the `CREATE VIEW` statement, as in the following:

```
view
```

When you use the `WITH CHECK OPTION`, it prevents users from inserting rows or updating columns that do not conform to the where clause, as in the following example:

```
CREATE VIEW  employee_view_by_state AS
SELECT name, address, city, state, zip
FROM employee
WHERE state = 'VA' OR state = 'MA'
WITH CHECK OPTION
```

Through this view, users can only add rows with a VA or MA state code and they can only update a state code to MA or VA. If users try to change the state code to something other than VA or MA, they will receive the following message:

```
Msg 550, Level 16, State 2
The attempted insert or update failed because the target view either
specifies WITH CHECK OPTION or spans
a view which specifies WITH CHECK OPTION and one or more rows resulting
from the operation did not
qualify under the CHECK OPTION constraint.
Command has been aborted.
```

Note

The WITH CHECK OPTION is new to SQL Server 6.0.

HOW VIEWS AND PERMISSIONS WORK TOGETHER

When you grant object permissions to a view, you do not need to grant permissions to the underlying tables in the view. Therefore, users can SELECT employee data from the employee_view, even though they do not have SELECT permission for the employee table. This feature can simplify administration when the view consists of multiple tables.

Tip

You may be asking yourself "Why not use column level permissions to prevent access to the employee_ssn, salary, last_updated_by, and last_update_datetime columns?" (refer to Figure 11.11). Good question! Both views and column level permissions can prevent a user from accessing restricted columns.

The reason for using a view rather than column level security is that the view allows a user to issue the SELECT * statement without receiving error messages while still providing column level security. Consider the following examples:

11

MANAGING SQL SERVER SECURITY

Example A:

1. John's SELECT permission has been revoked from the employee_ssn column in the employee table.

2. When John issues SELECT * FROM employee, he will receive the following error message:

```
Msg 230, Level 14, State 1
SELECT permission denied on column employee_ssn of object employee, data-
base xxx, owner dbo
```

3. To avoid the error message, John explicitly names each column in the SELECT statement.

Example B:

1. A view has been developed for John to use. The view does not include the employee_ssn column.

2. John can issue a SELECT * statement against the view and he will only see the columns specified in the view. He will not receive any error messages.

STORED PROCEDURES FOR DATA SECURITY

The advantage of using stored procedures to access and modify data is that users only need the EXECUTE permission to run a stored procedure; they do not need access to the tables and views that make up the stored procedure. This alleviates the headache of assigning permissions to all underlying tables and views referenced within a stored procedure. The following syntax is an example of a stored procedure that returns all rows in the employee table:

```
CREATE PROCEDURE usp_employee AS
SELECT * FROM EMPLOYEE
```

To run the procedure, the user only needs the EXECUTE permission for usp_employee. The user does *not* need the SELECT permission for the employee table.

GOING TO EXTREMES (BUT IT MAY BE WORTH IT!)

You can really clamp down on end-user data modifications by implementing stored procedures to handle all data modifications. To implement this strategy, you must design your applications to only use stored procedures and not embedded SQL to handle data modifications. Next, you need to revoke all UPDATE, DELETE, and INSERT (and maybe even SELECT) privileges to *all* tables and views in the database. End-users will now be denied access whenever they try to modify data. For this approach to be successful, it requires extensive use of stored procedures, careful planning, and tight coordination between the application developers and the DBA.

Triggers for Audit Trails

Triggers are comprised of Transact SQL statements that automatically execute when a table is modified through INSERT, UPDATE, or DELETE statements. Because a trigger is automatically executed, it can be a useful facility for auditing data changes. Additionally, you do not need to grant a user the privilege to execute a trigger.

An often used type of trigger is one that tracks who made the last change to a table and when the change occurred. For example, to track this information use the following syntax:

```
CREATE TRIGGER tiu_employee ON dbo.employee
FOR INSERT,UPDATE,DELETE
AS
UPDATE employee
SET employee.last_updated_by = USER_NAME(),
employee.last_update_datetime = GETDATE()
FROM inserted,employee
WHERE inserted.employee_ssn = employee.employee_ssn
```

Whenever an INSERT, UPDATE, or DELETE statement is run against the employee table, the column last_updated_by will be set to the name of the user that made the change and the column last_update_datetime will be set to time the change was made.

Warning

BCP will bypass triggers! Therefore, any audit trail that is maintained through a trigger will have to be manually updated after using BCP.

Between the Lines

The following are some of the important tips and tricks to read between the lines for security:

◆ Use the Enterprise Manager or Transact SQL commands to grant and revoke permissions. For ease-of-use, the Enterprise Manager is generally preferred over Transact SQL commands.

11

◆ When an object (table, view, stored procedure) is first created, only the creator of the object or the SA can access and manipulate the object. Object permissions must be assigned to users so that they can access the object.

◆ Object and statement permissions take effect immediately. Unlike other systems, a user does not have to log out and log back into SQL Server for the change to take effect.

◆ Permissions are object-specific, not database-specific. Therefore each object (tables, view, or stored procedure) must be assigned the appropriate permission.

◆ By default, the SA automatically has all permissions to all objects. You do not need to assign permissions to the SA.

◆ Use SETUSER to impersonate another user within the system. This is an easy way to test permission changes without having to log out and log in again.

◆ Use groups to implement security, but don't forget that a user can belong to only one user-defined group (the user will automatically belong to the public group).

◆ Use the public group to assign object permissions to a table, view, or stored procedure to which everyone needs access.

◆ Use views to control column and row access.

◆ Use stored procedures to control data modifications.

◆ Use triggers for audit trails.

SUMMARY

You now should have a good understanding of object and database security. By having a solid understanding of SQL Server's security architecture, you can lock down your data and ward off unauthorized data changes. In the next chapter, you will discover how to implement data replication.

CHAPTER 12

Replication

One of the exciting new features of SQL Server 6.0 (that ships with the product) is *data replication*.

Note

I throw in the fact it ships with the standard product because several other RDBMS vendors treat replication as a separate product that you must pay extra for!

In a nutshell, replication is the capability to reliably duplicate data from a source database to one or more destination databases. Using Microsoft SQL Server replication, you can automatically distribute read-only, transaction-based data from one server to many different servers via ODBC (Open Database Connectivity). When would you want to use SQL Server replication? Here are some examples:

◆ To distribute the workload across servers (such as moving ad hoc query and reporting capability from a source server).

◆ To move specific subsets of data (such as a company department, one month's worth of data) from a main central server.

◆ When you have a central database that is updated and the updates need to be moved out to other databases (such as a department store changing prices for an item).

◆ Environments in which several servers are importing similar flat file information use a central database to import the flat file and replicate the information to the other sites.

SQL Server replication uses a loose consistency distributed data model. *Loose consistency* means that the data synchronization between the source and destination server does not occur simultaneously. Before going into more detail, look at another distributed data model: tight consistency. A *tight consistency* distributed data model can be accomplished with SQL Server using two phase commits. In a tight consistency model, all transactions are committed or rolled back on all the servers so that the data is in synch 100 percent of the time. In a loose consistency model, transactions are committed or rolled back on a source server. The transactions on the source server are then replicated asynchronously to subscribing servers. The big difference between the tight consistency model and the loose consistency model is that there is some lag time between changes made to the source server and replication to the destination servers (that is, the databases are temporarily out of synch).

SQL Server replication is not designed to be used in a hot backup server situation (that is, another machine that is used when the primary machine goes down). The loose consistency model used by SQL Server replication does not keep the two servers "in-synch" at all times.

OVERVIEW

SQL Server is able to perform replication by using the existing transaction log. If a table is marked for replication, the changes made to the table will automatically be replicated to other servers. It sounds simple, but in reality, the replication process is a little more complicated. Before getting into the details of replication, it is important to understand some of the terminology used when discussing SQL Server replication. In Figure 12.1, SQL Server A is replicating data from the pubs database to several other servers. Using Figure 12.1, review the terminology used in SQL Server replication.

Figure 12.1.
Overview of replication.

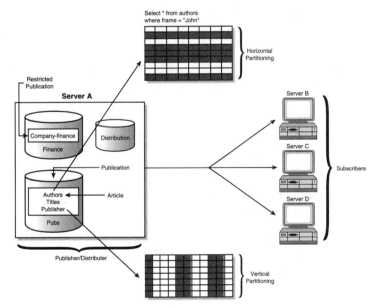

PUBLISH AND SUBSCRIBE

SQL Server replication uses a *publish and subscribe* metaphor. Servers publish publications that other servers can subscribe to. A SQL Server that makes data available to other servers for subscribing purposes is called a publisher. For example, Server A in Figure 12.1 is a publisher. A SQL Server that subscribes to a publication published by another SQL Server is said to be a subscriber (an example of a subscription server is Server B in Figure 12.1). A SQL Server that contains the distribution database is said to be a distributor (the distribution server is Server A in Figure 12.1).

PUBLICATION AND ARTICLES

A publisher publishes a collection of one or more articles called a publication. The publication shown in Figure 12.1 is called `Author_Publisher` and contains the authors and publishers table. An article is the basic unit of replication and can be a table or a subset of the table.

Note

Articles are always associated with a publication and cannot be published by themselves.

Publications can contain one or more of the following:

♦ Tables
♦ Vertically partitioned tables
♦ Horizontally partitioned tables
♦ Horizontally and vertically partitioned tables

A vertically partitioned table is an article using a filter that selects only certain columns of a table. A horizontally partitioned table is an article based on a filter that selects only specific rows in the table.

Note

The following cannot be published:

♦ The database's model, tempdb, and msdb
♦ The system tables in the master database
♦ The SQL Server identity columns and timestamp columns
♦ Tables without a primary key

Data replication only provides limited support for text and image columns passing NULL values, unless you replicate using the table refresh method.

SQL Server replication provides a level of security. For example, publications can be selectively marked restricted or unrestricted to different subscribing servers. In Figure 12.1, Server B has been restricted from viewing the company_finance publication.

Note

Subscribing servers can only see publications they have access to.

SERVER ROLES

SQL Server can play one or more of the following roles during the replication process:

- ◆ Publisher
- ◆ Subscriber
- ◆ Distributor

PUBLISHER

A publisher server is responsible for maintaining its source databases, making the data available for replication, and sending the data to the distribution database to be replicated to subscribing servers.

SUBSCRIBER

A subscriber server is a server that receives and maintains published data.

DISTRIBUTION

The distribution server maintains the distribution database, which is responsible for the store and forward capabilities of SQL Server replication. The job of the distribution server is to replicate data from the distribution database to the appropriate subscribing servers.

REPLICATION MODELS

As you can tell by now, SQL Server can participate in one or more replication roles. For example, in many cases a publication server also serves as a distribution server and can also subscribe to other publications from other publishers, in which case the same server that was acting as a publisher and distributor is also acting as a subscriber. When setting up replication, there are several publisher and subscriber models you can use. Figure 12.1 is an example of a single publisher providing information to multiple subscribers. Figure 12.2 shows a single publisher server using a distribution server to replicate data to subscribers.

The replication model pictured in Figure 12.3 shows multiple publishers and multiple subscribers.

Figure 12.2.
Replication model:
single publisher using
a distribution server.

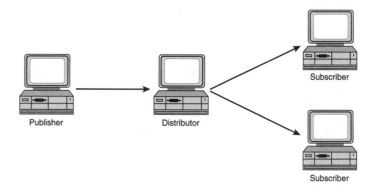

Figure 12.3.
Replication model:
multiple publishers
and multiple sub-
scribers.

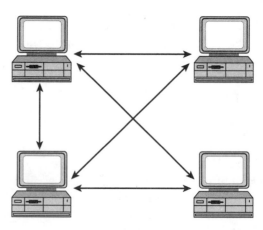

Another replication model similar to Figure 12.3 is multiple publishers to a single subscriber. The important point to understand is that there are many ways to set up SQL Server replication. Study the various replication models and plan before implementing!

Tip

Microsoft SQL Server documentation covers the different replication models in detail. Make sure you review the replication chapters before implementing replication.

WALKING THROUGH THE REPLICATION PROCESS

Now that you have a general understanding of replication terminology, walk through the SQL Server replication process using Figure 12.4.

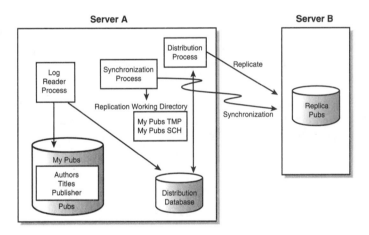

Figure 12.4.
Overview of SQL Server
replication.

To begin the overview of SQL Server replication, assume that Server A has published the entire pubs database in a publication titled MyPubs for replication. Server A is also the distribution server. Before you begin your walk-through, you need to learn about some of the components that make up SQL Server replication.

LOG READER PROCESS

The *log reader* process searches the transaction log of published databases for transaction log entries that are marked for replication. The log reader process moves the marked transactions to the distribution database.

DISTRIBUTION DATABASE

The *distribution database* stores all the transactions that are to be replicated to subscribing servers and acts as a store and forward database for replicated transactions. Transactions stay in the distribution database until all subscribers have successfully received the transaction.

SYNCHRONIZATION PROCESS

The synchronization process ensures that the published database and the subscribing database are in synch with one another before data replication begins.

DISTRIBUTION PROCESS

The distribution process distributes the transactions stored in the distribution database to the subscribing servers.

Note

The log reader process, synchronization process, and the distribution process are all part of the SQL Executive service.

Now that the review of the components of the distribution server is complete, walk through two of the main replication processes: synchronization and replicating data. Referring to Figure 12.4, Server B subscribes to the MyPubs publication. Before data replication can begin between the two databases, the synchronization process must complete successfully.

SERVER A AND SERVER B PERFORM SYNCHRONIZATION

When Server B subscribes to Server A's pubs database publication, the subscriber, Server B, has the choice of accepting several different synchronization modes:

◆ Automatic
◆ Manual
◆ No Synchronization
◆ Snapshot Only

SYNCHRONIZATION MODES

The default synchronization mode is automatic, which means that SQL Server will perform the synchronization process automatically during a scheduled interval.

Manual synchronization requires you to synchronize the databases and notify SQL Server when the synchronization process has completed.

Tip

> Use manual synchronization when dealing with very large tables or a slow communications line. The files required for synchronization can be copied to a tape or other media and applied to the destination server(s).

No synchronization assumes that the articles in the source are already in synch with articles in the destination. SQL Server will do nothing to verify that the databases are synchronized—that task is up to you. The last option, Snapshot Only, is also referred to as a *table refresh*. If a snapshot synchronization is selected, then SQL Server ignores any changes to the published articles and instead performs the synchronization process at defined intervals (that is, refreshing the destination tables).

WALKING THROUGH AUTOMATIC SYNCHRONIZATION

For our example, assume Server B selects automatic synchronization during the subscription process. The distribution server creates two files referred to as a synchronization set in the replication working directory (the default is \REPLDATA in the SQL Server home directory). The synchronization set consists of a BCP data file with the actual data of the subscribed articles and the article's table schema file.

Tip

> Schema files created for replication have a .SCH extension and the data files have a .TMP file extension.

Once the synchronization set is created, a synchronization job is added to the distribution database. The distribution process reads the distribution database and applies the synchronization file set to the subscribing server, Server B in this example. First, the schema file is applied to create the table schema. The table information is then copied to the subscribing server using BCP. The distribution server is notified that synchronization has completed and Server A can begin to replicate the publication MyPubs to Server B.

12

REPLICATION

Note

Once all other subscriptions have acknowledged successful synchronization, the .TMP files are removed from the replication working directory.

Any transactions that occurred to the published articles after the subscribing server first subscribed but before the synchronization process occurred are then replicated to the subscriber.

Warning

Be careful when trying to perform synchronization with tables that exist on the publishing and the subscribing server, such as the pubs database. The distribution process attempts to drop a table on the subscribing server if it exists during the synchronization process. If the table being dropped has declarative referential integrity defined and is referenced—for example by a foreign key constraint from another table—then the table cannot be dropped and the synchronization process will fail. If this occurs, use the manual synchronization, no synchronization modes, or do not drop the table during synchronization.

ARTICLES ON SERVER A ARE MODIFIED AND REPLICATED

The two servers, shown in Figure 12.4, are synchronized. Modifications are made to articles (tables) on Server A. Because the tables are published, the transactions are marked in the pubs database transaction log for replication. The log reader process, searching transaction logs for marked transactions, creates SQL statements for any marked transactions found and sends the SQL statements to the distribution database.

Note

Transactions marked for replication in a published database's transaction log will remain in the transaction log until the distribution process copies the marked transactions to the distribution database. That is, transaction log backups will not truncate the transactions in the transaction log marked for replication until they have been copied to the distribution database.

The distribution process replicates the transactions found in the distribution database to the subscriber (Server B), using the preconstructed SQL statements or stored procedures. It also removes the transactions from the distribution database and updates the `Mslast_job_info` table on the subscription server.

Note

Using SQL statements to perform the data modifications rather than sending the actual data, greatly reduces the network traffic required to perform replication. The use of SQL statements makes it quite clear why the databases must be synchronized first. Using SQL statements also highlights the point of keeping subscribing databases read-only in practice so that SQL statements applied on the source database have the same effect on the records in the destination database.

PLANNING FOR DATABASE REPLICATION

Unlike many other database operations that you perform using SQL Server, replication requires some planning before implementing. Let's review the requirements before setting up replication.

TRUSTED NETWORK CONNECTIONS ARE REQUIRED

SQL Servers participating in replication are required to use a *trusted connection*, which means that you must have trusted relationships established for NT servers residing in other domains. The SQL Server that is acting as the distribution server must have a client configuration default protocol setting of named-pipes or multi-protocol.

Note

SQL Server replication works with any of the security modes—standard, integrated, or mixed. But, since replication uses a trusted connection, the distribution server always connects to the subscribing servers in an integrated security mode.

32-BIT ODBC DRIVERS INSTALLED

SQL Server replication uses ODBC (Open Database Connectivity) to replicate the data. The 32-bit ODBC drivers must be installed on all SQL Servers involved with replication.

Note

The ODBC drivers are installed automatically during setup. You do not have to configure the ODBC sources.

MEMORY REQUIREMENTS

If the server is a distribution server or both a distribution server and publication server, then the NT server requires at least 32MB of memory with 16MB of memory assigned to SQL Server.

SAME CHARACTER SET

The character set on all servers participating in replication (distribution, publication, and subscriber) must have the same character set. It is recommended, but not required, that they have the same sort order.

Warning

Make sure you check that all servers participating in replication have the same character set or you will find out late in the game that you cannot replicate to other servers due to a different character set. SQL Server will allow you to set up publications and subscribe to servers with different character sets, but the replication process will fail during synchronization.

ADEQUATE TRANSACTION LOG SPACE FOR PUBLISHER DATABASES

Because transactions will remain in the transaction log until moved to the distribution database, your publishing databases may require extra space for the added overhead of active replication transactions in the log.

ALL TABLES YOU WANT TO PUBLISH HAVE PRIMARY KEYS

You cannot publish a table that does not have a primary key declared for the table (for example, tables without primary keys will not appear when selecting articles for publication).

CHECKLIST

The following is a checklist you can use before setting up replication:

Pre-Replication Setup Checklist

TRUSTED NETWORK

- ☐ Default network protocol on distribution server client configuration ___ named-pipes ___ multi-protocol
- ☐ 32-bit ODBC drivers installed

MEMORY REQUIREMENTS

- ☐ NT Server 32MB (Total including SQL Server)
- ☐ SQL Server 16MB

SAME CHARACTER SET

- ☐ Distribution server character set
- ☐ Distribution server sort order (Optional)
- ☐ All subscribers and publishers use the same character set as distribution server
- ☐ Adequate transaction log space for publisher databases
- ☐ All tables you want to publish have primary keys

CREATING THE DISTRIBUTION DATABASE

Now it's time to walk through the steps required to set up replication. First, we will examine how to set up the distribution database. Following are the steps required to create the distribution database, using the SQL Enterprise Manager:

1. Select the server onto which you want to install the distribution database.

2. From the SQL Enterprise Manager Menu, select Server and then select the Replication Configuration option. A drop-down menu will appear (see Figure 12.5).

   Select the Install Publishing... option. The Install Replication Publishing dialog box appears (see Figure 12.6).

3. To install the distribution database, use the default option, Local - Install New Local Distribution Database (see Figure 12.6). Select an existing device for the data and the transaction log of the distribution database using the combo selection boxes, or create a new device by selecting <new> in the Data Device and Log Device combo box.

Figure 12.5.
Replication Configura-
tion menu and option
list.

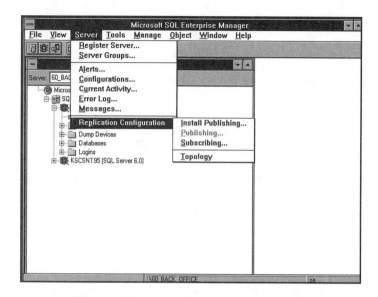

Figure 12.6.
Install Replication
Publishing dialog box.

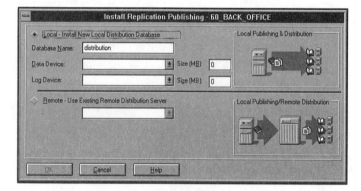

Note

In most cases that you encounter, you typically will be using a distribution server that has already been set up, so you would be selecting
the second option shown in Figure 12.6 (Remote - Using Existing
Remote Distribution Server).

4. Once you have selected the proper devices, enter the size for the database
   and transaction log and click on the OK button to create the distribution
   database (see Figure 12.6).

Tip

Like every database, put the transaction log for the distribution database on a separate device.

A Distribution Completion dialog box will appear when the process completes.

Note

The recommended minimum size for the distribution database is 30MB for the data and 15MB for the transaction log. To help determine the correct amount of space, determine the number of transactions, average transaction size, and the retention time of the data (that is, typical database size requirements).

TROUBLESHOOTING DISTRIBUTION DATABASE SETUP

While creating the distribution database, you can easily run into a few gotchas. I have listed a few of the problems encountered while setting up replication distribution databases.

◆ Do not try to create the distribution database while connected to a SQL Server that is on the same machine as the Enterprise Manager using the default server name of (local). You will get midway through the distribution process and encounter error number 21271 (see Figure 12.7 for actual error message). Make sure you connect to the server using the server name!

Figure 12.7. Error Number 21271 message box.

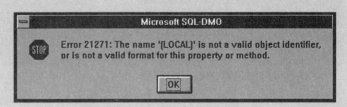

> **Microsoft SQL-DMO**
>
> STOP Error 21271: The name '[LOCAL]' is not a valid object identifier, or is not a valid format for this property or method.
>
> [OK]

◆ Make sure you are using a trusted connection.

◆ If you run into problems while creating the distribution database, check the file INSTDIST.OUT in the \INSTALL directory for errors.

12

> ◆ If your SQL Server is not configured with at least 16MB of memory, you will be warned and will be unable to build the distribution database until you allocate at least the minimum amount.

The process of creating a distribution database can be performed manually by performing the following steps:

1. Create the distribution database and transaction log on separate devices.
2. Run the install script INSTDIST.SQL from the distribution database. The script file will add all the required system tables and stored procedures.
3. Dump the transaction log for the distribution database using the NO_LOG option.
4. Use the system stored procedure sp_serveroption to set the option dist to TRUE for the server.

WHAT HAPPENS WHEN THE DISTRIBUTION DATABASE IS CREATED?

When you create the distribution database, you create a SQL Server database named *distribution*. The distribution database is created with the standard database system tables, as well as the following user tables:

Msjob_commands: Used by the distribution process, the Msjob_commands table contains one command for each transaction.

Msjob_subscriptions: Associates a subscriber with an article.

Msjobs: Contains the transactions used for replication.

Mssubscriber_info: Used by the SQL Executive for passing jobs.

Mssubscriber_jobs: Stores information that associates each subscriber with the commands they need to receive.

Mssubscriber_status: Stores status information about batches of transactions sent to subscribing servers.

CONFIGURING REPLICATION PUBLISHING AND DISTRIBUTION OPTIONS

Once the distribution database has been successfully installed, or you have been given permission to publish to a remote distribution server, you can then configure a server to be a publisher. Using the SQL Enterprise Manager you can set up which servers can subscribe to published databases, which publisher servers can use the distribution server as a remote distribution server, as well as set up the replication schedule used to replicate the data to each subscribing server.

Note

In order to setup SQL Server as a publisher, you must have one of the following:

◆ A local distribution database

◆ Access to a remote distribution database

If you have a local distribution database on your server (that is, your server is acting as a distribution server) you can perform the following:

◆ Set distribution working directory

◆ Allow other servers access to your distribution database for publishing

Both distribution servers and publisher servers can control which servers will allow access to published articles and which databases on your local server can publish articles.

CONFIGURING PUBLISHING

To set up publications options, perform the following steps:

1. Select the server from the Enterprise Manager.

2. From the SQL Enterprise Manager Menu, select Server and then select Replication Configuration. From the drop-down list box, select Publishing. The Replication Publishing dialog box appears (see Figure 12.8).

3. To enable a database for publication, check the Enable checkbox by the appropriate database.

4. To enable a server to subscribe, check the server's Enable checkbox.

5. To save the changes, click the OK button. To ignore changes made, click the Cancel button.

SETTING DISTRIBUTION OPTIONS

Using the Replication Publishing dialog box, you can administer various distribution options (refer to Figure 12.8). The distribution options can be changed for each subscriber by clicking the Distribution Options button, which displays the Distribution Options dialog box (see Figure 12.9).

12

Figure 12.8.
Replication Publishing
dialog box.

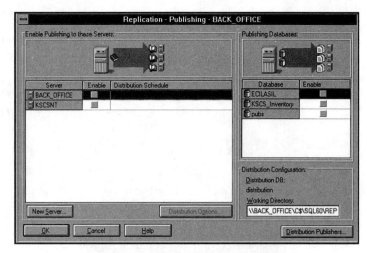

Figure 12.9.
Distribution Options
dialog box.

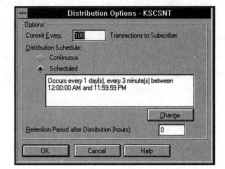

The Distribution dialog box enables you to set replication scheduling to subscribing servers. Using a Continuous schedule, for example, transactions are replicated continuously to the subscribing servers. If you do not want continuous replication, then you can set up a schedule for how often transactions are replicated to the subscribing service. To allow a remote publisher server to use this server as a remote distribution server, click the button Distribution Publishers. The Replication - Distribution dialog box will appear (see Figure 12.10).

To allow a remote publishing server to use the local server as a distribution server, mark the Enable checkbox by the appropriate remote server and click the OK button.

Figure 12.10.
Replication -
Distribution
dialog box.

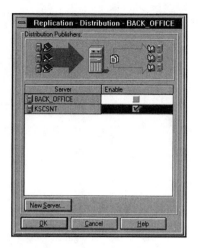

CONFIGURING REPLICATION SUBSCRIBING

To allow local databases to subscribe to publications or to allow publishing servers to replicate data to the local server requires enabling permissions for the publication servers and the local databases using the SQL Enterprise Manager.

Note

Setting up subscribers enables you to determine which databases can receive published articles and which remote publisher servers you can receive publications from.

To set up subscription options, perform the following steps:

1. Select the server from the Enterprise Manager.
2. From the SQL Enterprise Manager Menu, select *Server* and then select Replication Configuration option. From the drop-down list box, select Subscribing. The Replication - Subscribing dialog box appears (see Figure 12.11).
3. Check the Enabled checkbox located by the server's or database's name to enable. When you are done, click the OK button.

*Figure 12.11.
Replication -
Subscribing
dialog box.*

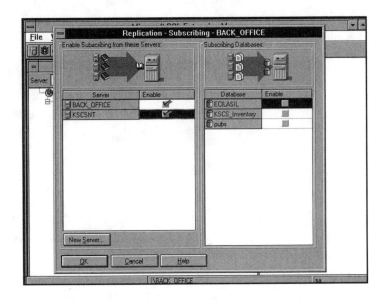

VIEWING REPLICATION TOPOLOGY

Once you have set up your replication, you can view the overall replication topology.
Using the SQL Enterprise Manager, perform the following steps:

1. Select the server from the Enterprise Manager.

2. From the SQL Enterprise Manager Menu, select Server, and then select
   Replication Configuration option. From the drop-down list box, select
   Topology. The Replication Topology dialog box appears (see Figure 12.12).

*Figure 12.12.
Replication Topology
dialog box.*

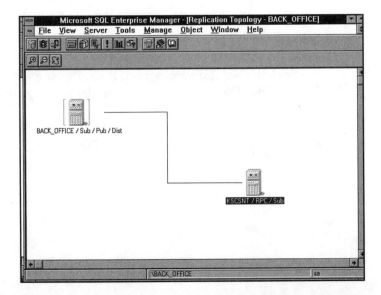

Tip

The Replication Topology dialog box gives you a graphical view of how replication is set up between servers. If a server is a distribution server, the server will have the abbreviation DIST by its picture. Publishing servers have the abbreviation Pub and subscribing servers have the abbreviation Sub.

MANAGING PUBLICATIONS

After you set up your SQL Server as a publisher, you can create publications to which other SQL Servers can subscribe. Changes made to your published databases are then replicated to subscribing databases. Remember, a publication consists of one or many articles (tables). To create a publication using the SQL Enterprise Manager, perform the following steps:

1. Select the server from the Enterprise Manager.
2. From the SQL Enterprise Manager Menu, select Manage, and then select Replication. From the drop-down list box, select Publications. The Manage Publications dialog box appears (see Figure 12.13).

Figure 12.13.
Manage Publications dialog box.

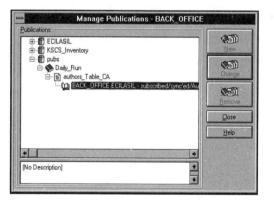

Published databases are displayed in the Publications list box. The databases have the typical SQL Server Enterprise Manager drill-down features. Drilling down on a database displays the publications in the database. Drilling down on a publication shows the articles in the publication. If you drill down on the article(s), you can see the current subscribers.

3. To create a new publication, click on the database to add the publication and then click on the New button (see Figure 12.13). The Edit Publications dialog box appears (see Figure 12.14).

12

To remove a publication, use the Remove button (refer to Figure 12.13). To modify a publication, use the Change button (refer to Figure 12.13).

*Figure 12.14.
Edit Publications
dialog box.*

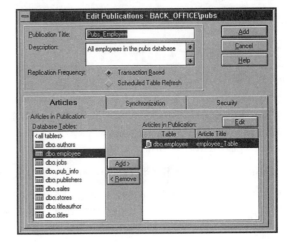

The Edit Publications dialog box enables you to create a new publication and assign articles to the publication.

4. To create a publication, enter the name of the publication in the Publication Title text box. In the Description box, enter the description for the publications.

5. To add tables to the publication, select a table and click on the Add button (refer to Figure 12.14). The table is then added to the Articles in the Publication list box.

6. To remove an article from the publication, select the article and click on the Remove button. The Replication Frequency frame, shown in Figure 12.14, displays the different methods of replication for the publication.

If you select the Transaction Based Replication Frequency radio button, changes in the transaction log are marked and copied to the distribution database and later applied to the destination databases. The Scheduled Table Refresh checkbox is applied at scheduled intervals and sometimes is referred to as a *snapshot*. When a table refresh is performed, the destination table is dropped and re-created. The data in the source table is copied into the destination (a snapshot) table.

7. To add a new publication, click the Add button.

8. To edit the article, to apply a filter, or add scripts, click on the Edit button (refer to Figure 12.14). The Manage Article dialog box appears (see Figure 12.15).

Figure 12.15.
Manage Article
dialog box.

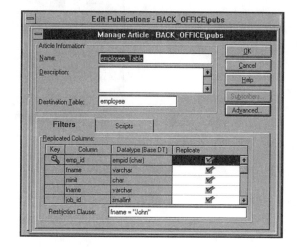

MANAGING ARTICLES

Using the Manage Article dialog box, you can set up filters on the table to perform vertical partitioning by deselecting columns in the table listed in the Replicated Columns Box or you can perform horizontal partitioning by applying a filter in the text box Restriction Clause (refer to Figure 12.15). For example, in Figure 12.15, a restriction has been added to the pubs database employee table column `fname`, to select records where `fname` is equal to John. If you want to further tune the article by adding stored procedures or editing a script, click on the Scripts tab shown in Figure 12.15. The Manage Article dialog box with the Scripts tab active is shown in Figure 12.16.

The Scripts tab enables you to specify the type of replication mechanism used by SQL Server during replication.

The checkboxes marked Insert Command, Update Command, and Delete Command represent the default replication mechanism used by SQL Server when constructing SQL Statements for each of the commands. Checking the Custom checkbox enables you to make one of the following two choices:

◆ Enter NONE in the Custom text box to prevent the type of transaction from being replicated. For example, if you check Custom in the Updated Command row and enter NONE in the Custom text box, any transactions that are updated commands will not be replicated.

◆ Enter a stored procedure to perform the proper SQL command UPDATE, INSERT, or DELETE. You must enter the stored procedure in the format Call stored_procedure_name.

Figure 12.16.
The Scripts tab in
the Manage Article
dialog box.

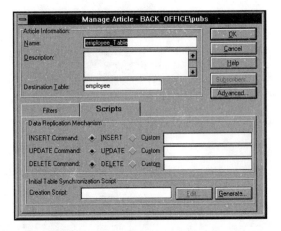

Tip

Use stored procedures to improve the performance of the replication process. The use of stored procedures will improve performance by using precompiled SQL statements during replication. Network traffic is reduced as well since you are only passing the stored procedure name and parameters to the other servers instead of the entire SQL statement. If you use stored procedures for replication, all subscribing servers must have the stored procedures in the subscribing database.

If you are editing an existing article, the Creation Script text box will contain the path and filename of the synchronization schema file (refer to Figure 12.16). To generate the schema file, click the Generate button.

Tip

To set the schema options, such as table index options, truncating the table, dropping or not dropping the table during synchronization, or include the primary key, click the Generate button shown in Figure 12.16 to display a schema option dialog box.

The Advanced button allows you to add a stored procedure to filter the replication results. You may want to use these feature to further limit the results of an article that has already been partioned horizontally or vertically. The stored procedure must follow the following format:

```
If Sql Statement Return 1 Else Return 0
```

When you have completed any modifications or changes to the article, click the OK button to save your changes or click the Cancel button to ignore your changes. Review the other tab options available on the Edit Publications dialog box.

SYNCHRONIZATION OPTIONS

To set synchronization options for a publication, use the Synchronization tab in the Edit Publications dialog box (see Figure 12.17). You can control the type of BCP formats used, Native or Character format, and you can schedule the frequency of automatic synchronization by clicking the Change button.

Figure 12.17.
The Synchronization
tab in the Edit Publi-
cations dialog box.

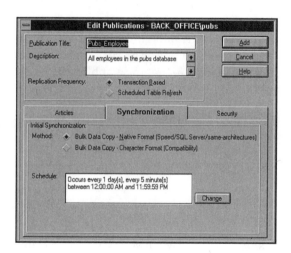

SECURITY OPTIONS

The Security tab in the Edit Publications dialog box enables you to restrict which servers can view the publication (see Figure 12.18). The default is unrestricted.

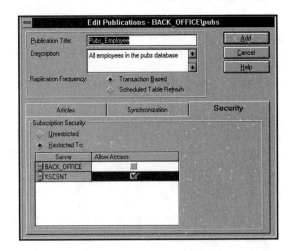

Figure 12.18.
The Security tab in
the Edit Publications
dialog box.

MANAGING SUBSCRIPTIONS

SQL Server supports two types of subscription methods: a *pull subscription* and a *push subscription*. A pull subscription is when you are managing the subscribing server and you select one or more publications to subscribe to. A push subscription occurs when you are managing a publication server and you set up subscribers from the publication server (that is, you push the article out to other servers).

Note

Push subscriptions cannot be performed at the publication level. Only articles can be pushed.

PULL SUBSCRIPTIONS

A *pull subscription* is when you are the subscribing server and you subscribe to one or more publications. To manage a pull subscription, perform the following steps:

1. Select the server from the Enterprise Manager.

2. From the SQL Enterprise Manager menu, select Manage and then select Replication. From the drop-down list box, select Subscriptions. The Manage Subscriptions dialog box appears (see Figure 12.19).

3. To subscribe to a publication or an article, click on a publication or an article in the Publications list box. To subscribe to the selected publication or article, click the Subscribe button. The Subscription Options dialog box appears (see Figure 12.20).

Figure 12.19.
Manage Subscriptions
dialog box.

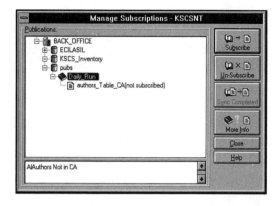

Figure 12.20.
Subscription Options
dialog box.

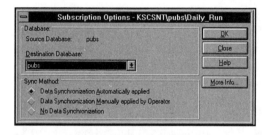

Note

Use the Un-Subscribe button to remove a subscription. The Sync
Completed button informs SQL Server that the synchronization
process has been completed (use only for manual synchronization).

4. Select the destination database for the replicated publication in the Destination Database combo box. Select the synchronization method and then
   click the OK button. The subscription has been added. The process is
   completed when the data synchronization occurs. Then replication will
   occur between the source and destination databases.

Tip

In most cases, you probably will want to use automatic synchronization methods and allow SQL Server to handle the required synchronization steps. There are exceptions, however. If the database you are
replicating is extremely large or the servers you are replicating to are
linked via a slow data line, use the manual replication mechanism

12

> instead. If you are creating a duplicate database on another server using a current backup of the database or you are positive the two databases participating in replication are identical, you may want to perform the no synchronization option.

PUSH SUBSCRIPTIONS

In a *push subscription*, you set up subscribers from the publication server (that is, you push the article out to other servers).To manage a push subscription, perform the following steps:

1. Select the server from the Enterprise Manager.

2. From the SQL Enterprise Manager menu, select Manage, and then select Replication. From the drop-down list box, select Publications. The Manage Publications dialog box appears (refer to Figure 12.13). Access the Edit publications dialog box (refer to Figure 12.14). Select an article and click on the Edit button. The Manage Article Dialog dialog box appears (refer to Figure 12.15). Click on the Subscribers button and the Publication Subscribers dialog box appears (see Figure 12.21).

Figure 12.21.
Publication Subscribers dialog box.

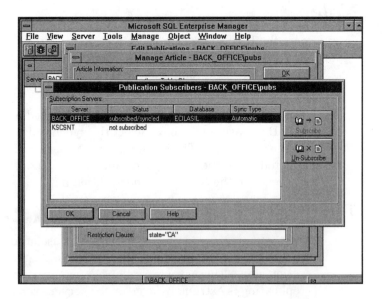

3. Select a server to push the article to and click the Subscribe button. The Subscription Options dialog box appears (see Figure 12.22).

Figure 12.22.
Subscription Options
dialog box.

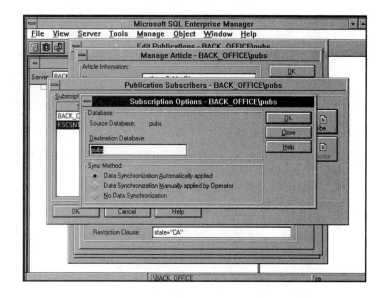

4. Type the name of the database and select the synchronization method.
   Click on OK to push the subscription to the selected server and database.

WRAPPING UP

In wrapping up, review a few last pointers/tips/reminders when dealing with SQL Server replication.

SUBSCRIBING (REPLICATED) DATABASES ARE READ-ONLY

As stated earlier, databases that are subscribed from a publisher server should not be modified on the subscribing server and should be used only for read-only purposes. SQL Server will not prevent you from modifying the data, but if you do modify data in the replicated databases, then the database will become out of synch with the published database. Also, any changes you make in the replicated database can easily be overwritten by changes made in the published database. Suppose that you modify an amount field in row one of a table called `bank_account` on the subscribing server's replicated database. You set the value of the field to $1,000.00. A few minutes later, someone on the publishing database modifies the same record but they set the value to -$1000.00. A few minutes later, the changed record is replicated to your database, overwriting your changes—unknown to you! The values in your database are no longer valid (another reason to use SQL Server replication for read-only databases). SQL Server does *not* have a mechanism that allows you to replicate records to various databases and make changes on any of the databases (subscriber or publisher). Then replicate all the changes back to subscribing servers, notifying users of record conflicts (records modified by more than one server). Do not get discouraged—the read-only database replication scheme is very powerful and useful in many real world scenarios.

DATABASE READ-ONLY OPTION

Replication cannot occur on a subscribing database if the read-only database option is set to true.

REPLICATION IS TRANSACTION-DRIVEN

It is important to remember that SQL Server replication is transaction-driven. Keep this in mind as you publish and subscribe various articles and monitor the number of transactions that are replicated. Pay close attention to update transactions. If SQL Server performs a deferred update on a table, then the update consists of a delete followed by an insert. So updating 10,000 records could translate to 10,000 deletes and 10,000 inserts for a total of 20,000 transactions. If you intend to perform many updates, you may want to examine the rules SQL Server uses to perform direct updates, better known as updates in place. Rather than performing a delete and insert, SQL Server updates the record in place.

DEADLOCKS

Due to exclusive table lock conditions, deadlocks can sometimes occur between the distribution process and the log reader. If you experience deadlocks between the two processes, try reducing the commit batch size using the Enterprise Manager or reduce the frequency of the distribution process.

BETWEEN THE LINES

Following are some of the important things to remember for SQL Server replication:

- ◆ SQL Server replication is transaction-based and follows a loose consistency data distribution model.
- ◆ Replication uses a publisher/subscriber metaphor.
- ◆ Subscribing databases should be treated as read-only.
- ◆ NT servers participating in replication require a trusted connection.
- ◆ SQL Server uses ODBC for replication.
- ◆ A server can play multiple roles and be a subscriber, publisher, or distributor.

♦ You can tune or schedule the frequency of replicating publications.

♦ Use stored procedures instead of SQL statements for replication to enhance performance.

SUMMARY

Replication is a new and exciting technology that will play an important part in many real-world solutions. As a Microsoft SQL Server DBA, you will need to fully understand how to correctly set up and administer database replication and how to correctly use replication to benefit your company or organization.

CHAPTER 13

Backups

Backups are copies of SQL Server databases or transaction logs used to recover a database in the event the database becomes corrupt or is lost in a catastrophic event. The task of backing up and protecting the data is probably the number one job responsibility of the DBA. I have been to many organizations where the sole job responsibility of the DBAs are backups and database maintenance. Being able to recover a database when several disk drives crash or a table or database becomes corrupted is where the good DBA earns his keep. Keep in mind, the capability to recover relies on current backups of your databases. In this chapter, you learn about the different methods available to you to back up SQL Server databases and transaction logs. Even more important, you will create a backup and recovery strategy.

Note

Database and transaction log backups are commonly referred to as *dumps* (that is, database dump or transaction log dump). The name *dump* comes from the SQL Server Transact SQL command used to back up databases and transaction logs, the DUMP command.

Better Safe than Sorry!

I learned the value of having a good set of database backups, the hard way! Several years ago, while working on a Sybase 4.2 UNIX system, I was hired as a contractor to help out an organization with several large Sybase databases. They had recently lost several key MIS employees and were short-handed.

I was working with a gentleman who I'll just refer to as Don "The Man," one of the few really good jack-of-all trades (UNIX system administrator, Sybase DBA, and Client/Server developer) individuals I have met. I had only been at the organization for two days. Don and I were busy trying to get a clean set of backups for the database and the UNIX system. The nightly UNIX backup had failed for the last two days and the database backups were going slow, because several databases were flagged with errors during DBCC (database consistency check).

We were busy working with Sybase tech support to correct the database problems. Don was busy working on one of the larger databases preparing it for a backup when I heard him exclaim, "Oh No! I can't believe I did that, I can't believe what I just did. We are doomed!"

It turned out that Don had entered a SQL statement incorrectly and had started one large transaction that was deleting all the rows of a table with about four million rows! I said, "No problem, we will just recover from a database backup." It was then that Don informed me that the only database backup was 30 days old and outdated! What to do?

Well, because Don had blocked the delete within a single transaction, we killed the server before it could complete the operation and commit the transaction. The server took a while to come back up as several thousand transactions were rolled back. We then verified the table row count from some numbers taken earlier that day to verify no data had been lost (information was always added to the table, never updated).

At this point, Don and I realized that we needed backups—NOW. We stayed late that night verifying previous backup tapes that we found could not be read because of media problems! We continued to work early into the morning and created a whole new set of UNIX system backups and database backups.

The moral of the story is "backups are serious business!" Too often I have heard someone say, "The nightly backup did not run. I'm not sure why, but I'll run it again tonight." Big mistake. Remember, you know not the hour, day, or minute when the disk drive will give up, the building will be hit by a natural disaster, or someone like Don will issue a SQL command that will ruin the production database! If you don't have a good backup, you will find yourself trying to explain to your boss how you lost a day's worth of data because the nightly backup did not work and you did nothing about it that morning!

WHAT IS A DATABASE BACKUP (DUMP)?

Think of a database backup as a full backup of a database. When you perform a database backup, SQL Server copies all user-defined objects, system tables, and data to the backup device including the transaction log. Remember from Chapter 8, backup devices are called dump devices and can be files, floppy drives, or tape drives. SQL Server 6.0 supports dump devices on a Novell file server and the capability to perform striped backups to multiple devices.

Tip

> You can dump (backup) a database while the database is in use. When a database DUMP command is issued, SQL Server writes all completed transactions to disk and then begins to copy the database. Any incomplete transactions or transactions that occur after the database dump process is started, are *not* backed up. To get changes that occurred while the backup process was running requires dumping the transaction log after the backup completes. Backing up a database will slow SQL Server down, so consider performing backups during non-peak hours.

WHAT IS A TRANSACTION LOG BACKUP (DUMP)?

If you think of a database dump as a full backup, think of a transaction log dump as an incremental database backup (as stated in Chapter 9, a transaction log contains all the various transactions that have occurred on a database prior to the last transaction log dump).

Note

> If you create your database and transaction log on the same device, you will not be able to perform an "incremental" (transaction log) backup.

A transaction log dump performs one or both of the following operations depending on the dump options selected:

◆ Copies the inactive part of the transaction log to the backup device

◆ Truncates (clears and frees up space) the inactive part of the transaction log

The inactive part of the transaction log is all the completed transactions up to and not on the same page as the earliest outstanding transaction or the earliest transaction that has not been moved to the distribution database and is marked for replication.

Note

> Performing a full database dump (backup) does not clear out the inactive part of the transaction log. If you only perform database

13

dumps, eventually your transaction log will fill up and you will be unable to perform any transactions in the database (insert, update, delete, and so on) until you dump the transaction log. You have to perform transaction log dumps, even if you rely on full database backups, to clear out the inactive part of the transaction log!

PERFORMING DATABASE AND TRANSACTION LOG BACKUPS

Examine the steps required to perform a database backup and/or transaction log backup using the SQL Server Enterprise Manager.

Note

Earlier versions of SQL Server used the SQL Administrator to perform database and transaction log backups.

From the SQL Enterprise Manager, select Tools and then select Backup/Restore. The Database Backup/Restore dialog box appears (see Figure 13.1).

Dump Device frame

*Figure 13.1.
Database Backup /
Restore dialog box.*

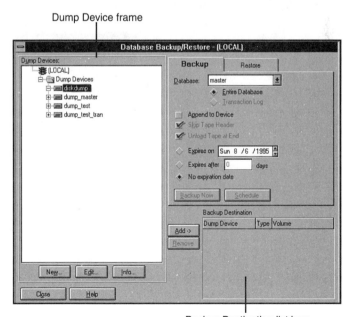

Backup Destination list box

Note

When SQL Server performs a database or transaction log backup, SQL Server reads one extent at a time (eight 2KB data pages), skipping unallocated extents and writes the extent to the database device.

Take a quick review of the Database Backup/Restore dialog box (refer to Figure 13.1).

BACKUP AND RESTORE TABS

The Database Backup/Restore dialog box has two different tabs: the Backup tab and the Restore tab. In this chapter, you will concentrate on the functionality provided with the Backup tab, and in Chapter 14, you will learn about the functionality in the Restore tab.

DUMP DEVICES FRAME

The Dump Devices frame contains a list of different SQL Servers and the dump devices on each server (refer to Figure 13.1). The format of the Dump Devices frame follows the standard drill down approach of the SQL Enterprise Manager. Clicking on the + of a dump device expands the view to show the current information of the dump device (see Figure 13.2).

Figure 13.2.
Expanded disk dump
devices.

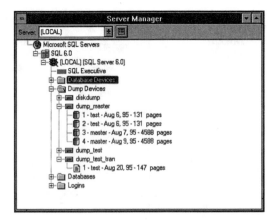

The functions performed by the three buttons located at the bottom of the Dump Devices frame are as follows.

13

New Button and Edit Button

The New button allows you to add a new dump device to the selected server. The Edit button allows you to modify an existing device. Adding and modifying dump devices was covered extensively in Chapter 8.

Info Button

The Info button displays the dump device Header Information dialog box (see Figure 13.3).

Figure 13.3.
Header Information
dialog box.

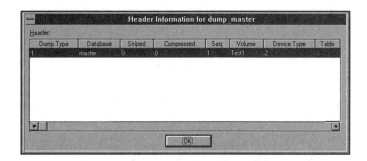

The header information provides you with dump device information, such as the size of the dump device, the database and transaction logs currently on the dump device, and the date/time the database or transaction log was dumped to the device.

Note

One of the more exciting new features of SQL Server 6.0 is the enhanced features added when backing up to a disk file as opposed to a tape. Many of the features that existed for tape backups in previous versions such as displaying header information or multiple dumps to a single tape, have now been implemented with disk file dump devices. Now the procedures to back up to the tape or disk file dump devices are almost identical except for one or two option flags specific to tape drives.

Header information can be displayed for any type of dump devices. The transact SQL Command to display the header information of a dump device is LOAD HEADERONLY and has the following format:

```
LOAD HEADERONLY
From dump device
```

To back up a database or transaction, perform the following steps:

1. From the Database Backup/Restore dialog box, select a dump device in the Dump Device frame by clicking on the device (refer to Figure 13.1).

2. Using the Database drop-down combo box, select the database on which you want to perform the database or transaction log backup.

3. Check the Entire Database checkbox to perform a database dump (backup) or check the Transaction Log checkbox to perform a transaction log dump.

4. To append to an existing backup on the selected device, check the Append to Device checkbox. The Skip Tape Header and Unload Tape at End checkboxes are specific to tape drive devices. If the Skip Tape Header box is checked, SQL Server will skip reading the ANSI label on the tape. If the Unload Tape at End checkbox is checked, SQL Server rewinds and unloads the tape at the end of the backup.

Note

The capability to append database and transaction log dumps to a disk file dump device is another welcome addition to SQL Server 6.0 and backups. Previous versions of SQL Server did not have this capability and many DBAs were forced to write script files that would execute after a dump was executed and move the disk dump file to another directory and/or rename the file so that the next backup would not overwrite the previous backup. I have seen some very good disk dump file management schemes using directories and filenaming conventions. Being able to append to an existing dump device should eliminate many script files and the problem of overwriting previous backups. However, be careful about how much information is appended to a single backup device. The danger in using a single large dump device for an extended period of time with many different databases and transaction log dumps introduces the possibility of losing all your backups with a single media failure.

5. Set one of the following three checkboxes to determine at what time an existing dump device tape or file can be overwritten with new information:

   ◆ **Expires on**: Sets the date the tape or file can be overwritten.

   ◆ **Expires after**: Sets the number of days before the tape or file can be overwritten.

   ◆ **No expiration date**: The file or tape can be overwritten immediately.

13

Tip

Use the Expires On or the Expires After options to protect your database and transaction log dumps from being accidentally over-written.

6. Select the dump device to backup the transaction log or database to by selecting a device in the Dump Devices frame and then clicking on the Add button to add the device to the Backup Destination list box (see Figure 13.4).

Figure 13.4
Selected Device in the
Backup Destination
Device list box.

To add a volume label to the dump, enter the name of the Volume in the Volume column. Volume labels can be up to six ASCII characters with the default name SQ0001.

7. To start the database or transaction log backup, click the Backup Now button (refer to Figure 13.4). The database or transaction log is written to the selected devices in the BackUp Destination list box with the selected options.

Note

To dump a database or transaction log to the floppy disk dump devices diskettedumpa or diskettedumpb requires running the Console utility program from a DOS shell. As an alternative, you can dump the database or transaction log to a disk file dump device and then copy the dump file to the floppy.

The Transact SQL command used to back up the database and transaction log is the DUMP command, which has the following format for a database:

```
DUMP DATABASE {dbname ¦ @dbname_var}
TO dump_device [, dump_device2 [..., dump_device32]]
[WITH [[,] {UNLOAD ¦ NOUNLOAD}]
[[,] {INIT ¦ NOINIT}]
[[,] {SKIP ¦ NOSKIP}]
[[,] {{EXPIREDATE = {date ¦ @date_var}}
```

```
¦ {RETAINDAYS = {days ¦ @days_var}}]
[[,] STATS [ = percentage]]]
```

To dump a transaction log, use the following format:

```
DUMP TRANSACTION {dbname ¦ @dbname_var}
[TO dump_device [, dump_device2 [..., dump_device32]]]
[WITH {TRUNCATE_ONLY ¦ NO_LOG ¦ NO_TRUNCATE}
[[,[{UNLOAD ¦ NOUNLOAD}]
[[,] {INIT ¦ NOINIT}]
[[,] {SKIP ¦ NOSKIP}]
[[,] {{EXPIREDATE = {date ¦ @date_var}}
¦ {RETAINDAYS = {days ¦ @days_var}}]]
```

SQL Server also recognizes the following short cut syntax to dump the transaction log:

```
DUMP TRAN
```

(rather than DUMP TRANSACTION)

For both the DUMP DATABASE and DUMP TRANSACTION command, dump_device has the following format:

```
{dump_device_name ¦ @dump_device_namevar}
¦ {DISK ¦ TAPE ¦ FLOPPY ¦ PIPE} =
{'temp_dump_device' ¦ @temp_dump_device_var}}
[VOLUME = {volid ¦ @volid_var}]
```

The optional parameters INIT and NOINIT, available with tape devices on 4.2*x* versions of SQL Server, are now available for other dump devices on SQL Server Version 6.0. Use the INIT option to overwrite the information stored on a dump device. Use NOINIT to append the information. Remember, the capability to overwrite a device also depends upon the expiration and retention date set for the dump device.

TEMPORARY DUMP DEVICES

SQL Server 6.0 enables you to create and use temporary dump devices. A temporary dump device is a dump device that is created at the time of the DUMP command and has not been added to the system table sysdevices with the system stored procedure sp_addumpdevice. To dump a database to a temporary dump device, you must specify the type of media the dump device is on using the options DISK, FLOPPY, TAPE, or PIPE, and then specify the complete path and filename. In the case of PIPE, you must specify the name of the named pipe used in the client application. You can use variables to create a temporary dump device. Look at some examples using temporary devices.

Example: Dump the master database to a temporary disk dump device called tdump_master.dat, located in the directory C:\SQL60\DATA.

Using the path and filename:

```
DUMP DATABASE master
to DISK='C:\SQL60\DATA\tdump_master.dat'
```

Using a variable:

```
Declare @temp_dump varchar[255]
Select @temp_dump = 'C:\SQL60\DATA\tdump_master.dat'
DUMP DATABASE master
to DISK = @temp_dump
```

DUMP TRANSACTION OPTIONS

The different options available for a transaction log and when to use the different options can be confusing to new DBAs. Examine each of the options individually and determine the correct time to use them.

TRUNCATE_ONLY

TRUNCATE_ONLY removes the inactive part of the transaction log (truncates) without backing up (copying) the log to a dump device. You do not need to specify a dump device when using TRUNCATE_ONLY because the log is not copied to a dump device. For example, the syntax to dump the master database transaction log with the TRUNCATE_ONLY option is as follows:

```
DUMP TRANSACTION master
WITH TRUNCATE_ONLY
```

Use the TRUNCATE_ONLY option in the following cases:

♦ If you do not use the transaction log for recovery purposes and rely on full database backups, then use TRUNCATE_ONLY immediately after a full database backup has been performed to clear out the inactive part of the transaction log

♦ To truncate the transaction log when the database and the transaction log share the same device (the master database, for example)

Warning

Always perform a full database backup before using the TRUNCATE_ONLY option. If you use the TRUNCATE_ONLY option without a full database backup, you will not be able to recover the completed transactions in the inactive part of the transaction log at the time the DUMP TRAN with TRUNCATE_ONLY command was issued.

NO_LOG

When a DUMP TRANSACTION command is issued with the NO_LOG, option SQL Server truncates the inactive part of the transaction log without logging the DUMP TRANSACTION command.

Warning

After using the NO_LOG option, always perform a full database backup; otherwise, the changes that had been in the transaction log at the time the logged was truncated with the NO_LOG option will not be recoverable.

Use the NO_LOG option only when the transaction log has become so full that you cannot dump the transaction log normally to free up space. This occurrs when SQL Server is attempting to log the DUMP TRANSACTION command with no room left in the transaction log. Like the TRUNCATE_ONLY option, the NO_LOG option does not require a database device since the log is not copied to a device.

Tip

Microsoft SQL Server has added a feature, available with the first NT release, called a *threshold dump*. The threshold dump monitors the space in the transaction log and prevents the log from filling up by performing a transaction dump when the log reaches a user-defined threshold. See Chapter 24 to learn how to set up a transaction log threshold. Once you have set up SQL Server to automatically dump transaction logs, you should not have to use the NO_LOG option.

NO_TRUNCATE

Use the NO_TRUNCATE option when the database you are trying to access is corrupted and you are about to rebuild the database. To use NO_TRUNCATE, the following must be true:

◆ The transaction log must reside on a separate device from the database
◆ The master database is not corrupted

The NO_TRUNCATE option writes all the transaction log entries from the time of the last transaction dump up to the point of the database corruption. You can then load the transaction log dump as the last dump in the recovery process for up-to-the-minute data recovery.

Tip

Become familiar with the NO_TRUNCATE option. I have run in to many DBAs who were unfamiliar with the option or were not sure when to use it.

PERFORMING STRIPED BACKUPS

SQL Server 6.0 adds the capability to perform a database or transaction log dump to multiple dump devices called *parallel striped backups*. A parallel striped backup speeds up the amount of time required to back up a database or transaction log by creating a single thread for each dump device. The dump device threads read an allocated extent in a round robin fashion and then writes the extents to the thread's assigned dump device, taking advantage of asynchronous I/O capabilities. An example of a parallel striped backup is shown in Figure 13.5.

Figure 13.5.
Example of parallel
striped backup.

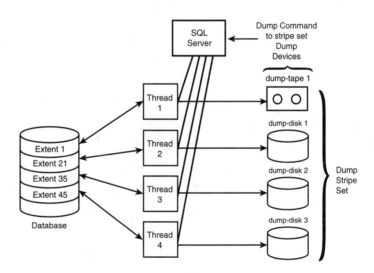

The database or transaction log can be dumped to multiple devices of the same or different type of dump device (tape, floppy, disk, and so on) called the *striped set*. If a database or transaction log is dumped to multiple devices, then it must also be read from multiple devices during restoration. SQL Server can perform parallel backups from 2 to 32 database dump devices. To perform a parallel striped dump to multiple devices using the dump database command, list the dump devices separated by a comma. For example, to dump the master database to three disk dump devices called dump1, dump2, and dump3, the syntax would be as follows:

```
DUMP DATABASE master
to dump1, dump2, dump3
```

To use the SQL Server Enterprise Manager to perform a parallel striped backup, access the Database Backup/Restore dialog box (refer to Figure 13.1). Select the database you wish to backup and set the appropriate dump options for the database or transaction log. To create a striped dump set perform the following:

1. Select a dump device displayed in the Dump Device frame, and click on the Add button.

2. Continue to select dump devices that are to be part of the dump striped set and click on the Add button, adding them to the Backup Destination list box (see Figure 13.6). To back up the database to the selected devices, click the Backup Now button.

Figure 13.6
Database Backup /
Restore dialog box, set
up to perform a parallel
striped backup.

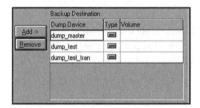

Use the striped parallel backup features when you have very large databases or are in a production environment with little or no downtime.

Warning

Remember, when using a striped dump set, restoring the transaction log or database requires reading the entire striped set. If any of the striped devices fail, you will be unable to recover the data.

SCHEDULING BACKUPS

Microsoft SQL Server 6.0 excels with new and improved scheduling capabilities (the new scheduling capabilities and improvements are covered in Chapter 24). Setting up SQL Server to automatically perform database and transaction log backups is a snap!

Note

SQL Server 6.0 backup scheduling capabilities have improved substantially over SQL Server 4.21. SQL Server 4.21 scheduling involved running the SQL Monitor. I heard many complaints and problems about scheduled backups and the SQL Monitor under SQL Server

13

> 4.21. For example, if a backup took an extended period of time and the SQL Monitor properties in the system registry for the backup time were not set high enough to allow the backup to complete, SQL Monitor would halt the backup. I also ran into a few people who used the NT scheduler and AT command instead of SQL Monitor to schedule backups. SQL Server 6.0 scheduling has improved substantially and I would recommend using the new features along with the SQL Server Executive service.

To use SQL Server scheduling requires running the SQL Server Executive service that is installed during SQL Server installation. Backups are scheduled from the Database Backup/Restore dialog box (refer to Figure 13.1). To schedule a database or transaction log for backup, the database to backup, the appropriate options, and the dump device(s), click the Schedule button. The Schedule Backup Dialog dialog box appears (see Figure 13.7).

Figure 13.7.
Schedule Backup
dialog box.

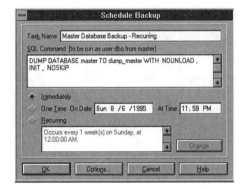

To schedule the backup, perform the following steps:

1. Enter a name for the scheduled task in the Task Name text box shown in Figure 13.7.

Tip

> Use a descriptive name for the scheduled task. Using a descriptive name makes it easier to identify the task later in the NT event log or the SQL Server Scheduled task history log.

2. The transact SQL command that is scheduled to be executed when the scheduled task runs is displayed in the SQL Command list box. You can edit the SQL command by typing over the existing text or entering new text.

Tip

If you were wondering how to perform a DUMP TRANSACTION with NO_LOG, TRUNCATE_ONLY, or NO_TRUNCATE with SQL Enterprise Manager, you won't find any checkbox options like the ones in SQL Server 4.21 SQL Administrator! Instead, you must select the device and database for the transaction log dump, click the Schedule button, and then edit the command in the SQL Command list box, adding the transaction log dump options.

If you do not backup the transaction log for recovery purposes and rely on full database dumps, you may want to add a DUMP TRANSACTION with a TRUNCATE_ONLY command before or after the DUMP DATABASE command in the SQL Command list box. That way, the inactive part of the transaction log will be cleared out when the database is dumped and is scheduled as a single task.

3. The next step is to select when you want the scheduled backup to occur. For the backup to occur immediately as a background task, check the Immediately checkbox. For the task to occur one time only, check the One Time checkbox and then set the date and time you want the backup to occur. To set up a recurring backup, check the Recurring checkbox. To schedule the recurring backup, click on the Change button. The Task Schedule dialog box appears (see Figure 13.8).

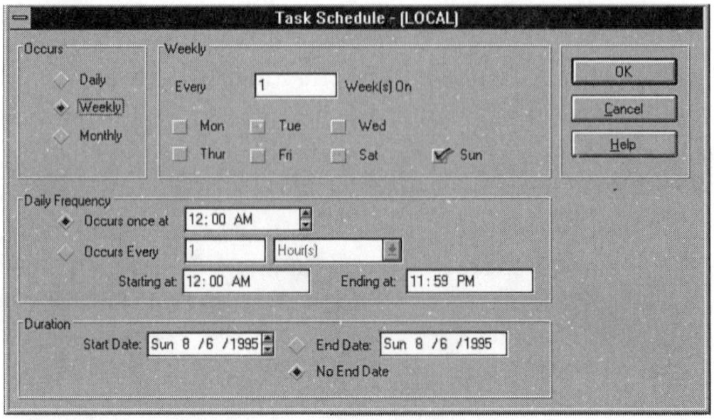

Figure 13.8.
Task Schedule
dialog box.

13

Using the Task Scheduled dialog box, you can easily schedule the backup to occur daily, weekly, or monthly on a given day or time. (The Schedule dialog box is covered in detail in Chapter 24.)

4. After you choose when you want the backup to occur, click OK to schedule the backup.

Note

The Options button allows you to set up e-mail notification on the success or failure of the scheduled backup and is covered in detail in Chapter 24.

The success and failure of the scheduled task can be viewed from the scheduling window using the SQL Enterprise Manager. Scheduled backups and user initiated backups are now written to the NT Event log (see Figure 13.9).

Figure 13.9.
Windows NT Event
Log, showing Master
Database dump.

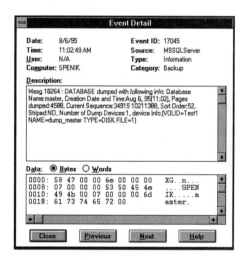

DATABASE OPTIONS AND THE TRANSACTION LOG

The following database options affect your capability to perform transaction log dumps on a database:

◆ trunc. log on chkpt.

◆ select into/bulkcopy

TRUNC. LOG ON CHKPT.

If the trunc. log on chkpt. option is set on a database, SQL Server performs the equivalent of a DUMP TRANSACTION with the TRUNCAT_ONLY command when SQL Server's checkpoint handler or a user performs a checkpoint on the database. How often a checkpoint is performed on a database by the checkpoint handler depends on the SQL Server configuration parameter recovery interval. If the trunc. log on chkpt. option is set, you will get an error message if you attempt to perform a transaction log dump. If you have the trunc. log on chkpt. option set, you must rely on full database dumps for backups. Use the trunc. log on chkpt. option in a development environment where you are not concerned about the potential loss of data.

SELECT INTO / BULKCOPY

The SELECT INTO/BULKCOPY option enables you to perform operations, such as select into or bulk copy operations using BCP. Operations such as SELECT INTO and fast BCP are non-logged operations (that is, the changes to the database are not logged in the transaction log). If a non-logged operation is performed on a database, you will not be able to perform a transaction log dump on the database. To use the DUMP TRANSACTION command requires you to use the DUMP DATABASE command to back up the database with the non-logged operations. Once you have successfully performed a full database dump, you can then use the DUMP TRANSACTION command until a non-logged operation is performed in the database.

USING DATABASE DUMPS AND TRANSACTION LOG DUMPS TO RECOVER A DATABASE

Before discussing how to create a backup database schedule, it is important for you to understand how to use database dumps and transaction log dumps to restore a database with up-to-the minute information. To help you understand how to use database and transaction dumps in the real world, walk through the following example (see Figure 13.10).

Using the example in Figure 13.10, the backup schedule for a database is as follows:

◆ Full database backup performed daily at 9:00 p.m.

◆ Transaction log backups performed daily at 12:00 (noon) and 6:00 p.m.

The backup schedule was set up accordingly because the majority of the people working on the database go to lunch at noon and go home for the evening before 6:00 p.m. The two incremental backups and the daily full database backup meet the user's recovery needs. Follow through the drawing starting with Day 1.

Figure 13.10.
Example of database
and transaction log
dumps.

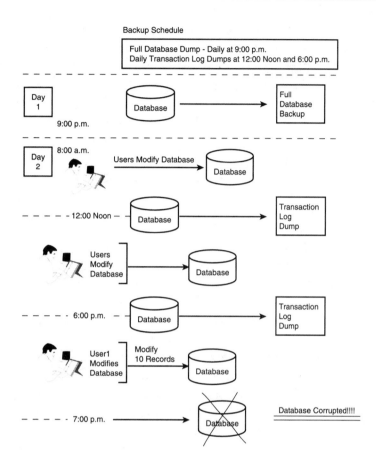

DAY 1: FULL DATABASE BACKUP OCCURS

Day 1 is a starting point for this example. All you are concerned about is that at 9:00 p.m. on Day 1, SQL Server successfully performs a full database backup.

DAY 2: DATABASE MODIFIED, DATABASE CORRUPTED

Between 8:00 a.m. and 11:59 a.m., the database users begin to log onto the database and make minor modifications and changes to the data stored in the database.

Between 12:00 noon and 12:59 p.m., many of the database users are off to lunch, although some continue to work. The SQL Executive kicks off the scheduled transaction log dump. The transaction log of the database is dumped to a dump device, saving all the changes made to the data since the last full backup at 9:00 p.m. the previous evening.

Between 1:00 p.m. and 5:59 p.m., the database users continue to make minor modifications to the data in the database. By 6:00 p.m., the majority of the users have logged off the database and are on their way home.

Between 6:00 p.m. and 6:59 p.m., the SQL Executive starts the evening transaction log dump, saving all the committed transactions made to the database prior to the previous transaction log dump at noon. Shortly after the transaction log backup completes, User 1 modifies ten records on the database.

At 7:00 p.m. the database becomes corrupted and users are no longer able to access the database. The DBA is called in to remedy the problem. Now what?

USING THE DUMPS TO RECOVER THE DATABASE

In Chapter 14, the commands and detail requirements to recover a corrupted database are discussed in detail. In this chapter, an example of a high-level walk through of restoring the database using the available dumps is covered (refer to Figure 13.10). So where do you start?

The first thing to do is to dump the transaction log with the NO_TRUNCATE option and then drop the corrupted database and re-create it. Once the database has been recreated, you are ready to restore the data.

First, you must load a full database backup to the newly created database. So, you load the database dump performed on Day 1 at 9:00 p.m. The new database now exists in the exact same state as the corrupted database on Day 1 at 9:00 p.m. How do you get back the work that was done on Day 2? You guessed it, you use the incremental database dumps (that is, the transaction log dumps).

Transaction log dumps are sequenced and must be loaded in the correct order. You load the first transaction log dump that was made at 12:00 noon on Day 2. Loading a transaction log (also referred to as *applying* the transaction log) causes the transactions in the transaction log to re-execute. When the transaction load has completed, the database is now in the exact state the database was in as of 12:00 noon on Day 2.

To regain the 12:00 noon until 6:00 p.m. transactions, you load the second transaction log dump performed at 6:00 p.m. on Day 2. Once the second transaction log successfully loads, the database is in the same state as the original database at 6:00 p.m. on Day 2. What about the ten records modified by User 1 after the transaction log dump completed but before the database was corrupted? If the database and transaction log were on the same device or you forgot to run the DUMP TRANSACTION with the NO_TRUNCATE command, then they are lost because you do not have a transaction log dump or a full database dump with the modifications in them. User 1 would have to manually go back and update the records! But, since you had the database and transaction log on separate devices and you executed the DUMP TRANSACTION with the

NO_TRUNCATE command, you load the transaction log dump produced by the NO_TRUNCATE dump command, and the database is back in the same state (including the ten modified records) as the original database just prior to failing! You now know how transaction logs and database dumps are used to recover a database but, when should you dump your databases and transaction logs?

WHEN TO DUMP A DATABASE AND TRANSACTION LOG

You know how to schedule and dump transaction logs and databases, but when should you dump them? To answer that question, you are now going to create two separate categories. Category 1 consists of actions that are performed in a database that warrant an immediate database dump. Category 2 consists of the dumps required to meet your recovery needs.

CATEGORY 1: ACTIONS THAT WARRANT DUMPING A DATABASE

You are aware that in general, you should perform database backups on a timely schedule. Backups should also be performed after certain actions are performed in a database to ensure full and easy recovery.

USER DATABASES

When you perform certain actions on a user database, you should dump the database as soon as possible to guarantee the recovery of your changes. For example, perform a database backup in the following cases:

- ◆ After the database is created
- ◆ After performing non-logged operations such as fast BCP, SELECT INTO, or DUMP TRANSACTION with NO_LOG or TRUNCATE_ONLY
- ◆ After you make substantial database modifications (new triggers, stored procedures, tables, and so on)
- ◆ After you create a large index, this will speed up the recovery process because SQL Server will not have to rebuild the index during the recovery process.

THE MASTER DATABASE

Of course, the master database has its own set of rules for when it should be backed up! Remember, keeping a healthy master database is a high priority, so backing up the master database regularly is a must. The master database should be backed up when changes are made to system tables. A list of the commands that modify the system tables can be found in the SQL Server documentation. A sample of some the commands is as follows:

- `ALTER DATABASE`
- `DISK INIT`
- `DISK MIRROR`
- `DISK RESIZE`
- `sp_addlogin`
- `sp_droplogin`

Because many of you will use the SQL Enterprise Manager to perform your database administrative task, you may be unaware of the SQL Server commands and system stored procedures being executed. So in SQL Enterprise Manager lingo, back up the master database after you have done the following:

- Added/removed devices or database
- Altered the size of a database
- Added system login ids
- Modified system configuration parameters

CATEGORY 2: SCHEDULED DATABASE DUMPS

Unfortunately, there is no exact formula to tell you when you should dump your databases. Why? Because, each database has its own backup requirements. For example, in the backup and recovery example you stepped through earlier, transaction log dumps were performed twice a day. In the example, it was acceptable to lose a half a day's work if the example SQL Server suddenly lost all it's databases, including the master. Many organizations cannot afford to lose any data and require up-to-the minute recovery.

As another example, maybe you are in a development environment where a bi-monthly database backup is all that is required. Your backup strategy should enable you to recover any of your databases within the acceptable amount of time and data loss limit for each database. Before discussing backup strategies, I would like to point out that it is just as important to perform routine database and table maintenance (database maintenance plans are discussed in more detail in Chapter 23).

In general, you can find more information on setting up appropriate backup schedules in the documentation that ships with SQL Server or white papers found on Microsoft Technet. Now review a few questions and suggestions you can use to help you setup a backup plan.

Note

In my opinion, a backup and recovery plan are one and the same. To test and verify your backup plan requires you to use the database backups to restore your SQL Server databases; thus, the two go hand-in-hand! Also, don't forget that databases require routine maintenance, including DBCC commands.

SYSTEM DATABASES

Having up-to-date, valid database backups can save you a lot of time, especially if you need to restore a system database (such as the master database). Take special care with the master database and consider mirroring the master device for added protection. I would recommend at the minimum backing up the following system databases daily:

- ◆ master
- ◆ msdb
- ◆ model
- ◆ distribution database (for distribution replication servers)

TRANSACTION LOG THRESHOLD ALERTS

All database transaction logs should have threshold events scheduled to prevent the database transaction logs from filling up (enough said)!

HOW OFTEN SHOULD I DUMP THE TRANSACTION LOG DATABASE?

If the database and the transaction log both became corrupted, how many transactions could you afford to lose? How many transactions are performed in an hour? A day? You will need to ask and answer these questions and more to determine how often you should dump the transaction log and database. Try and perform your database and transaction log dumps during non-peak hours.

Also keep in mind what is required to recover a database using full database dumps and transaction logs. For example, if you performed transaction log dumps (incremental backups) six times a day and a full database backup every five days, what would you have to do to recover the database? Depending on when the database became corrupted, you stand the possibility of having to load a full database backup and 0 to 30 transaction log dumps. Is this acceptable? Get the picture? You may have a database that is not updated very often and performing a biweekly transaction log dump and a weekly database dump will meet your requirements.

How Do I Manage the Dumps?

How are you going to manage the various different database and transaction log dumps that are on tapes or dump files and how long are you going to keep your backups? Believe me, this is a problem in organizations with several databases! Organization is the key here. Come up with a consistent naming convention and filing system for your backups. You will want to keep old backups around for several weeks or months. Organization makes it easy to find dumps that are several weeks or months old.

How Long Will It Take to Recover the Database?

If your database becomes corrupted, how long will it take to recover the database and is the recovery time acceptable? If you find the recovery time is not acceptable, you may need to consider a hot backup.

In What Other Ways Is the Database Protected?

It never hurts to have more than one level of data protection for very sensitive data. For example, is the database on a device that is mirrored or resides on a RAID 5 drive configuration? Is the SQL Server shut down weekly and the SQL Server directory and database devices backed up to tape by a system administrator? Always know what other recovery options are available to you, just in case your well-constructed backup and recovery plans fail.

Test and Practice

Once you have created a backup plan, don't stop there and say, "Well I've got a plan— I'm done." Make sure you test your backup plan by actually recovering the databases. And when you are done testing, test your recovery plan again! When the day comes and a database fails, you should feel very comfortable and confident in your ability to recover the database. The bottom line is, test and practice your backup and recovery plans!

Between the Lines

For database backups, keep in mind the following:

◆ A SQL Server backup is commonly referred to as a dump.

◆ Database dumps are full backups of the data and database objects.

◆ Transaction log dumps are incremental backups that reflect the changes in the database since the previous transaction log dump.

◆ Users can still use the database during backups.

13

- Use the header information on dump devices to display important information about the currently stored dumps.
- You can append dumps to disk dump devices as well as tape dump devices.
- SQL Server 6.0 allows you to use temporary dump devices.
- Review the section on the DUMP TRANSACTION log options, TRUNCATE_ONLY, NO_LOG, and NO_TRUNCATE.
- To decrease the amount of time required for database backups, use the new parallel striped backup features of SQL Server 6.0.
- Backups can be reliably and easily scheduled from the SQL Enterprise Manager.
- Create a backup and recover plan to protect your databases. Make sure to test and practice the plan.
- Back up the master database at least once a day.

SUMMARY

Maintaining a good set of database backups is one of the most important responsibilities of a DBA. Use the ideas and suggestions put forth in this chapter to help you build your own backup plan. The next chapter examines the other side of the coin and looks at how to use the database and transaction log backups to restore or move a database.

CHAPTER 14

Recovery

In the previous chapter, you learned how to back up a database and transaction log and set up a backup schedule to prevent data loss. In this chapter, you learn how to use the database and transaction log backups to restore a corrupted database or move a database to another server. This chapter builds on what you learned in the previous chapter and puts your backup and recovery plan(s) to the test. When you think of database recovery you probably think of a database becoming corrupted and the DBA following a series of steps to restore (recover) the database. SQL Server also performs another type of database recovery called *automatic recovery*.

AUTOMATIC RECOVERY

Whenever SQL Server is started, a process called automatic recovery occurs. The automatic recovery process consists of SQL Server checking each database for uncommitted transactions to roll back or for committed transactions to roll forward.

You may be wondering what it means to roll a transaction back or to roll a transaction forward. First, you must understand what a transaction is. In simple database terminology, a *transaction* is defined as a unit of work. A transaction can consist of a single SQL statement that modifies one row or 10,000 rows or a transaction can consist of many SQL statements that are bunched together as a single unit of work. Look at an example of each.

The following is a single SQL statement:

```
Insert jobs
Values(12, "Write SQL Books", 1,4)
```

The following are multiple SQL statements:

```
Begin TRAN
Insert jobs
Values(12, "Write SQL Books", 1, 4)
if(@@error != 0)
begin
Rollback tran
else
Update employee
set job_id = 12
end
if(@@error = 0)
Commit TRAN
else
Rollback TRAN
```

Note

Data modification statements such as Insert, Delete, and Update are treated as transactions. To group several data modifications together to be treated like a single transaction, use the following syntax:

```
BEGIN TRAN
```

or

```
BEGIN TRANSACTION
```

To commit the changes (that is, save them in the database), use the following syntax:

```
COMMIT TRAN
```

or

```
COMMIT TRANSACTION
```

To roll back the changes (that is, do not save them in the database), use the following syntax:

```
ROLLBACK TRAN
```

or

```
ROLLBACK TRANSACTION
```

If a transaction is written to the database, the transaction is said to be *committed*. A transaction is said to be *rolled back* when the transaction is written to the data cache and transaction log and then removed from the log without being written to the database. Using the diagrams in Figure 14.1, walk through a series of transactions and a SQL Server automatic recovery.

STEP 1: START TRANSACTIONS

Figure 14.1 shows two users issuing two separate transactions to SQL Server called TRAN1 and TRAN2. SQL Server receives the transactions and marks the start of the transactions TRAN1 and TRAN2 in the transaction log. TRAN1 modifies page 5 in the cache and TRAN2 modifies page 7 in the cache. No data has been written to the transaction log or the database.

STEP 2: COMMIT TRANSACTION *TRAN1*

User 1 sends a statement to SQL Server to commit TRAN1. SQL Server writes the committed transaction to the transaction log and marks page 5 in the cache as a *dirty* page. The transaction is still not written to the database.

Note

SQL Server uses a write-ahead log scheme. Data is written to the transaction log first before it is written to the database. The term *dirty*

14

refers to a page in the disk cache that has been modified by a committed transaction and the page has been written to the transaction log but not to the database (pages modified by uncommitted transactions are considered active and not dirty).

Figure 14.1.
Transactions and
automatic recovery.

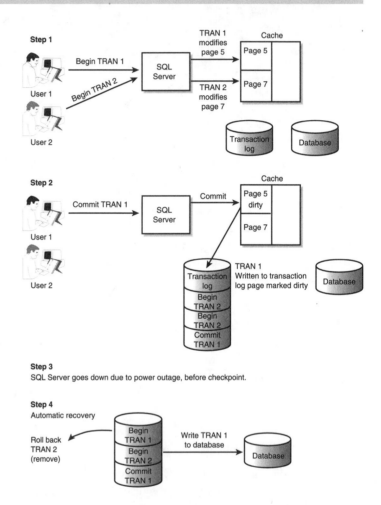

STEP 3: POWER OUTAGE - SQL SERVER UNEXPECTEDLY SHUTS DOWN

Before SQL Server issues a checkpoint in the database and User 2 can commit TRAN2, a power outage occurs, bringing down the NT server and SQL Server.

Note

Dirty pages are written to the database when SQL Server performs an automatic checkpoint or when a user (database owner or SA) issues a CHECKPOINT command in the database. A checkpoint causes all dirty pages to be written to the database and typically takes a second or two to execute. The frequency of automatic checkpoints is dependent upon the SQL Server configuration parameter recovery interval. The parameter recovery interval determines the maximum number of minutes required to recover a database. The checkpoint process checks every minute to see which databases have matched or exceeded the recovery interval and performs a checkpoint in each of these databases. For more information on the recovery interval, see Chapter 18.

STEP 4: RESTART AND AUTOMATIC RECOVERY

In this step, the NT server is restarted and restarts SQL Server. SQL Server begins to go through the automatic recovery process. First, the master database is checked. The model database and the temporary database are cleared. The scheduling database is recovered, followed by the pubs database, and the distribution database for servers configured as replication distributor. Last, but not least, the user databases are recovered. In the user database (refer to Figure 14.1), the committed transaction TRAN1 is *rolled forward*, or written to the database. The uncommitted transaction, TRAN2, is *rolled back*, or removed from the transaction log without being written to the database. You can view the results of SQL Server's automatic recovery process by viewing the error log as shown in Listing 14.1 or by viewing the NT event log.

LISTING 14.1. PARTIAL ERROR LOG LISTING OF SQL SERVER AUTOMATIC RECOVERY PROCESS.

```
95/08/07 20:27:40.67 spid10    Recovering database 'pubs'
95/08/07 20:27:40.69 spid11    Recovering database 'msdb'
95/08/07 20:27:40.70 spid12    Recovering database 'test'
95/08/07 20:27:40.74 spid11    Recovery dbid 5 ckpt (1283,20) oldest tran=(1283,19)
95/08/07 20:27:40.75 spid11    1 transactions rolled forward in dbid 5.
95/08/07 20:27:40.75 spid10    Recovery dbid 4 ckpt (777,24) oldest tran=(777,23)
95/08/07 20:27:40.76 spid10    1 transactions rolled forward in dbid 4.
95/08/07 20:27:40.77 spid12    Recovery dbid 6 ckpt (1522,27)
95/08/07 20:27:41.62 spid1     Recovery complete.
```

LOADING A DATABASE DUMP OR APPLYING A TRANSACTION LOG DUMP

Before covering the steps required to recover a corrupted database, examine how to use the SQL Enterprise Manager to load a previous database or apply a transaction log dump (backup).

Note

The following steps can be performed to load or recover databases. You can load the master database using the following steps, but to recover a damaged master database requires running a special utility covered later.

From the SQL Enterprise Manager, select Tools and then select Backup/Restore. The Database Backup/Restore dialog box appears (see Figure 14.2).

*Figure 14.2.
Database Backup/
Restore dialog box.*

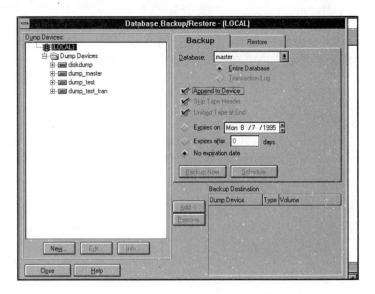

Click on the Restore tab (see Figure 14.3).

Note

For detailed information on the dump devices, frame, and buttons, refer to Chapter 13.

Figure 14.3.
The Restore tab in the
Manage Database
Backup/Restore
dialog box.

Dump Device frame—

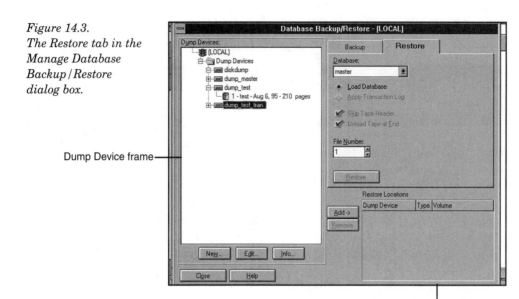

Restore Locations list box

14

To load a database or transaction log backup, perform the following steps:

1. Using the Database drop-down combo box, select the database you want to
   load the database or transaction log dump.

2. To load a database dump, check the Database checkbox. For a transaction
   log dump, check the Apply transaction log box.

3. The Skip Tape Header and Unload Tape at End checkboxes are specific to
   tape drive devices. If the Skip Tape Header box is checked, SQL Server will
   skip reading the ANSI label on the tape. If the Unload Tape at End
   checkbox is checked, SQL Server rewinds and unloads the tape at the end
   of the load.

4. If the dump device you are loading the database or transaction log dump
   from contains multiple dumps (see Figure 14.4), use the File Number box to
   select the correct dump to load.

5. Select the dump device to load the transaction log or database dump from
   by selecting a device in the Dump Devices frame and then clicking on the
   Add button to add the device to the Restore Locations list box (see Figure
   14.5).

Figure 14.4.
Multiple dumps on
dump device.

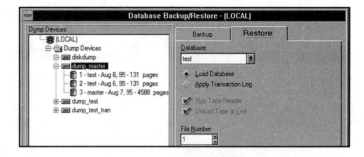

Figure 14.5.
Devices in the Restore
Locations list box.

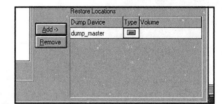

Note

If the database or transaction log dump was performed using a parallel striped set, the dump must be loaded using the same stripe set.

6. To restore the database or apply the transaction log, click the Restore button (refer to Figure 14.3).

Note

A new feature of SQL Server 6.0 that speeds up the load and recovery process is loading database or transaction dumps in 64KB chunks.

The Transact SQL command to load a database backup is the LOAD DATABASE command, which has the following syntax:

```
LOAD DATABASE { dump_device_name ¦ @dump_device_namevar}
¦ {DISK ¦ TAPE ¦ FLOPPY ¦ PIPE} =
{'temp_dump_device' ¦ @temp_dump_device_var}}
[VOLUME = {volid ¦ @volid_var}]
FROM dump_device [, dump_device2 [..., dump_device32]]
[WITH [[,] {UNLOAD ¦ NOUNLOAD}]
[[,] {SKIP ¦ NOSKIP}]
[[,] {FILE = fileno}]
[[,] STATS [ = percentage]]]]
```

Tip

You can load dumps from temporary dump devices.

The Transact SQL command to load a transaction log is the LOAD TRANSACTION command, which has the following syntax:

```
LOAD TRANSACTION { dump_device_name ¦ @dump_device_namevar}
¦ {DISK ¦ TAPE ¦ FLOPPY ¦ PIPE} =
{'temp_dump_device' ¦ @temp_dump_device_var}}
[VOLUME = {volid ¦ @volid_var}]
FROM dump_device [, dump_device2 [..., dump_device32]]
[WITH [[,] {UNLOAD ¦ NOUNLOAD}]
[[,] {SKIP ¦ NOSKIP}]
[[,] {FILE = fileno}]
```

Tip

You can load a database dump from SQL Server 4.2x to SQL Server 6.0, but you cannot load a SQL Server 6.0 database to a 4.2x SQL Server. You cannot load 4.2x transaction log dumps or a 4.2x master database dump to a 6.0 SQL Server.

PREPARING FOR A DATABASE LOAD

Whether you are trying to recover a corrupted database or moving a database to another server, certain conditions must be met to load the dump. First, any existing data in the database is overwritten by the loaded dump. A dump cannot be loaded while the database is in use and the SQL Server to which you are loading the dump must have the same sort order and character set as the SQL Server that dumped the database. The database to which you are loading the dump must be at least as large or larger than the database that created the dump.

Tip

If you are creating a database to load a database backup, use the new SQL Server 6.0 feature FOR LOAD option on the CREATE DATABASE Transact SQL command. The FOR LOAD option saves time when creating the database by not initializing the data pages.

One of the most overlooked aspects of preparing a database for recovery is that the database must not only be the same size or larger than the dump database but must also have the same device allocation order and size.

THE RESTORE DATABASE MYTH

Requiring the exact device size and allocation is one of the deep, dark secrets of SQL Server database recovery. I have run into many DBAs who were trying to restore databases and were having problems because the device allocation was not the same. Many assumed the database only had to be the same size or larger!

What does having the same device allocation and size mean? Now look at a few examples to help you understand. In the first example, you create a database called test1 that is created with 40MB for data on data_dev1 and 10MB for the transaction log on log_dev1. To load a database dump of the database test1 to another database would require you to create a database at least 50MB in size with 40MB of data followed by at least 10MB for the transaction log. Now suppose that you performed an ALTER DATABASE command and added 5MB for data on data_dev2, 2MB for log on log_dev2, and 10MB of data on data_dev1. Now the test1 database contains many different device fragments (that is, the space allocated to the database via create and alter statements) as shown in the Table 14.1:

TABLE 14.1. DATABASE TEST1 DEVICE FRAGMENT MAP.

Device Type	Size
Data	40
Log	10
Data	5
Log	2
Data	10
Total Database Size	67MB

To create a database to load the test1 database dump requires a database at least 67MB in size with a 40MB data fragment followed by a 10MB log fragment, followed by 5MB data fragment, followed by a 2 MB log fragment, followed by at least a 10MB data fragment—get the picture?

Note

To load or recover a database from a dump, the actual device on which the database is located is not important; however, the size and type of device fragmentation allocation are. The actual device(s) on which a

> database resides is important should a device fail and need to be re-created.

To determine the device allocation for a database, perform the following query in the master database. (Note that the following query is for the database test1. Substitute your database name for test1):

```
select segmap 'fragment type', size 'fragment size'
from sysusages
where dbid = (select dbid
from sysdatabases
where name = "test1")
```

Running the query on SQL Server displays the following output:

```
Fragment Type Fragment Size
3              1024
4               512
```

The fragment type column just shown translates as follows:

- ◆ 3 = Data Device
- ◆ 4 = Log Device
- ◆ 7 = Log and Data are on the same Device

Note

Any other values are user defined segments.

The fragment size is displayed in 2K blocks (512K = 1MB). If you don't want to compute the size of the device segment, execute the system stored procedure sp_helpdb, which has the following syntax:

```
sp_helpdb [database name]
```

Following is the output of the sp_helpdb command on the test1 database:

```
name  db_size  owner  dbid created  status
---------------------- ----------- ------------------------ ------ ---------- --
------------------------------------------------------------------------------
------------------------------------------------------------------------------
-------
test1  3.00 MB sa  6  Aug  6 1995 no options set

device_fragments  size  usage
-------------------------------- ----------- -------------------
test1                            2.00 MB data only
test1_log                        1.00 MB log only
```

Tip

Keep device fragment maps and device allocation for each database. In the event of a recovery or a simple database move, you will have the size and device fragments handy, speeding up the process.

RECOVERING A DATABASE

Now that you understand how to use the tools and commands used to load a database, review the following steps to recover a damaged database:

1. If the transaction log for the corrupt database is on a separate device, use the DUMP TRANSACTION command with the NO_TRUNCATE clause to dump the transaction log to a dump device so that the transactions can be recovered (that is, load as the last transaction log).

2. Perform the device allocation query described earlier to determine the correct fragment map required to re-create the database.

3. Drop the damaged database with the SQL Enterprise Manager or the DROP DATABASE command. If the DROP DATABASE command fails, use the DBCC DBREPAIR (database name, DROPDB) or the system stored procedure, sp_dbremove.

4. Create the database with the correct device fragments using the CREATE DATABASE command or the SQL Server Enterprise Manager and, if necessary, the ALTER DATABASE command.

5. Reload the database using the SQL Enterprise Manager or the LOAD DATABASE command.

LOADING TRANSACTION LOGS

After you load the most recent database backup, you can begin to load (apply) the transaction log dumps to the database. When you load a transaction log dump, database modifications made in the transaction log are re-executed in the database. To maintain database integrity, transaction logs must be loaded in correct order. SQL Server checks the timestamp value of each transaction log and ensures that the transaction sequence is correct. If you try to load a transaction log out of sequence, you will get an error and the transaction load will halt. To load transaction logs, use the SQL Enterprise Manager or the LOAD TRANSACTION command.

MOVING A DATABASE

If you plan to move a database to another server or another database using a database dump, follow the guidelines outlined earlier in the section "Preparing for a Database Load." Create the database using the correct segment map and load the database.

SQL Server provides another tool to move a database, discussed in Chapter 15, the Transfer Manager. Use the Transfer Manager to move a database when the character set or sort order of the two database servers is different. You can also use the Transfer Manager to transfer databases between servers on different platforms such as from an Intel platform to an Alpha platform.

Warning

If you use the DUMP command and then the LOAD command to move a database from one server to another, remember that the database user ids travel with the database and the mappings between the server login ids, and that database ids may not be correct on the new server. Use aliases to correct the problem.

RECOVERING THE MASTER DATABASE

You probably guessed by now that the master database is definitely not just another database, and as such, to recover the master database requires a separate recovery procedure. You will know when the master database is corrupted either from a DBCC output, an error message in the error log or the NT event log, or SQL Server will not start.

Note

The procedure to restore the master database is different in SQL Server 6.0 from previous versions and much improved. You no longer have to use the utility buildmaster or run the installmaster and installmodel scripts! As a matter of fact, they are no longer shipped with SQL Server.

To rebuild the master database, use the SQL Setup program. Start the SQL Setup program and perform the following steps:

1. Select the Rebuild Master Database checkbox in the SQL Server Setup programs dialog box and click the Continue button (see Figure 14.6).

Figure 14.6.
SQL Server Setup
program dialog box.

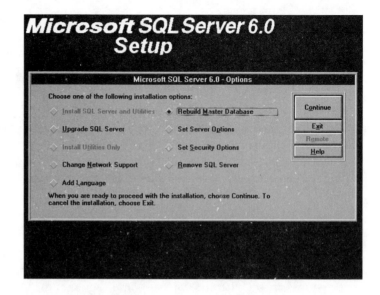

The Rebuild Master Database dialog box appears (see Figure 14.7).

Figure 14.7.
Rebuild Master
Database dialog box.

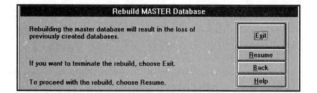

Note

The Rebuild Master Database dialog box, shown in Figure 14.7, warns that you will lose all previously created databases. You will recover the previous databases by loading a backup of the master database later in the rebuild process.

2. Click the Resume button. The SQL Server 6.0 Rebuild Options dialog box appears (see Figure 14.8).

Figure 14.8.
SQL Server 6.0 Rebuild
Options dialog box.

3. To recover the master database and all your other databases, you must select the same sort order and character set of the corrupted master database. Once you have selected the correct character set and sort order, click the Continue button.

4. The SQL Server Installation Path dialog box appears (see Figure 14.9). Select the correct path of your current SQL Server installation and click the Continue button. The Rebuild Master Device dialog box appears (see Figure 14.10).

Figure 14.9.
SQL Server Installa-
tion Path dialog box.

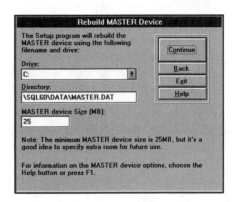

Figure 14.10.
Rebuild Master Device
dialog box.

5. Enter the path and the size of your current master device and click the Continue button. The master device and database will then be re-created. When the process finishes, a completion dialog box appears. Click the Exit to Windows NT button.

6. Start SQL Server and log on to the server using the SQL Enterprise Manager. The master database is in the same state as when SQL Server was first installed. You now must use a previous database dump of the master database to restore it. Add to the master database the dump device from which you plan to restore.

7. Shut down SQL Server. To load the master database, either with the SQL Enterprise Manager or from an `isql` command prompt, requires starting SQL Server in single-user mode. To start SQL Server in single-user mode,

use the SQL Setup program and the Set Server Options selection to add the single-user flag /m or enter the following on the command line:

```
startserver /c /dpath and filename of the master device /m
```

8. Once SQL Server is started in single-user mode, use the Enterprise Manager of the LOAD DATABASE command to load a backup of the master database. When the load operation completes, the Server Connection Broken dialog box appears (see Figure 14.11).

Figure 14.11.
Server Connection
Broken dialog box.

The Server Connection Broken dialog box appears because SQL Server shuts down after the master database load process completes. Restart SQL Server in multi-user mode. The master database has now been successfully rebuilt. If changes, such as new logins or database modifications, have been made since the master database backup, you will have to manually apply the changes or use a script file. Some changes, such as new devices that were added after the loaded backup, can be recovered using the DISK REINIT command.

To recover database CREATE or ALTER database statements, use the DISK REFIT command. Remember, if you loaded from a current master database dump, then the recovery is complete! *Always* maintain a current backup of the master database.

Tip

If you are a new DBA or a DBA in training, find a test system on which you can practice recovering the master database. Think about how crucial the master database is to the proper operation of your SQL Server. The first time you rebuild the master database should not be on a production database while you are under a lot of stress and pressure to get the database back and running. Practice makes perfect!

I contracted once for a Fortune 500 company that was using a UNIX Sybase system (prior to the release of Windows NT). The DBA was new and inexperienced and the UNIX system had many problems during the first month with the system and drives. The DBA had to rebuild the master database twice. (Unfortunately I was not allowed to help since I was contracted to support another group!) The first time resulted in failure, frustration, and then just an "Oh heck, it's not production. Let's reinstall." The second time the DBA had learned from the previous experience and was able to rebuild the master database. Fortunately for us, Microsoft has made rebuilding the master database a simple and graphical task!

BETWEEN THE LINES

◆ Automatic recovery is performed on all the databases when SQL Server is started.

◆ Use the SQL Enterprise Manager to load transaction log and database dumps.

◆ When creating a database that will be loaded with a database backup, use the FOR LOAD option on the CREATE DATABASE command.

◆ Restoring from a stripe dump set requires reading from the stripe set.

◆ Loading a database dump requires the new database to have the same size and device fragment allocation.

◆ When moving or loading databases, the SQL Server must have the same character set and sort order as the SQL Server that produced the database dump.

◆ Use the SQL Setup program to rebuild the master database.

◆ Practice performing database recovery procedures.

SUMMARY

Database backups and recovery are serious business and an important part of a DBA's job responsibility. Set up a database backup plan and from time to time, practice your recovery procedures, so that in the event of an emergency, you will be prepared to properly recover the database.

14

RECOVERY

CHAPTER 15

Importing and Exporting Data

Various methods can be used to import and export SQL Server data. Almost all systems require some type of data transfer. BCP is the utility provided by SQL Server to transfer data. This chapter will discuss in detail the BCP utility and also cover alternatives to BCP.

BCP

BCP stands for *Bulk Copy Program*. It is the only tool SQL Server provides (with the exception of a few tricks discussed later in the chapter) to import and export data. Data can be in either native mode (SQL Server specific) or character mode (ASCII text). ASCII text data is commonly used to share data between SQL Server and other systems (see Figure 15.1).

Figure 15.1.
Common uses of BCP.

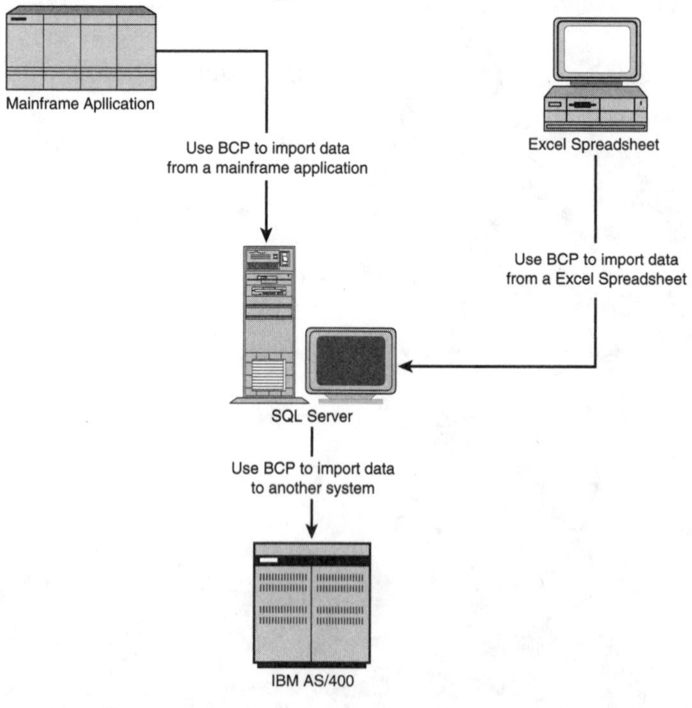

Mainframe Apllication

Use BCP to import data
from a mainframe application

Excel Spreadsheet

Use BCP to import data
from a Excel Spreadsheet

SQL Server

Use BCP to import data
to another system

IBM AS/400

IS IT LOVE OR HATE?

As a DBA you will probably have a love/hate relationship with BCP. BCP is limited in scope, and lacks common file formats, but it does provide excellent performance.

For those new to SQL Server, the following list will provide some insight into BCP. These are the reasons why I like BCP.

♦ **Performance**: BCP is one the fastest raw data loaders around. I have seen BCP turn in impressive performance numbers compared to other import/export products.

♦ **Minimal Overhead**: Because BCP is command-line-based, it requires a nominal amount of memory to run compared to today's memory intensive GUI applications. This leaves memory for other tasks.

Now for the drawbacks of BCP. These are the reasons why I hate it.

♦ **Unforgiving Syntax**: BCP's switches are case- and order-sensitive. This is because BCP's origins stem back to Sybase and the UNIX world where commands are case-sensitive. I wish that Microsoft would break with tradition and implement a user-friendly version of BCP.

♦ **Minimal File Support**: Basically, the choices are ASCII text, native SQL Server format, or nothing at all. Do not try loading an Excel spreadsheet or Access database directly into SQL Server; it will never work! To load non-SQL Server data, you need to export the data as ASCII text and then import the text file into SQL Server. It would be nice if BCP could directly import/export today's popular file formats such as Access, Excel, dBASE, and so on.

♦ **Inadequate Error Messages**: BCP's error messages are minimal and too generic. I wish that Microsoft would enhance BCP's error messages to be more informative and specific.

As you can see, BCP is far from perfect, but it is the only utility provided by SQL Server to import/export data. Oh well! With this in mind, hopefully the remainder of this chapter will provide you with some useful tips and tricks to make your life easier when using BCP.

15

IMPORTING AND EXPORTING DATA

BCP SYNTAX

Use the following syntax to perform BCP operations.

```
bcp [[database_name.]owner.]table_name {in | out} datafile
[/m maxerrors] [/f formatfile] [/e errfile]
[/F firstrow] [/L lastrow] [/b batchsize]
[/n] [/c] [/E]
[/t field_term] [/r row_term]
[/i inputfile] [/o outputfile]
/U login_id [/P password] [/S servername] [/v] [/a packet_size]
```

Note

With BCP you can use - or / to preface a switch. For example,

```
bcp pubs..sales out sales.out /c /Usa /P
```

is the same as

```
bcp pubs..sales out sales.out -c -Usa -P
```

BCP syntax explanation:

Syntax	Explanation
database_name	Name of the database being accessed.
	Database name is optional; if the database name is omitted, the user's default database will be used (optional).
owner	Owner of the table or view being accessed (optional).

Tip

Use the .. symbol to specify ownership. The .. syntax is more generic than specifying an owner (for example: pubs..authors).

table_name	Name of the table or view being accessed (required).

Tip

Use the # or ## symbol to copy a temporary table.

in ¦ out	Direction of data transfer where in means import; ¦ out means export (required).
datafile	Name of data file for an import or the name of the file that will created during an export. A path may be included with this statement, such as c:\sql\binn\authors.txt (required).
/m maxerrors	Maximum number of errors that can occur before the BCP operation is terminated. Each failed insert counts as one error. Default value is 10 (optional).
/f formatfile	Name of format file used to import or export data. A path may be included with this statement, such as c:\sql\binn\authors.fmt (optional).

/e *errfile*	Name of error file to store BCP error messages and unsuccessfully transferred rows. A path may be included with this statement, such as `c:\sql\binn\authors.err` (optional).

Tip

Error files are useful for pinpointing BCP errors during unattended operations such as nightly data imports.

/F *firstrow*	Number of the first row to copy (optional).
/L *lastrow*	Number of the last row to copy (optional).

Tip

The /F and /L switches are useful when copying portions of data. For example, to export the first 1000 records from a table, use the following syntax:

`/F 1 /L 1000`

/b *batchsize*	The number of rows transferred in a batch. The default setting is the number of rows in the data file (optional).
/n	Native data mode. Native data is SQL Server–specific. Native data mode does not prompt the user for field information (optional).
/c	Character data mode. Character data (ASCII) can be transferred to and from SQL Server tables and other non-SQL Server products. Character mode does not prompt the user for field information. By default, fields are tab delimited and rows are new line delimited (optional).

Tip

Character data mode is usually easier to work with than native data mode.

/E	Used when importing data into a table that contains an identity datatype and you want to populate the column with values from the data file. If this switch is omitted, SQL Server will automatically populate the identity

15

IMPORTING AND EXPORTING DATA

column and will ignore the field's corresponding data values in the import file (optional). The following example illustrates how the /E switch impacts data imports.

```
Sample table structure:
id int identity(1,1)
descr char(15)
Sample data file:
5    xxx
6    yyy
7    zzz
BCP syntax WITHOUT the /E switch:
bcp sales..table2 in
table2.txt /c /U sa /P
Results:
id          descr
---------- --------------------------------
1           xxx
2           yyy
3           zzz
```

Notice the values in the id column. SQL Server populated the id column with an automatically incremented data value. It ignored the values 5,6,7 in the data file.

The following is BCP syntax with the /E switch:

```
bcp sales..table2 in
table2.txt /c /E /U sa /P
Results:
id          descr
---------- -----------
---------------------
5           xxx
6           yyy
7           zzz
```

With the /E switch, the values in the text file were observed and SQL Server did *not* automatically generate a set of data values for the id column.

Tip

Use the /E switch to preserve data values when you are unloading and reloading data in a table that contains an identity datatype. Otherwise, SQL Server will automatically populate the identity column with its own set of values.

Note

The /E switch is new with Version 6.0.

/t *field_term*	Field terminator (optional). See Table 15.1 for BCP terminators.
/r *row_term*	Row terminator (optional) See Table 15.1 for BCP terminators.
/i *inputfile*	File to redirect input. This switch is not generally used (optional).
/o *outputfile*	File to redirect BCP output (optional).

Tip

Use the /o switch to log BCP output during unattended BCP operation. This creates a useful trail of BCP output that can be used to monitor and diagnose BCP performance and execution.

/U *login_id*	SQL Server login id (required).
/P *password*	SQL Server password. If the password is omitted, BCP will prompt you for a password (required).

Note

If you are using integrated security or your SQL Server login does not have a password, BCP will still prompt you for a password. To bypass BCP's prompt, use the /P switch without a password, as in the following example:

```
BCP pubs..authors in authors.txt /U sa /P
```

/S *servername*	Name of server that contains the database and table you are working with. The /s servername switch is required if you are using BCP from a remote client on a network (optional).
/v	Displays the version of DB-Library in use (optional).

Note

If you are concurrently running SQL Server Version 6.0 and Version 4.2x, be certain that you are using the correct version of BCP. To determine which version of BCP is in use, type **BCP** /v. Version 6.0's copyright date will be greater than or equal to 1995.

15

IMPORTING AND EXPORTING DATA

/a *packet_size*   Number of bytes contained in a network packet. The default value for Windows NT servers and Windows NT clients is 4096. The value for MS-DOS clients is 512. Valid sizes are 512 to 65,535 bytes (optional).

Tip

Depending your network architecture, you may be able to improve BCP performance by increasing the packet size. Try setting the packet size between 4096 and 8192 bytes. Use the statistics returned by BCP (clock time and rows per second) to help tailor this setting.

TABLE 15.1. VALID BCP TERMINATORS.

Terminator Type	Syntax
tab	\t
new line	\n
carriage return	\r
backslash	\\
null terminator	\0
user-defined terminator	character (^, %, *, and so on)

PERMISSIONS REQUIRED TO RUN BCP

No permissions are required to run the BCP command line utility. However, to BCP data into a table the user must be granted INSERT permission to the target table. To export data from a table, the user must be granted SELECT permission on the source table.

CHARACTER MODE VERSUS NATIVE MODE

BCP can import/export data in a character file format or native file format. Character mode is plain old ASCII text. Use the /c switch or a format file to specify character mode. Native mode uses special formatting characters internal to SQL Server to represent data. It should only be used when you are transferring data between SQL Server tables. Use the /n switch to specify native mode. The following is sample output from character mode BCP:

```
bcp pubs..jobs out jobs.txt /c /U sa /P

1       New Hire - Job not specified    10    10
2       Chief Executive Officer         200   250
3       Business Operations Manager     175   225
```

Tip

Character mode is usually easier to work with than native mode because you can view the contents of a character mode data file with a standard text editor.

INTERACTIVE BCP

Interactive BCP is used to selectively import or export data. Interactive mode is automatically activated when the following switches are *not* included in the BCP statement:

/n (native format)

/c (character format)

/f (format file)

Through the use of interactive prompts, you can tailor BCP to your import and export specifications.

Note

The default values provided with interactive BCP are the same as those produced by using native mode BCP (/n). This means that if you accept *all* default prompts you are running native mode BCP.

Interactive BCP will prompt you for four pieces of information:

◆ File storage type

◆ Prefix length

◆ Field length

◆ Field and row terminator

The following are sample interactive BCP prompts:

```
Enter the file storage type of field discounttype [char]:
Enter prefix-length of field discounttype [0]:
Enter length of field discounttype [40]:
Enter field terminator [none]:
```

Tip

> When importing data, you can skip a column by entering 0 for prefix length, 0 for length, and no terminator. You cannot skip a column when exporting data.

At the end of an interactive BCP session, you will receive the following prompt.

```
Do you want to save this format information in a file? [Y/n]
Host filename [bcp.fmt]:
```

If you answer **yes** at this prompt, your interactive responses will be saved to a format file. This enables you at a later time to specify the /f switch (format file) to automatically reuse the information from your interactive BCP session.

FILE STORAGE TYPE

File storage type specifies the datatypes used to read from and write to data files. Table 15.2 lists valid file storage types.

Tip

> When working with ASCII files, set all file storage types to char, regardless of the table's datatypes.

TABLE 15.2. FILE STORAGE TYPES.

char

varchar

text

binary

varbinary

image

datetime

smalldatetime

decimal

numeric

float

real

int

File Storage Types
smallint
tinyint
money
smallmoney
bit
timestamp

PREFIX LENGTH

SQL Server uses prefix length to store compacted data. When working in native mode, accept the default values whenever possible.

Tip

When working with fixed width ASCII data, set the prefix length to 0.

FIELD LENGTH

Field length specifies the number of bytes required to store a SQL Server datatype. Use default field lengths whenever possible, otherwise data truncation or overflow errors may occur. Table 15.3 lists default field lengths.

TABLE 15.3. DEFAULT FIELD LENGTHS.

Datatype	Length In Bytes
bit	1
char(*n*)	*n*
datetime	26
decimal	28
float	25
int	12
money	24
numeric	28
real	25
smalldatetime	26

continues

15

IMPORTING AND EXPORTING DATA

TABLE 15.3. CONTINUED

Datatype	Length In Bytes
smallint	6
smallmoney	24
tinyint	3
varchar(*n*)	*n*

Tip

When importing/exporting ASCII fixed width data files, you may need to modify the field length to match your import/export specification. For example, to export a char(15) column as a 25-byte piece of data, specify a field length of 25. This will pad the data length to 25 bytes.

FIELD TERMINATOR

The field terminator prompt controls how field data is delimited (separated). The default delimiter is no terminator. See Table 15.4 for valid field terminators.

Tip

The last field in a table acts as a row terminator. To separate rows with a new line delimiter, specify \n at the field terminator prompt.

Note

At the BCP command line, you can also use the \t (field terminator) and \r (row terminator) switches to specify terminators.

TABLE 15.4. VALID FIELD TERMINATORS.

Terminator Type	Syntax
tab	\t
new line	\n
carriage return	\r

Terminator Type	Syntax
backslash	\\
null terminator	\0
user-defined terminator	character (^, %, *, and so on)

FORMAT FILES

A format file is a template for BCP to use when you import/export data. With this template you can define how BCP should transfer your data.

The easiest way to create a format file is to initiate an interactive BCP session (interactive mode is initiated when you do *not* specify one of the following switches):

- ◆ /n (native format)
- ◆ /c (character format)
- ◆ /f (format file)

At the end of your interactive session, you will receive the following prompt:

```
Do you want to save this format information in a file? [Y/n] y
Host filename [bcp.fmt]:sample.fmt
```

At this prompt, enter a filename to save the format information. SQL Server will then create a format file, which is really just an ASCII text file (see Figure 15.2). You can make modifications to an existing format file by using a standard text editor.

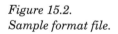

Tip

Use a .fmt extension when saving format files. This will simplify file identification.

Figure 15.2.
Sample format file.

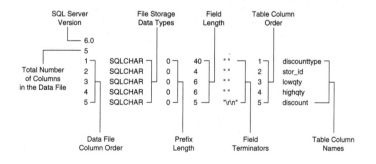

Once you have saved the format file, you can reuse the format file by specifying the /f (format file) switch, as in the following example:

```
bcp sales..discounts in discount.txt /f sample.fmt /U sa /P
```

> **Note**
>
> If a table has a corresponding format file, any column modification to the table must be reflected in the format file. For example, if you drop a column from a table, you must also remove the column from the format file.

SAMPLE BCP SCRIPTS

This section discusses how to use BCP to perform typical import and export routines. The examples discussed in this section use the pubs..discounts table.

The following is a discounts table structure:

```
discounttype varchar (40)
stor_id varchar
lowqty smallint
highqty smallint
discount decimal(0, 0)
```

The following is discounts table data:

```
discounttype                                stor_id lowqty highqty discount
--------------------------------------------- ------ ------ ------ --------
Initial Customer                            (null)  (null) (null)  10.50
Volume Discount                             (null)  100    1000    6.70
Customer Discount                           8042    (null) (null)  5.00
```

SIMPLE IMPORT

This example uses the /c switch to load a data file that contains tab delimited fields and new line delimited rows. For this example, the import data is contained in a file named disc.txt. Following are the contents of the sample import file.

```
Preferred Customer 6380 200 800   5.5
Valued Customer    7896 100 1000 8.5
```

The following syntax illustrates how to import the contents of the disc.txt file into the discounts table:

```
bcp pubs..discounts in disc.txt /c /U sa /P
```

SIMPLE EXPORT

This example uses the /c switch to export data to a file with tab delimited fields and new line delimited rows.

The following syntax illustrates how to export the contents of the discounts table to the discount.out file:

```
bcp pubs..discounts out discount.out /c /U sa /P
```

Following is the output:

```
Initial Customer                                10.50
Volume Discount         100     1000    6.70
Customer Discount       8042                    5.00
```

COMMA DELIMITED IMPORT

This example imports a data file that contains comma delimited fields and new line delimited rows. The /t switch specifies a comma delimiter and the /r\n switch specifies a new line row delimiter. For this example, the import data is contained in a file named disc2.txt. Following are the contents of the sample import file.

```
Preferred Customer,6380,200,800,5.5
Valued Customer,7896,100,1000,8.5
```

The following syntax illustrates how to import the contents of the disc2.txt file into the discounts table.

```
bcp pubs..discounts in disc2.txt /c /t, /r\n /U sa /P
```

COMMA DELIMITED EXPORT

This example exports the discounts table to a file that contains comma delimited fields and new line row delimiters.

The following syntax illustrates how to export the contents of the discounts table to the disc3.txt file.

```
bcp pubs..discounts out disc3.txt /c /t, /r\n /U sa /P
```

Following is the output:

```
Initial Customer,,,,10.50
Volume Discount,,100,1000,6.70
Customer Discount,8042,,,5.00
```

FIXED LENGTH IMPORT

This example uses a fixed-length ASCII text file named `disc4.txt`. Table 15.5 lists the layout of the text file.

TABLE 15.5. `disc4.txt` FILE LAYOUT.

Column Name	File Length	File Position
discounttype	40	1–39
stor_id	4	40–43
lowqty	6	44–49
highqty	6	50–55
discount	5	56–60

The following is `disc4.txt` sample data:

```
12345678901234567890123456789012345678901234567890123456789

Preferred Customer                    6380200   800    5.5
Valued Customer                       7896100   1000   8.5
```

For fixed-length data transfers, SQL Server needs to know the field positions in the data file. An easy way to do this is to use interactive BCP. To begin interactive BCP use the following command.

Sample BCP syntax:

```
bcp sales..discounts in disc4.txt /U sa /P
```

For the first two prompts, you can accept the default values because they match the layout in the data file. For the third, forth, and fifth prompts, you have to override the default prompts (see Figure 15.3).

Note

When importing fixed-length ASCII data, *always* use char for the file storage type and 0 for the prefix length!

FIXED LENGTH EXPORT

Suppose that you need to export the discount table in a fixed-length file format and the format needs to follow the specification used in the previous example. No problem; you can reuse the format file that you created in the previous example (see Figure 15.4).

Figure 15.3.
Interactive BCP
responses.

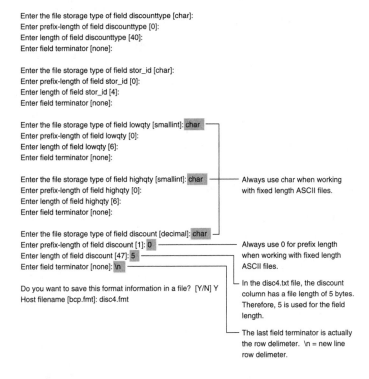

```
Enter the file storage type of field discounttype [char]:
Enter prefix-length of field discounttype [0]:
Enter length of field discounttype [40]:
Enter field terminator [none]:

Enter the file storage type of field stor_id [char]:
Enter prefix-length of field stor_id [0]:
Enter length of field stor_id [4]:
Enter field terminator [none]:

Enter the file storage type of field lowqty [smallint]: char
Enter prefix-length of field lowqty [0]:
Enter length of field lowqty [6]:
Enter field terminator [none]:

Enter the file storage type of field highqty [smallint]: char
Enter prefix-length of field highqty [0]:
Enter length of field highqty [6]:
Enter field terminator [none]:

Enter the file storage type of field discount [decimal]: char
Enter prefix-length of field discount [1]: 0
Enter length of field discount [47]: 5
Enter field terminator [none]: \n

Do you want to save this format information in a file?  [Y/N] Y
Host filename [bcp.fmt]: disc4.fmt
```

Always use char when working with fixed length ASCII files.

Always use 0 for prefix length when working with fixed length ASCII files.

In the disc4.txt file, the discount column has a file length of 5 bytes. Therefore, 5 is used for the field length.

The last field terminator is actually the row delimeter. \n = new line row delimeter.

The following syntax illustrates how to export the contents of the `discounts` table to the disc4.out file.

```
bcp pubs..discounts out disc4.out /c /f disc4.fmt /U sa /P
```

Figure 15.4.
disc4.fmt format file.

```
6.0
5
1    SQLCHAR    0    40    " "     1    discounttype
2    SQLCHAR    0    4     " "     2    stor_id
3    SQLCHAR    0    6     " "     3    lowqty
4    SQLCHAR    0    6     " "     4    highqty
5    SQLCHAR    0    5     "\r\n"  5    discount
```

SKIPPING FIELDS ON IMPORT

Suppose that you want to skip the columns `stor_id`, `lowqty`, and `highqty` when you load the disc4.txt ASCII file. In order to do this, you need to modify your format file. To skip a column, enter 0 for the table column order (see Figure 15.5).

After you modify your format file, you can use the following BCP syntax to load the data.

```
bcp pubs..discounts in disc4.txt /c /f disc4.fmt /U sa /P
```

15

Figure 15.5.
Format file used to skip
columns.

```
6.0
5
1    SQLCHAR    0    40    " "    1    discounttype
2    SQLCHAR    0    4     " "    0    stor_id
3    SQLCHAR    0    6     " "    0    lowqty
4    SQLCHAR    0    6     " "    0    highqty
5    SQLCHAR    0    5     "\r\n" 5    discount
```

A 0 indicates
that the column
should be skipped

SKIPPING FIELDS ON EXPORT

BCP does not allow you to skip a column in a table during an export. However, you can trick BCP into skipping a column by creating a view that only references the columns you wish to export, thus skipping unwanted columns. Then use BCP to export the data from the view.

The following syntax illustrates how to export only the `discounttype` and `discount` columns in the `discounts` table.

```
create view discounts_view as
select output = convert(char(40),discounttype) + convert(char(5),discount)
from discounts
```

Next, create a format file that contains one column (see Figure 15.6). Only one column is listed in the format file because the view concatenates the `discounttype` and `discount` columns together.

Figure 15.6.
Format file used to
export data from a
view.

```
6.0
1
1    SQLCHAR    0    45    "\r\n"    1    output
```

Finally, use BCP to export the data from the view:

```
bcp pubs..discounts_view out discview.txt /f discview.fmt /U sa /P
```

The following is sample output:

```
Initial Customer                    10.50
Volume Discount                     6.70
Customer Discount                   5.00
```

MODES OF OPERATION

When importing data, BCP has two modes of operation: fast mode and slow mode. As you probably guessed, the fast mode runs faster than the slow mode. The performance difference is due to the logging of transactions. Fast mode bypasses the transaction log, while slow mode posts all data inserts to the transaction log.

> *Note*
>
> You only need to be concerned with fast and slow mode BCP when you are importing data. BCP does not use a fast or slow mode when you export data.
>
> When you run BCP, SQL Server automatically decides which mode of BCP to run. There is *not* a BCP switch that allows you to toggle between fast and slow mode.

ACHIEVING FAST MODE BCP

Three factors determine whether BCP can run in fast mode: SELECT INTO/BULKCOPY, indexes, and triggers. For BCP to run in fast mode, the following three conditions must be true.

- ◆ The database option SELECT INTO/BULKCOPY must equal TRUE.
- ◆ Indexes must not exist on the target table.
- ◆ Triggers must not exist on the target table.

If any of these conditions are FALSE, BCP will run in the slow mode (see Figure 15.7).

WHY YOU SHOULD BE CONCERNED WITH WHICH MODE OF BCP IS RUNNING

You may be asking yourself, "Why not always run the fast mode of BCP?" The answer is based on the following three factors:

- ◆ Backup strategy
- ◆ Window of opportunity
- ◆ Available database space

BACKUP STRATEGY

To run the fast mode of BCP, you must have the SELECT INTO/BULKCOPY option set to TRUE. By setting this option to TRUE, you may be sacrificing data recovery for BCP performance. When SELECT INTO/BULKCOPY is set to TRUE, you *cannot* back up the transaction log for a database. Instead, you can only back up the entire database. This means that you will be unable to use the transaction log to provide up-to-the-minute data recovery.

15

WINDOW OF OPPORTUNITY

Fast mode BCP requires that the target table not contain any indexes or triggers. This means that you must consider the downtime involved with dropping the indexes, loading the data, and re-creating the indexes. For a table that requires 24-hour data access, it is not feasible to be dropping and re-creating indexes.

Figure 15.7.
How SQL Server
determines which mode
of BCP to run.

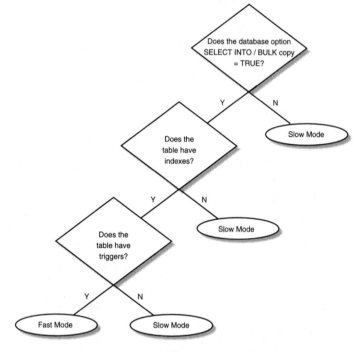

Tip

To significantly reduce the time required to create a clustered index, have your import data presorted on the fields that make up your clustered index. Then use the WITH SORTED_DATA option to create the clustered index, as in the following example:

```
CREATE CLUSTERED INDEX pk_idx ON table1 (id) WITH SORTED_DATA
```

AVAILABLE DATABASE SPACE

A clustered index requires free space equal to approximately 120 percent the size of the table. For example, a 100MB table requires approximately 120MB free database space to create the clustered index. If you are tight on disk space, you may not be able to drop and re-create a clustered index for a large table.

See Table 15.6 to help clarify the differences between the two modes.

TABLE 15.6. FAST BCP VERSUS SLOW BCP.

	Fast Mode	Slow Mode
PROS	Fast! Operations are not logged	Maximum recoverability
	Don't have to worry about filling up the transaction log	
CONS	Zero recoverability	Slow! Every insert is written to the transaction log
	Must dump the database after using BCP	Cannot dump the transaction log
	Need time to rebuild clustered index	Can easily fill up the transaction log during large data imports, thus complicating the import process

> *Note*
>
> BCP may or may *not* notify you as to which mode it is using! You will *not* receive a message that slow mode is in use when you import data into a table with an existing index or trigger.

BCP AND ENFORCEMENT OF TRIGGERS, RULES, DEFAULTS, CONSTRAINTS, AND UNIQUE INDEXES

When using BCP to import data into a SQL Server table, it is important that you understand how triggers, rules, defaults, constraints, and unique indexes are enforced. Many people forget that certain types of objects are bypassed when using BCP to import data. See Table 15.7 for a summary of which objects are enforced when BCP is used to import data.

TABLE 15.7. ENFORCEMENT OF OBJECTS.

Object	Enforced
Default	Yes
Unique index/unique constraints	Yes
Primary key and foreign key constraints	Yes
Check constraint	No
Rule	No
Trigger	No

Warning

Do not forget that triggers, check constraints, and rules are not enforced when using BCP! To prevent data integrity problems, load your data into a work table and run it through a validation routine similar to the validation defined in your triggers, constraints, and table rules. Once you are satisfied that the data meets your integrity requirements, transfer your data to your target table.

Note

Prior to Version 6.0, you could only enforce primary key/foreign key relationships through the use of triggers. Because BCP bypasses triggers, additional steps were required to ensure that you did not violate primary key/foreign key integrity. This problem has been resolved in Version 6.0 through the use of primary key and foreign key constraints which are enforced by BCP.

COMMON BCP TRAPS

Be on the lookout for the following traps. They always seem to be lurking out there!

- ◆ **Invalid dates**: When importing data, a data file that contains dates represented as 00/00/00 and 000000 will fail. These are invalid SQL Server date formats. This problem often arises when data is transferred from a mainframe system to SQL Server. You must adhere to SQL Server date formats when importing date information into datetime columns.

- ◆ **Space-filled dates**: With a date column, SQL Server will convert spaces in a text file to 1/1/1900. This is probably not what you want! To avoid this problem, do not pad the column with any data; just follow the column with a delimiter. SQL Server will set the data column to NULL, which is presumably more in line with what you expected.

◆ **Improper delimiter**: Do not use a delimiter that exists in your data or you will have problems. For example, if first and last name are stored as one field and a user enters Smith, Mike, a comma delimiter should not be used. For this example, use a tab or another type of delimiter.

BCP TIPS

Use the following tips to help simplify data imports and exports.

◆ Use views to export data: This allows increased flexibility to filter, sort, and physically arrange your data. For example, to export only the date portion of a datetime column, use a VIEW and the CONVERT function.

Sample table:
```
emp_id char(3)
hire_date datetime
```
Sample view:
```
CREATE VIEW date_example_view AS
SELECT emp_id,convert(char(12),hire_date,1)
FROM sample_table
```

Note

See the CONVERT function in Appendix D for other date formats.

The following is a sample BCP statement:
```
bcp sales..date_example_view out sample.out /c /U sa /P
```

◆ Always issue an UPDATE STATISTICS command after importing data into a table with existing indexes. An index's statistics will not reflect the data that was loaded with BCP. This may cause the optimizer to overlook a useful index. To avoid this problem, you must use the UPDATE STATISTICS command.

Note

You do not need to issue an UPDATE STATISTICS command if the table's indexes are dropped before the BCP operation is performed and re-created after the BCP operation. Under this scenario, the statistics will be up-to-date.

◆ Echo BCP output and errors to a text file. To capture BCP's output, use the /o switch. To capture BCP's error messages, use the /e switch.

◆ Many systems import data on a recurring basis. Once the data is loaded into the system, various routines are run to summarize the data, generate reports, and so on. Any easy way to automate this process is to create a stored procedure that calls BCP and then runs the subordinate processes. The advantage of creating a single stored procedure to run your import process is that you can schedule it through SQL Server's Task Scheduler. The following syntax is an example of a stored procedure that calls BCP to load data into the system and then executes summary procedures against the data:

```
CREATE PROCEDURE usp_load_example AS
/* flush out work table */
truncate table table1

/* BCP in data */
exec master..xp_cmdshell "bcp sales..table1 in C:\sql60\binn\table1.txt /c
/U sa /P"

/* run summary procedures */
exec usp_summary1
exec usp_summaryN
```

Warning

Do not use xp_cmdshell to call BCP from within a user-defined transaction in a stored procedure. This can lead to endless blocking!

ALTERNATIVES TO BCP

This section discusses alternatives to BCP. These alternatives are simple tips and tricks that may simplify data transfers.

SELECT INTO AND *INSERT* COMBINED WITH A *SELECT*

The SELECT INTO statement creates a new table with a structure identical to the structure in the SELECT statement, along with any matching data. For example, the following SQL statement copies the authors table from the pubs database to the sales database.

```
SELECT *
INTO sales..authors
FROM pubs..authors
```

Note

The database option SELECT INTO/BULKCOPY must be set to TRUE to use SELECT INTO to create a new table in a database. However, the SELECT INTO/BULKCOPY setting has no impact on the capability to create a temporary table in SQL Server.

An INSERT statement combined with a SELECT statement will append data into a target table with data from the source table. For example, the following SQL statement will copy any rows returned from the SQL statement into the *target_table*:

```
INSERT INTO target_table
SELECT * FROM source_table
```

Tip

Sometimes you must drop and re-create a table to perform a table modification. Most people will BCP out the data, drop and re-create the table, and then BCP back in the data. Under this scenario, it may be complicated to use BCP to reload your data if you made extensive changes to your table. An alternative to using BCP would be to use SELECT INTO to create a working copy of your table. Drop and re-create your table and then use INSERT INTO to reload the data from your work table.

SAVE SQL OUTPUT AS A TEXT FILE

An easy method to save data in a fixed-width format is to issue a SQL SELECT query from the Query window in the Enterprise Manager. The query results will be displayed in the Results tab. Click on the Save Query/Result button to save the query's output. The output will be saved in an ASCII text file in a fixed-width data format with new line separators (see Figure 15.8).

Tip

Use Query Options to prevent column names and row counts from being displayed in the Results tab. From the Query dialog box, click on the Query options button. This will take you to the Query Options dialog box. From this dialog box, select the Query Flag tab. Set No Count Display to TRUE and from the Format Options tab, set Print Headers to FALSE.

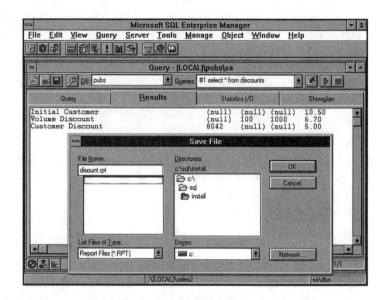

Figure 15.8.
Saving SQL output as
a text file.

SQL SERVER 4.2x's OBJECT MANAGER

For some inexplicable reason, the graphical version of BCP found in SQL Server 4.2's Object Manager was not included in the initial release of SQL Server Version 6.0. This is unfortunate because the graphical version of BCP in Version 4.2x's Object Manager greatly simplified BCP usage. However, you can still run Version 4.2x's Object Manager against SQL Server 6.0, thus taking advantage of graphical BCP. The following steps explain how to install and use Version 4.2x's Object Manager to graphically BCP data.

Warning

The Object Manager will only work with Version 6.0 tables that use Version 4.2x datatypes. This means that you cannot BCP tables that use identity, decimal, or other 6.0 enhancements.

1. Load the object2.sql script included with Version 4.2x from SQL Server 6.0 (see Figure 15.9). In Version 4.2x, the default installation for the file was the \sql\install\ directory. Ignore any error messages generated by the script.

2. Click on the SQL Object Manager icon in the SQL Server for Windows NT group (see Figure 15.10).

Figure 15.9.
Object2.sql script.

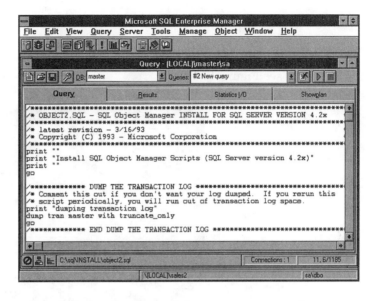

Note

SQL Object Manager is a 4.2x product that was not included with SQL Server 6.0.

Figure 15.10.
SQL Object Manager
icon.

3. In the Connect Server dialog box, enter the server name, login id, and password for SQL Server 6.0. Click on the Connect button to connect to SQL Server 6.0.

Tip

To determine which version of SQL Server you are logged into, use the @@version global variable. For example:

```
SELECT @@version.
```

Following is the output:

```
Microsoft SQL Server 6.0 - 6.00.121 (Intel X86)
Jun 13 1995 11:32:40
Copyright (c) 1988-1995 Microsoft Corporation
```

4. Select a database.

5. Click on the Transfer button in the Object Manager. This displays the Transfer Data dialog box. From this dialog box, you can graphically BCP data (see Figure 15.11).

Figure 15.11.
Object Manager's
Transfer Data
dialog box.

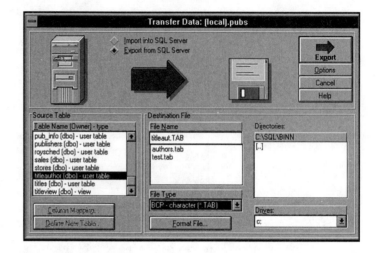

TRANSFER MANAGER

The *Transfer Manager* is a graphical tool used to transfer databases and objects. These objects can be transferred between different databases, different servers, and even different versions of SQL Server. Following are the types of objects that can be transferred:

◆ Tables (including data)

◆ Views

◆ Triggers

◆ Rules

◆ Defaults

◆ User datatypes

◆ Stored procedures

◆ Segments

◆ Logins (including permissions)

Tip

> The Transfer Manager is useful for moving a database from a development server to a production server or for moving a table and its data between the two servers.

Note

> The Transfer Manager allows you to transfer objects and data between SQL Server 6.0 and SQL Server 4.2x. Be aware that several new reserved words were added with Version 6.0. If a reserved word is present in your 4.2x Transact-SQL statement, the transfer to Version 6.0 will fail.
>
> The Transfer Manager also enables you to transfer a SQL Server 6.0 database to a SQL Server 4.2x server. However, the database cannot contain any 6.0 language enhancement, such as identity datatypes, decimal datatypes, declarative referential integrity, and so on.

The following steps explain how to use the Transfer Manager:

1. Double-click on the SQL Transfer Manager icon in the Microsoft SQL Server 6.0 (Common) group (see Figure 15.12). This will take you to the SQL Transfer Manager dialog box.

Figure 15.12.
SQL Transfer
Manager icon.

2. From the SQL Transfer Manager dialog box, enter the names of the Source Server and Destination Server (see Figure 15.13). Click on the Connect button to establish a connection to both servers. This will take you to the SQL Transfer Manager dialog box.

Tip

> Your Source Server and Destination Server can be the same server. Use this feature to transfer objects between different databases on the same server.

Figure 15.13.
SQL Transfer Manager
dialog box.

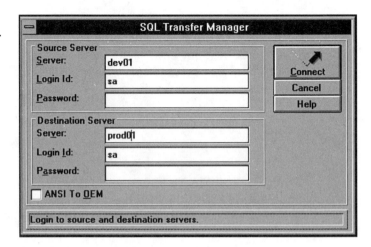

3. From the SQL Transfer Manager dialog box, select the source database and target database. Select the types of objects you want to transfer. Enter a directory for the generation of scripts. Click on the Transfer button to initiate the transfer (see Figure 15.14).

Note

To transfer individual objects, deselect the All Objects checkbox. This enables the Available Objects list box. From this list box, you can select individual objects to transfer.

Figure 15.14.
SQL Transfer Manager
dialog box.

Between the Lines

◆ BCP uses two file types to transfer data: character mode and native mode. Character mode is ASCII text and native mode is a SQL Server file type. Character mode is usually easier to work with.

◆ When working with fixed-length ASCII files, always use the `char` datatype and `0` prefix length.

◆ To skip a column in interactive BCP, enter `0` for prefix length, `0` for length, and no terminator.

◆ When importing data, BCP has two modes of operation: fast and slow mode. Fast mode bypasses the transaction log, while slow mode posts all data inserts to the transaction log.

◆ To achieve fast mode BCP, set the database option `SELECT INTO/BULKCOPY` to `TRUE` and drop all indexes and triggers on the target table.

◆ The capability to continuously run fast mode BCP is dependent upon your backup and data access requirements in your production environment.

◆ Check constraints, rules, and triggers are not enforced when using BCP.

◆ When importing data into a date column, spaces in a data file will convert to `1/1/1900`.

◆ Always `UPDATE STATISTICS` after using BCP to import data into a table that contains indexes.

Summary

As you can see from reading this chapter, you need to know a lot when it comes to importing and exporting data in SQL Server. The next chapter discusses common SQL Server errors.

CHAPTER 16

Troubleshooting
SQL Server

Each chapter of this book has covered common problems and resolutions. This chapter steps back for a moment and focuses on how SQL Server alerts you to possible problems with databases, objects, or the server; how to find more information about the problem; how to fix the problem; or how to get help in determining/ fixing your problem. You also will learn about several tools that ship with SQL Server to help you track and debug problems, as well as other resources that are readily available to aid in problem resolution. Start by taking a look at SQL Server error messages.

SQL ERROR MESSAGES

If you run a query and accidentally make a mistake entering a table that does not exist in the database, what happens? SQL Server returns an error message. Actually SQL Server reacts to errors in the same manner, be it user-, database-, object-, or system-generated. SQL Server will return a formatted error message and/or write the error message to the error log and/or event log. Go through a quick example by executing a SQL statement to update a nonexistent table in the pubs database. The SQL statement for the example is as follows:

```
UPDATE new_authors
Set author1 = "Spenik,
author2 = "Sledge",
title="Microsoft SQL Server DBA Survival Guide"
```

When the statement is executed, the following error message is returned:

```
 Msg 208, Level 16, State 1
Invalid object name 'new_authors'.
```

The preceding error message demonstrates the standard message format for error messages returned by SQL Server.

Tip

The first thing you notice in the error message is the message number, severity level, and the state. To most users, these numbers are just garbage to ignore, so they skip down to the message and try to resolve the problem. In reality, the error message number is very useful for obtaining more error information. The severity levels can be used to help find errors that need to be handled. When tracking a problem, always write down all the error information, including the message number, severity level, and state. In many cases, these will be of more assistance than the actual message.

Examine the format of a standard SQL Server error message.

ERROR MESSAGE NUMBER

Each error message displayed by SQL Server will have an associated error message number that uniquely identifies the type of error.

ERROR SEVERITY

The error severity levels provide a quick reference for you on the nature of the error. The severity levels range from 0-25.

0-10	Messages with a severity level of 0-10 are informational messages.
11-16	Severity levels 11-16 are generated as a result of user problems and can be fixed by the user. For example, the error message returned in the invalid update query used earlier had a severity level of 16.
17	Severity level 17 indicates that SQL Server has run out of a configurable resource, such as user connections or locks. Severity error 17 can be corrected by the DBA and, in some cases, by the database owner.
18	Severity level 18 indicates nonfatal internal software problems.

Note

Severity errors 19 through 25 are fatal errors. When a fatal error occurs, the running process that generated the error is terminated (nonfatal errors continue processing). For error severity levels 20 and greater, the client connection to SQL Server is terminated.

19	Severity level 19 indicates a nonconfigurable resource limit has been exceeded.
20	Severity level 20 indicates a problem with a statement issued by the current process.
21	Severity level 21 indicates SQL Server has encountered a problem that affects all the processes in a database.
22	Severity level 22 means a table or index has been damaged. To try and determine the extent of the problem, stop and restart SQL Server. In the event that the problem is only in the cache and not on the disk, the restart will correct the problem. Otherwise, use DBCC to determine the extent of the damage and the required action to take.

16

TROUBLESHOOTING SQL SERVER

23	Severity level 23 is a suspect database. To determine the extent of the damage and the proper action to take, use the DBCC commands.
24	Severity level 24 is a hardware problem.
25	Severity level 25 indicates some type of system error.
state number	The error state number indicates the source that issued the error.
error message	The error message is a description of the error that occurred. The error messages are stored in the sysmessages system table. Figure 16.1 shows a query result of the sysmessages table.

Figure 16.1.
Query results of
sysmessage using the
Query Analyzer.

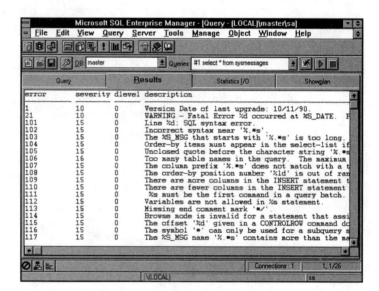

USING THE ERROR MESSAGE NUMBER TO RESOLVE THE ERROR

Earlier, it was stated that by using the error message number, you could quickly retrieve detailed information on the error and possible ways to resolve the error. How, you ask? *Books Online!*

INFORMATION AT YOUR FINGERTIPS

Isn't technology great! I believe that to really appreciate Microsoft's Books Online, you have to have been a Sybase DBA from the 4.2 UNIX days. When an error occured that displayed the error number, you would jot down the error number and then try to locate the error messages and troubleshooting guide. Of course, the book was never in the same place. And if you had my luck, once you found the book, the error number was never in the book; it always fell under that section "reserved" or something similar. New DBAs starting with SQL Server 6.0 will truly be spoiled by Microsoft's Books Online!

Hopefully, when you installed SQL Server or the utilities, you included the Books Online utility shown in Figure 16.2.

Figure 16.2.
SQL Server Books
Online.

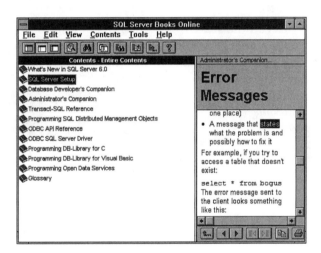

To see how to use Books Online to find more information on the error message number displayed during your invalid query example, error message number 208, perform the following steps:

1. Select Find from the Tools menu in the SQL Server Books Online window. The Find dialog box appears (see Figure 16.3).

Figure 16.3.
Find dialog box.

2. The Find dialog box allows you to quickly search the Books Online for specific information. In the combo box labeled Query, enter the error message number **208**. In the Scope of Search frame, check the Entire CD radio button. In the Topic Area To Search frame, select the Title Only radio button.

3. To run the search, click the Find button. The query will run searching for 208 in the title of any of the book topics. If one or more items are found, they will be displayed in a Find Results dialog box (see Figure 16.4).

Figure 16.4.
Find Results
dialog box.

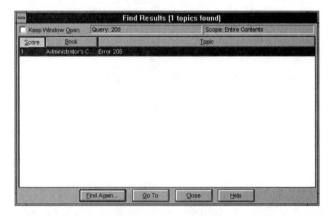

4. To view the document(s) found in the search, double-click on the item or click the Go To button. The detailed information for the error message number, including a detailed explanation and the action to take, is displayed in the document. You can even print the document. Just think, no more trying to locate a troubleshooting or error message book. No more flipping through pages searching for error messages, and if the error number is not in the book, you know immediately! The detailed information found for error number 208 is displayed in Figure 16.5.

Figure 16.5.
Detailed Books Online
description of error
message 208.

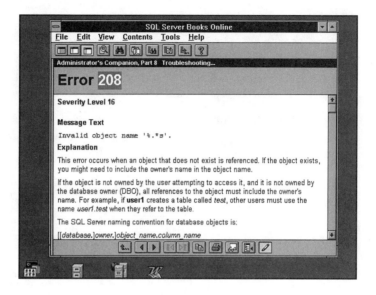

DECIPHERING THE ERROR LOG

The error log is a standard text file that holds SQL Server informational and error messages and can provide meaningful information to help you track down problems or to alert you to potential or existing problems. SQL Server maintains the current error log and the six previous error log files. The current error log filename is ERRORLOG and the previous error log files are named ERRORLOG.1 (most recent) to ERRORLOG.6 (the oldest). The default location of the error log file is in the \LOG directory off of the SQL Server home directory. The following is an example of a SQL Server error log:

```
95/09/01 22:16:03.92 spid1    Recovering database 'model'
95/09/01 22:16:03.94 spid1    Recovery dbid 3 ckpt (259,26)
95/09/01 22:16:04.05 spid1    Clearing temp db
95/09/01 22:16:05.93 kernel   Read Ahead Manager started.
95/09/01 22:16:05.96 kernel   Using 'SQLEVN60.DLL' version '6.00.000'.
95/09/01 22:16:06.14 kernel   Using 'OPENDS60.DLL' version '6.00.01.02'.
95/09/01 22:16:06.17 kernel   Using 'NTWDBLIB.DLL' version '6.00.121'.
95/09/01 22:16:06.18 ods      Using 'SSNMPN60.DLL' version '6.3.0.0' to listen on
                              '\\.\pipe\sql\query'.
95/09/01 22:16:08.21 spid10   Recovering database 'pubs'
95/09/01 22:16:08.23 spid12   Recovering database 'test'
95/09/01 22:16:08.24 spid11   Recovering database 'msdb'
95/09/01 22:16:08.26 spid12   Recovery dbid 6 ckpt (1028,6)
95/09/01 22:16:08.27 spid11   Recovery dbid 5 ckpt (1304,18) oldest tran=(1304,17)
```

The error log output includes the time and date the message was logged, the source of the message, and the description of the error message. If an error occurs, the log will contain the error message number and description.

Tip

Spend some time looking at and understanding the messages in the
error log, especially the proper startup sequence messages. This
knowledge will come in handy in times of trouble!

You can view the error log using any text editor, such as Notepad, or you can use the
SQL Server Enterprise Manager. To use the Enterprise Manager, select Error Log
from the Server menu. The Server Error Log dialog box appears (see Figure 16.6).

Figure 16.6.
Server Error Log
dialog box.

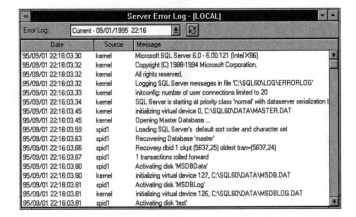

USING THE EVENT VIEWER

SQL Server also logs information and error messages to the Windows NT event log.
The event log is used by NT as a repository for the operating system and applications
to log informational and error messages. The Event Viewer is located in the
Windows NT Administrative Tools group. The advantage of using the Event Viewer
over the error log is that errors are easy to spot because NT highlights all error
messages with a red stop sign and information messages with a blue exclamation
mark (see Figure 16.7).

To view the detail error message description, severity level, and state, double-click
on the line item. A detail error dialog box appears. The Event Viewer also provides
a search utility that enables you to search for specific types of events in the event
log. For example, you can search for all the error messages in the event log.

Figure 16.7.
Windows NT Applica-
tion Event Log.

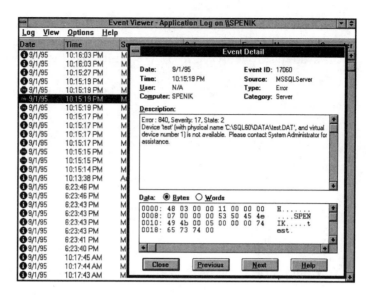

KILLING A PROCESS

A SQL Server *user process* is a task or request made to SQL Server by a user. Occasionally, you maybe required to halt (stop) a user process before it completes. Maybe the user has incorrectly formatted a query or launched a massive transaction that will take hours to complete and blocked out other users from necessary table information. Whatever the case may be, you can bet that sooner or later someone will ask you to stop his or her process or someone else will complain about not getting any information back. You name it—the list goes on! The proper terminology for halting a process is called *killing* a process, which sounds much more severe than just halting or stopping. When you kill a process, you completely remove the process from SQL Server.

Tip

The number one reason to kill a process is interference with other users' processing (that is, preventing them from getting to the required information by "blocking" them out, as in exclusive table locks, for a lengthy transaction).

SQL Server assigns each task a unique identity number called a *spid* (system process id). To view the currently running processes and their spids, you can issue the system stored procedure sp_who, which has the following format:

```
sp_who [login id ¦ 'spid']
Where login_id is a specfic user login id to report activity and spid is a specfic
process id to report activity.
```

Issuing the sp_who command with no parameters displays a report on all the current processes on SQL Server in the following example:

```
spid   status     loginame    hostname   blk   dbname    cmd
------ --------   --------    --------   ----  --------   --------------------
1      sleeping   sa                     0     master    MIRROR HANDLER
2      sleeping   sa                     0     master    LAZY WRITER
3      sleeping   sa                     0     master    CHECKPOINT SLEEP
4      runnable   sa                     0     master    RA MANAGER
10     sleeping   sa          SPENIK     0     master    AWAITING COMMAND
11     runnable   sa          SPENIK     0     master    SELECT
```

To kill a process, you use the KILL command, which has the following syntax:

```
KILL spid
```

where *spid* is the system process id of the process you want to kill.

You can only kill one spid at a time and the statement cannot be reversed. Once you have issued the command, the process will be killed. To kill the spid 11 shown in the previous sample, for example, you would issue the following command:

```
KILL 11
```

> ## Note
>
> In pre-system 10 versions of Sybase and pre-Windows NT versions of Microsoft SQL Server, the KILL command did not always work! If the spid was a sleeping process, the only way to kill the process was to shut down the server! The inability to kill a process with the KILL statement was kind of a joke among DBAs but also a problem when a process really did need to be shut down and the KILL command was ineffective. Microsoft corrected the problem in SQL Server for Windows NT 4.21.

You also can kill a process using the SQL Server Enterprise Manager by performing the following steps:

1. After you select a server, from the Enterprise Manager select Current Activity from the Tools menu. The Current Activity dialog box appears (see Figure 16.8).

Figure 16.8.
Current Activity
dialog box.

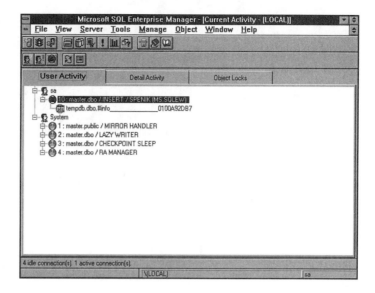

2. The current processes running on SQL Server as well as the spid of each process are displayed in the Current Activity dialog box.

Tip

You can view the last command executed by a process or the resource usage of the process (CPU and disk usage) by double-clicking on the process shown in the Current Activity dialog box (refer to Figure 16.8).

3. To kill a process, click on the process you want to terminate and then click on the Kill Process toolbar button in the Current Activity dialog box (see Figure 16.9). The selected process will be terminated.

16

TROUBLESHOOTING SQL SERVER

Figure 16.9.
Kill Process toolbar
button in the Current
Activity dialog box.

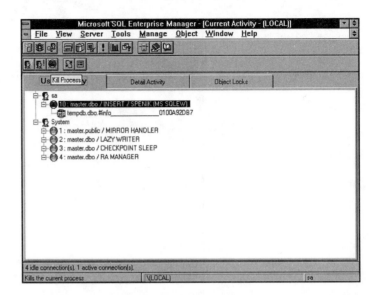

USING DBCC TO TROUBLESHOOT

DBCC stands for *Database Consistency Checker*. DBCC consists of a series of commands that perform many different functions on databases and database objects. You will use DBCC commands to perform database and database object maintenance but you also will use the output of DBCC commands to find errors, and in some cases, fix them.

For starters, when tracking for errors or problems, you will want to examine the output of your daily DBCC maintenance commands for standard SQL Server error messages. If you find an error message in a DBCC output, treat the error message like any other SQL Server error messages and use Books Online or technical support to resolve the error. When you call technical support or find the error number in the Books Online, one or many of the resolution steps may be to execute DBCC command(s) to resolve the problem. Suppose that you are trying to create an index in sorted order on the authors table, column au_lanme, in the pubs database, and the CREATE INDEX statement fails with the following error message:

```
Msg 1520, Level 18, State:1
Sort failed because dpages in the Sysindexes row for table 'authors' in database
'pubs' had an incorrect value. Please run DBCC CHECKTABLE on this
table to correct the value, then re-run your command.
```

The description in the error message suggests that you execute the DBCC command with the option CHECKTABLE. If you search Books Online for 1520, you will see a more detailed description of why the error message occurred and the following Action section (taken from Administrator's Companion, Books Online):

```
Action
To correct the page count, use one of the following statements:
dbcc tablealloc(tablename)
dbcc newalloc(databasename)
dbcc checktable(tablename)
After running DBCC, you should be able to create the index.
```

Become familiar with the DBCC commands. Use the correct DBCC options (if any) to fix a problem in your database when instructed to do so.

TABLE FRAGMENTATION

I have seen a lot of noise on various SQL Server forums about table fragmentation. *Table fragmentation* occurs on tables that have a lot of insert/update/delete activity. As the table is modified over a period of time, the fullness of each data page begins to vary (that is, pages are not full). You can defragment the table by dropping and re-creating the clustered index on the table, which will pack each page (with the fill factor amount) of data. Not only does this improve performance when reading the table, it also can increase the amount of available database space. Because rebuilding a clustered index on a very large table can take a fair amount of time, SQL Server 6.0 now provides the DBCC SHOWCONTIG command that enables you to determine how fragmented a table or index is (that is, whether you need to rebuild it). The SHOWCONTIG option has the following format:

```
DBCC SHOWCONTIG (table id, [index id])
```

where `table id` and `index id` are the ids of the object found in the `sysobjects` table of the database. For example, the following is the command line and output from a DBCC SHOWCONTIG command performed on the `authors` table in the pubs database:

```
DBCC SHOWCONTIG(16003088)
DBCC SHOWCONTIG scanning 'authors' table...
[SHOW_CONTIG - SCAN ANALYSIS]
--------------------------------------------------------------------
Table: 'authors' (16003088)  Indid: 1  dbid:4
TABLE level scan performed.
- Pages Scanned................................: 1
- Extent Switches..............................: 0
- Avg. Pages per Extent........................: 1.0
- Scan Density [Best Count:Actual Count].......: 100.00% [0:1]
- Avg. Bytes free per page.....................: 89.0
- Avg. Page density (full).....................: 95.58%
- Overflow Pages...............................: 0
- Disconnected Overflow Pages..................: 0
DBCC execution completed. If DBCC printed error messages, see your System Adminis-
trator.
```

OTHER SOURCES OF HELP AND INFORMATION

Microsoft has done a good job in SQL Server 6.0 of providing useful and valuable information in Books Online, but as a DBA, it is important to know that there are many other good sources of information for Microsoft SQL Server (such as this book). But what happens when the problem is beyond the scope of published resources? The following sections discuss some of the options available to you.

TECHNICAL SUPPORT

When you run across a problem that is not covered in the book or is of a very critical and urgent nature, it's time to get in touch with your tech support company. If you have purchased SQL Server, hopefully, you have purchased a support agreement with Microsoft or with a Microsoft Solution Provider to help you in the event of an emergency. If not, Microsoft will still provide help and charge you per incident. My experience with Microsoft tech support has been very good. In general, Microsoft support contracts and agreements are much less expensive than some of the other RDBMS companies. A Microsoft Solution Provider is an independent organization that provides consulting and integration services for Microsoft products and also can provide support. Before calling tech support, be sure to have all the information required to start an incident report. You should have the following information:

◆ Hardware platform

◆ Version of Windows NT

◆ Version of SQL Server (you can get this from the error log or the @@Version global variable)

◆ Complete error message (number, level, state, and description)

◆ Type of environment (production/development)

◆ Urgency of problem resolution

◆ Description and scenario of the problem and the cause

Tip

If the problem is one that can be reproduced by using SQL commands or a sequence of events, have this information written down so that the tech support person can duplicate the results.

MICROSOFT TECHNET

Before there was SQL Server 6.0 Books Online, there was *Microsoft TechNet*. Microsoft TechNet is a monthly CD subscription containing a wealth of information about Microsoft products. TechNet provides product white papers, release notes, current patches and drivers, and a knowledge base of product information and problem resolution. TechNet costs only a few hundred dollars (I won't quote a price since it's subject to change).

Tip

TechNet is my second line of defense. If I can't resolve the problem based on my knowledge and the Books Online, I check TechNet for a information on the problem. Do yourself a favor and subscribe!

The advantage of TechNet is that it is a monthly CD, so problem resolution that was not available when SQL Server 6.0 shipped can be placed in the TechNet knowledge base for your immediate use. TechNet's search facility looks identical to the Books Online search facility (or should I say vice versa since TechNet was here first!), as shown in Figure 16.10. Like Books Online, you can perform searches on error numbers or keywords and get a list of articles that contain the keyword or error number.

Figure 16.10.
Microsoft TechNet.

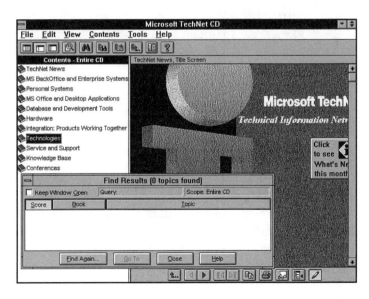

ONLINE SERVICES

To obtain interactive support without using your tech support, try one of the interactive Microsoft SQL Server forums. Currently, forums exist on CompuServe (GO MSSQL) and on the new Microsoft Network. Using the online services, you can search for existing messages that deal with problems you are experiencing. You also can post messages asking for help from your peers. I find the online services to be very useful and well worth the small monthly fee. Many individuals have their problems resolved on the online services, but most of these are of a noncritical nature since turn-around time on a posted question is an unknown.

USER GROUPS

SQL Server user groups can provide a forum to discuss problems or issues with your local peers. They also tend to enlighten you on current products and future releases.

BETWEEN THE LINES

- ◆ SQL Server displays error messages in the following format: Msg #, Level #, State #, Description.
- ◆ If an error occurs, write down the entire message, not just a part of it.
- ◆ Use Books Online and the Microsoft TechNet search facilities to help resolve problems.
- ◆ Make a point to understand the SQL Server error log.
- ◆ Check the Windows NT Event Log for errors by using the Event Viewer search facility.
- ◆ Stop user processes with the KILL command.
- ◆ Stay informed by taking advantage of user groups and online services.

SUMMARY

You should now know where to search for SQL Server error messages and understand the format and meaning of SQL Server error messages. In Chapter 23, you will learn how to perform maintenance on your SQL Server. This chapter set up the foundation for you in understanding how to interpret and research the potential error messages that you may receive during routine maintenance. Another important point is to be a good DBA, get involved in your local SQL Server user group or spend a few hours a week on an online service, interacting with your peers and learning more about SQL Server.

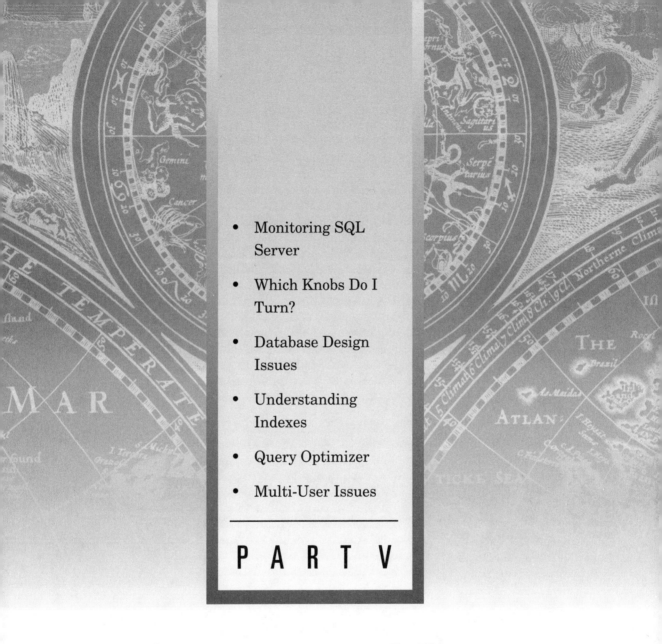

- Monitoring SQL Server

- Which Knobs Do I Turn?

- Database Design Issues

- Understanding Indexes

- Query Optimizer

- Multi-User Issues

PART V

Performance and Tuning

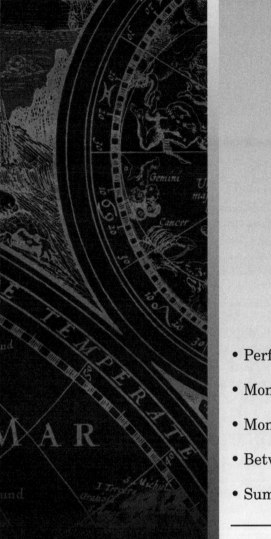

- Performance Monitor

- Monitoring

- Monitoring Users

- Between the Lines

- Summary

CHAPTER 17

Monitoring SQL Server

SQL Server provides several utilities that allow you to easily monitor SQL Server and its interaction with the operating system. These utilities can help a DBA quickly isolate bottlenecks and determine hardware deficiencies.

PERFORMANCE MONITOR

The *Performance Monitor* is an excellent tool for monitoring SQL Server and the Windows NT operating system. The advantage of the Performance Monitor is that it is tightly integrated with the operating system. This enables you to track real time statistics about SQL Server and Windows NT. Together these statistics can be used to isolate bottlenecks and track performance.

Note

The Performance Monitor may slightly degrade system performance. The overhead incurred from the Performance Monitor has been found to be 5 percent or less on single processor machines and insignificant on multiple processor machines.

USING THE PERFORMANCE MONITOR

The following steps explain how to use the Performance Monitor.

1. Double-click on the SQL Performance Monitor icon in the Microsoft SQL Server 6.0 program group.

Figure 17.1.
SQL Performance
Monitor icon.

Click here ———

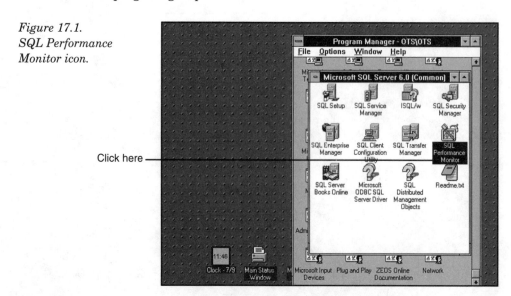

This displays the Performance Monitor dialog box (see Figure 17.2).

Figure 17.2.
Performance Monitor
dialog box.

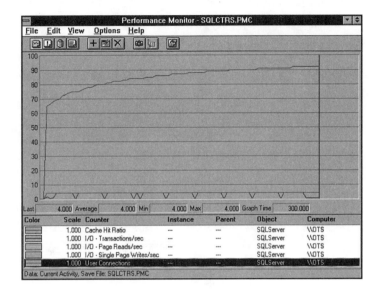

By default, the Performance Monitor for SQL Server will track the following five predefined counters:

◆ Cache Hit Ratio

◆ I/O - Transactions/sec

◆ I/O - Page Reads/sec

◆ I/O - Single Page Writes/sec

◆ User Connections

Note

The five default counters are useful, but they do not give a complete picture of SQL Server or Windows NT. Therefore, you will likely want to add additional counters to get a clearer understanding of system performance.

ADDING ADDITIONAL COUNTERS

The following steps explain how to add additional counters to the Performance Monitor.

1. From the Performance Monitor dialog box, select Add To Chart from the Edit menu.

2. Select the object type and counter type. Click on the Add button to add the counter to the chart (see Figure 17.3).

Figure 17.3.
Adding counters
to a chart.

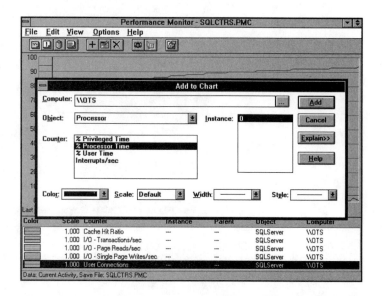

Note

Chart settings are only valid for the life of the chart. You must manually save the chart if you want to save your chart settings. From the File menu, select Save or Save As to save the current chart to disk.

MONITORING

The Performance Monitor may be overwhelming because it provides so much information. You can track over 40 different counters in regards to SQL Server and hundreds of different counters in regards to Windows NT. Trying to track this much information will drive you crazy!

Instead of trying to track everything at once, you should monitor the following five key areas (see Figure 17.4):

◆ Memory

◆ Processor

◆ Disk I/O

◆ User Connections

◆ Locks

These five indicators will quickly clue you in to performance bottlenecks. After you determine the general bottleneck source, you should look into the other types of counters not mentioned in this chapter (use the *Windows NT Resource* Guide for additional information).

Note

When using the Performance Monitor, it is important to monitor key counters over time and establish patterns before making rash decisions. Be sure to understand the types of operations being performed by SQL Server before adding a new processor or additional memory. Otherwise, a hardware improvement based on incomplete data may not yield the desired improvement in performance.

Figure 17.4.
Recommended counters
to watch.

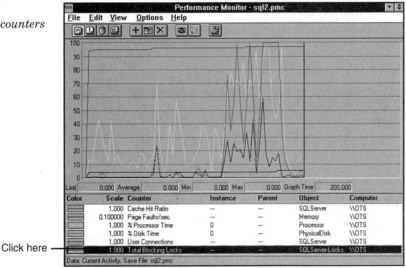

Click here

MEMORY

SQL Server likes memory. It uses memory to hold data and frequently accessed objects. An increase in memory may allow SQL Server to place more data into the memory cache. This may result in better performance.

When diagnosing memory, the following counters are useful to monitor:

◆ SQLServer: Cache Hit Ratio

◆ Memory: Page Faults/sec

◆ SQLServer: I/O - Lazy Writes

SQLSERVER: CACHE HIT RATIO

This counter monitors the hit rate in which data was found in the data cache. If the data is not in the data cache, the server will have to read the data from disk. This counter generally provides an accurate indication of memory allocation that can be used to determine whether you have sufficient memory.

A number consistently less than 85 percent may indicate that you have insufficient memory. Performance may suffer because SQL Server will have to read the data from physical disk. Reading data from the physical disk is an expensive operation. When evaluating this counter it is important to base it on the type of operation being performed on the machine and when the operation occurs. In a transaction processing environment, you can probably improve the cache hit ratio by adding more memory. In a batch environment that uses very large databases, the cache hit ratio may never go above 85 percent. Under this scenario, additional memory may not substantially improve performance.

MEMORY: PAGE FAULTS / SEC

This counter monitors the number of times a virtual page was not found in memory. When a page is not found in memory, the operating system must retrieve the page from disk. The time it takes to retrieve a page from disk will always be longer than the time required to retrieve the page from memory.

After the SQL Server has stabilized, this number should remain at or near 0. If the number is consistently greater than 0, this indicates that too much memory is allocated to SQL Server and not enough memory is allocated to Windows NT. Therefore, you should reduce the amount of memory allocated to SQL Server.

SQLSERVER: I/O - LAZY WRITES

This counter monitors the number of flushed pages per second by the Lazy Writer.

A number constantly greater than 0 indicates that Lazy Writer is constantly working to flush buffers to disk. This means that the data cache is too small which indicates that you have insufficient memory.

PROCESSOR

SQL Server is CPU intensive. Continuously high utilization rates may indicate that your CPU is the bottleneck. The best way to determine if your CPU is the bottleneck is to use the % Processor Time counter.

PROCESSOR: % PROCESSOR TIME

This counter monitors the amount of time the CPU spends processing a thread.

A steady state value above 80–90 percent may indicate that a CPU upgrade or the additional processors can significantly improve performance.

Note

Scalability (the capability to gain performance through additional processors) has been greatly improved with SQL Server Version 6.0. Previous versions of SQL Server did not scale well when multiple processors were added to the computer. Benchmark tests have shown that in an On-Line Transaction Processing (OLTP) environment, SQL Server 6.0 will scale in a relatively linear fashion up to four processors.

DISK I/O

You always want to minimize disk I/O when working with SQL Server. However, when SQL Server does read and write to the hard disk, you want to ensure adequate disk performance. If you are not achieving adequate disk I/O, transaction throughput will suffer.

To help detect disk I/O bottlenecks you should monitor the following two counters:

◆ PhysicalDisk: % Disk Time
◆ PhysicalDisk: Disk Queue Length.

Note

You must run the diskperf command before you can monitor disk performance statistics. To enable diskperf, go to the command prompt and type the following:

    diskperf -y,

and shut down and restart the computer.

Warning

Disk I/O values will vary from one type of disk system to another. You should contact your disk manufacture to determine acceptable counter values.

PHYSICALDISK: % DISK TIME

This counter monitors the percentage of elapsed time that the disk is busy with read/write activity.

A consistently high value indicates that your disk system is a possible bottleneck.

PHYSICALDISK: DISK QUEUE LENGTH

This counter monitors the number of outstanding requests on disk.

A consistently high value for one physical disk combined with a consistently low value for your other physical disks indicates that redistributing your data may improve performance. Examine your device and segment configuration. Sustained queue lengths greater than 3 may indicate a potential bottleneck.

USER CONNECTIONS

How many times have you been hit with the following problem?

> System performance crawls during peak business hours. These are the hours when everyone in the company is banging away on the system. Transactions are being processed at a snail's pace and your phone is ringing off the hook with irate users.

I think every DBA, at one time or another, has experienced this problem. It is no secret that as the number of active users increases, the likelihood of performance degradation also increases.

To help track why and when user connection bottlenecks occur I suggest using the following counters:

◆ `SQLServer: User connections`

◆ `SQLServer: Net - Network Reads/sec.`

SQLSERVER: USER CONNECTIONS

This counter monitors the number of active user connections.

Use this counter to help determine when the number of active users exceeds the capabilities of your system. You may find that performance is exceptional with 50 users, adequate with 75 users, and horrendous with more than 100 users.

Tip

The SQLServer: User connections counter can also be used to help determine the appropriate configuration value for user connections. If the number of active user connections is significantly below the number of available user connections, you are probably wasting memory. Each connection uses 37K of memory, regardless of connection status.

SQLSERVER: NET - NETWORK READS / SEC

This counter monitors the number of data packets read from the network.

If you are currently not using stored procedures and you find that this counter is high and you're transaction rate is low, you may be able to improve performance by implementing stored procedures. Stored procedures will help reduce the amount of network traffic. If this counter is extremely high for an extended period of time, you may be able to improve performance by using faster Network Interface Cards.

LOCKS

SQL Server uses locks to ensure data consistency in a multi-user environment. You often will see various degrees of locking activity during normal processing. Be on the lookout for *blocking locks*. A blocking lock is a lock that forces another process to wait until the current process is complete. When monitoring blocking, use the SQLServer-Locks: Total Blocking Locks counter.

SQLSERVER-LOCKS: TOTAL BLOCKING LOCKS

This counter monitors the number of all locks that are blocking other processes.

An occasional block or two is usually unavoidable. Be on the lookout for blocking levels consistently greater than zero. This usually indicates serious transaction problems. Blocking can be caused by a variety of factors. Some of the basic causes of blocking are inefficient query design, poor table design, and slow throughput due to inadequate hardware.

MONITORING USERS

In addition to monitoring SQL Server activity, it may be useful to monitor individual user activity. Through the Enterprise Manager you can view user connections, locks, process numbers, and user commands.

Note

> The capability to graphically monitor detailed information about user information is new to Version 6.0 of SQL Server. Previous versions provided limited user activity information.

USING THE USER ACTIVITY MONITOR

One of the best features of the User Activity Monitor is the capability to view more information about a process. This is a major plus for DBAs! It gives you all the information you need to know about a process. You can use this information to help kill a process or to pinpoint a query that is a burden to the system.

The following steps explain how to use the User Activity Monitor.

1. Click on the Current Activity toolbar button from the Enterprise Manager window (see Figure 17.5). This displays the Current Activity dialog box (see Figure 17.6).

Figure 17.5.
Current Activity toolbar button.

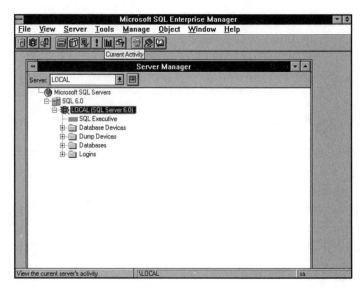

Figure 17.6.
Current Activity
dialog box.

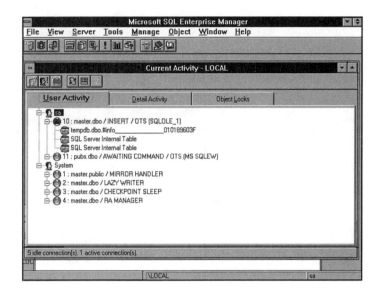

2. From the Current Activity dialog box, you can view three types of information: User Activity, Detail Activity, and Objects Locks. Click on the corresponding tab in the Current Activity dialog box window to view each type of information (see Figures 17.7, 17.8, and 17.9).

Figure 17.7.
User activity.

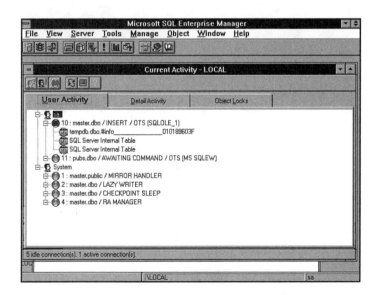

Figure 17.8.
Detail activity.

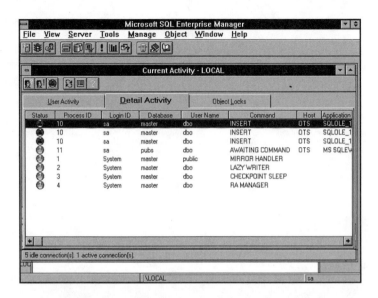

Figure 17.9.
Object locks.

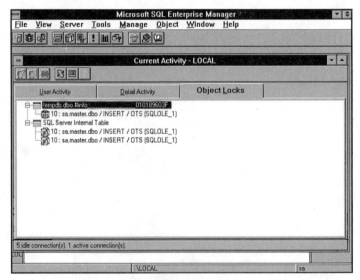

Tip

Click on the Toggle Legend toolbar button to display a legend for
activity information (see Figure 17.10).

17

Figure 17.10.
Activity Legend.

Tip

Be on the lookout for blocking when users are complaining that their transactions are hung. Select the Detail Activity tab from the Current Activity dialog box to view blocked processes.

4. From within the Current Activity dialog box, click on the More Info toolbar button to view more information about a process. This displays the Process Information dialog box (see Figure 17.11). From this dialog box, you can view the last statement issued by the user, kill a process, and send a message to the user.

Note

The send message feature is only available for Microsoft networks.

Figure 17.11.
Process Information
dialog box.

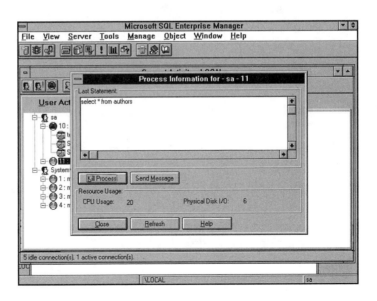

Tip

The Transact SQL commands sp_who, sp_lock, KILL, and DBCC INPUTBUFFER and OUTPUTBUFFER can be used to perform functions similar to the functions found in the User Activity monitor.

BETWEEN THE LINES

The following are some of the important tips and trick to read between the line when monitoring SQL Server:

- ◆ The Performance Monitor is an excellent tool for monitoring SQL Server and the Windows NT operating system.

- ◆ On a single processor machine, the Performance Monitor may slightly degrade system performance.

- ◆ Don't let the Performance Monitor drive you crazy! Rather than trying to track a multitude of counters, track five to eight key performance indicators. Anything over eight to ten different counters makes it difficult to determine what is going on.

- ◆ Following are some useful counters to track:
    - ◆ SQLServer: Cache Hit Ratio
    - ◆ Processor: % Processor Time
    - ◆ PhysicalDisk: % Disk Time
    - ◆ SQLServer: User connections
    - ◆ SQLServer: Net - Network Reads/sec
    - ◆ SQLServer-Locks: Total Blocking Locks

- ◆ You must run diskperf before you can monitor disk performance statistics.

- ◆ Use the User Activity monitor to track user connections, locks, and process numbers. The User Activity monitor can also be used view the SQL commands issued from each user.

SUMMARY

The Performance Monitor and User Activity monitor are two valuable tools for tracking server utilization and pinpointing bottlenecks. All DBAs should keep an eye on their system by tracking a few key counters. The next chapter discusses server configuration and tuning.

CHAPTER 18

Which Knobs Do I Turn?

You now have SQL Server installed and running. Maybe you are about to roll out your first production database and your boss is breathing down your neck asking, "Mr. (or Madam) DBA, have you tuned and optimized the server?" You tell your boss no, but tuning and optimizing SQL Server was next on your list. You bring up the SQL Enterprise Manager. You begin to stare at the Enterprise Manager configuration screen and ask yourself, "So, which knobs do I turn?"

In this chapter, you will learn how to modify SQL Server's configuration parameters. Each configuration parameter and its function and effect on SQL Server performance and tuning will be examined. When SQL Server is installed, the configuration parameters are given an initial default value. Microsoft has done a good job of selecting default values for the configuration parameters. In many cases, the default values will provide the optimum performance for your database server. SQL Server enables you to set over 45 parameters. We will use tips to highlight the most commonly tuned parameters. This is not to say that you do not want to touch the other parameters, but in general, the default settings will be sufficient.

To Tune Or Not To Tune?

Keep in mind as you start to tune SQL Server that you are tuning the database server. Other factors, such as the hardware configuration chosen for the database, the network the database clients and SQL Server belong to, and the overall size and structure of your databases, affect the performance of the database server.

I have a friend who used to work for a Fortune 500 company that was bringing several SQL Servers online. He had spent some time tuning SQL Server and everything was up and running quite smoothly. As the days went on, the organization started to experience problems with a particular application running progressively slower. Upper management thought the problem must be a SQL Server configuration problem. My friend tried to explain to them that the problem was not a SQL Server tuning issue but an application issue. He explained how they had done everything right: researched and purchased a very fast RAID 5 machine, tuned Windows NT Server, and then used SQL Server tools to properly configure SQL Server.

Management didn't buy it, so they brought in another consulting firm with a highly certified and expensive specialist. The specialist examined the SQL Server and did not change any configurations parameters because they were all reasonably set. So, the hired guns ended up leaving without fixing anything and upper management were left scratching their heads. I stopped by to see if I could help them out, and as it turned out, their problem was failure to issue a simple command that needed to be executed on three of their tables (UPDATE STATISTICS, what else?)!

The moral of the story is that many things affect the overall performance of SQL Server. Performance issues start from square one when you research and purchase the machine and set up Windows NT Server. Too often, the real problems are not understood and tuning SQL Server is the answer. Tuning SQL Server enables the Server to use the available resources on the machine optimally but will not prevent problems resulting from poor database and application design or failure to perform periodic maintenance. It is important to understand the value and limitations of tuning SQL Server. Oh yeah, when queries are running slow and the table has the correct indexes—remember the UPDATE STATISTICS command. In many cases, it will fix the problem!

Configuring SQL Server

Before discussing the many different configuration parameters, you next learn how to modify SQL Server parameters using the Enterprise Manager. Start up the Enterprise Manager, select a SQL Server, and perform the following steps:

1. From the Enterprise Manager, select Configurations from the Server menu. The Server Configuration/Options dialog appears (see Figure 18.1).

2. Click the Configuration tab in the Server Configuration/Options dialog box to display the Configuration tab (see Figure 18.2).

The Configuration tab displays the SQL Server configuration parameters. The Configuration column displays the SQL Server configuration parameter. The Minimum and Maximum columns display the minimum acceptable value for the configuration parameter and the maximum acceptable value for the configuration parameter. The value currently in use by SQL Server is displayed in the Running column. The Current column contains the current value of the SQL Server configuration parameter.

Figure 18.1.
Server Configuration /
Options dialog box.

Figure 18.2.
The Configuration tab
in the Server
Configuration / Options
dialog box.

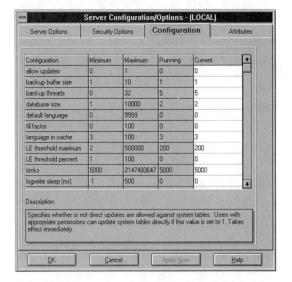

Note

What is the difference between the Running column and the Current column? Most of the time, the two values will be the same. As you start to change and modify SQL Server configurations, however, the Current column will reflect changes that you have made. These changes will not become the running value until you choose the OK button on the Server Configuration/Options dialog box or for some configuration variables, shut down and restart the server.

3. To edit a configuration parameter, enter the new value in the Current column of the configuration value you want to modify. Make sure the value entered is within ranges displayed in the Maximum and Minimum columns.

Tip

Take advantage of the description that appears in the description box when you select a configuration parameter. The description text gives a summary of the configuration value and when the changed value will take effect (such as immediately or requires stopping and restarting SQL Server). Special thanks to the Microsoft development team whp put this screen together! It makes configuring SQL Server so much easier (anyone that has had to use sp_configure and look up minimum and maximum values knows what I mean)!

4. To change the configuration value immediately and stay in the Server Configuration/Options dialog box, click the Apply Now button.

To change the modified variables and exit the Server Configuration/Options dialog box, click on the OK button. To cancel any modifications made, click on the Cancel button.

Warning

If you modify a configuration parameter(s) and then select the Apply Now button, the changes are made to SQL Server. If you then click on the Cancel button, the changes are *not* rolled back!

When you click on the Apply Now or OK buttons, the current value of the modified configuration parameters is changed. The running value is changed if the value can be modified without stopping and restarting SQL Server.

STRANGER THAN FICTION!

While I was modifying a configuration value that could be updated immediately, I noticed that the value displayed in the Running column of the Server Configuration/Options dialog box did not change to the Current column value when I clicked the Apply Now button. I thought this was pretty strange since *apply now* means just that—

change the configuration and running value now if the value can be changed without restarting SQL Server. So I pressed F1 to display the help screen, which states

"Apply Now - Applies the information you have specified. For values that take effect immediately, you must close the Server Configuration/Options dialog box for the value to take effect."

After reading the help, I was even more confused because now I can't determine the difference between the OK button and the Apply Now button. Do they both take effect when you close out the Server Configurations/Options dialog box? Well, I brought up a second instance of the Enterprise Manager and did some testing using the Server Configuration/Options dialog box on one instance to change values and the second instance using sp_configure to check values. Guess what I found. The configuration values do take effect when you click the Apply Now button; however, the Server Configurations/Options dialog box is not refreshed! The configuration value takes effect when you click the Apply Now button, not when you close the window! Closing the window forces you to redisplay the Server Configuration/Options dialog box (that is, refreshing the display) to see the changed values. Hmmm, since it's in the help file, it must be a feature not a bug, right?

To change system configuration parameters the way those poor folks stuck in the dark ages of ISQL (Sybase) do, use the system stored procedure sp_configure, which has the following syntax:

```
sp_configure [configuration_name [, configuration_value]]
```

where

configuration_name is the configuration parameter name you wish to change

configuration_value is the new value for the configuration parameter

Note

Using sp_configure with no parameters displays the current SQL Server configuration.

SQL Server configuration values are stored in the system table sysconfigures. If you use sp_configure to modify an option , you must use the RECONFIGURE command to make the change take effect. RECONFIGURE has the following syntax:

```
RECONFIGURE [WITH OVERRIDE]
```

where WITH OVERIDE is only required when setting the allow updates configuration parameter to 1. This provides an added security check to make sure you really want to modify `allow updates`.

We have mentioned several times configuration parameters that can take effect without restarting SQL Server. These configuration parameters are referred to as *dynamic configuration variables* and are as follows:

- `allow updates`
- `backup buffer size`
- `cursor threshold`
- `free buffers`
- `LE threshold Maximum`
- `LE threshold Minimum`
- `LE threshold Percent`
- `logwrite sleep`
- `max lazywrite IO`
- `max worker threads`
- `network packet size`
- `RA cache hit limit`
- `RA cache miss limit`
- `RA delay`
- `RA pre-fetches`
- `RA slots per thread`
- `recovery interval`
- `remote login timeout`
- `remote query timeout`
- `resource timeout`
- `show advanced options`
- `sort pages`
- `spin counter`

CONFIGURATION PARAMETERS

The following sections examine in alphabetical order each of the SQL Server configuration parameters, except in special cases, such as when parameters will be grouped together (memory configuration parameters, for example). Also, the advanced options will be reviewed separately from the standard options. Start with the most important tunable configuration parameters—memory.

MEMORY PARAMETERS

By this time, you have already made several decisions that will affect the performance of your SQL Server, such as the type of computer and disk system you have chosen. Now comes the question, "Which knobs do I turn?" or "Which parameters do I change?" As a Microsoft SQL Server DBA, the most important parameters to configure are the memory parameters. In general, SQL Server loves memory; that is, the performance of your SQL Server system can be enhanced by adding more memory. SQL Server is not a memory hog and is very smart with memory usage, particularly data caching. How does SQL Server use memory? Look at Figure 18.3 to understand how memory is allocated.

Figure 18.3.
Windows NT and SQL
Server memory usage.

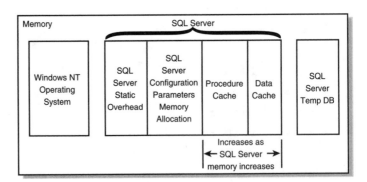

Before you can give memory to SQL Server, you must allocate enough memory for Windows NT Server to run sufficiently. The minimum memory requirement for Windows NT Server is 12MB but the amount of memory required by Windows NT will vary, depending on the overall use of the NT Server. For a dedicated SQL Server machine, I like to start out with 16MB of memory for the NT Server and then work my way up, if necessary. When the operating system requirements are met, you then can allocate memory for SQL Server. SQL Server will request the memory configuration parameter amount of memory from the Windows NT operating system and then use the allocated memory to set up shop. SQL Server uses the memory as follows.

First, a certain amount of memory is allocated for SQL Server overhead, which includes the size of the SQL Server executable. The amount of SQL Server static overhead is roughly 2MB and is not affected in any way by configuration parameters.

SQL Server then allocates memory for various configuration options, such as user connections and open databases (for example, each user connection configured in

SQL Server requires 37K of memory up front). The remaining amount of memory is then used for the procedure cache (stores most recent stored procedures and query trees) and the data cache (stores the most recently used data and index pages). As you increase the amount of SQL Server memory, the size of the procedure cache and disk cache increase, boosting performance because SQL Server can retrieve more information from memory without performing disk I/O to retrieve the information. If the temporary database (tempdb) has been placed in RAM, SQL Server requests the memory to create the database from the Windows NT operating system during startup.

Warning

An important point to remember, if the temporary database, tempdb, is placed in RAM, the memory allocated to the temporary database is *not part of the memory configured* for SQL Server! I have seen many SQL Server systems fail to start because someone had switched the temporary database to RAM, and allocated all the remaining memory to SQL Server, assuming that tempdb in RAM was taken from SQL Server's memory allocation!

If you find yourself in this situation, you can restart SQL Server using the default settings by adding the startup parameter -f to the SQL Server startup parmeter list. You can find the startup parameter list under the option Set Server Options in the SQL Setup program.

MONITORING MEMORY

This section offers some tips to help you determine the correct amount of memory for your SQL Server. The primary tools are the SQL Performance Monitor and the DBCC MEMUSAGE command. To determine whether you have enough memory or too much memory, use the Performance Monitor and watch the counters shown in Table 18.1.

TABLE 18.1. PERFORMANCE MONITOR COUNTER FOR TUNING SQL SERVER MEMORY.

Performance Monitor Object	Counter
Memory	Page Faults/sec
SQLServer	Cache Hit Ratio
SQLServer	I/O Page Reads/sec

The first step, and one of the most important steps when trying to tune SQL Server for memory, is to make sure that you are running your typical processes and work loads on SQL Server while you are using the Performance Monitor. The idea behind tuning SQL Server for memory is to keep a high `Cache Hit Ratio` (that is, data being retrieved is in the cache), low physical I/O (disk I/O is low since data pages are in memory), and no page faults (a page fault occurs when not enough memory has been allocated to Windows NT, causing Windows NT to rely heavily on virtual memory). If your `Cache Hit Ratio` is below 85 to 90 percent, your SQL Server may benefit from increased memory. If the number of `I/O Page Reads/sec` remains high during your tuning sessions, then you may have an insufficient amount of memory allocated to SQL Server (or a sub-standard disk drive system). An `I/O Page Reads/sec` counter value of `0` reflects the data being retrieved is in memory. If you are continuously experiencing page faults, then you have allocated too much memory to SQL Server and not enough to Windows NT. The problem can be corrected by reducing the amount of memory allocated to SQL Server or by adding more physical memory to be used by Windows NT. Before tuning for memory, configure your procedure cache and data cache first and then use the Performance Monitor to determine the correct amount of memory.

Note

When tuning SQL Server memory as just described, in many of the different counter scenarios the word *may* was used instead of *will* to describe whether or not adding more memory would benefit your SQL Server. Why so vague? In many cases, adding additional memory to SQL Server will increase the performance of you system by keeping more information in the cache. However, other factors come into play that cannot be accounted for in a generalized sense. You need to be aware of the type of actions taking place on SQL Server while you are watching the performance monitor and tuning SQL Server. For example, if the work load executing on SQL Server is accessing the same values in a table over and over, you should see a high `Cache Hit Ratio` indicating that you have sufficient memory allocated to SQL Server. But, if in your actual production environment, many different tables and databases are being accessed instead of one table, your tuning session did not reflect your production environment and your assumption of sufficient memory may have been wrong.

This can also work in reverse. Your tuning session may access many different tables and databases simultaneously, indicating insufficient memory allocation. However, in your actual production environment the typical situation is that the same data is being retrieved over and over (that is, enhancing the chance of being in the cache), which would change your assumption of your required memory allocation. Make sure you tune to your production environment and carefully evaluate your results.

To determine the actual memory pages used by the procedure cache and the data cache, subtract the total SQL Server static overhead and overhead from SQL Server configuration values from the total amount of memory allocated to SQL Server. To get the size of the procedure cache, multiply the total cache page value by the default percentage value of the procedure cache. For the data cache, subtract the procedure cache from the total cache value. For example, a SQL Server system has a configuration value of 16MB of memory. Assume the static and configuration values overhead are 3MB. The amount of memory available for the caches is 16MB – 3MB = 13MB.

To determine the size of the procedure cache using the default value of 30, 13MB × 30% (.30) = 3.9MB for the procedure cache. The data cache is 13MB – 3.9MB (size of procedure cache) = 9.1MB data cache.

Note

To determine the amount of memory consumed by configuration variables, multiply the configured values for each of the following configuration parameters by the approximate amount of memory consumed by object and add the totals:

Locks	32 bytes
User Connections	37K
Open Databases	4K
Open Objects	40 bytes
Devices	127.5K

Total for 255 configured devices in SQL Server 6.0

To double-check your memory computations, use the DBCC MEMUSAGE command to get the exact sizes of SQL Server and configuration overhead, as well as the size of the procedure and data cache. The following partial listing is actual output from a DBCC MEMUSAGE command:

LISTING 18.1. PARTIAL DBCC MEMUSAGE OUTPUT.

```
Memory Usage:

                        Meg.      2K Blks     Bytes

   Configured Memory:  8.0000      4096      8388608
          Code size:   1.7166       871       800000
   Static Structures:  0.2385       123       250048
              Locks:   0.2480       127       260000
       Open Objects:   0.1068        55       112000
     Open Databases:   0.0031         2         3220
```

continues

LISTING 18.1. CONTINUED

User Context Areas:	0.8248	423	864824
Page Cache:	3.3020	1691	3462416
Proc Headers:	0.0795	41	83326
Proc Cache Bufs:	1.3359	684	1400832

Using the terminology established earlier to compute the SQL Server memory breakdown, the DBCC MEMUSAGE output translates as follows:

```
Configured Memory = Total Amount of Memory Allocated to SQL Server
Code Size + Static Structures = SQL Server Overhead
Locks + Open Objects + Open Databases + User Context Areas = Configuration Overhead
Page Cache = Data Cache
Proc Headers + Proc Buffers = Procedure Cache
```

The DBCC MEMUSAGE command also prints out the 20 buffered tables and indexes in the cache, as well as the top 20 items in the procedure cache. Listing 18.2 shows a partial listing of the top 20 procedures from a DBCC MEMUSAGE command output.

LISTING 18.2. DBCC MEMUSAGE PARTIAL LISTING: ITEMS IN PROCEDURE CACHE.

```
Procedure Cache, Top 20:

Procedure Name: sp_MSdbuserprofile
Database Id: 1
Object Id: 233051866
Version: 1
Uid: 1
Type: stored procedure
Number of trees: 0
Size of trees: 0.000000 Mb, 0.000000 bytes, 0 pages
Number of plans: 2
Size of plans: 0.144749 Mb, 151780.000000 bytes, 76 pages

Procedure Name: sp_help
Database Id: 1
Object Id: 1888009757
Version: 1
Uid: 1
Type: stored procedure
Number of trees: 0
Size of trees: 0.000000 Mb, 0.000000 bytes, 0 pages
Number of plans: 1
Size of plans: 0.051249 Mb, 53738.000000 bytes, 27 pages
```

MEMORY

The memory configuration parameter sets the amount of memory allocated to SQL Server from the operating system. The values are represented in 2K (2048 byte) units. For example, 16MB would be 16MB/2K = 8192 pages. In general, adding memory to SQL Server increases the performance of your system.

Use the Performance Monitor and the DBCC command MEMUSAGE to help you properly configure your SQL Server with the appropriate amount of memory.

Tip

Is it possible to have too much memory? The answer is yes! If you allocate too much memory to SQL Server, you can decrease the performance of your SQL Server by causing excessive paging. To determine whether you have allocated too much memory to SQL Server, use the Performance Monitor and watch the counter Page Faults/sec. If page faults are being generated, then you are running SQL Server with too much memory. Reduce the configuration amount and check again.

Microsoft prints out a table of suggested memory allocation for SQL Server, based on amount of memory on the computer, which can be found on the Books Online. Remember that the table is just a suggested starting point; you should always determine the correct amount of memory by monitoring your SQL Server.

Minimum: 1000 (2MB)
Maximum: 1048576 (2GB)
Default: Depends on setup, 8 MB for computers < 32MB, 16MB for computers with > 32MB
Dynamic Variable: No

Warning

Be careful about allocating more memory to SQL Server and Windows NT than is physically available (that is, relying on virtual memory). Configuring SQL Server so that it uses virtual memory exceeding a ratio of 1:1 can hurt SQL Server performance and will show up as excessive paging in the Performance Monitor.

TEMPDB IN RAM

The temporary database, tempdb, is used by SQL Server, applications, and developers as a temporary work area for creating temporary tables or storing temporary information. For example, a developer may create a temporary work table in a stored procedure or SQL Server may create a temporary work table as a result of a query with a group by or order by clause. The temporary database resides on disk as part of the master device and has a default size of 4MB. Like a regular database, the size of tempdb can be increased via the ALTER database command. In SQL Server 4.21 for Windows NT, Microsoft included the option to allow the temporary database to reside in memory.

Minimum: 0
Maximum: 2044 (Note: Depends on the size of your temporary database)
Default: 0
Dynamic Variable: No

DEVELOPERS FEEL THE NEED FOR TEMPDB IN RAM

When this feature first came out, I was working with a group of developers who had SA privileges on one of the development servers. They could not wait to put the temporary database in RAM to help speed up their stored procedures, which made heavy use of temporary tables. The problem was the development machine had only a modest 32MB of memory. SQL Server had been configured as 16MB of memory and tempdb had the default size of 4MB. At the time, the developers thought that the memory from tempdb was part of the 16MB configured with SQL Server, since in 4.21 it was not well documented exactly where the memory for tempdb in RAM was coming from.

These guys placed tempdb in RAM, stopped and restarted the system, and were as happy as could be thinking they had just got a huge performance boost. Later on, they had to shut down SQL Server and when they tried to restart SQL Server, it would not start. This is where I came in. Turns out they had several other applications running on the NT Server that grabbed the memory needed to create the tempdb in RAM.

When SQL Server failed while creating the tempdb, the server halted. I was able to shut down the other processes and restart the server and place tempdb back on disk. The moral of the story is, "Watch out for the developers; they will do everything they can to convince you they need tempdb in RAM!"

Microsoft recommends that you not place tempdb in RAM unless your NT Server has at least 64 to 128 MB of memory. I would make the same recommendation because it has been my experience that in systems with less memory, the available memory is better used as part of the data or procedure cache. If you have enough memory to place tempdb in memory, then make sure by running a series of benchmark tests with your queries or stored procedures that use the temporary database. Be sure that placing the temporary database in memory will give you the benefits you want.

If you find substantial performance gains, then leave tempdb in RAM; otherwise, place tempdb back on disk and use the memory for a larger procedure and data cache.

PROCEDURE CACHE

Tip

> The procedure cache configuration parameter is an often tuned parameter to enhance SQL Server performance.

If you refer to Figure 18.3, you will see that SQL Server maintains two cache areas that increase as the amount of memory is increased: the procedure cache and the data cache. The procedure cache stores the most recently used stored procedures and also is used for compiling SQL for ad hoc queries. The data cache is used to store the most recently used data or index pages. Both caches use a LRU-MRU management scheme (least recently used/most recently used) to determine what stays in the cache and what is overwritten.

So how do you know whether you have the correct values for your procedure cache? First, you need to understand that stored procedures are not re-entrant; that is, if the same stored procedure is executed simultaneously by two users, SQL Server will have a separate copy of the compiled stored procedure in the procedure cache one for each user (that is, the two users cannot share the same stored procedure). So, if 50 users run the same or different stored procedures simultaneously, you have 50 copies of the stored procedures in the procedure cache.

STRANGER THAN FICTION!

In the SQL Server Books Online section "Estimating SQL Server Overhead," the default size of the procedure cache is incorrectly listed at 20 rather than the correct default value of 30. Other parts of the documentation have the correct default value for the procedure cache.

Minimum: 1
Maximum: 99
Default: 30
Dynamic Variable: No

Tip

Because the procedure cache is of a limited size, it is possible to run out of available memory in the procedure cache causing an error 701 to occur. For example, if your procedure cache is large enough to run 200 stored procedures, and 200 stored procedures are being executed, the next stored procedure or query tree that attempts to load in the cache will be rejected for lack of space. If this occurs frequently, increase the size of your procedure cache.

Now that you understand how users affect the number of stored procedures or query trees in the procedure cache, what about the size of a stored procedure? The minimum size of a stored procedure is 2K. To determine the correct size of a stored procedure, use the DBCC MEMUSAGE command. The following formula, found in the Microsoft SQL Server *Administrator's Companion*, can be used to size the procedure cache:

```
Procedure Cache = (Max. Number of Concurrent Users) x
                       (Size of Largest Plan) x 1.25
```

To come up with the configuration value, use the following:

```
Procedure Cache Config. Value = (Procedure Cache/(SQL Server Memory - (Static
                             Overhead + Configuration Overhead) ) ) x 100%
```

A better method is to determine the most widely used stored procedures and use an average size of the procedures in the preceding formula rather than the size of the largest procedure. If your SQL Server has a large amount of memory available for the cache (> 64MB), you may want to consider lowering the percentage. For example, if you had a 100MB available and use the default setting, your procedure cache would be 30MB. If the maximum number of concurrent users 175 with an average plan size of 55K, then the following would be true:

```
Procedure Cache = 175 users x (55k plan size) x 1.25 = 12 MB
Procedure Cache Config Value = (12 MB/100 MB) x 100% = 12
```

By using the formulas, you find that you could probably get by with a procedure cache configuration value of 12 percent instead of 30 percent, freeing up an additional 18MB of memory for the disk cache! Determining the correct size of the procedure cache involves trial and error, but getting it right enhances the performance of your system.

Tip

You have spent some time determining the correct size of the data cache and now it's time to tune the procedure cache; however, here's the catch. If you modify the procedure cache configuration value, then you change the data cache! If you add more memory to SQL Server, then you change the size of the data cache and the procedure cache. To size either the procedure cache or data cache without changing the other cache value requires setting both the memory configuration value and the procedure cache value simultaneously, adjusting the two values so that the other cache remains the same. Use this technique when fine tuning the correct cache values.

ALLOW UPDATES

If the value of allow updates is set to 1, then the SQL Server system tables can be modified. First, do not set this configuration value to 1, unless told to do so by Microsoft Technical Support.

Warning

Directly updating system tables is risky business and could prevent your SQL Server from running.

If you need to update system tables, use the system stored procedures. If you do need to turn on this option, start SQL Server in single-user mode (command-line option -m) to prevent any other users from accidentally modifying the system tables.

Minimum: 0
Maximum: 1
Default: 0
Dynamic Variable: Yes

Note

Stored procedures created to modify system tables while the allow updates option is on can always modify the system tables, even after the allow updates option is turned off.

BACKUP BUFFER SIZE

A new SQL Server 6.0 option, backup buffer size, enables you to set the size of the buffer used to load/dump a database to increase the performance of backup/load operations. The value is in 32-page increments.

Minimum: 1
Maximum: 10
Default: 1
Dynamic Variable: Yes

BACKUP THREADS

Another new feature added to speed up dump/load processing, `backup threads` configuration value specifies to reserve a number of threads to be used for parallel striped backups and recoveries.

Minimum: 0
Maximum: 32
Default: 5
Dynamic Variable: No

DATABASE SIZE

This option determines the default size allocated to each new database that is created without specifying the database size. The configuration values are in megabytes.

Minimum: 1
Maximum: 10000
Default: 2
Dynamic Variable: No

DEFAULT LANGUAGE

This option determines the number of the language used to display system messages.

Minimum: 0
Maximum: 9999
Default: Varies (`US_English = 0`)
Dynamic Variable: No

FILL FACTOR

The fill factor specifies how densely packed you want your index and data pages while creating an index. The default is 0, which leaves room on the nonleaf pages with the leaf pages 100 percent full. Use a low fill factor to spread data over more pages.

Minimum: 0
Maximum: 100
Default: 0
Dynamic Variable: No

> ### Note
>
> The fill factor is not maintained by SQL Server after index creation and is only maintained when the index is built.

LANGUAGE IN CACHE

This option determines the number of languages that can be held simultaneously in the language cache.

Minimum: 3
Maximum: 100
Default: 3
Dynamic Variable: No

LE THRESHOLD MAXIMUM

> ### Tip
>
> LE threshold maximum is a new configuration parameter, which will help in easing potential locking problems in environments with extremely large tables.

LE threshold maximum stands for *Lock Escalation threshold maximum* and is a new SQL Server 6.0 configuration parameter. In previous versions of SQL Server, when many page lock requests began to pile up on a table, SQL Server would escalate the lock request to a table lock, preventing other users from accessing the table. The magical number, regardless of the size of the table, was 200 and could not be tuned. Developers working in environments with large amounts of data are penalized because the majority of their transactions may affect over 200 pages. Now you can tune the level of the number of page locks SQL Server will hold before a table lock is placed on the table!

Minimum: 2
Maximum: 500000
Default: 200
Dynamic Variable: Yes

> ## Note
>
> The configurable locking parameters are just some of many ways SQL Server 6.0 has improved SQL Server locking capabilities and available options to the developer and DBA. I take my hat off to the guys in Redmond!

LE THRESHOLD PERCENT

The LE threshold percent (new for SQL Server 6.0) enables you to control locking escalation as a percentage rather than a fixed number. A 0 value causes a table lock to occur when the LE threshold minimum is reached.

Minimum: 1
Maximum: 100
Default: 0
Dynamic Variable: Yes

LOCKS

The locks configuration variable sets the number of available locks. If you are getting error messages that the SQL Server is out of locks, increase the number.

> ## Tip
>
> The locks configuration parameter is an often tuned parameter.

Minimum: 5000
Maximum: 214748364
Default: 5000
Dynamic Variable: No

LOGWRITE SLEEP (MS)

This option specifies the number of milliseconds to delay before writing to disk a buffer that is not full, in hopes that other users will fill up the buffer before it is written to disk.

Minimum: -1
Maximum: 500
Default: 0
Dynamic Variable: No

STRANGER THAN FICTION!

This option is listed in the Microsoft SQL Server documentation as *Advanced option*, yet it shows up on the regular configuration menu when advanced options are turned off. So which is it? I would guess it probably belongs with the advanced options.

MAX ASYNC *IO*

This option is the number of outstanding asynchronous I/Os that can be issued. Modify only if you have databases that span multiple physical drives or are using disk striping and your database server has separate disk controllers or a smart disk controller like a Compaq smart array.

> **Minimum:** 1
> **Maximum:** 255
> **Default:** 8
> **Dynamic Variable:** No

MAX WORKER THREADS

Worker threads are used by SQL Server for things such as checkpoints, users, and network support. The configuration parameter sets the maximum number of worker threads SQL Server can use. If the configured value is greater than the number of concurrent user connections, all user connections will have their own thread; otherwise, the user will share a pool of worker threads.

> **Minimum:** 10
> **Maximum:** 1024
> **Default:** 255
> **Dynamic Variable:** Yes

MEDIA RETENTION

This option sets the number of days you want to retain backup media before overwriting with a new dump. If you attempt to overwrite the media before the number of retention days has expired, you will get a warning message.

Minimum: 0
Maximum: 365
Default: 0
Dynamic Variable: No

NESTED TRIGGERS

When this option is set to 1, a trigger can call another trigger (that is, nesting). When set to 0, calling a trigger from another trigger is prohibited.

Minimum: 0
Maximum: 1
Default: 1
Dynamic Variable: Yes

> *Note*
>
> You can have up to 16 levels of nesting!

NETWORK PACKET SIZE

This option was first introduced in SQL Server 4.21 for Windows NT, but with the major restriction that it could only be set using NETBUI. With Version 6.0, however, you can now set the packet size for any of the network protocols supported by SQL Server. If you have a network that will support large packet size, then you can increase the network performance with SQL Server by increasing the packet size. The default of 4096 bytes is a welcome change to the anemic 512 byte packet size used in previous versions.

Minimum: 512
Maximum: 32767
Default: 4096
Dynamic Variable: Yes

OPEN DATABASES

This option specifies the maximum number of databases that can be open at one time on SQL Server. If you receive error messages that indicate that you have exceeded the number of open databases, increase the number. The overhead is fairly insignificant (about 4K per configured open database).

Minimum: 5
Maximum: 32767
Default: 20
Dynamic Variable: No

> *Note*
>
> Unlike locks, which are not shared and are per user/per object, the open databases configuration is for the entire server, regardless of the number of users.

OPEN OBJECTS

This option specifies the maximum number of database objects that can be open at one time on SQL Server.

Minimum: 100
Maximum: 2147483647
Default: 500
Dynamic Variable: No

RECOVERY FLAGS

Setting recovery flags to 0 displays minimum information during the SQL Server recovery process at startup. When this option is set to 0, a recovery message, along with the database name, is displayed. Setting this option to 1 results in the display of more informational messages (information about individual transactions).

Minimum: 0
Maximum: 1
Default: 0
Dynamic Variable: No

RECOVERY INTERVAL

SQL Server uses the recovery interval, the database truncate log on checkpoint setting, and the amount of database activity to determine when a checkpoint should be performed to write the "dirty pages" (modified pages not yet flushed to disk). The recovery interval specified is not the amount of time between SQL Server checkpoints, but the maximum amount of time per database that SQL Server needs to recover the database in the event of a system failure. The checkpoint process checks each database every minute to see whether the database needs to be checkpointed, based on the criteria mentioned previously.

> **Tip**
>
> The recovery interval configuration parameter is an often tuned parameter.

Minimum: 1
Maximum: 32767
Default: 5
Dynamic Variable: Yes

REMOTE ACCESS

This option controls the logins from remote SQL Servers. When set to 1, users from remote SQL Servers have access to the server.

Minimum: 0
Maximum: 1
Default: 1
Dynamic Variable: No

SHOW ADVANCED OPTIONS

This option displays the advanced configuration options when using the SQL Server Enterprise Manager or the sp_configure system stored procedure.

Minimum: 0
Maximum: 1
Default: 0
Dynamic Variable: Yes

USER CONNECTIONS

This option specifies the maximum number of simultaneous user connections allowed on SQL Server. If the maximum number is exceeded, you will get an error and will be unable to establish the new connection until one becomes available. Be careful about setting this parameter too high because each user connection takes up approximately 40K of memory overhead, regardless of whether the connection is used.

> **Tip**
>
> The user connections configuration parameter is an often tuned parameter.

Minimum: 5
Maximum: 32767
Default: 20
Dynamic Variable: No

PARAMETER OVERKILL

I was once at a site with a well-configured machine (128MB of memory for SQL Server), and those at the site were wondering whether they had properly configured SQL Server for optimum performance. I issued a DBCC MEMUSAGE command to get an overview of how things looked in memory and I was astounded to see a very large amount of memory being used for user connections (40MB)! It turned out that someone had bumped up the number of user connections to 1000, not realizing how SQL Server allocated the memory up front for user connections. The funny thing was they only had 30 users, with at most 60 connections at any one time. We quickly got back an extra 38MB of memory for the data and procedure cache!

Warning

The following configuration parameters are considered to be advanced configuration parameters and can only be seen by turning on the show advanced options configuration option. I highly suggest leaving them alone. Microsoft has done a good job setting the default values and you could easily hinder the performance of your SQL Server by incorrectly setting one of the advanced configuration options. If you do modify them, make sure you fully understand the option and the overall impact of your changes!

CURSOR THRESHOLD

This option determines how the keyset for a cursor is generated. If the option is set to -1, all cursor keysets are generated synchronously (which is good for small cursor sets). If the option is set to 0, all cursor keysets are generated asynchronously. Otherwise, the query optimizer compares the number of expected rows in the cursor set and if it exceeds the cursor threshold configuration variable, then the keyset will be built asynchronously.

Minimum: -1
Maximum: 2147483647

Default: -1
Dynamic Variable: Yes

> ### STRANGER THAN FICTION!
>
> When using the SQL Enterprise Manager and reviewing this option in the Configuration tab on the Server Configuration/Options dialog box, I noticed they left out the description for this option! Maybe in the next release...

DEFAULT SORTORDER ID

This option shows the current sort order id installed on SQL Server. Do *not* use sp_configure or the SQL Enterprise Manager Configuration dialog box to change the sort order! Changing the sort order is done through the SQL Setup program and is a major change to your SQL Server!

Minimum: 0
Maximum: 255
Default: Varies
Dynamic Variable: No

FREE BUFFERS

This option determines the threshold of free buffers available to SQL Server. The values will automatically change as the SQL Server memory is changed. The value will equal approximately 5 percent of the available memory.

Minimum: 20
Maximum: Varies
Default: Varies
Dynamic Variable: Yes

HASH BUCKETS

You use this option to create the number of buckets available for hashing to speed access time when retrieving data residing in the data cache. The standard default is sufficient for systems with less then 160MB of memory.

Minimum: 4999
Maximum: 265003
Default: 7993
Dynamic Variable: No

LE THRESHOLD MINIMUM

This option sets the minimum number of locked pages required before escalating to a table lock.

> **Minimum:** 2
> **Maximum:** 500000
> **Default:** 20
> **Dynamic Variable:** Yes

MAX LAZYWRITE IO

Use this option to tune the priority of batched asynchronous I/O performed by the lazy writer process. Do not modify unless told to do so by Microsoft Tech Support!

> **Minimum:** 1
> **Maximum:** 255
> **Default:** 8
> **Dynamic Variable:** Yes

PRIORITY BOOST

If the `priority boost` configuration value is set to `1`, SQL Server will run at a higher priority on the Windows NT server.

> **Minimum:** 0
> **Maximum:** 1
> **Default:** 0
> **Dynamic Variable:** No

Warning

Even if you have a dedicated machine for SQL Server, do not boost the priority of SQL Server. It will run fine as a regular Windows NT server and boosting the priority can cause some unexpected problems when trying to bring down SQL Server or use other NT tools on the server.

REMOTE LOGIN TIMEOUT

This option specifies the number of seconds to wait before returning from a remote login attempt. The default of `0` specifies an infinite timeout value.

Minimum: 0
Maximum: 2147483647
Default: 0
Dynamic Variable: Yes

REMOTE QUERY TIMEOUT

This option specifies the number of seconds to wait before timing out as a result of a remote query. The default of 0 specifies an infinite timeout value.

Minimum: 0
Maximum: 2147483647
Default: 0
Dynamic Variable: Yes

RESOURCE TIMEOUT

This option specifies the number of seconds to wait for a resource to be released.

Minimum: 5
Maximum: 2147483647
Default: 1
Dynamic Variable: Yes

SET WORKING SET SIZE

If the value of the working set option is set to 1 when SQL Server starts, Windows NT locks all the memory in the memory configuration value and tempdb value (if in RAM), as a working set to increase performance. You can disable the creation of the memory working set by setting the option to 0. When this option is disabled, SQL Server ask the cache manager for memory as needed up to the value in the memory configuration parameter. Memory is still reserved for tempdb (if in RAM).

Minimum: 0
Maximum: 1
Default: 0
Dynamic Variable: No

SMP CONCURRENCY

This option determines the number of threads SQL Server will release to Windows NT for execution. The default value for this parameter assumes a dedicated computer for SQL Server, allowing SQL Server to automatically configure itself in an SMP environment or single processor environment for the best performance.

Minimum: -1
Maximum: 64
Default: -1
Dynamic Variable: No

SORT PAGES

This option specifies the maximum number of pages allowed a user performing a sort. This option may require adjusting if the SQL Server performs large sorts.

Minimum: 64
Maximum: 511
Default: 64
Dynamic Variable: Yes

SPIN COUNTER

This option specifies the maximum number attempts a process will make to obtain a resource.

Minimum: 1
Maximum: 2147483647
Default: 10000
Dynamic Variable: Yes

STRANGER THAN FICTION!

In the *Administrative Companion* that ships with SQL Server 6.0 and found in the Books Online, mention is made of an advanced configuration parameter called *time slice* that controls the amount of time a user process can pass a yield point without yielding. Modifying the configuration parameter time slice will be difficult, because it appears time slice does not exist. The value does not show up in the output of `sp_configure` or the SQL Enterprise Manager. If you try to set the value using `sp_configure 'time slice'` or even `sp_configure 'timeslice'`, you will be told that the option does not exist. It just goes to show that you cannot believe everything you read!

ASYNCHRONOUS READ AHEAD CONFIGURATION PARAMETERS

SQL Server 6.0 ships with an exciting new feature called *Parallel Data Scan*, also referred to as *Asynchronous Read Ahead*. The read ahead technology (RA for short), decreases the time required to perform logical sequential data reads, which translates to improved performance for table scans, index creation, DBCC commands, UPDATE STATISTICS, and covered queries. Microsoft claims the RA technology (depending upon the hardware platform, databases, and so on) can boost performance up to a factor of three on some queries over Version 4.21! The idea behind the parallel data scan is simple. Using separate threads, SQL Server reads extents (8 data pages or 16K) into memory before the thread running the query needs the extent. When the extent is needed to satisfy the query, the data pages are already in the memory cache thanks to the read ahead. Look at Figure 18.4 for an idea of how RA works.

Figure 18.4.
Parallel data scan.

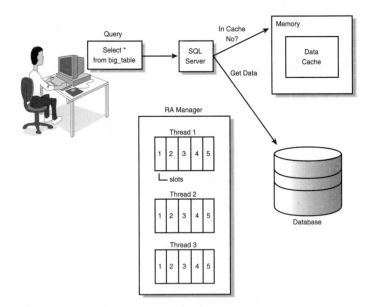

A user issues a query that performs a table scan on a table called big_table. SQL Server gets the query request and begins to process the query. When SQL Server goes to retrieve the first data page, SQL Server first checks to see whether the data page is already in the data cache (memory). If the page is not in memory, SQL Server reads the page from disk and places it in the data cache.

Regardless of whether RA is available, SQL Server always checks the data cache first before reading the data page. So, how does the RA technology fit in? First there is a Read Ahead Manager that operates in the background that manages several threads that perform the asynchronous data reads. SQL Server also has several configuration variables that determine how the read ahead will work. For example, there is a parameter to determine the number of read ahead threads that exist and the number of slots handled per each thread. There also is a parameter that determines how many cache misses can occur in a sequential data operation before the RA manager will assign a thread to prefetch the data into the data cache.

Look again at Figure 18.4. The query `Select * from big_table` is being executed by SQL Server. SQL Server checks to see whether the data page is in the data cache. The page is not in the cache, so SQL Server goes out to disk. The RA manage counts 1 cache hit miss and compares the number of misses to the SQL Server configuration parameter RA cache miss limit, which defaults to 3 (the value used for this example).

Because the number of cache misses is less than the configuration parameter, nothing happens. The query continues to run and SQL Server checks to see whether the next data page is in the data cache. Again, it's not, so SQL Server reads the page and the RA manager checks the number of cache misses with the configuration value.

This continues until the number of cache misses exceeds the configuration value. Then the RA manager checks thread 1 for an empty slot and assigns the slot to handle read aheads for the `big_table` query. Thread 1 then begins to prefetch an extent 16K (8 data pages) into the data cache, as shown in Figure 18.5.

Figure 18.5.
Read Ahead Manager
using a thread to
prefetch data.

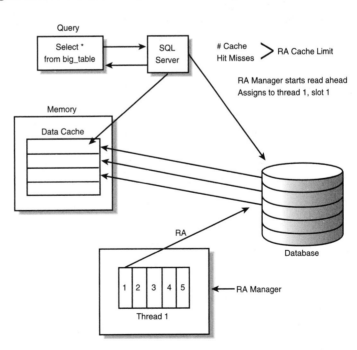

When the query checks to see whether the next page is in the data cache, the answer is yes. The thread performing the query does not have to wait for SQL Server to read the data page into memory!

The RA thread will prefetch up to a configuration amount of extents into the cache before becoming idle and maintains the number of extents ahead of the operation. If another request comes along and thread 1 has an empty slot, the new request also will be assigned to thread 1. Thread 2 will not have any request assigned until all the slots in thread 1 are filled. The next section examines the different configuration parameters for the RA technology.

RA CACHE HIT LIMIT

Warning

SQL Server 6.0 documentation recommends that you do not modify this parameter unless instructed to do so by your primary SQL Server support provider.

This option specifies the number of cache hits that a read ahead request can have before it is canceled.

Minimum: 1
Maximum: 255
Default: 4
Dynamic Variable: Yes

RA CACHE MISS LIMIT

Warning

SQL Server 6.0 documentation recommends that you do not modify this parameter unless instructed to do so by your primary SQL Server support provider.

This option specifies the number of cache misses that can occur before the read ahead manager assigns a thread and slot to begin to prefetch data.

Minimum: 1
Maximum: 255
Default: 3
Dynamic Variable: Yes

RA DELAY

This option sets the amount of time in milliseconds to wait between the time the read ahead event is set and when the read ahead thread is awakened by the operating system. This configuration parameter is only required in non-SMP systems.

Minimum: 0
Maximum: 500
Default: 15
Dynamic Variable: Yes

RA PREFETCHES

The RA prefetches configuration parameter specifies the number of data extents the read ahead thread pre-fetches in the data cache before becoming idle.

Minimum: 1
Maximum: 1000
Default: 3
Dynamic Variable: Yes

RA SLOTS PER THREAD

This option specifies the number of slots maintained by each RA thread. A slot corresponds to a RA request and each RA thread will simultaneously manage the number of RA slots per thread.

Minimum: 1
Maximum: 255
Default: 5
Dynamic Variable: No

RA WORKER THREADS

This option specifies the number of threads available to handle read-ahead requests.

Minimum: 0
Maximum: 255
Default: 3
Dynamic Variable: No

BETWEEN THE LINES

In this chapter, all the possible SQL Server configuration parameters have been examined. Following are some of the more important points to remember about tuning and configuring SQL Server.

◆ Take the time to learn how SQL Server uses memory.

◆ Make sure when tuning SQL Server via the Performance Monitor, that the SQL Server is running against the expected real-world work load.

◆ Learn how to start SQL Server with the -f startup option to reset incorrectly configured parameters that may prevent SQL Server from starting.

◆ It is highly recommended that you spend some time tuning the memory parameters such as memory and procedure cache. Verify your settings using the Performance Monitor and DBCC MEMUSAGE.

◆ Understand the impact of changing configuration parameters before modifying them.

SUMMARY

The answer to the question "Which knobs do I turn?" is "Not many!" The nice thing about SQL Server is that many of the default values provide optimal SQL Server performance for most database installations right out of the box. I also noticed with the newer versions of SQL Server, that Microsoft increased the default values for several configuration parameters to meet more real-world needs (and probably reduce the number of calls to Tech support). For example, the default size of the procedure cache is 30 instead of 20, and they removed the configuration value devices (old default value 10) increasing the number of devices to the previous versions configured maximum of 255—these are just a few. I'm sure if you are familiar with previous versions of SQL Server or a Sybase SQL Server you will also notice the differences. Tune your SQL Server installation for the best possible performance but do not forget that tuning is a many-phased process. It starts with the hardware, operating system installation, SQL Server tuning and installation, and the overall design of the databases and applications.

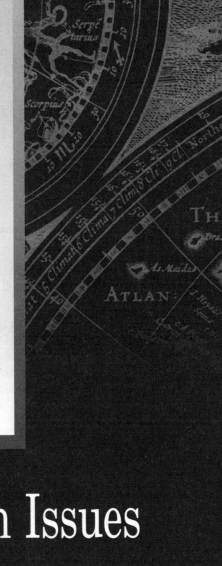

- Problems that
  Can Arise from an
  Improperly Designed
  Database

- Normalization

- Denormalization

- Between the Lines

- Summary

CHAPTER 19

Database Design Issues

A properly designed database can increase data integrity and simplify data maintenance. To help you better understand how to design a database, the following concepts are discussed in this chapter:

◆ Problems that may arise from an improperly designed database

◆ How to correctly design a database

◆ How to take a properly designed database a step backward in order to improve performance

Problems that Can Arise from an Improperly Designed Database

The following are problems that can occur from an improperly designed database:

◆ Redundant data

◆ Limited data tracking

◆ Inconsistent data

◆ Update anomalies

◆ Delete anomalies

◆ Insert anomalies

Redundant Data

As you can see in Figure 19.1, `manager name` and `training description` are continuously repeated. This increases the amount of physical storage required to track training data.

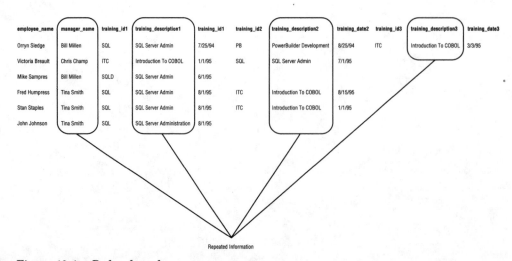

Figure 19.1.   Redundant data.

LIMITED DATA TRACKING

The table design in Figure 19.2 is limited to tracking three classes per employee. Additional columns must be added to the table if you want to track more than three classes.

This table allows a maximum of 3 training courses to be tracked.

employee_name	manager_name	training_id1	training_description1	training_data	training_id21	training_description2	training_date2	training_id3	training_description3	training_date3
Orryn Sledge	Bill Millen	SQL	SQL Server Admin	7/25/94	PB	PowerBuilder Development	8/25/94	ITC	Introduction To COBOL	3/3/95
Victoria Breault	Chris Champ	ITC	Introduction To COBOL	1/1/95	SQL	SQL Server Admin	7/1/95			
Mike Sampres	Bill Millen	SQLD	SQL Server Admin	6/1/95						
Fred Humpress	Tina Smith	SQL	SQL Server Admin	8/1/95	ITC	Introduction To COBOL	8/15/95			
Stan Staples	Tina Smith	SQL	SQL Server Admin	8/1/95	ITC	Introduction To COBOL	1/1/95			
John Johnson	Tina Smith	SQL	SQL Server Administration	8/1/95						

Figure 19.2.   Limited data tracking.

INCONSISTENT DATA

Consider the likelihood of a training class being misspelled when a new record is added to the employee_training table (see Figure 19.3). As more records are added to the table, the potential for inconsistent data from keying errors increases.

employee_name	manager_name	training_id1	training_description1	training_date1	training_id2	training_description2	training_date2	training_id3	training_description3	training_date3
Orryn Sledge	Bill Millen	SQL	SQL Server Admin	7/25/94	PB	PowerBuilder Development	8/25/94	ITC	Introduction To COBOL	3/3/95
Victoria Breault	Chris Champ	ITC	Introduction To COBOL	1/1/95	SQL	SQL Server Admin	7/1/95			
Mike Sampres	Bill Millen	SQLD	SQL Server Admin	6/1/95						
Fred Humpress	Tina Smith	SQL	SQL Server Admin	8/1/95	ITC	Introduction To COBOL	8/15/95			
Stan Staples	Tina Smith	SQL	SQL Server Admin	8/1/95	ITC	Introduction To COBOL	1/1/95			
John Johnson	Tina Smith	SQL	SQL Server Administration	8/1/95						

Are these two different training classes or is this a data entry error?

Figure 19.3.   Inconsistent data.

UPDATE ANOMALIES

You just realized that the SQL Server Admin class should be named SQL Server Administration (see Figure 19.4). To change the class name, you will need to update it in five different places. Wouldn't it be easier if you could change the name in one place and have it automatically reflected throughout the application?

19

DATABASE DESIGN ISSUES

employee_name	manager_name	training_id1	training_description1	training_date1	training_id2	training_description2	training_date2	training_id3	training_description3	training_date3
Orryn Sledge	Bill Millen	SQL ①	SQL Server Admin incorrect	7/25/94	PB	PowerBuilder Development	8/25/94	ITC	Introduction To COBOL	3/3/95
Victoria Breault	Chris Champ	ITC	Introduction To COBOL	1/1/95	SQL ⑤	SQL Server Admin incorrect	7/1/95			
Mike Sampres	Bill Millen	SQLD ②	SQL Server Admin incorrect	6/1/95						
Fred Humpress	Tina Smith	SQL ③	SQL Server Admin incorrect	8/1/95	ITC	Introduction To COBOL	8/15/95			
Stan Staples	Tina Smith	SQL ④	SQL Server Admin incorrect	8/1/95	ITC	Introduction To COBOL	1/1/95			
John Johnson	Tina Smith	SQL	SQL Server Administration correct	8/1/95						

You just realized that "SQL Server Admin" should be "SQL Server Administration."
To change the class name you will need to update it in 5 different places.

Figure 19.4.   Update anomalies.

DELETE ANOMALIES

Suppose that you are no longer interested in tracking the "Introduction To COBOL" training class, so you delete matching records (see Figure 19.5). But wait…you just realized that you deleted other important information. The removal of more than one type of information from a table is considered a *delete anomaly*.

employee_name	manager_name	training_id1	training_description1	training_date1	training_id2	training_description2	training_date2	training_id3	training_description3	training_date3
Orryn Sledge	Bill Millen	SQL	SQL Server Admin	7/25/94	PB	PowerBuilder Development	8/25/94	ITC	Introduction To COBOL	3/3/95
Victoria Breault	Chris Champ	ITC	Introduction To COBOL	1/1/95	SQL	SQL Server Admin	7/1/95			
Mike Sampres	Bill Millen	SQLD	SQL Server Admin	6/1/95						
Fred Humpress	Tina Smith	SQL	SQL Server Admin	8/1/95	ITC	Introduction To COBOL	8/15/95			
Stan Staples	Tina Smith	SQL	SQL Server Admin	8/1/95	ITC	Introduction To COBOL	1/1/95			
John Johnson	Tina Smith	SQL	SQL Server Administration	8/1/95						

You are no longer interested in tracking the "Introduction To COBOL" training class so you delete
matching records. But wait . . . you just realized that you deleted other important information.

Figure 19.5.   Delete anomalies.

INSERT ANOMALIES

Suppose that you want to track a new training course titled "Database Design" and you designate the code "DD" for training_id1. What values will you use for employee_name and manager_name when you insert the record into the sample table (see Figure 19.6)? Do you leave the values blank? Do you insert a special code such as "unknown" for employee_name and manager_name?

employee_name	manager_name	training_id1	training_description1	training_date1	training_id2	training_description2	training_date2	training_id3	training_description3	training_date3
Orryn Sledge	Bill Millen	SQL	SQL Server Admin	7/25/94	PB	PowerBuilder Development	8/25/94	ITC	Introduction To COBOL	3/3/95
Victoria Breault	Chris Champ	ITC	Introduction To COBOL	1/1/95	SQL	SQL Server Admin	7/1/95			
Mike Sampres	Bill Millen	SQLD	SQL Server Admin	6/1/95						
Fred Humpress	Tina Smith	SQL	SQL Server Admin	8/1/95	ITC	Introduction To COBOL	8/15/95			
Stan Staples	Tina Smith	SQL	SQL Server Admin	8/1/95	ITC	Introduction To COBOL	1/1/95			
John Johnson	Tina Smith	SQL	SQL Server Administration	8/1/95						
??	??	DD	Database Design							

You want to track a new training course called "Database Design." Where do you insert the record?

Figure 19.6.   Insert anomalies.

NORMALIZATION

Normalization is a set of standard rules that test the soundness of database design. It can help prevent the problems discussed in the previous section. By applying these standard rules, you can pinpoint design flaws that may jeopardize data integrity and complicate data maintenance.

HOW TO NORMALIZE A DATABASE

There are three standard normalization rules. After a design successfully passes a rule, it is said to be in # normal form (# = 1st, 2nd, or 3rd). Rules are cumulative. For example, for a design to be in 3rd normal form, it must satisfy the requirements of 3rd normal form plus the requirements for 2nd, as well as 1st normal forms.

Technically speaking, there are other types of normalization rules beyond 3rd normal form. However, for most database designs the first three normal forms are sufficient. Seldom will you need to apply the other types of normalization. Therefore, this topic will only concentrate on the 1st, 2nd, and 3rd normal forms of database design.

- ◆ **1st normal form**: No repeating groups
- ◆ **2nd normal form**: No nonkey attributes are dependent upon a portion of the primary key
- ◆ **3rd normal form**: No attributes are dependent on other nonkey attributes

Now that you know the rules regarding normalization, apply them to a sample application.

For this application, you are tracking training classes taken by each employee. Figure 19.7 contains a denormalized listing of the data tracked by this application. Each employee may have taken *0* or *N* (zero or many) classes.

employee_id	char(5)
employee_name	char(35)
employee_address	char(35)
employee_city	char(35)
employee_state	char(2)
employee_zip	char(11)
manager_id	char(5)
manager_name	char(35)
training_id1	char(5)
training_description1	char(25)
training_date1	datetime
training_id2	char(5)
training_description2	char(25)
training_date2	datetime
training_id3	char(5)
training_description3	char(25)
training_date3	datetime

Figure 19.7.   *Denormalized database design.*

1ST NORMAL FORM

Look at the `training_id`, `training_description`, and `training_date` attributes of Figure 19.8. See how they are repeated? This violates the concept of 1st normal form: No repeating groups.

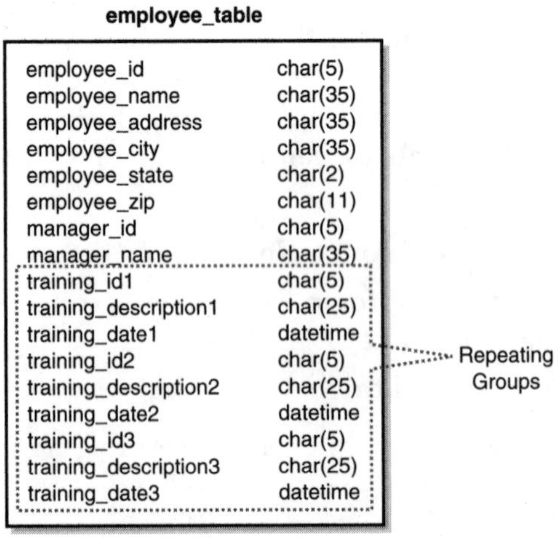

employee_table

employee_id	char(5)
employee_name	char(35)
employee_address	char(35)
employee_city	char(35)
employee_state	char(2)
employee_zip	char(11)
manager_id	char(5)
manager_name	char(35)
training_id1	char(5)
training_description1	char(25)
training_date1	datetime
training_id2	char(5)
training_description2	char(25)
training_date2	datetime
training_id3	char(5)
training_description3	char(25)
training_date3	datetime

Repeating Groups

Figure 19.8.   *Repeating groups.*

Move the training information into a separate table called `employee_training` and create a relationship between the `employee` table and the `employee_training` table. Now the table design meets the requirements of 1st normal form (see Figure 19.9).

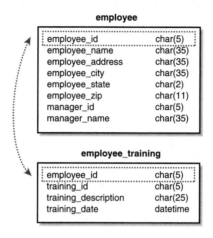

Figure 19.9.   1st normal form.

2ND NORMAL FORM

Notice in Figure 19.10 how the `training_description` attribute is only dependent upon the `training_id` attribute and not the `employee_id` attribute in the `employee_training` table. This violates 2nd normal form: No nonkey attributes are dependent upon a portion of the primary key (the primary key for this table is `employee_id` + `training_id`). This rule is only applied to entities that have compound primary keys (a primary key consisting of more than one attribute).

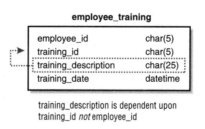

Figure 19.10.   A nonkey attribute is dependent upon a portion of the primary key.

Move the `training_description` attribute into a separate table called `training`. Relate the `training` table to the `employee_training` table through the `training_id` attribute. Now the design satisfies 2nd normal form (see Figure 19.11).

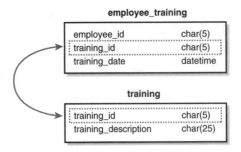

Figure 19.11.   2nd normal form.

3RD NORMAL FORM

Look at the manager_name attribute for the employee table in Figure 19.12. The primary key for the employee table is the employee_id attribute. Is the manager_name attribute dependent on the employee_id attribute? No! This violates 3rd normal form: No attributes are dependent upon other nonkey attributes.

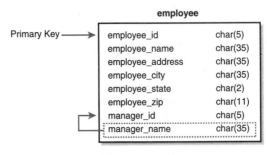

Figure 19.12.   An attribute is dependent on a nonkey attribute.

Move the manager_name attribute into a separate table called manager. The manager table can be related to the employee table through the manager_id attribute. By making this change, the design meets the requirements of 3rd normal form (see Figure 19.13).

Now you have completed the normalization process (see Figure 19.14). This process helped isolate design flaws that would have lead to an awkward and inefficient database design.

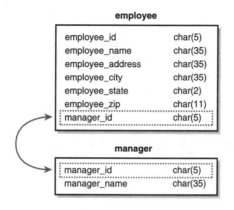

Figure 19.13.   3rd normal form.

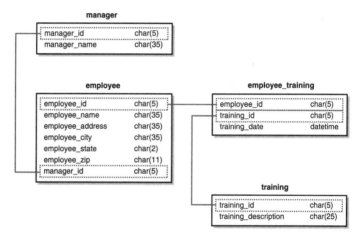

Figure 19.14.   Normalized database design.

DENORMALIZATION

Denormalization means that you are purposely designing your database so that it is *not* in 3rd normal form. This is done to maximize performance or to simplify end-user reporting. Whenever you denormalize a database, you must be willing to forego the benefits gained from 3rd normal form.

PERFORMANCE

A database design in 3rd normal form may require more table joins to process a query than a design in 2nd or 1st normal form. These additional table joins can be expensive in terms of CPU and disk I/O.

Suppose that you need a report that lists the training classes taken by each employee (see Figure 19.15).

employee name	manager name	training description	training date
Orryn Sledge	Bill Millen	SQL Server Admin	7/25/94
		PowerBuilder Development	8/25/94
		Introduction To COBOL	3/3/95
Victoria Breault	Chris Champ	Introduction To COBOL	1/1/95
		SQL Server Admin	7/1/95
Mike Sampres	Bill Millen	SQL Server Admin	6/1/95
Fred Humpress	Tina Smith	SQL Server Admin	8/1/95
		Introduction To COBOL	8/15/95
Stan Staples	Tina Smith	SQL Server Admin	8/1/95
		Introduction To COBOL	1/1/95
John Johnson	Tina Smith	SQL Server Admin	8/1/95

Figure 19.15.   Sample report.

To retrieve the data from your fully normalized database, you would need to create the following query, which is a sample query for a fully normalized database:

```
SELECT a.employee_name, d.manager_name, c.training_description,b.training_date
FROM employee a, employee_training b, training c, manager d
WHERE a.emp_id = b.emp_id
 AND b.training_id = c. training_id
 AND a.manager_id = d.manager_id
```

As you can see, this simple report requires four tables to be joined. Assume that each table contains one million rows. Can you imagine the work involved to join four tables, each containing one million rows? You can be assured that performance will suffer.

In order to maximize performance, you sometimes have to step back to 2nd or 1st normal form. If you denormalized your data into a single table, you could use the following query, which is a sample query for an unnormalized database:

```
SELECT employee_name, manager_name, training_description, training_date
FROM training_summary
```

AD HOC REPORTING

Another reason to denormalize a database is to simplify *ad hoc* reporting. Ad hoc reporting is the unstructured reporting and quering performed by end users. End users often get confused when they have to join a significant number of tables. To avoid the confusion, DBAs can create a special set of tables designed for ad hoc reporting. If the data is used for reporting and not online processing, you may avoid some of the problems associated with a denormalized design.

Tip

Views can sometimes be used as an alternative to denormalization. They can present your data in a denormalized manner, which can simplify ad hoc reporting.

DENORMALIZATION TECHNIQUES

Following is brief summary of various techniques that can be used to denormalize a database:

◆ **Duplicate data**: Duplicate data can reduce the number of joins required to process a query, thus reducing CPU and disk I/O usage.

◆ **Summary data**: Summary data can provide improved query performance by reducing or eliminating the steps required to summarize your data.

◆ **Horizontal partitioning**: Horizontal partitioning is the splitting of a table into two separate tables at the record level, thus reducing the number of rows per table (see Figure 19.16).

◆ **Vertical partitioning**: Vertical partitioning is the splitting of a table into two separate tables at the column level, thus reducing the number of columns per table (see Figure 19.17).

id	name	favorite_food	favorite_color	shoe_size
111-11-1111	Orryn Sledge	Pizza	Blue	9.5
222-22-2222	Victoria Breault	Ice Cream	Peach	6.0
333-33-3333	Mike Sampres	Pizza	Silver	9.0
444-44-4444	Fred Humpress	Fish	Red	10.0
555-55-5555	Stan Staples	Meat	Red	8.0
666-66-6666	John Johnson	Poultry	Black	9.0
777-77-7777	Mary Douglous	Pizza	White	6.0
888-88-8888	Jack Johnson	Pizza	Blue	10.0
999-99-9999	Jan Smithe	Pizza	Blue	10.0

With horizontal partitioning, a table is split into two tables at the row level. Usually, the split occurs at a predefined key value.

id	name	favorite_food	favorite_color	shoe_size
111-11-1111	Orryn Sledge	Pizza	Blue	9.5
222-22-2222	Victoria Breault	Ice Cream	Peach	6.0
333-33-3333	Mike Sampres	Pizza	Silver	9.0
444-44-4444	Fred Humpress	Fish	Red	10.0
555-55-5555	Stan Staples	Meat	Red	8.0

id	name	favorite_food	favorite_color	shoe_size
666-66-6666	John Johnson	Poultry	Black	9.0
777-77-7777	Mary Douglous	Pizza	White	6.0
888-88-8888	Jack Johnson	Pizza	Blue	10.0
999-99-9999	Jan Smithe	Pizza	Blue	10.0

Figure 19.16.   Horizontal partitioning.

id	name	favorite_food	favorite_color	shoe size
111-11-1111	Orryn Sledge	Pizza	Blue	9.5
222-22-2222	Victoria Breault	Ice Cream	Peach	6.0
333-33-3333	Mike Sampres	Pizza	Silver	9.0
444-44-4444	Fred Humpress	Fish	Red	10.0
555-55-5555	Stan Staples	Meat	Red	8.0
666-66-6666	John Johnson	Poultry	Black	9.0
777-77-7777	Mary Douglous	Pizza	White	6.0
888-88-8888	Jack Johnson	Pizza	Blue	10.0
999-99-9999	Jan Smithe	Pizza	Blue	10.0

With vertical partitioning, a table is split into two separate tables and joined by a common key.

id	name
111-11-1111	Orryn Sledge
222-22-2222	Victoria Breault
333-33-3333	Mike Sampres
444-44-4444	Fred Humpress
555-55-5555	Stan Staples
666-66-6666	John Johnson
777-77-7777	Mary Douglous
888-88-8888	Jack Johnson
999-99-9999	Jan Smithe

id	favorite_food	favorite_color	shoe size
111-11-1111	Pizza	Blue	9.5
222-22-2222	Ice Cream	Peach	6.0
333-33-3333	Pizza	Silver	9.0
444-44-4444	Fish	Red	10.0
555-55-5555	Meat	Red	8.0
666-66-6666	Poultry	Black	9.0
777-77-7777	Pizza	White	6.0
888-88-8888	Pizza	Blue	10.0
999-99-9999	Pizza	Blue	10.0

Figure 19.17.   Vertical partitioning.

BETWEEN THE LINES

The following are some of the tips and tricks to reading between the lines when designing databases.

◆ Strive for 3rd normal form. This will maximize data consistency and minimize update anomalies.

◆ When a significant number of tables must be joined to process a query, you may want to selectively denormalize the database in order to improve performance.

SUMMARY

Tangible benefits can be gained by understanding and following the rules of normalization. When a normalized design is not feasible, you should selectively denormalize. Keep in mind the concepts discussed in this chapter when you read the next chapter. Your normalization strategy might influence your indexing strategy.

CHAPTER 20

Understanding Indexes

You maybe asking yourself, "What in the world is a chapter on indexes and index selection doing in a book about database administration?" My experience as a DBA has shown me that it is important to understand indexes and how SQL Server uses indexes to help developers when they are stuck and come to the DBA looking for some words of wisdom and advice. Not only can you seem like a SQL Server guru by helping a developer quickly tune a query by adding an index, you need to be aware of the disk space requirements of indexes and the performance impact of too many indexes on a single table by an overzealous developer.

This chapter will give you a very basic understanding of an index, the type of structures used by indexes, and how to help developers select the proper indexes for their applications.

To get started, you need to know what an index is. An index is a separate physical database structure created on a table that facilitates faster data retrieval when searching on a indexed column. SQL Server also uses indexes to enforce uniqueness on a row or column in a table or to spread out the data on various data pages to help prevent page contention.

GENERAL PRINCIPAL BEHIND INDEXES

Take a high-level look at how indexing can help speed up data retrieval. Figure 20.1 depicts a single table called School Employee that lists the name and occupation of each employee in the school.

Figure 20.1.
School Employee table.

School Employee

row	name	occupation
1	John	Janitor
2	David	Principal
3	Adam	Bus Driver
4	Gary	Teacher
5	Lisa	Janitor
6	Chris	Teacher
7	Debbie	Guidance Counselor
8	Denise	Assistant Principal
9	Bryan	Janitor

Using the table shown in Figure 20.1, what would you do if you wanted to select all the names in the School Employee table that were janitors? You would have to read every row in the table and display only the name where the occupation in the row is Janitor. The process of reading every row or record in a table to satisfy a query is called a *table scan*. Now, let's add an index to the occupation column. Figure 20.2 shows the index on the Occupation column of the School Employee table.

Figure 20.2.
Index on Occupation
column of the School
Employee *table.*

occupation	row pointer
Assistant Principal	8
Bus Driver	3
Guidance Counselor	7
Janitor	1
Janitor	5
Janitor	9
Principal	2
Teacher	4
Teacher	6

The type of index shown in Figure 20.2 contains a pointer to the data. Using the index shown in this figure, walk through the same query to find the names of all employees that are janitors. Rather than performing a table scan on the School Employee table, you read the first row of the index and check the occupation until you find Janitor. When a row contains Janitor, you use the value in the row pointer column to find the exact row number in the School Employee table of a Janitor. You continue to read the index, as long as the occupation is Janitor. When the occupation is no longer Janitor, you stop reading the index! Pretty simple right?

Apply to SQL Server this little bit of knowledge of tables and indexes just described. For starters, SQL Server stores data and index information on a data page (see Figure 20.3).

Figure 20.3.
SQL Server data page.

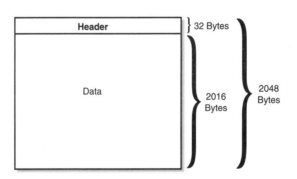

A data page is 2048 bytes in size with a 32-byte header. The remaining 2016 bytes are used for data (that is, table or index information).

Tip

SQL Server allocates space for tables and indexes eight pages at a time, which is called an *extent*. When the extent is filled, another extent (8 pages) is allocated. Remember this tip if you take your Microsoft SQL Server certification test. The odds are that you will be asked a question on index and table space allocation.

Suppose the `School Employee` table, used earlier, contained other information, such as the employee's home address, phone number, spouse's name, education, and number of years of service. The size of a single row of information for the `School Employee` table is around 480 bytes and the maximum size of the `Occupation` column is 25 bytes. Using these row and column sizes, place the `School Employee` table (shown in Figure 20.1) and the index (shown in Figure 20.2) on SQL Server data pages (see Figure 20.4).

Note

The layout of the table information and index information on the data pages shown in Figure 20.4 are not the actual index and table layouts used by SQL Server, but are used to help you understand the general idea behind data pages, table scans, and indexes.

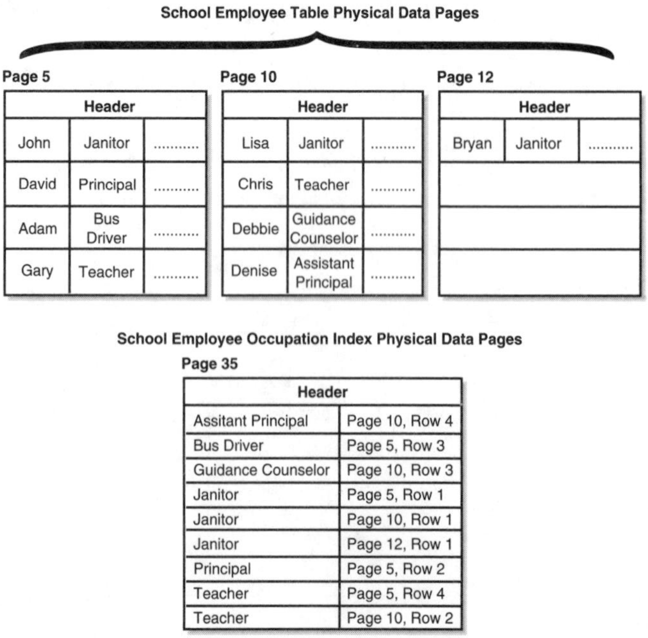
School Employee Table Physical Data Pages
Page 5
Header
John
Janitor
David
Principal
Adam
Bus Driver
Gary
Teacher
Page 10
Header
Lisa
Janitor
Chris
Teacher
Debbie
Guidance Counselor
Denise
Assistant Principal
Page 12
Header
Bryan
Janitor
School Employee Occupation Index Physical Data Pages
Page 35
Header
Assitant Principal
Page 10, Row 4
Bus Driver
Page 5, Row 3
Guidance Counselor
Page 10, Row 3
Janitor
Page 5, Row 1
Janitor
Page 10, Row 1
Janitor
Page 12, Row 1
Principal
Page 5, Row 2
Teacher
Page 5, Row 4
Teacher
Page 10, Row 2

Figure 20.4.
`School Employee` table and index on SQL Server data pages.

Using the diagram shown in Figure 20.4, how would SQL Server find all the employee names whose occupation is Asst Principal without the index? First, SQL Server would read data page 5 and search each record for an employee with an occupation equal to Asst. Principal. No records are found on the first page. SQL Server reads the second data page (page 10), searches each record, and displays the fourth record. Because SQL Server has no way of knowing how many records there are with the occupation of Asst. Principal, SQL Server reads and searches the third and final page, page 12.

So what happened? SQL Server performed a table scan, reading all the data pages. In this example, a table scan did not seem all that bad because SQL Server only had to read three data pages. But what if the School Employee table had 1,000 times more records for a total of 9,000 records (a small amount for SQL Server)! SQL Server would have to read 3,000 data pages rather than 3 data pages to find all the Asst. Principals, even if there were only one employee who was an Asst. Principal and were located on the first data page!

Walk through the same query using the index. First, SQL Server reads the index page and begins to search for Asst. Principal. The first row read is Asst. Principal. SQL Server then checks the pointer, which tells SQL Server that the record is located on data page 10, row four. SQL Server read data page 10 and goes to the fourth row and displays the name.

The next row in the index page is checked and because the occupation is not Asst. Principal, SQL Server stops. The number of pages read using the index is two pages as opposed to three pages in the table scan example.

What about the Janitor query used earlier? Performing a table scan would require reading all three data pages. Using the index would require reading all three data pages plus the index page, for a total of four data pages, which is one more than a table scan! In some cases, a table scan may be faster than using the index. It's the job of the SQL Server query optimizer to determine which index to select or when to perform a table scan.

Tip

You will read many recommendations in this book about keeping indexes small and the row width of a table small for maximum performance. All too often, the reasoning behind small row and index width is left out! It boils down to data pages and how many data pages SQL Server has to read to fulfill a query.

20

UNDERSTANDING INDEXES

Suppose that you have a table with 500,000 rows and the size of a row (with overhead bytes) is 250 bytes or (2048 bytes in a data page – 32 bytes of overhead) / 250 bytes = 8) 8 records per data page. The number of data pages required for all 500,000 records is (500,000 / 8 = 62,500) 62,500 data pages.

Suppose that you look at your overall table design and you are able to shrink the size of the maximum row width just over 10 percent so that 9 rather than 8 records will fit on a data page. The number of data pages is reduced almost 7,000 data pages! An index data page is the same. Indexing a 20-character field (with overhead) and a 6-byte field (with overhead), for example, is the difference of 100 keys per data page or 336 keys per data page.

The larger index requires SQL Server to read three times as many data pages to access the same number of keys. (This does not take into account the added B-tree levels caused by a larger index key!) Normalize your tables and select smart indexes!

STRUCTURE OF SQL SERVER INDEXES

SQL Server maintains indexes with a B-tree structure (see Figure 20.5). B-trees are multilevel, self-maintaining structures.

Figure 20.5.
B-tree structure.

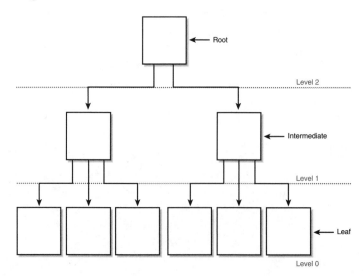

A B-tree structure consists of a top level, called the *Root* and a bottom level called the *Leaf* (always level 0) and 0 to many intermediate levels. (Note that the B-Tree shown in Figure 20.5 has one intermediate level.) In SQL Server terms, each square shown in Figure 20.5 represents an index page (or data page). The greater number of levels in your index, the more index pages you must read in order to retrieve the records you are searching for (that is, performance degrades as the number of levels increases). SQL Server maintains two different types of indexes: a clustered index and a nonclustered index.

CLUSTERED INDEX

A *clustered index* is a B-tree structure where level 0, the leaf, contains the actual data pages of the table and the data is physically stored in the logical order of the index.

> **Note**
>
> When a clustered index is created, the data pages are ordered, the index pages are created, and the non-ordered data pages are deleted. Creating a clustered index requires you to have free space in the database that amounts to approximately 1.2 times the data in the table.

Figure 20.6 shows a clustered index on the Name column in the School Employee table. Notice that the data pages are the leaf pages of the clustered index and that the data is stored in logical order on the data pages.

Figure 20.6.
Clustered index on the
School Employee table:
the Name column.

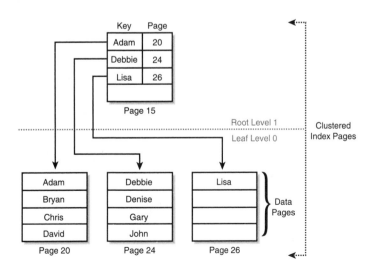

Note

Because data is physically ordered on the data pages, you can only have one clustered index per table. Select the clustered index wisely.

NONCLUSTERED INDEX

With a nonclustered index, the leaf level pages contain pointers to the data pages and rows, not the actual data such as the clustered index. A nonclustered index does not reorder the physical data pages of the table. Therefore, nonclustered indexes do not require the large amounts of free disk space associated with creating a clustered index. Figure 20.7 shows a nonclustered index on the School Employee table. Notice that the data in the data pages is in the order the data was inserted, not in the order of the index key. Also note that the nonclustered index adds one more level by always arriving at the leaf and then having to read the data page.

Figure 20.7.
Nonclustered index on
the School Employee
table: the Name column.

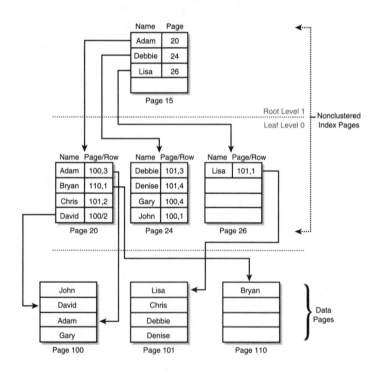

Tip

You can have up to 249 nonclustered indexes on a table, although you would *never* want to create anywhere near 249 indexes on a single table. A large number of indexes on a single table will affect the performance of other operations, such as UPDATE, DELETE, and INSERT. An index cannot exceed 256 bytes in width or 16 columns. Again, you would *never* want an index that is 256 bytes in width or contains 16 columns.

Remember, use narrow width indexes to maximize the number of index keys on a data page. This improves performance by requiring less disk I/O to scan the index. Try not to exceed 4 columns when creating indexes. A table can have both clustered and nonclustered indexes. Because you are only allowed to have a single clustered index on a table, you can meet your other indexing needs with nonclustered indexes. Try not to over-index; in many cases, a clustered index and 2 to 4 nonclustered indexes is more than suffecient.

DATA MODIFICATION AND INDEX PERFORMANCE CONSIDERATIONS

It is widely known that an index can help speed up data retrievals and from time to time, you may hear someone say that indexes will slow down other operations, such as inserts, updates, and deletes, which is true. It has been mentioned that B-tree data structures are, for the most part, self-maintaining data structures, meaning that as rows are added, deleted, or updated, the indexes also are updated to reflect the changes, thus requiring extra I/O to update the index pages.

What happens when a new row is added to a table without a clustered index? The data is added at the end of the last data page. What happens when a new row is added to a clustered index? The data will be inserted into the correct physical and logical order in the table and other rows might be moved up or down, depending on where the data is placed, causing additional disk I/O to maintain the index.

As the index pages and data pages grow, they may be required to split (which is beyond the scope of this book), requiring slightly more disk I/O.

In general, you should not worry about the time required to maintain indexes during inserts, deletes, and updates. Be aware that extra time is required to update the indexes during data modification and that performance can become an issue if you over-index a table. On tables that are frequently modified, I try to restrict the tables to a clustered index and no more than three to four nonclustered indexes. If you find the need to index beyond these numbers, run some benchmark tests to check for performance degradation.

CREATING INDEXES

You can create an index using the SQL Enterprise Manager.

Note

You cannot create an index on the following data types:

`bit`

`text`

`image`

Indexes cannot be created on a view.

Using the SQL Enterprise Manager, select a database. (The following example uses the pubs database.)

1. Select Indexes from the Manage menu. The Manage Indexes dialog box appears (see Figure 20.8).

Figure 20.8.
Manage Indexes
dialog box.

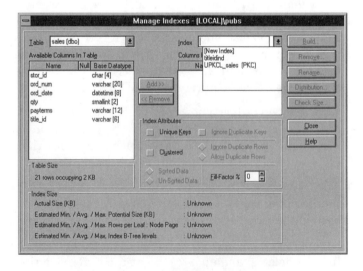

2. Using the *Index* drop-down combo box, shown in Figure 20.8, select the New Index option. The Index drop-down combo box will go blank. Now, in the Index drop-down combo box, enter the name of the new index.

Tip

Use a meaningful naming convention for indexes and stick with it. I like to prefix my index with *cidx* for a clustered index and *idx* for a nonclustered index. If the index is on the primary key table, I add *pk*. If the index is a foreign key, I add *fk*. I then use the column or columns name(s) to remind me at a glance which column(s) make up the index. For a clustered index on the primary key column on the authors table, au_id, in the pubs database, for example, I would name the index cidx_pk_au_id. The maximum number of characters you can use for an index is 30.

3. Select the column you want to add to the index by single clicking on the column in the Available Columns In Table list box. Click the Add button to move the selected column to the Columns in Index list box (see Figure 20.9). You also can move a column from the Available Columns in Table list box to the Columns in Index list box by double-clicking on the selected column.

Figure 20.9.
Adding columns to an index with the Manage Indexes dialog box.

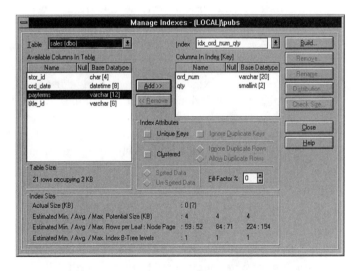

Note

An index that consists of more than one column is called a *composite index*. When creating a composite index, the order of the columns in the index makes a difference. SQL Server keeps density statistics on all columns that make up the index, but only histogram statistics on the first column of the composite index. As a result, if the first column of a composite index has very few unique values, the index may not be used for index selection by the query optimizer. When creating a composite index, select the column with the most unique values for the first column of a composite index.

4. To add the index, click the Build button. The Index Build dialog box appears (see Figure 20.10).

Figure 20.10.
Index Build dialog box.

The Index Build dialog box enables you to create the indexes immediately, by clicking the Execute Now button or to schedule the index build for a later time by clicking the Schedule As Task button. Being able to schedule the index build for a later time is a great new feature of SQL Server 6.0.

Warning

The table the index is being created on is locked during index creation. Creating indexes on very large tables or creating clustered indexes, which may reorder the data pages, may take some time to complete. While the index is being created, you will not be able to access the table until the index creation is complete. Try to create clustered indexes and very large nonclustered indexes during non-peak hours.

When an index is added, a row is placed in the sysindexes database system table.

Tip

Always build your clustered index before building your nonclustered index. When a clustered index is built, all nonclustered indexes currently on the table are rebuilt! You also can build an index on a temporary table.

The Transact SQL statement used to create an index is the CREATE INDEX command, which has the following syntax:

```
CREATE [UNIQUE] [CLUSTERED ¦ NONCLUSTERED] INDEX index_name
ON [[database.]owner.]table_name (column_name [, column_name]...)
[WITH [FILLFACTOR = x][[,] IGNORE_DUP_KEY][[,] {SORTED_DATA ¦ SORTED_DATA_REORG}]
[[,] {IGNORE_DUP_ROW ¦ ALLOW_DUP_ROW}]]
[ON segment_name]
```

Note

SQL Server 6.0 provides another method to create indexes called *constraints*. A constraint is added to a table during the table creation and can be used to maintain referential integrity. The primary key constraint places a unique index, clustered or nonclustered, on the columns defined as the primary key. You cannot drop a constraint index via the SQL Enterprise Manager (using the Manage Index dialog box). To remove a constraint requires using the ALTER TABLE command.

Let's examine in more detail some of the options and information displayed in the Manage Index Window dialog box and the CREATE INDEX command (see Figure 20.11). Start with the Index Attributes frame.

Figure 20.11.
Manage Index
dialog box.

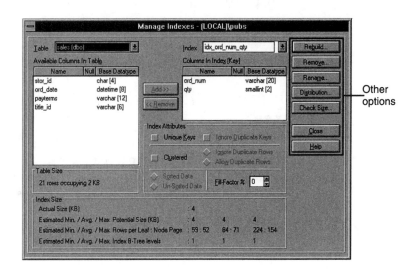

Other
options

INDEX ATTRIBUTES FRAME

The Index Attributes frame, shown in Figure 20.11, contains checkboxes that enable you to specify the type of index you want to create and relate to many of the options used in the CREATE INDEX command.

UNIQUE KEYS CHECKBOX

The Unique option creates an index that will enforce uniqueness on the indexed column(s). Use the Unique option when uniqueness is an attribute of the data (for example, the primary key of the table).

Warning

If you try to create a unique index on a column with duplicate data, the index creation will fail. You must remove the duplicate data entries to build the index.

IGNORE DUPLICATE KEYS CHECKBOX

The Ignore Duplicate Keys checkbox does not enable you to create a unique index with duplicate values, but if an attempt is made to insert or update a duplicate row, the duplicate row is ignored and an informational message is displayed. If the insert or update is part of a transaction, the transaction continues rather than rolling back on a duplicate key error.

CLUSTERED CHECKBOX

When the Clustered checkbox is selected, a clustered index with the selected columns is created on the table. Remember, you can only have one clustered index per table. When the option is not selected, a nonclustered index is created.

IGNORE DUPLICATE ROWS AND ALLOW DUPLICATE ROWS CHECKBOXES

These options are only relevant to clustered indexes. The Ignore Duplicate Row checkbox prevents duplicate rows from being added by ignoring the duplicate. The Allow Duplicate Rows checkbox enables you to create a non-unique clustered index on a table with duplicate rows and allows duplicate rows to be inserted or updated.

SORTED DATA AND UN-SORTED CHECKBOXES

The Sorted Data checkbox and Un-Sorted Data checkbox are used for a clustered index. If the data is already in a sorted order, check the Sorted Data checkbox to skip sorting the data while building the index. If a value is found out of order, the index creation will halt. Checking the Un-Sorted Data checkbox specifies to sort the data during the index creation process.

FILL FACTOR

The Fill factor specifies how densely packed you want your index and data pages while creating an index. The default is 0, which leaves room on the nonleaf pages with the leaf pages 100 percent full. Use a low fill factor to spread data over more pages.

Note

The fill factor is not maintained by SQL Server after index creation and is only maintained when the index is built.

TABLE SIZE AND INDEX SIZE

The Table Size and Index Size frames supply useful information, such as the current size of the table and the amount of disk space used by the index. You can use the information in these two frames to help you determine whether to use indexes on a table and if there may be performance problems with the indexes created.

The Table Size frame displays the number of rows and the amount of space occupied by the data. Remember, if the table contains a small number of rows, SQL Server will not use indexes and will perform a table scan instead. There is no minimum or maximum number of rows before an index or table scan occurs; you will have to test your queries and look at the query plan used by the optimizer.

For an index that already exists, the size of the index in disk space is displayed in the Actual Size field and the Estimated Min./Avg./Max. Potential Size field.

The Estimated Min./Avg./Max. Rows Per Leaf:Node Page label is displayed for nonclustered indexes and provides the estimated minimum, average, and maximum number of rows that are on the leaf pages and the nonleaf pages of the index B-tree. For a clustered index, the label reads Estimated Min./Avg./Max. Rows Per Index Page. The leaf pages are excluded because they are the actual data pages. Estimated Min./Avg./Max. Index B-Tree levels displays the number of levels for the expected index B-tree.

Tip

The levels of the B-tree can point to possible performance problems or poor index selection. A B-tree with a large number of levels will require more time to find rows because each level adds more data pages that must be read to get to the leaf pages.

20

UNDERSTANDING INDEXES

You can reduce the number of B-tree levels by reducing the width of the indexed columns, which increases the number of index keys per page.

OTHER INDEX OPERATIONS

Quickly review other index operations you can perform from the Manage Index dialog box shown in Figure 20.11.

Rebuild button	Rebuilds the currently selected index.
Remove button	Removes the selected index and frees up the space in the database allocated to the index, and removes the entry for the index from the database system table sysindexes. The Remove button performs the same operation as the transact SQL command DROP INDEX, which has the following format:

```
DROP INDEX [owner.]table_name.index_name
[, [owner.]table_name.index_name...]
```

Rename button	Enables you to rename an existing index. The Rename button performs the same operation as the SQL Server system stored procedure sp_rename, which has the following syntax:

```
sp_rename objname, newname [, COLUMN ¦ INDEX ]
```

Distribution button	Clicking the Distribution button displays the Index Distribution Statistics dialog box (see Figure 20.12).

Figure 20.12.
Index Distribution
Statistics dialog box.

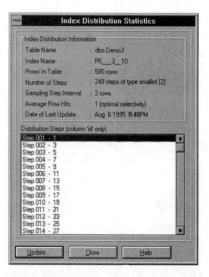

The Index Distribution Statistics dialog box displays the distribution page used by the query optimizer to determine which index or whether an index should be used to optimize performance when executing a query. For tables with more then 200 rows, a rating system is displayed to classify the usability of the selected index in most examples. The rating system is listed in Table 20.1.

TABLE 20.1. INDEX SUBJECTIVITY RATINGS.

Index Rating	# of Rows Returned	Comment
Optimal	1 row	Good candidate for primary key
Very Good	> 1 row	< 0.5% of rows
Good	> 0.5% of rows	< 1% of rows
Fair	> 1.0% of rows	< 2.5% of rows (Check with query showplan.)
Poor	> 2.5% of rows	< 5% of rows (Do not index.)
Very Poor	> 5% of rows	No way!

Tip

I'm really impressed with the information provided in the Index Distribution Statistics dialog box. It helps remove some of the guess work about the data distribution of a table. For developers and DBAs, being able to see the distribution page information and the subjective index rating will help in making a sound decision on whether a possible column(s) is a good index candidate.

Use the information in the Index Distribution Statistics dialog box, along with the Query Analyzer dialog box showplan option, described in the next chapter, to further tune your index selection.

Check Size   Use the Check Size button to check and verify the actual size of the index.

SUGGESTED INDEX STRATEGIES

Index selection is based on the design of the tables and the queries that are executed against the tables. Before you create indexes, make sure that the indexed columns are part of a query or are being placed on the table for other reasons, such as preventing duplicate data. The following sections discuss some suggested indexing strategies.

WHAT TO INDEX

The following list shows criteria you can use to help determine which columns will make good indexes:

◆ Columns used in table joins

◆ Columns used in range queries

◆ Columns used in order by

◆ Columns used in group by

◆ Columns used in aggregate functions

WHAT NOT TO INDEX

The following list shows cases in which columns or indexes should not be used or should be used sparingly:

◆ Tables with a small number of rows

◆ Columns with poor selectivity (that is, wide range of values)

◆ Columns that are very large in width (I try to limit my indexes to columns < 25 bytes in size.)

◆ Tables with heavy transaction loads (many inserts and deletes) but very little decision support operations

◆ Columns not used in queries

CLUSTERED OR NONCLUSTERED INDEX

As you are well aware, you can only have one clustered index per table. Following are some situations in which a clustered index works well:

◆ Columns used in range queries

◆ Columns used in order by or group by queries

◆ Columns used in table joins

◆ Queries returning large result sets

Nonclustered indexes work well in the following situations:

◆ Columns used in aggregate functions

◆ Foreign keys

◆ Queries returning small result sets

◆ Information frequently accessed by a specific column in table joins (order by or group by)

◆ Primary keys that are sequential surrogate keys (identity columns, sequence numbers)

COMPUTING SELECTIVITY

You can determine whether a column is a good candidate for an index by performing some simple math and computing the selectivity of the column. First, you need to determine the total number of rows in the table being indexed. You can obtain this information from the Table Size frame shown Figure 20.11 or use the following SQL command:

```
Select COUNT(*) FROM table_name
```

Next, you need to determine the number of unique values for the column you want to index. To determine this number, execute the following SQL command:

```
Select COUNT(DISTINCT column1_name) FROM table_name
```

To determine the number of expected rows returned by using the indexed column, perform the following formula:

```
expected number of rows = (1/number of unique values) * Total number of rows in the
table
```

If the expected number of rows is low relative to the total number of rows in the table, the column will be a good candidate for an index. You can further validate this by computing a percentage, as follows:

```
Percentage of rows returned = (expected number of rows/total number of rows in the
table) * 100
```

and compare this value to the values shown in Table 20.1.

COMPOSITE INDEXES

Composite indexes are indexes created with two or more columns (the maximum number of columns per an index is sixteen columns). SQL Server 6.0 keeps distribution page information on all the columns that make up the composite index, but the histogram of data distribution used by the query optimizer is only kept on the first key, so the order of the keys does matter. Use the key with the most unique values as the first key (best selectability). Try not to get carried away by creating composite indexes with a large number of columns (I try to keep them under four columns). Too many columns affect performance and make the index key large, thus increasing the size of the index.

INDEX COVERING

Index covering is a term used to explain a situation in which all the columns returned by a query and all the columns in the WHERE clause are the key columns in a single nonclustered index. SQL Server does not have to read the data pages to satisfy the query, instead returning the values on the leaf page of the index. In some cases, a covered nonclustered index can outperform a clustered index.

The downside to index covering is the added overhead to maintain the indexes. Also, it is very difficult to create indexes to cover the many different queries executed by your users. Avoid creating indexes to cover queries. You are better off creating single column or narrow composite indexes for the query optimizer to use.

BETWEEN THE LINES

Following are important points to remember about SQL Server indexes:

- ◆ SQL Server maintains indexes with a B-tree structure
- ◆ In a clustered index, the leaf contains the actual data pages of the table and the data is physically stored in the logical order of the index
- ◆ The SQL Server query optimizer will select at most one index to resolve a query
- ◆ Composite indexes are indexes created with two or more columns
- ◆ Select indexes carefully

SUMMARY

It is important that you grasp the basic ideas behind indexes that are used in SQL Server. In the next chapter, you will build on the basic concepts of this chapter and learn about the query optimizer. Understanding indexes and the query optimizer will enable you to provide valuable support to developers.

CHAPTER 21

Query Optimizer

The key to extracting maximum query performance is to understand SQL Server's optimizer. By understanding the optimizer, you will be able write queries that run faster, build better indexes, and resolve performance problems.

Note

SQL Server uses an *intelligent* cost-based optimizer. Don't be misled by the word *intelligent*! I have yet to meet a query optimizer that is more intelligent than a good DBA! Although SQL Server has an excellent query optimizer, there is no way it will ever be able to understand all the nuances and intricacies of your data. Therefore, do not put blind faith in the query optimizer. Instead, try to understand how the optimizer works and how you can finesse it into delivering better performance.

Note

SQL Server's optimizer has been significantly improved in Version 6.0. Following is a summary of notable enhancements.

Enhanced Index Usage: Version 6.0 has an improved optimizer that will take better advantage of useful indexes. This can reduce the amount of tuning effort required to achieve maximum performance.

Reverse Traversal of Indexes: When you perform a sort in descending order (ORDER BY...DESCENDING), the optimizer will look for useful indexes. Previous versions of SQL Server would process the query by using a worktable and a table scan.

Improved Subquery Optimization: Subqueries are now optimized in regard to the tables in the main query.

DISTINCT Statement: An index can now be used to process a query with the DISTINCT statement.

Optimizer Hints: The optimizer can be forced into using an index specified in the FROM clause.

WHY SQL SERVER USES A QUERY OPTIMIZER

SQL Server uses a cost-based query optimizer to generate the optimal execution path for an INSERT, UPDATE, DELETE, or SELECT SQL statement. The "optimal" execution path is the path that offers the best performance. Before the query is run, the optimizer will assign a cost based on CPU and disk I/O usage for different execution paths. The optimizer then will use the least expensive execution path to process the query. See Figure 21.1 for examples of execution paths.

Figure 21.1.
Examples of execution paths.

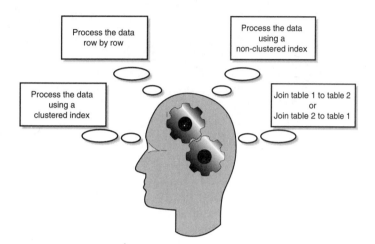

The advantage of the query optimizer is that it relieves users from the tedious process of having to decide how their SQL statements should be constructed to use indexes and in what order the data should be accessed. The query optimizer enables users to build SQL statements that *automatically* take advantage of indexes and *automatically* determine the optimal order to process table joins.

UPDATE STATISTICS

Whenever you create an index, SQL Server creates a set of statistics about the data contained within the index. The query optimizer uses these statistics to determine whether it should use the index to help process the query. You will find that over time, your statistics will become less representative of your data in tables that are frequently modified. In turn, this will cause the optimizer to ignore useful indexes.

In order to keep statistics up to date, the UPDATE STATISTICS command should be run whenever a large percentage of the table's index keys have changed. Operations such as BCP, batch inserts, deletes, and updates can cause an index's statistics to become outdated.

```
UPDATE STATISTICS [[database.]owner.]table_name [index_name]
```

If you do not include the [index_name] parameter, all indexes attached to the table will automatically be updated.

Tip

In a transaction-oriented environment, it can be advantageous to automate UPDATE STATISTICS (see Chapter 24 for more information on automating UPDATE STATISTICS). This will help keep your index statistics current.

Use the Task Scheduler included with the Enterprise Manager to schedule UPDATE STATISTICS.

To determine when an index's statistics were last updated, use STATS_DATE() or DBCC SHOW_STATISTICS, as in the following:

```
STATS_DATE (table_id, index_id)
        DBCC SHOW_STATISTICS (table_name, index_name)
```

BASIC QUERY OPTIMIZATION SUGGESTIONS

The following is a list of suggestions that concentrate on the basics of query optimization. By concentrating on the basics, you can improve performance.

◆ Target queries that run slow and are run frequently. By simply adding an index or updating statistics, you often will see a dramatic improvement in query performance.

◆ Understand your data. To use advanced optimization tricks, you must understand your query and how it relates to your data. Otherwise, your lack of knowledge may hamper your ability to effectively rewrite a query.

◆ Record statistics about the existing query. Before you begin to optimize a query, record a showplan and I/O statistics. This will serve as a benchmark to measure the success of your revisions.

◆ Start with the basics. Look for the obvious when you start to optimize a query. Do useful indexes exist? Have the statistics been updated recently? Are triggers being executed when the query is run? Does the query reference a view? Does the query use nonsearch arguments?

◆ Understand the output from a showplan. It is important to understand what is relevant and what is not when evaluating a showplan. (Use Table 21.1 to help determine relevant showplan output.)

◆ Throw conventional wisdom out the window. Sometimes you need to break the rules to optimize a query. The capability to extract maximum query performance is a mix between art and science. What works on one query may not work on another query. Therefore, you occasionally have to go against conventional wisdom to maximize performance.

TOOLS TO HELP OPTIMIZE A QUERY

The following optimizer tools can be used to help optimize a query.

- ◆ Showplan
- ◆ Statistics I/O
- ◆ No Execute
- ◆ Stats Time

SHOWPLAN

A *showplan* provides insight as to how SQL Server is going to process a SQL statement. The showplan can be one of the most confusing aspects of SQL Server. Its output is cryptic and based on technical jargon. Yet, if you know how to interpret its cryptic output, it can be useful for tuning queries.

SQL Server provides two facilities to generate a showplan: graphical and text-based.

The first facility is the *graphical* showplan. The graphical showplan is a subset of the output produced from a text-based showplan.

Warning

Not all showplan information is displayed in the graphical version. Showplan information, such as `The update mode is deferred`, and `The update mode is direct`, will not be displayed. Sometimes you may need to use the text-based showplan to get a full understanding of how the optimizer is handling your query.

To generate a graphical showplan, click on the Display Showplan button within the Query dialog box from the Enterprise Manager (see Figure 21.2).

After you execute your query, click on the Showplan tab to view the showplan output (see Figure 21.3).

To generate a text-based showplan, click on the Query Options button within the Query dialog box from the Enterprise Manager. Select the Show Query Plan option from the Query Flags tab (see Figure 21.4).

Figure 21.2.
Generating a graphical
showplan.

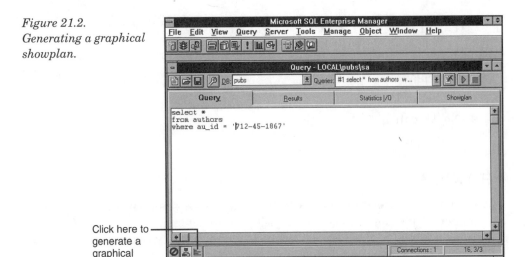

Click here to
generate a
graphical
showplan

Figure 21.3.
Graphical showplan.

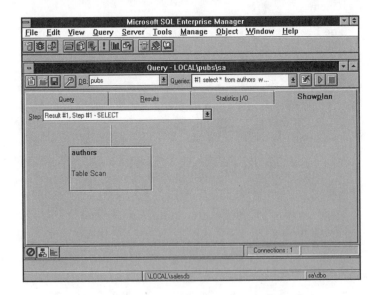

After you execute your query, the output from the showplan will appear in the Results window (see Figure 21.5).

Figure 21.4.
Setting query options.

Figure 21.5.
Text-based showplan.

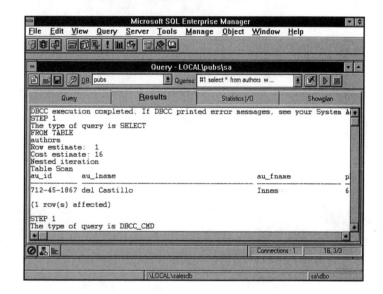

STATISTICS I/O

Statistics I/O is useful in determining the amount of I/O that will be used to process a query. The less I/O you have, the faster your query will run. When tuning queries, you want to try to minimize the amount of I/O used by the query. SQL Server uses I/O statistics to help determine the optimal query execution path.

When you generate statistics I/O, you will get back three types of I/O measurements: *scan count*, *logical reads*, and *physical reads*. See Figure 21.6 for an explanation of I/O measurements.

Figure 21.6.
Statistics I/O output.

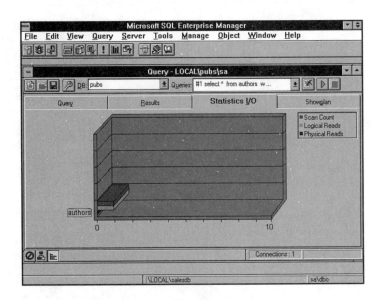

scan count equals the number of table scans required to process the query.

logical reads equal the number of pages accessed to process the query.

physical reads equal the number of times the disk was accessed to process the query.

Note

Each time a query is run, the data used to process the query may become loaded into the data cache. This can reduce the number of *physical reads* required to process the query when it is run again. You can detect whether the data is loaded into the data cache by monitoring the *logical reads* and *physical reads* for a query. If *physical reads* is less than *logical reads*, it means that some or all of the data was in the data cache.

SQL Server provides two facilities to generate I/O statistics: graphical and text-based.

To generate graphical statistics I/O, click on the Display Statistics I/O button within the Query dialog box from the Enterprise Manager (see Figure 21.7).

Figure 21.7.
Generating graphical
statistics I/O.

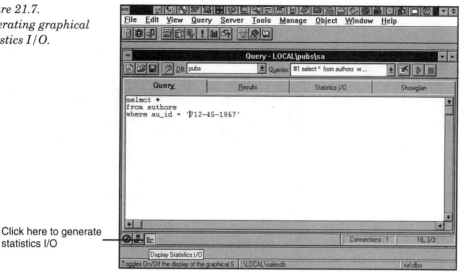

Click here to generate
statistics I/O

After you execute your query, click on the Statistics I/O tab to view I/O statistics
output (see Figure 21.8).

Figure 21.8.
Graphical statis-
tics I/O.

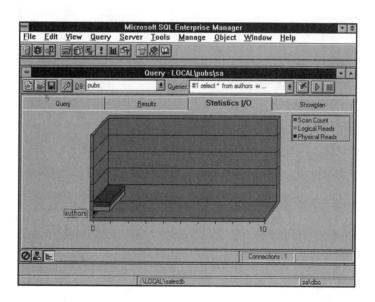

To generate text-based statistics I/O, click on the Query Options button within the Query dialog box from the Enterprise Manager. Select the Show Stats I/O option from the Query Flags tab. (Refer to Figure 21.4 for information on setting query options.)

Figure 21.9.
Text-based statis-
tics I/O.

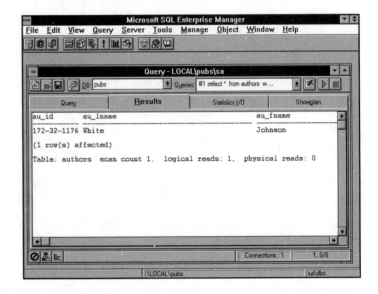

After you execute your query, the output from the statistics I/O will appear in the Results window.

NO EXECUTE

No Execute is an excellent tool for optimizing long running queries. By using this option, you can determine the showplan for a query without having to actually run the query. When you use this option, the syntax of the query will be validated, a showplan can be generated, and any error messages will be returned.

To use the No Execute option, click on the Query Options button within the Query dialog box from the Enterprise Manager. Select the No Execute option from the Query Flags tab (refer to Figure 22.4 for information on setting query options).

STATS TIME

Setting the Stats Time displays the time required by SQL Server to parse, compile, and execute a query.

To use the Stats Time option, click on the Query Options button within the Query dialog box from the Enterprise Manager. Select the Show Stats Time option from the Query Flags tab. (Refer to Figure 21.4 for information on setting query options.)

READING THE SHOWPLAN

The showplan provides insight as to how SQL Server is going to process a SQL statement. If you know what to look for in a showplan, the information it provides can be useful for tuning queries.

> **Note**
>
> For those new to SQL Server, don't be dismayed by the jargon used in the showplan. For example, the showplan will use words such as SCALAR AGGREGATE. This is just a fancy way of saying that the query contains an aggregate function, such as AVG(), COUNT(), MAX(), MIN(), or SUM(). After you get past the lingo used by the showplan, you will find it to be a useful tool for optimizing queries.

> **Note**
>
> A large amount of irrelevant information may be generated by a showplan. When you read a showplan, it is important to know what to look for. Use Table 21.1 to help weed out the irrelevant information.
>
> Items in Table 21.1 that are considered irrelevant are those that you cannot control. For example, if you use an aggregate function, such as COUNT(), you will *always* get the words SCALAR AGGREGATE or VECTOR AGGREGATE in the showplan. Therefore, I consider SCALAR AGGREGATE and VECTOR AGGREGATE to be irrelevant to query tuning because no matter how you modify your indexes or revamp your query, it will include these words.

TABLE 21.1. RELEVANT SHOWPLAN OUTPUT.

Text-based showplan output	Relevant
EXISTS TABLE : *nested iteration*	No
FROM TABLE	Yes
GROUP BY	No
Index : *<index name>*	Yes
Nested iteration	No
SCALAR AGGREGATE	No
STEP *n*	Yes
Table Scan	Yes

continues

TABLE 21.1. CONTINUED

Text-based showplan output	Relevant
The type of query is SELECT	No
The type of query is INSERT	No
The type of query is UPDATE	No
The type of query is DELETE	No
The type of query is SELECT (into a worktable)	Yes
The update mode is deferred	Yes
The update mode is direct	Yes
This step involves sorting	Yes
TO TABLE	No
Using Clustered Index	Yes
Using Dynamic Index	Yes
Using GETSORTED	Yes
VECTOR AGGREGATE	No
Worktable	No
Worktable created for DISTINCT	No
Worktable created for ORDER BY	Yes
Worktable created for REFORMATTING	Yes
Worktable created for SELECT_INTO	No

The following sections explain showplan output.

EXISTS TABLE : NESTED ITERATION

What it Means: The query contains an EXISTS, IN, or ANY clause.

Tip: Ignore this output

Relevant: No

FROM TABLE

What it means: The source of the data for the query

Tips: Use this output to determine the order in which the optimizer is joining the tables. On complex table joins (usually more than four tables), sometimes you can improve performance by rearranging the order of the tables in the FROM clause and

21

the WHERE clause. To force the optimizer to follow the table order in the FROM clause, you must use the SET FORCEPLAN command.

Relevant: Yes

GROUP BY

What it means: Query contains a GROUP BY clause

Tip: Ignore this output

Relevant: No

INDEX : <INDEX NAME>

What it means: The optimizer found a useful nonclustered index to retrieve the rows

Tips: Generally speaking, a query that uses an index will run faster than a query that does not use an index. An exception to this rule is a table with a small number of rows. Under this scenario, a table scan may be faster than using an index; however, the optimal access plan will always depend on the number of rows and columns in the table being accessed.

Relevant: Yes

NESTED ITERATION

What it means: Default approach for queries with WHERE criteria or table joins.

Tip: Ignore this output

Relevant: No

SCALAR AGGREGATE

What it means: Query contains an aggregate function: AVG(), COUNT(), MAX(), MIN(), or SUM(), and does not contain a GROUP BY clause.

Tip: Ignore this output

Relevant: No

STEP N

What it means: The number of steps required to process the query. Every query will have at least one step.

Tips: Fewer steps means better performance. GROUP BY clause will always require at least two steps.

Relevant: Yes

TABLE SCAN

What it means: Each row in the table is processed.

Tips: Look out for this plan on large tables. It may slow down your query because each row in the table will be processed. This can lead to a high degree of I/O.

To avoid a table scan, try to build a useful index that matches the WHERE clause.

On small tables, the optimizer may choose to ignore an index and perform a table scan. Under this scenario, a table scan may process faster than using an index to retrieve the data. On very large tables, you will want to avoid table scans.

Relevant: Yes

DISCUSSION ON TABLE SCAN

The table scan is dreaded when working with large tables in an OLTP (On-Line Transaction Processing) environment. It can lead to poor performance and result in table blocking.

The following example shows the difference in showplans for a retrieval based on a table scan versus a retrieval that can use an index:

```
Table:
CREATE TABLE sales
          (sales_id int not null,
          descr char(50) null)
Primary Key: sales_id
Indexes: None
Row Count: 1,000,000
Query:
SELECT * FROM sales
          WHERE sales_id = 450
Showplan:
STEP 1
The type of query is SELECT
FROM TABLE
sales
Nested iteration
Table Scan
```

Now consider the inefficiencies involved with a table scan. The user only wants one row returned from the table, but the server had to process *every row* in the table (see Figure 21.10)!

To prevent the table scan in this example, create a clustered index on the column sales_id. By creating the index, the optimizer can generate a showplan that will directly access the data without having to look at each row of data (see Figure 21.11). This will significantly improve performance!

Figure 21.10.
Table scan on
a 1,000,000
row table.

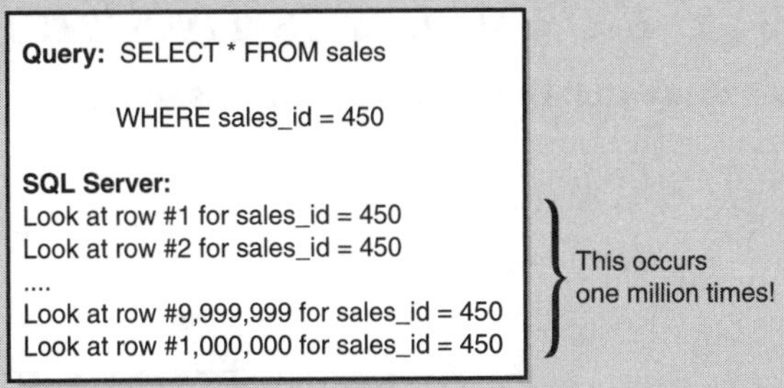

Query: SELECT * FROM sales

         WHERE sales_id = 450

SQL Server:
Look at row #1 for sales_id = 450
Look at row #2 for sales_id = 450
....
Look at row #9,999,999 for sales_id = 450
Look at row #1,000,000 for sales_id = 450

This occurs
one million times!

```
Index:
CREATE UNIQUE CLUSTERED INDEX sales_idx ON sales(sales_id)
Showplan:
The type of query is SELECT
FROM TABLE
sales
Nested iteration
Using Clustered Index
```

Figure 21.11.
Clustered index to find
data on a 1,000,000
row table.

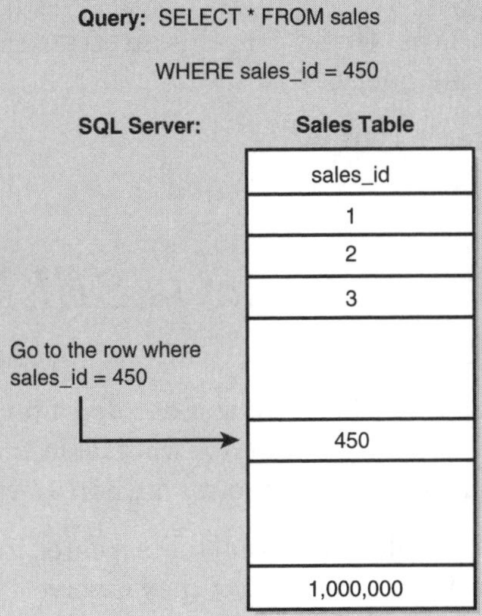

Query: SELECT * FROM sales

         WHERE sales_id = 450

SQL Server: **Sales Table**

sales_id
1
2
3
450
1,000,000

Go to the row where
sales_id = 450

THE TYPE OF QUERY IS *SELECT*

What it means: Query contains a SELECT clause

Tip: Ignore this output

Relevant: No

THE TYPE OF QUERY IS *INSERT*

What it means: Query contains an INSERT clause or a worktable that must be used to process the query.

Tip: Ignore this output

Relevant: No

THE TYPE OF QUERY IS *UPDATE*

What it means: Query contains an UPDATE clause or a worktable that must be used to process the query

Tip: Ignore this output

Relevant: No

THE TYPE OF QUERY IS *DELETE*

What it means: Query contains an DELETE clause or a worktable that must be used to process the query.

Tip: Ignore this output

Relevant: No

THE TYPE OF QUERY IS *SELECT (INTO A WORKTABLE)*

What it means: The optimizer decided a temporary worktable needs to be built to efficiently process the query. A worktable is always created when a GROUP BY clause is used and sometimes generated when an ORDER BY clause is used.

Tips: A worktable is an actual table created in the tempdb database. Worktables can degrade performance because they involve additional disk I/O. When the process is complete, the workable table is automatically deleted. A worktable is unavoidable when using a GROUP BY clause.

Relevant: Yes

THE UPDATE MODE IS DEFERRED

What it means: Two passes are required to update the data. The first pass generates a log of the changes and the second pass applies the changes. UPDATE, DELETE, and INSERT statements can generate this plan.

Tip: Update deferred is slower than update direct (see the sidebar entitled *"update mode is deferred* versus *update mode is direct"* for more information).

Relevant: Yes

UPDATE MODE IS DEFERRED VERSUS *UPDATE MODE IS DIRECT*

Update mode is often overlooked when trying to tune queries. Even the designers of the graphical showplan overlooked this aspect. You must run the text-based showplan to determine the update mode. By tweaking your table definition, indexes, and SQL statements, you can improve your UPDATE, INSERT, and DELETE performance.

It is important to determine the type of update mode in use because a direct update is always faster than a deferred update. When a deferred update is used, SQL Server takes two passes to update the data. The first pass generates a log of the changes and the second pass applies the changes. A direct update does not generate a log, thus it can be directly applied to the data.

The following is a list of requirements for SQL Server to run a direct update:

- ◆ The column containing the clustered index cannot be updated.
- ◆ The table being updated cannot contain an UPDATE trigger.
- ◆ The table being updated cannot be marked for replication.

The following rules apply to single row updates:

- ◆ If the column being modified is variable length, the row must fit on the same page as the old row.
- ◆ When updating a column that is part of a nonunique, non-clustered index, the column must be a fixed-length column. If the column being updated is part of a unique, nonclustered index, the column must be fixed-length and have an exact match in the WHERE clause.
- ◆ The modified row size must not differ from the original row size by more than 50 percent.

> The following rules apply to multiple row updates:
> - ◆ The column being modified must be fixed-length.
> - ◆ The column being modified must not be part of a unique, nonclustered index.
> - ◆ If the column is part of a non-unique, clustered index, it must be fixed-length; otherwise, the update will be deferred.
> - ◆ The table must not contain a timestamp datatype.

THE UPDATE MODE IS DIRECT

What it means: The data can be directly updated. UPDATE, DELETE, INSERT, and SELECT INTO statements can generate this plan.

Tip: Update direct is always faster than update deferred (see the sidebar title *"update mode is deferred* versus *update mode is direct"* for more information).

Relevant: Yes

THIS STEP INVOLVES SORTING

What it means: Query contains a DISTINCT or ORDER BY clause. To process the query, a worktable is created to sort the data.

Tips: This step is unavoidable if the query contains the DISTINCT clause. If the query contains the ORDER BY clause, you may be able to eliminate this step by creating a useful index.

Relevant: Yes

TO TABLE

What it means: The target table for data modifications. UPDATE, DELETE, INSERT, and SELECT INTO statements can generate this plan.

Tip: Ignore this output

Relevant: No

USING CLUSTERED INDEXES

What it means: The optimizer decided to use a clustered index to retrieve the record.

Tips: When working with a large table and retrieving a single record, this usually is the fastest and easiest strategy to implement for data retrieval.

Relevant: Yes

COMPOUND CLUSTERED INDEXES

The rules regarding compound clustered index optimization sometimes cause confusion. A compound clustered index is an index comprised of more than one column. This index uniquely identifies the record in the table.

Following is the structure of a table that will be used for this discussion.

```
Table:
CREATE TABLE table1
        (col1 int not null,
        col2 int not null,
        col3 int not null,
        description char(50) null)
Primary Key:
col1 + col2 + col3
Index:
CREATE UNIQUE CLUSTERED INDEX table1_idx ON table1(col1,col2,col3)
Number of rows:
1000
```

When working with a large table, the optimizer will take advantage of the clustered index when one of the following is true:

◆ All columns in the clustered index are referenced in the WHERE clause and they contain useful search arguments.

◆ The first column in the clustered index is referenced in the WHERE clause with a useful search argument.

For example, the following queries can take advantage of a clustered index:

```
SELECT *
        FROM table1
        WHERE col1 = 100
        and col2 = 250
        and col3 = 179


SELECT *
        FROM table1
        WHERE col1 = 100
        and col2 = 250


SELECT *
        FROM table1
        WHERE col1 = 100
```

```
SELECT *
        FROM table1
        WHERE col1 = 100
        and col3 = 250
```

For example, the following queries cannot take advantage of a clustered index:

```
SELECT *
        FROM table1
        WHERE col2 = 100
        and col3 = 250


SELECT *
        FROM table1
        WHERE col2 = 100


SELECT *
        FROM table1
        WHERE col3 = 100
```

USING DYNAMIC INDEX

What it means: The optimizer decided to build a temporary index to help process the query. This strategy is chosen when the query contains an OR clause or an IN clause.

Tips: A dynamic index is usually faster than a table scan on a large table, but slower than using an existing index. Use the OR clause and IN judiciously on large tables—a higher degree of I/O will be involved to process the query.

Relevant: Yes

USING GETSORTED

What it means: Query contains a DISTINCT or ORDER BY clause. To handle the sort, a worktable will be created.

Tips: This step is unavoidable if the query contains the DISTINCT clause. If the query contains the ORDER BY clause, you may be able to eliminate this step by creating a useful index.

Relevant: Yes

VECTOR AGGREGATE

What it means: Query contains an aggregate function and a GROUP BY clause. Aggregate functions are AVG(), COUNT(), MAX(), MIN(), and SUM().

Tip: Ignore this output

Relevant: No

WORKTABLE

What it means: The optimizer decided that a worktable must be created to process the query.

Tips: The use of worktable requires additional overhead, which can decrease performance. A GROUP BY clause will always generate a worktable, so don't spend any time trying to get rid of the worktable if your query has a GROUP BY clause.

Relevant: Yes

WORKTABLE CREATED FOR DISTINCT

What it means: Query contains the DISTINCT clause. A worktable is always used when the query contains the DISTINCT clause.

Tip: Ignore this output

Relevant: No

WORKTABLE CREATED FOR ORDER BY

What it means: Query contains an ORDER BY clause. The optimizer could not find a suitable index to handle the sort.

Tip: Evaluate your indexing strategy. A index may help eliminate this step.

Relevant: Yes

> ### WORKTABLE CREATED FOR ORDER BY
>
> If the ORDER BY clause is generating a worktable, you can use the following strategies to help eliminate the need for a worktable.

> ◆ Sort on the column(s) that contain the clustered index. This will always eliminate the need for a worktable. With a clustered index, the data is physically stored in sorted order; therefore, a worktable isn't required to handle the sort.
>
> ◆ Sort on a column that contains a nonclustered index. This may or may not eliminate the worktable. The optimizer will look at the cost of performing a table scan versus the cost of using the non-clustered index. It will choose the nonclustered index if the cost is less than a table scan.

WORKTABLE CREATED FOR *REFORMATTING*

What it means: This strategy is used when large tables are joined on columns that do not have useful indexes. The table with the fewest number of rows is inserted into a worktable. Then the worktable is used to join back to the other tables in the query. This reduces the amount of I/O that is needed to process the query.

Tips: This is an easy one to fix! Whenever the optimizer chooses this strategy, you need to look at your indexes. Chances are good that indexes do not exist or the statistics are out of date. Add indexes to the columns you are joining on or issue an UPDATE STATISTICS command. The optimizer will only use this strategy as a last resort. Try to avoid this strategy.

Relevant: Yes

WORKTABLE CREATED FOR *SELECT_INTO*

What it means: Query contains the SELECT..INTO clause. A worktable will always be created when SELECT..INTO is used.

Tip: Ignore this output

Relevant: No

OVERRIDING THE OPTIMIZER

Use the following commands to override the optimizer.

◆ Index Hints

◆ SET FORCEPLAN ON

INDEX HINTS

New to Version 6.0 is the capability to override the optimizer. Now you can force the optimizer into using an index or force it to not choose an index.

You usually will want to let the optimizer determine how to process the query. However, you may find it beneficial to override the optimizer should you find that it is not taking advantage of useful indexes. Following is the syntax to override the optimizer:

```
SELECT ...
FROM [table_name] (optimizer_hint)
```

where *optimizer_hint* is

```
INDEX={index_name ¦ index_id}
```

index_name is any valid name of an existing index on the table.

index_id is 0 or 1. 0 will force the optimizer to perform a table scan. 1 will force the optimizer to use a clustered index.

To force the optimizer to use a clustered index, use the following:

```
select *
from authors (1)
where au_id = '213-46-8915'
```

To force the optimizer to perform a table scan, use the following:

```
select *
from authors (0)
where au_id = '213-46-8915'
```

To force the optimizer to use the au_fname_idx nonclustered index, use the following:

```
select *
from authors (INDEX = au_fname_idx)
where au_fname = 'Marjorie'
```

Tip

> The capability to override the optimizer should be used with prudence. Only in cases where SQL Server is choosing a sub-optimal execution plan should the optimizer be overridden.

SET FORCEPLAN ON

SET FORCEPLAN ON forces the optimizer to join tables based on the order specified in the FROM clause. Normally, you will want to let the optimizer determine the order in which to join tables; however, if you feel that the optimizer is selecting an inefficient join order, you can use SET FORCEPLAN ON to force the join order.

When forcing SQL Server to use a predefined join order, you will usually want the table with the fewest number of qualifying rows to come first in the FROM clause (or the table with the least amount of I/O if you are dealing with a very wide or a very narrow table). The table with the second lowest number of qualifying rows should be next in the FROM clause, and so on.

The following example shows how SET FORCEPLAN ON can impact query optimization:

```
SET FORCEPLAN ON
select *
from  titleauthor , authors
where titleauthor.au_id = authors.au_id
SET FORCEPLAN OFF
```

The following is showplan output with SET FORCEPLAN ON:

```
STEP 1
The type of query is SELECT
FROM TABLE
titleauthor
Nested iteration
Table Scan
FROM TABLE
authors
JOINS WITH
titleauthor
Nested iteration
Table Scan
```

Notice that with SET FORCEPLAN ON, the optimizer processes the titleauthor table before processing the authors table.

Following is the query:

```
select *
from  titleauthor , authors
where titleauthor.au_id = authors.au_id

Showplan:
STEP 1
The type of query is SELECT
FROM TABLE
authors
Nested iteration
Table Scan
FROM TABLE
titleauthor
JOINS WITH
authors
Nested iteration
Table Scan
```

Notice that without using SET FORCEPLAN ON, the optimizer processes the authors table before processing the titleauthor table.

21

Tip

Whenever you use SET FORCEPLAN ON, be sure to turn it off. It will remain in effect for your current connection until the connection is broken or until it is explicitly turned off.

Warning

Use the SET FORCEPLAN ON option as a last resort. You usually will want to let the optimizer determine the order in which to process tables.

OTHER TUNING TRICKS

Whenever you are trying to optimize a query, you should be on the lookout for obstructions that can lead to poor performance. The following sections discuss common causes of poor query performance.

ARE YOU TRYING TO TUNE AN *UPDATE*, *DELETE*, OR *INSERT* QUERY?

If so, does the table have a trigger? Your query may be okay, but the trigger may need improvement. An easy way to determine whether the trigger is the bottleneck is to drop the trigger and run the query. If query performance improves, you need to tune the trigger.

DOES THE QUERY REFERENCE A VIEW?

If so, you need to test the view to determine whether it is optimized. An easy way to test whether the view is optimized is to run a showplan on the view.

ARE YOUR DATATYPES MISMATCHED?

If you are joining on columns of different datatypes, the optimizer may not be able to use useful indexes. Instead, it may have to choose a table scan to process the query, as in the following example:

```
Table:
CREATE TABLE table1
(col1 char(10) not null)
Index: CREATE INDEX col1_idx ON table1(col1)
Row Count: 1000
Table:
```

```
CREATE TABLE table2
(col1 varchar(10) not null)
Index: CREATE INDEX col1_idx ON table2(col1)
Row Count: 1000
Query:
SELECT *
FROM table1, table2
WHERE table1.col1 = table2.col2
```

This query will result in a table scan because you are joining a char(10) column to a varchar(10) column. Internally, SQL Server must convert these values to process the query and this will result in a table scan.

Mismatched datatypes can also cause an UPDATE to be deferred instead of being direct.

Does the Query Use a Nonsearch Argument?

Nonsearch arguments force the optimizer to process the query with a table scan. This is because the search value is unknown until runtime.

Following are some common examples of queries that use nonsearch arguments and how to convert them to search arguments that can take advantage of an index:

```
Table:
CREATE TABLE table1
(col1 int not null)
Index: CREATE UNIQUE CLUSTERED INDEX col1_idx ON table1(col1)
Row Count: 1000 rows
```

The following is a nonsearch argument query:

```
select *
from table1
where col1 * 10 = 100
```

The following is a search argument query:

```
select *
from table1
where col1 = 100/10
```

The following is a nonsearch argument query:

```
select *
from table1
where convert(char(8),col1) =  '10'
```

The following is a search argument query:

```
select *
from table1
where col1 =  convert(int,'10')
```

21

Tip

A method to help reduce the use of a nonsearch argument is to keep the table column on the left side of the equation and to keep the search criteria on the right side of the equation.

Does Your Query Use More Than One Aggregate Function?

If your query has more than one aggregate function in the SELECT clause, it may be forced to perform a table scan *regardless* of available indexes. The following query uses the two aggregate functions, MIN() and MAX().

```
Table:
CREATE TABLE table1
(id int not null)
Index: CREATE UNIQUE CLUSTERED INDEX id_idx ON table1(id)
Query:
SELECT MIN(id),MAX(id)
FROM table1
```

If you find that a table scan is being performed, you can rewrite the query by using a subquery in the SELECT statement, as in the next example. This query avoids a table scan by searching the index for both the MIN and MAX aggregate request.

```
SELECT MIN(ID), (SELECT MAX(ID) FROM TABLE1) FROM TABLE1
```

Are You Trying to Optimize a Stored Procedure?

If you are trying to optimize a stored procedure you *must* keep in mind the following rules.

◆ A stored procedure's query plan is stored in memory when the stored procedure is first executed. Therefore, if you add an index after the query plan has been generated, it may not be used by the stored procedure. Whenever you make changes to the tables used by a stored procedure and the stored procedure does not contain the WITH RECOMPILE statement, *always* use sp_recompile or drop and re-create the stored procedure. This is the only way to ensure that the optimizer has re-evaluated the query plan.

Note

A stored procedure will automatically recompile its query plan whenever you drop an index used by a table within a stored procedure.

◆ Parameters used in the WHERE clause of a stored procedure may produce inconsistent query plans. As mentioned in the preceding rule, a stored procedure will save its query plan in memory. Therefore, if the first execution of the procedure uses a parameter that is atypical, the optimizer may place in memory a query plan that is not advantageous for your typical parameter. This may degrade performance when you execute your stored procedure with your typical parameter. Look at the following example:

```
CREATE PROCEDURE usp_example @search_name char(50) AS
SELECT au_lname
FROM authors
WHERE au_lname like @search_name + '%'
Index: CREATE INDEX au_lname_idx ON authors(au_lname)
```

Consider what happens when a user executes the query with 'B' as a parameter.

```
EXEC usp_example 'B'
```

If the table contains numerous records that have a last name beginning with the letter 'B', the optimizer is likely to perform a table scan.

Next, consider what happens when a user executes the query with 'BREAULT' as a parameter.

```
EXEC usp_example 'BREAULT'
```

If the table contains only a couple of records that have a last name = 'BREAULT', the optimizer is likely to use an index.

As you can see, the optimizer is choosing different query plans based on the value of the parameter passed into the stored procedure. The problem arises when the first query plan is stored in memory. By default, different users will receive the same query plan based on the first execution of the stored procedure. If the first user of the stored procedure was to pass the 'B' as a parameter, the query plan would be very inefficient for other users that specify 'BREAULT' as a parameter.

To avoid this problem, use the WITH RECOMPILE option when you execute the procedure. This will force the procedure to regenerate its query plan, as in the following:

```
EXEC ... WITH RECOMPILE
```

The revised query plan will only be available for the current execution of the procedure. Subsequent executions of the procedure without the recompile option will revert back to the old query plan.

Additionally, you can also use the `WITH RECOMPILE` option when you create the procedure, as in the following:

```
CREATE PROCEDURE ... WITH RECOMPILE
```

This will force the optimizer to recompile the query plan each time the stored procedure is executed.

BETWEEN THE LINES

- ◆ You must understand SQL Server's optimizer to get maximum query performance.
- ◆ Don't forget to `UPDATE STATISTICS`.
- ◆ Keep in mind the following questions when you are trying to tune a query. Any questions that are answered with a "No" should be used as a starting point for tuning your query.

    - ◆ Have useful indexes been created?
    - ◆ Have the statistics been updated recently?
    - ◆ Does the query use search arguments?
    - ◆ Does the query join columns of the same datatype?

- ◆ Query optimization is part science, part luck. What works on one query may not work on another query. Try different techniques until you get the performance you expect.
- ◆ Use Showplan, Statistics I/O, No Execute, and Stats Time to help tune a query.
- ◆ Not all showplan information is displayed in the graphical showplan. You may need to run the text-based showplan to get a full understanding of your query.
- ◆ The top three items to look for in a showplan are: `Table Scan`, `Using Clustered Index`, and `Index: <index name>`.
- ◆ If you demand OLTP performance, do everything you can to prevent a table scan on a large table.
- ◆ A Clustered Index is usually your best bet for maximum retrieval performance.
- ◆ Use index hints to force the optimizer to use or not use an index.
- ◆ Stored procedures that do not contain the `WITH RECOMPILE` statement should be recompiled after you make an index change to a table used by the stored procedure.

SUMMARY

A good DBA needs to know how SQL Server's optimizer works. This will enable the DBA to turn an agonizingly slow query into a fast query. Consequently, knowledge of the optimizer can keep the DBA from creating needless indexes that are never used by the system. In the next chapter multi-user considerations are discussed.

- Locks

- Multi-User
  Configuration Options

- Between the Lines

CHAPTER 22

Multi-User Issues

How many times have you seen an application that works with a single user but when multiple users access the application, all sorts of performance and data problems occur? When these types of problems arise, it usually is up to the DBA to fix them. I know that you have been told many times that SQL Server is a high-performance database capable of handling 100 or more users. However, to extract maximum performance and data consistency, you must understand how SQL Server manages transactions in a multi-user environment. Otherwise, performance and data consistency will suffer. To help avoid these problems, the topics discussed in this chapter explain how to design multi-user databases that maximize transaction throughput while maintaining data consistency.

LOCKS

SQL Server uses *locks* to maintain data consistency in a multi-user environment. Locking behavior is automatically handled by SQL Server. However, Version 6.0 enables the DBA to control additional aspects of locking.

To help understand why locks are important, look at the simple banking example shown in Figure 22.1. Suppose that you decide to transfer $100 from checking to savings. Your bank decides to run a report that shows your combined balance for checking and savings. What happens if the report is run while the transfer is in progress? Would the report show a balance of $200 or $100?

Figure 22.1.
How locks maintain data consistency.

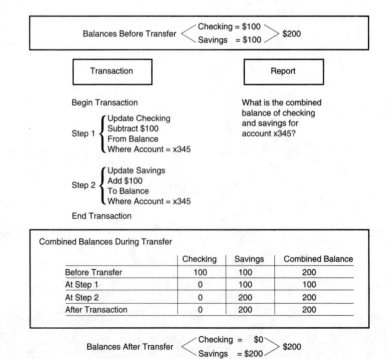

	Checking	Savings	Combined Balance
Before Transfer	100	100	200
At Step 1	0	100	100
At Step 2	0	200	200
After Transaction	0	200	200

The answer resides in how SQL Server uses locks to maintain data consistency. When transaction 1 is initiated, SQL Server will place a lock on the checking account information and on the savings account information. Other processes will be forced to wait until the transaction is complete before they can access the data.

These locks will force other users to wait until the locks are released before they can access the data. This prevents users from reading incomplete or pending changes. Therefore, the report will show the correct balance of $200.

Note

When pending changes can be read by a transaction, it is known as a *dirty read*. By default, SQL Server prevents dirty reads.

Without locks, the report could have showed a balance of $100, which is incorrect. For example, if the report read the data after the $100 was subtracted from checking but before it was added to savings, the report would show a combined balance of $100.

Understanding SQL Server's Locking Behavior

If locks are automatically handled by SQL Server you may be asking yourself, "Why we are having this discussion?" The answer is *blocking* and *deadlocks*! Whenever multiple users try to access or modify the same data, the potential for blocking and deadlocks increases.

By understanding SQL Server's locking behavior you can decrease the likelihood of blocking and deadlocks.

The following are some of the variables that can impact the frequency of blocking and deadlocks:

◆ Transaction management
◆ Query implementation
◆ Indexing scheme
◆ Table design
◆ Hardware configuration

Blocking

Blocking occurs when a process must wait for another process to complete. The process must wait because the resources it needs are exclusively used by another process. A blocked process will resume operation after the resources are released by the other process.

For this example, assume that the bank decides to eliminate the monthly service charge for all existing customers (see Figure 22.2). Therefore, the DBA sets the service_charge to $0.00 for all accounts. Not being a good DBA, he runs this transaction during prime hours. This forces transactions 2, 3, and 4 to wait until transaction 1 is complete. The waiting transactions are considered to be *blocked* by transaction 1.

Figure 22.2.
Blocking example.

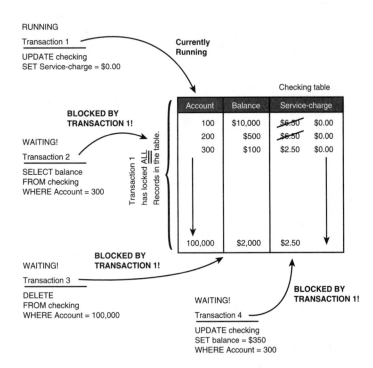

When blocking occurs, it looks like your machine is hung. What has happened is that SQL Server has put your process in a holding queue. The process will remain in the queue until it can acquire the resources it needs to complete its tasks.

BLOCKING PROBLEMS

I once was thrown into a project that involved converting a mainframe application to SQL Server. Management was eager to quickly convert the application. They did not want any time spent on table design or index strategy. I tried to explain to them that their existing database design could lead to blocking.

The day the application went into production was a prime example of how an application could dominate SQL Server. Whenever the application would run over 100, users were unable to process any transactions. This was due to blocking.

The reason the blocking was so severe was due to poor table design and index strategy. The main table used by the application was not properly normalized, thus making it very wide. Very wide tables can substantially slow processing throughput. Additionally, the table lacked any useful indexes. The combination of these factors is a sure-fire way to generate massive blocking.

After management realized what had happened, they were willing to allocate the resources to go back and redesign the table schema and re-evaluate the index strategy. After the redesign the blocking went away, and the application could be used without impacting other users.

DEADLOCK

Deadlock occurs when two users have locks on separate objects and each user is trying to lock the other user's objects. SQL Server automatically detects and breaks the deadlock. It terminates the process that has the least amount of CPU utilization. This enables the other user's transaction to continue processing. The terminated transaction will be automatically rolled back and an error code 1205 will be issued.

To help illustrate deadlock, look at Figure 22.3. Assume that transaction 1 and transaction 2 begin at the exact same time. By default, SQL Server automatically places exclusive locks on data that is being updated. This causes transaction 1 to wait for transaction 2 to complete, and transaction 2 will have to wait for transaction 1 to complete. This is deadlock! To resolve the deadlock, SQL Server automatically terminates one of the transactions.

Figure 22.3.
An example of
deadlock.

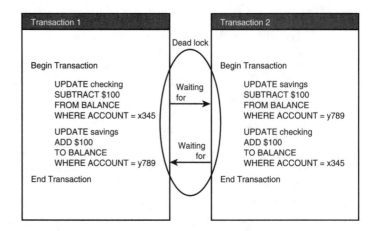

VIEWING LOCKS AND BLOCKING

The following are utilities provided by SQL Server to view locks:

Current Activity dialog box   The Current Activity dialog box in the Enterprise Manager provides graphical lock and blocking information (see Figure 22.4).

Figure 22.4.
Viewing locks from the
Current Activity dialog
box in the Enterprise
Manager.

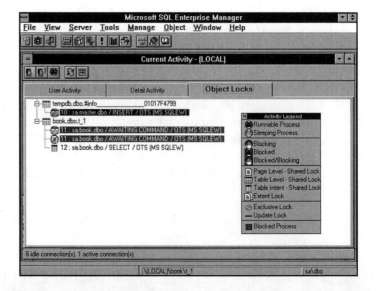

sp_lock   The system procedure sp_lock provides text-based lock information (see Figure 22.5).

Figure 22.5.
Sample output from
sp_lock.

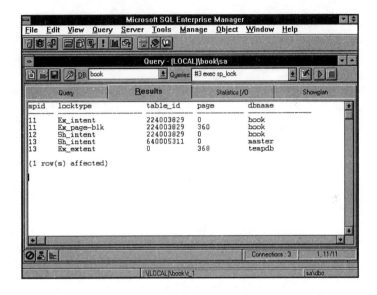

Performance Monitor   The Performance Monitor allows you to graphically track lock information (see Figure 22.6).

Figure 22.6.
Tracking locks with the
Performance Monitor.

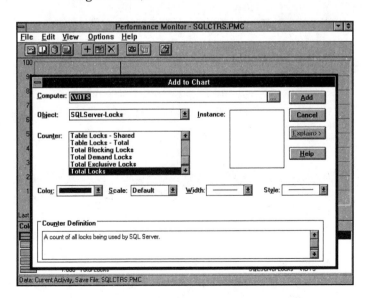

sp_who   The system procedure sp_who provides information about blocked processes (see Figure 22.7).

Figure 22.7.
Sample output from
sp_who.

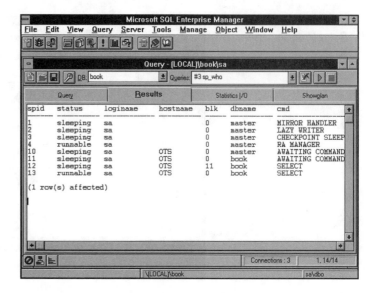

Trace flags   The trace flags shown in Table 22.1 provide extended insight into locking behavior.

TABLE 22.1. USEFUL TRACE FLAGS.

Trace flag	Output
1200	Displays process id and types of lock being requested
1204	Displays locks in use with a deadlock and the command involved in the deadlock
1205	Displays information about the commands used during a deadlock

Tip

The trace flag 1200 can be useful for tracking locking behavior. The easiest way to use the trace flag is to use the DBCC traceon() function. You also must turn on trace flag 3604 to echo trace information to the client workstation, as in the following example:

```
DBCC traceon(3604)
 DBCC traceon(1200)
 UPDATE t_1
 SET c_1 = 0
```

> The following is sample output from DBCC trace flag 1200:
>
> ```
> Process 11 requesting page lock of type SH_PAGE on 7 25
> Process 11 releasing page lock of type SH_PAGE on 7 25
> Process 11 releasing page lock of type SH_PAGE on 7 26
> Process 11 requesting table lock of type EX_TAB on 7 80003316
> Process 11 clearing all pss locks
> ```

LOCKING DETAILS

Now that you know why it is important to understand SQL Server's locking behavior and how to view active locks, you need to get in to the nuts and bolts of locking.

Any transaction that reads or modifies data (SELECT, INSERT, DELETE, UPDATE, CREATE INDEX, and so on) will generate some type of lock. The degree of locking is determined by the following two questions:

◆ Is the data being modified or read?

◆ How many rows are being accessed or modified?

To answer these questions, you must look at the two levels of physical locks: page locks and table locks.

PAGE LOCKS

A *page lock* is a lock on a 2K data page. Whenever possible, SQL Server attempts to use a page lock rather than a table lock. Page locks are preferred over table locks because they are less likely to block other processes. There are three main types of page locks.

SHARED

A *shared* page lock is used for read transactions (typically SELECT statements). If a page is marked as shared, other transactions can still read the page. A shared lock must be released before an exclusive page lock can be acquired. Shared locks are released after the page has been read, except when HOLDLOCK is specified. HOLDLOCK forces the page to remain locked until the transaction is complete.

EXCLUSIVE

An *exclusive* lock is used for write transactions (typically INSERT, UPDATE, or DELETE statements). Other transactions must wait for the exclusive page lock to be released before they can read or write to the page.

UPDATE

When an UPDATE or DELETE statement is initially processed, SQL Server will place update locks on the pages being read. It then escalates the update locks to exclusive locks before it modifies the data.

> Typically, read statements acquire shared locks and data modification statements acquire exclusive locks.

TABLE LOCKS

A *table lock* is when the entire table (data and indexes) is locked. When this happens, SQL Server has detected that it is faster to process the transaction by locking the table rather than incurring the overhead of locking numerous pages.

SQL Server usually will begin the transaction by placing page locks on the data being accessed. By default, if more than 200 pages are acquired within a transaction, SQL Server will automatically escalate the locks into a table lock.

> *Note*
>
> The 200-page limit can be overridden with SQL Server 6.0. See the topic "Lock Escalation" in the "Multi-User Configuration Options" section of this chapter for more information.

The drawback of table locking is that it increases the likelihood of blocking. When other transactions try to access or modify information in a locked table, they must wait for the table lock to be released before proceeding. There are three main types of table locks.

SHARED

A *shared* table lock differs from a shared page lock in that the lock is at the table level and not at the page level.

EXCLUSIVE

An *exclusive* table lock differs from an exclusive page lock in that the lock is at the table level and not at the page level.

Tip

In a multi-user environment, you want to avoid exclusive table locks during normal processing hours. An exclusive table lock on a commonly used table usually leads to blocking.

INTENT

An *intent* table lock occurs when SQL Server has the intention of acquiring an exclusive or shared table lock. SQL Server uses intent locks to keep other transactions from placing exclusive or table locks on the table in which it is currently processing.

Table 22.2 summarizes the different types of locks that can be placed on an object.

TABLE 22.2. OBJECT LOCK SUMMARY.

Object Lock Type
Page shared
Exclusive
Update
Table shared
Exclusive
Intent

PAGE AND TABLE LOCK SUMMARY

Table 22.3 summarizes the different types of page and table locks used by SQL Server. When viewing Table 22.3, be sure to notice the different locking strategies used in regard to indexes. When a useful index is present, SQL Server is less likely to choose a locking strategy that can lead to blocking.

TABLE 22.3. PAGE AND TABLE LOCK SUMMARY.

Using Index	Syntax	Table Level Locks	Page Level Locks
N/A	INSERT	Exclusive intent	Exclusive page
Yes	SELECT	Shared intent	Shared page
Yes	SELECT with HOLDLOCK	Shared intent	Shared page

continues

22

TABLE 22.3. CONTINUED

Using Index	Syntax	Table Level Locks	Page Level Locks
Yes	UPDATE	Exclusive intent	Update and exclusive
Yes	DELETE	Exclusive intent	Exclusive page
No	SELECT	Shared intent	Shared page
No	SELECT with HOLDLOCK	Shared table	None
No	UPDATE	Exclusive table	None
No	DELETE	Exclusive table	None
N/A	Create clustered index	Exclusive table	None
N/A	Create non-clustered index	Shared table	None

> *Note*
>
> Prior to Version 6.0, you could run out of extent locks when building clustered indexes on large tables. This problem has been resolved with Version 6.0.

10 TIPS TO HELP MINIMIZE LOCKING AND PREVENT DEADLOCKS

Try using the tips in this section when attempting to resolve locking problems. These tips can help minimize locking problems and prevent deadlocks.

TIP 1: USE AN INDEX WITH *UPDATE/DELETE* STATEMENTS

Whenever you issue an UPDATE or DELETE statement that does *not* use an index, an exclusive table lock will be used to process the transaction. The exclusive table lock may block other transactions.

To reduce the chance of an exclusive table lock, specify a WHERE clause that can take advantage of an existing index, preferably a clustered index. This may enable SQL Server to use page level locks instead of an exclusive table lock.

TIP 2: CONVERT A LARGE *INSERT* STATEMENT INTO A SINGLE *INSERT* STATEMENT WITHIN A LOOP

Inserting a large number of rows into a table may result in an exclusive table lock (for example, INSERT INTO table2 SELECT * FROM table1). To avoid this problem, convert the INSERT statement into an INSERT statement within a loop. For example, the following code opens a cursor and then initiates a loop that fetches the data from table1 into a variable and then inserts the contents of the variable into table2. This approach decreases the likelihood of blocking because it generates exclusive page locks rather than an exclusive table lock. It is important to note that this approach will run more slowly than a batch INSERT.

```
declare @col1 varchar(11)
declare sample_cursor cursor
 for select col1 from table1
open sample_cursor
fetch next from sample_cursor into @col1
while @@fetch_status = 0
 begin
 insert into table2 values (@col1)
 fetch next from sample_cursor into @col1
 end
deallocate sample_cursor
```

TIP 3: AVOID USING *HOLDLOCK*

HOLDLOCK is one of those keywords that almost every developer new to SQL Server has tried to use. Quite often, the developer will use HOLDLOCK without fully understanding the ramifications behind it.

When HOLDLOCK is used with a SELECT statement, all shared locks (remember that shared locks are acquired whenever a SELECT is issued) will remain in effect until the transaction is *complete*. This means additional locking overhead, which degrades performance and increases the likelihood of blocking or deadlocks. When the HOLDLOCK command is not used, SQL Server releases the shared locks as soon as possible rather than waiting for the transaction to complete.

What usually happens is that developers will use the HOLDLOCK command, thinking that they can temporarily prevent other users from reading the same data. What they do not realize is that HOLDLOCK only generates shared locks, not exclusive locks. Because the locks are shared, other users can still read the same data values.

TIP 4: PLACE CLUSTERED INDEXES ON TABLES THAT HAVE A HIGH FREQUENCY OF INSERTS

Whenever you insert data into a table without a clustered index, you increase the risk of contention for the last data page. In a high transaction environment with multiple users, this can lead to blocking.

Add a clustered index to your table to prevent this problem. By adding a clustered index, your inserted rows will be distributed across multiple pages. This significantly reduces the likelihood of contention for the same page.

TIP 5: KEEP TRANSACTIONS SHORT

Long running transactions, especially data modification transactions, increase the likelihood of blocking and deadlocks. Whenever possible, try to keep the length of a transaction to a minimum. Following are suggestions to help decrease the length of a transaction:

◆ **Break long-running transactions into multiple shorter running transactions.**

Whenever you can reduce the duration of a lock, you can reduce the possibility of blocking. For this example, assume that table t_2 has 100 records with a sequential id going from 1 to 100. The following is a long-running transaction:

```
INSERT INTO t_1
SELECT * FROM t_2
```

You can rewrite this long-running transaction into two shorter running transactions. This reduces the duration of locks in use.

```
INSERT INTO t_1
SELECT * FROM t_2
WHERE t_2.id <= 50
INSERT INTO t_1
SELECT * FROM t_2
WHERE t_2.id > 50
```

◆ **Minimize non-clustered indexes.**

Avoid unnecessary non-clustered indexes. Each index adds additional overhead that must be maintained whenever a record is inserted, deleted, or an indexed column is modified. This can decrease throughput.

◆ **Reduce the number of columns per table.**

An INSERT will process faster on a narrow table (a table with few columns) than a wide table (a table with many columns). The reduction of the overall width of a table enables more rows to exist on a page. This means that fewer pages will need to be accessed in order to process the transaction, thus shortening transaction times.

TIP 6: UNDERSTAND TRANSACTIONS

Two common misunderstandings in using transactions are nested transactions and user interaction within a transaction.

NESTED TRANSACTIONS

Look at the approach taken in Figure 22.8. Do you see any problems with the code?

Figure 22.8.
Nested transaction:
common (incorrect)
approach.

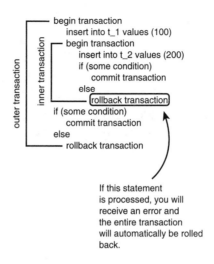

The problem is with the rollback statement for the inner transaction. If the inner transaction is rolled back, you will receive an error message and both INSERT transactions will automatically be rolled back by SQL Server, as in the following error message:

```
The commit transaction request has no corresponding BEGIN TRANSACTION.
```

To avoid the error message, use the SAVE TRANSACTION statement (see Figure 22.9).

Note

The COMMIT TRANSACTION statement must be issued after the ROLLBACK TRANSACTION INNER_TRANS statement.

Figure 22.9.
Nested transaction:
correct approach.

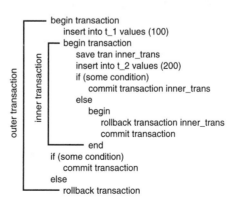

Now look at Figure 22.10. If the outer transaction is rolled back, do you think the inner transaction will also be rolled back? The answer is yes. SQL Server will always roll back the inner transaction when the outer transaction is rolled back, even though the inner transaction has been committed. This is how SQL Server handles nested transactions!

In my experience as a DBA, this often is contrary to what developers expect. Developers usually expect the inner transaction to not be rolled back because it has been committed. Make sure your developers understand how SQL Server handles nested transactions.

Figure 22.10.
The way in which SQL
Server handles nested
transactions.

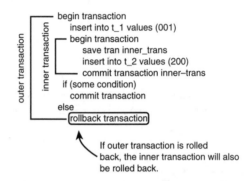

Note

Whenever you nest a transaction, all locks will be held for the duration of the transaction (see Figure 22.11). This means that when the inner transaction is committed, its locks will not be released until the outer transaction is committed. Be on the lookout for nested transactions; they increase the likelihood of blocking or deadlocks.

Figure 22.11.
The way in which locks
are held within a
nested transaction.

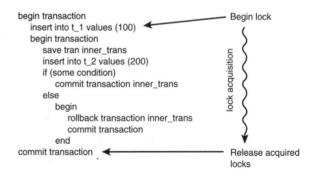

USER INTERACTION WITHIN A TRANSACTION

Keeping a watchful eye on transaction implementation can help ward off blocking. Consider the example in Figure 22.12. This virtually guarantees blocking in a multi-user environment. Always avoid user interaction within a transaction!

Figure 22.12.
User interaction within
a transaction.

You should rewrite the transaction to first prompt the user, and based on the user's response, perform the DELETE (see Figure 22.13). Transactions should always be managed within a single batch.

Figure 22.13.
Transaction rewritten
to avoid user inter-
action.

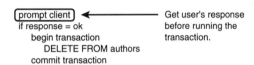

TIP 7: RUN TRANSACTIONS THAT MODIFY LARGE AMOUNTS OF DATA DURING THE OFF-HOURS

CREATE CLUSTERED INDEX and mass UPDATE/DELETE/INSERT statements should be processed during off-hours. These types of transactions require exclusive table locks and can be resource intensive.

TIP 8: ADD MORE MEMORY TO YOUR SERVER

By adding more memory, you will increase the amount of data that can remain in cache. This improves transaction performance, which reduces resource contention.

TIP 9: KNOW HOW TO SAFELY INCREMENT AN ID

Most applications require some type of auto-incrementing id to be used as a key field. Before a new record is inserted into the table, the application must get the next available id.

The easiest way to create an auto-incrementing id is to use the identity property. This data type has been optimized for performance and eliminates the need to have a separate table to track the next available id.

22

MULTI-USER ISSUES

Note

The identity data type is new with SQL Server 6.0.

If you are unable to use the identity property, you can use the following stored procedure to return the next id. Because the `update` statement is within a transaction, the risk of two users receiving the same id is eliminated. The following is a stored procedure that will return the next id:

```
CREATE PROCEDURE usp_next_id AS
declare @next_id integer
begin transaction
 update t_1
 set id = id + 1
 select @next_id = id from t_1
commit transaction
RETURN @next_id
```

The following is an example of how to use the `usp_next_id` stored procedure:

```
declare @next_id integer
exec @next_id = usp_next_id
select @next_id
```

TIP 10: TUNE THE LOCK ESCALATION THRESHOLD

The standard 200-page lock threshold limit may be unnecessarily low for very large tables. By tuning the lock escalation threshold level, you may be able to decrease the frequency of table locks. See the topic "Lock Escalation" in the "Multi-User Configuration Options" section of this chapter for more information.

MULTI-USER CONFIGURATION OPTIONS

SQL Server has several configuration options that allow you to tailor locking and other multi-user considerations. These options provide maximum control for multi-user access.

SERVER LEVEL

At the server level, you can configure the maximum number of locks, the maximum number of open objects, and the point at which lock escalation occurs.

All server level configuration options can be changed by using the Enterprise Manager or the `sp_configure` system procedure. The following the steps explain how to change a server configuration option with the Enterprise Manager:

1. Select a server.
2. Select Configurations from the Server menu bar. The Server Configurations/Options dialog box appears (see Figure 22.14).

Figure 22.14.
How to configure server
options using the
Enterprise Manager.

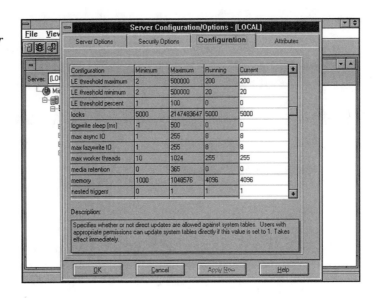

3. Click on the Configuration tab in the Server Configurations/Options dialog box.

4. Select the appropriate configuration option and enter the corresponding value.

MAXIMUM NUMBER OF LOCKS

This setting controls the maximum number of locks for a server. The default installation value is 5000. When setting this value, keep in mind that each lock uses 32 bytes of memory.

```
sp_configure 'locks', [value]
```

Tip

Use the Performance Monitor to track lock usage. You can use this value to help determine whether your lock configuration value is reasonable.

MAXIMUM OF OPEN OBJECTS

This setting controls the maximum number of open objects for a server. The default installation value is 500. Each open object uses 70 bytes of memory. The following is the syntax to configure open objects.

```
sp_configure 'open objects', [value]
```

LOCK ESCALATION

Lock escalation occurs when multiple page locks are converted into a single table lock. At this point, SQL Server determines that it is more efficient to process the transaction with a table lock rather than numerous page locks.

Note

The capability to configure lock escalation is new with SQL Server 6.0. Previous versions of SQL Server automatically escalated page locks to a table lock when 200 or more page locks had been acquired.

The default installation value for lock escalation is 200 pages. With a very large table, the default value may not be an optimal setting. For example, a modification to 1 percent of the data in a 200MB table automatically produces a table lock. This results in unnecessary table locking, which can lead to increased blocking.

By tuning the lock escalation point, you avoid unnecessary table locking. You can use the configuration settings shown in Table 22.4 to control lock escalation.

TABLE 22.4. LOCK ESCALATION.

Threshold Name	Threshold Type	Default Setting	Minimum Setting	Maximum Setting
LE threshold maximum	Maximum threshold value	200	2	500000
LE threshold minimum	Minimum threshold value	20	2	500000
LE threshold percent	Threshold value based on percentage of table size	0	1	100

Note

LE threshold minimum is an advanced option. To view and set advanced options, you must use the SHOW ADVANCED OPTION syntax with sp_configure. Following is the syntax to show advanced options:

```
sp_configure 'show advanced option',1
```

TRANSACTION ISOLATION LEVEL

With SQL Server, you can configure the transaction isolation level for a connection. A transaction isolation level will remain in effect for the life of the connection, unless the value is modified or the connection is broken.

Note

The capability to configure the transaction isolation level is new with SQL Server 6.0.

To set the transaction isolation level, use the SET TRANSACTION ISOLATION LEVEL command, as in the following syntax. (For an explanation of the differences among transaction isolation levels, see Table 22.5.)

```
SET TRANSACTION ISOLATION LEVEL {READ COMMITTED ¦ READ UNCOMMITTED ¦ REPEATABLE
READ ¦ SERIALIZABLE}
```

TABLE 22.5. TRANSACTION ISOLATION LEVELS.

Setting	Purpose
READ COMMITTED	SQL Server's default transaction isolation level. Prevents dirty reads but nonrepeatable reads may occur with this setting.
READ UNCOMMITTED	Minimizes locking by only issuing locks for UPDATE commands. Using this setting may result in dirty reads, phantom values and nonrepeatable reads.
REPEATABLE READ	See SERIALIZABLE.
SERIALIZABLE	Prevents dirty reads, phantom values, and nonrepeatable reads. In terms of performance, this setting is the least efficient option.

EXPLICIT LOCKING

With the SELECT statement, you can specify and sometimes override SQL Server's default locking behavior. To specify the locking behavior, use the keyword HOLDLOCK, UPDLOCK, NOLOCK, PAGLOCK, TABLOCK, or TABLOCKX. The following is the syntax to control explicit locking. See Table 22.6 for an explanation of the differences among explicit locking levels.

Note

With the exception of HOLDLOCK, the capability to explicitly control locking is new with SQL Server 6.0.

```
SELECT select_list
FROM table list [HOLDLOCK ¦ UPDLOCK ¦ NOLOCK ¦ PAGLOCK ¦ TABLOCK ¦ TABLOCKX]
```

TABLE 22.6. EXPLICIT LOCK SUMMARY.

Lock	Purpose
HOLDLOCK	Forces all locks to be held for the duration of the transaction.
NOLOCK	Turns off locking. Permits dirty reads.
PAGLOCK	Forces page locking rather than table locking.
TABLOCK	Forces table locking rather than page locking and uses a shared lock.
TABLOCKX	Forces table locking rather than page locking and uses an exclusive lock.
UPDLOCK	Forces an update lock to be issued rather than a shared lock. This type of lock ensures consistency when you intend to read data and then perform and update based on the values you just read.

BETWEEN THE LINES

The following are some of the important tips and tricks to read between the lines when addressing multi-user issues in SQL Server.

◆ Locks are used to maintain data consistency in a multi-user environment.

◆ Excessive locking can lead to blocking and deadlocks.

◆ Blocking occurs when a process must wait for another process to complete.

◆ Deadlock occurs when two users have locks on separate objects and each user is trying to lock the other user's objects.

◆ Use the Enterprise Manager, Performance Monitor, sp_lock, sp_who, and trace flags to help determine locking behavior.

◆ Almost every SQL operation against a table will result in some sort of lock.

◆ Page locks are preferable to table locks. They are less likely to cause blocking.

◆ Read statements acquire shared locks and data modification statements acquire exclusive locks.

◆ Page locks can escalate to table locks. At this point, it is more efficient for SQL Server to process the transaction with a table lock rather than a page lock.

◆ A clustered index can reduce contention during an insert.

◆ Always avoid user interaction within a transaction.

SUMMARY

I guarantee that as a DBA, you will run into blocking, deadlocks, and data consistency problems. The more users you have, the more likely you are to experience these problems. Hopefully, the topics discussed in this chapter will help you ward off these problems before they impact your production environment.

Speaking of your production environment, Chapter 23 will help you keep your databases up and running 24×7 (24 hours a day, 7 days a week).

22

MULTI-USER ISSUES

- Developing a SQL Server Maintenance Plan

- Automating Database Administration Tasks

- SQL OLE Integration

PART VI

Maintaining the Shop

- Areas of
  Maintenance

- Maintenance
  Checklist

CHAPTER 23

Developing a SQL Server
Maintenance Plan

Developing a SQL Server maintenance plan is a proactive approach that can help minimize system downtime. In terms of maintenance, SQL Server is no different than maintaining your car. Both require preventive maintenance and periodic tune ups. To help keep SQL Server motoring along, this chapter will discuss the types of maintenance that should be performed by a DBA.

AREAS OF MAINTENANCE

As a DBA, you will need to be concerned with four broad areas of maintenance:

◆ SQL Server maintenance
◆ Database maintenance
◆ Table/object maintenance
◆ Windows NT maintenance

SQL SERVER MAINTENANCE

The following list summarizes the types of maintenance that should be performed at the SQL Server database engine level:

◆ Monitor error logs
◆ Record configuration information
◆ Review the number of concurrent users
◆ Manage logins

MONITORING ERROR LOGS

A DBA should frequently review SQL Server's error log. When you review the error log, you should be looking for messages that do not appear under normal circumstances. Unfortunately, the error log contains more than just error messages. It also contains statements about the status of events, copyright information, and so on. This means that you have to know what to look for when you scan the error log. A good starting point is to look for the following key words:

◆ `error :`
◆ `table corrupt`
◆ `level 16`
◆ `level 17`
◆ `level 21`
◆ `Severity: 16`
◆ `Severity: 17`
◆ `Severity: 21`

Note

You can view the error log from within the Enterprise Manager or from within a text editor.

To view the error log from within the Enterprise Manager, click select Error log from the Server menu bar.

To view the current error log with a text editor, open the file `c:\sql60\log\errorlog`. You also can view the last six versions of the error log by opening the corresponding file (errorlog.1, errorlog.2, and so on).

The following example contains a sample error log. Items in bold indicate errors that a DBA may want to investigate:

Sample Error Log

```
95/09/21 20:20:27.04 kernel   Microsoft SQL Server 6.0 - 6.00.121 (Intel X86)
     Jun 13 1995 11:32:40
     Copyright (3) 1988-1995 Microsoft Corporation

95/09/21 20:20:27.05 kernel   Copyright (3) 1988-1994 Microsoft Corporation.
95/09/21 20:20:27.06 kernel   All rights reserved.
95/09/21 20:20:27.06 kernel   Logging SQL Server messages in file
                              'C:\SQL60\LOG\ERRORLOG'
95/09/21 20:20:27.08 kernel   initconfig: number of user connections limited to 20
95/09/21 20:20:27.09 kernel   SQL Server is starting at priority class 'normal'
                              with dataserver serialization turned on.
95/09/21 20:20:27.31 kernel   initializing virtual device 0,
                              C:\SQL60\DATA\MASTER.DAT
95/09/21 20:20:27.33 kernel   Opening Master Database ...
95/09/21 20:20:27.59 spid1    Loading SQL Server's  default sort order and charac-
                              ter set
95/09/21 20:20:27.74 spid1    Recovering Database 'master'
95/09/21 20:20:27.76 spid1    Recovery dbid 1 ckpt (6410,15) oldest tran=(6410,14)
95/09/21 20:20:27.79 spid1    1 transactions rolled forward
95/09/21 20:20:27.97 spid1    Activating disk 'dev1'
95/09/21 20:20:27.98 kernel   udopen: operating system error 2(The system cannot
                              find the file specified.) during the creation/opening
                              of physical device C:\SQL60\DATA\dev1.DAT
95/09/21 20:20:27.99 kernel   udactivate (primary): failed to open device
                              C:\SQL60\DATA\dev1.DAT for vdn 6
95/09/21 20:20:28.00 spid1    Activating disk 'dev2'
95/09/21 20:20:28.00 kernel   initializing virtual device 7, C:\SQL60\DATA\dev2.DAT
95/09/21 20:20:28.00 spid1    Activating disk 'dev3'
95/09/21 20:20:28.01 kernel   initializing virtual device 8, C:\SQL60\DATA\dev3.DAT
95/09/21 20:20:28.01 spid1    Activating disk 'distdb'
95/09/21 20:20:28.01 kernel   initializing virtual device 3,
                              C:\SQL60\DATA\distdb.DAT
95/09/21 20:20:28.01 spid1    Activating disk 'distlog'
95/09/21 20:20:28.02 kernel   initializing virtual device 4,
                              C:\SQL60\DATA\distlog.DAT
95/09/21 20:20:28.02 spid1    Activating disk 'MSDBData'
95/09/21 20:20:28.03 kernel   initializing virtual device 127,
                              C:\SQL60\DATA\MSDB.DAT
```

23

SQL Server Maintenance Plan

```
95/09/21 20:20:28.03 spid1    Activating disk 'MSDBLog'
95/09/21 20:20:28.03 kernel   initializing virtual device 126,
                              C:\SQL60\DATA\MSDBLOG.DAT
95/09/21 20:20:28.03 spid1    Activating disk 'sales'
95/09/21 20:20:28.04 kernel   udopen: operating system error 2(The system cannot
                              find the file specified.) during the creation/opening
                              of physical device C:\SQL60\DATA\sales.DAT
95/09/21 20:20:28.05 kernel   udactivate (primary): failed to open device
                              C:\SQL60\DATA\sales.DAT for vdn 5
95/09/21 20:20:28.05 spid1    Activating disk 'salesdev'
95/09/21 20:20:28.06 kernel   initializing virtual device 1,
                              C:\SQL60\DATA\salesdev.DAT
95/09/21 20:20:28.06 spid1    Activating disk 'saleslog'
95/09/21 20:20:28.06 kernel   initializing virtual device 2,
                              C:\SQL60\DATA\saleslog.DAT
95/09/21 20:20:28.10 spid1    server name is 'OTS'
95/09/21 20:20:28.19 spid1    Recovering database 'model'
95/09/21 20:20:28.20 spid1    Recovery dbid 3 ckpt (259,33)
95/09/21 20:20:28.24 spid1    Clearing temp db
95/09/21 20:20:29.97 kernel   Read Ahead Manager started.
95/09/21 20:20:29.97 kernel   Using 'SQLEVN60.DLL' version '6.00.000'.
95/09/21 20:20:30.12 kernel   Using 'OPENDS60.DLL' version '6.00.01.02'.
95/09/21 20:20:30.21 kernel   Using 'NTWDBLIB.DLL' version '6.00.121'.
95/09/21 20:20:30.31 ods      Starting Microsoft Mail session...
95/09/21 20:20:30.36 ods      Using 'SSNMPN60.DLL' version '6.3.0.0' to listen on
                              '\\.\pipe\sql\query'.
95/09/21 20:20:31.73 ods      Error : 17903, Severity: 18, State: 1
95/09/21 20:20:31.73 ods      MAPI login failure.
95/09/21 20:20:31.74 ods      Error : 17951, Severity: 18, State: 1
95/09/21 20:20:31.74 ods      Failed to start Microsoft Mail session.
95/09/21 20:20:32.27 spid11   Recovering database 'msdb'
95/09/21 20:20:32.28 spid12   Recovering database 'sales'
95/09/21 20:20:32.30 spid10   Recovering database 'pubs'
95/09/21 20:20:32.32 spid11   Recovery dbid 5 ckpt (1292,13) oldest tran=(1292,12)
95/09/21 20:20:32.33 spid11   1 transactions rolled forward in dbid 5.
95/09/21 20:20:32.35 spid12   Recovery dbid 6 ckpt (14651,11)
95/09/21 20:20:32.46 spid10   Recovery dbid 4 ckpt (1032,31) oldest tran=(1032,30)
95/09/21 20:20:32.46 spid10   1 transactions rolled forward in dbid 4.
95/09/21 20:20:32.73 kernel   udread: Operating system error 6(The handle is
                              invalid.) on device 'C:\SQL60\DATA\dev1.DAT'
                              (virtpage 0x06000018).
95/09/21 20:20:32.83 spid12   Error : 840, Severity: 17, State: 2
95/09/21 20:20:32.83 spid12   Device 'dev1' (with physical name
                              'C:\SQL60\DATA\dev1.DAT', and virtual device number
                               6) is not available.  Please contact System Admini-
                              strator for assistance.
95/09/21 20:20:32.85 spid12   Buffer a82678 from database 'marketing' has page
                              number 0 in the page header and page number 24 in the
                              buffer header
95/09/21 20:20:33.02 spid12   Unable to proceed with the recovery of dbid <8>
                              because of previous errors.  Continuing with the next
                              database.
95/09/21 20:20:33.04 spid11   Recovering database 'distribution'
95/09/21 20:20:33.07 spid11   Recovery dbid 7 ckpt (15967,14)
95/09/21 20:20:33.13 spid1    Recovery complete.
95/09/21 20:20:33.22 spid1    SQL Server's default sort order is:
95/09/21 20:20:33.22 spid1          'nocase' (ID = 52)
95/09/21 20:20:33.22 spid1    on top of default character set:
95/09/21 20:20:33.22 spid1          'iso_1' (ID = 1)
```

Tip

Use the Windows NT FINDSTR.EXE utility to search for text patterns in the error logs. (For the UNIX folks, FINDSTR.EXE is NT's equivalent of GREP.) This utility can help automate the process of scanning the log for errors. The following example shows how to scan the error log for the keyword `error` :.

```
C:\sql60\log>findstr /i /n /c:"error :" errorlog
```

The following is sample output:

```
C:\sql60\log>findstr /i /n /c:"error :" errorlog
34:95/09/16 11:24:20.42 ods      Error : 17903, Severity: 18, State: 1
36:95/09/16 11:24:20.43 ods      Error : 17951, Severity: 18, State: 1
53:95/09/16 11:24:35.53 ods      Error : 17903, Severity: 18, State: 1
55:95/09/16 11:24:35.54 ods      Error : 17951, Severity: 18, State: 1
```

Record Configuration Information

Two types of configuration information should be frequently generated and saved; Device Allocation Information and SQL Server Configuration.

Device Allocation Information

If you need to create a lost or damaged device to restore a database from a backup, you must know the size and type of device used by the database (for example, was the log on the same device as the database or was it on a different device?). If this information is used to re-create a lost device, it is important to remember that device fragments must be re-created in the same order as they were originally created. Use the following query to generate device allocation information:

```
select b.name 'db_name',a.segmap 'fragment type', a.size 'fragment size'
from master..sysusages a, master..sysdatabases b
where a.dbid = b.dbid
```

The following is sample output:

```
db_name                     fragment type fragment size
-------------------------   ------------- -------------
master                      7             1536
master                      7             7168
model                       7             512
msdb                        3             1024
msdb                        4             1024
pubs                        7             512
pubs                        7             1024
sales                       3             10240
sales                       4             2560
sales                       4             2048
tempdb                      7             1024
```

23

SQL Server Maintenance Plan

The following is an explanation for Fragment_type:

3   Data Device

4   Log Device

7   Log and Data are on the same device

Any other values are user-defined segments.

Fragment size is displayed in 2K blocks (512 = 1MB).

Tip

Use ISQL to generate device allocation information to a text file and then save the file as part of your nightly backup routine. The following example uses an input file named device.sql that contains the SQL statement to generate device information. The information will be saved in the file device_configure.txt.

The following is the device.sql statement:

```
select b.name 'db_name',a.segmap 'fragment type', a.size 'fragment size'
from master..sysusages a, master..sysdatabases b
where a.dbid = b.dbid
go
```

The following is the ISQL statement:

```
isql -U sa -P -i device.sql -o device_configuration.txt
```

SQL SERVER CONFIGURATION

When you are unable to start SQL Server, server configuration information may help Microsoft's technical support group get you back up and running.

Use the system procedure sp_configure to generate a list of configuration information, as in the following example:

```
exec sp_configure
```

The following is the output:

name	minimum	maximum	config_value	run_value
allow updates	0	1	0	0
backup buffer size	1	10	1	1
backup threads	0	32	5	5
cursor threshold	-1	2147483647	-1	-1
database size	1	10000	2	2
default language	0	9999	0	0
default sortorder id	0	255	52	52
fill factor	0	100	0	0
free buffers	20	524288	204	204
hash buckets	4999	265003	7993	7993
language in cache	3	100	3	3
LE threshold maximum	2	500000	200	200
LE threshold minimum	2	500000	20	20
LE threshold percent	1	100	0	0
locks	5000	2147483647	5000	5000
logwrite sleep (ms)	-1	500	0	0
max async IO	1	255	8	8
max lazywrite IO	1	255	8	8
max worker threads	10	1024	255	255
media retention	0	365	0	0
memory	1000	1048576	4096	8300
nested triggers	0	1	1	1
network packet size	512	32767	4096	4096
open databases	5	32767	20	20
open objects	100	2147483647	500	500
priority boost	0	1	0	0
procedure cache	1	99	30	30
RA cache hit limit	1	255	4	4
RA cache miss limit	1	255	3	3
RA delay	0	500	15	15
RA pre-fetches	1	1000	3	3
RA slots per thread	1	255	5	5
RA worker threads	0	255	3	3
recovery flags	0	1	0	0
recovery interval	1	32767	5	5
remote access	0	1	1	1
remote login timeout	0	2147483647	5	5
remote query timeout	0	2147483647	0	0
resource timeout	5	2147483647	10	10
set working set size	0	1	0	0
show advanced option	0	1	1	1
SMP concurrency	-1	64	0	1
sort pages	64	511	64	64
spin counter	1	2147483647	10000	0
tempdb in ram (MB)	0	2044	0	0
user connections	5	32767	20	20

Tip

Use ISQL and `sp_configure` to save configuration information to a text file and then save the file as part of your nightly backup routine. The following example creates a file named sp_configure.txt that contains configuration information:

```
isql -U sa -P -Q"sp_configure" -o sp_configure.txt
```

REVIEW THE NUMBER OF CONCURRENT USERS

It is a good idea to periodically monitor the number of concurrent user connections. This can help prevent a surprise phone call from a user complaining that he or she cannot log into the system because the maximum number of user connections has been exceeded. I recommend using the threshold feature of the Performance Monitor to track the number of active connections. If the threshold is exceeded, you can have an e-mail nofication sent to the DBA.

MANAGE LOGINS

As a DBA, you should periodically review who has access to SQL Server. In large organizations, people frequently change jobs. This means that you may have several SQL Server accounts that are not actively being used. You should inactivate these accounts to prevent unauthorized access to SQL Server.

DATABASE MAINTENANCE

The following list summarizes the types of maintenance that should be performed at the database level:

◆ Back up database and transaction log
◆ Test your backup strategy
◆ Run essential dbcc commands
◆ Audit database access

BACK UP DATABASE AND TRANSACTION LOG

In order to ensure database recovery, it is essential to frequently back up the database and transaction log. Devise a backup strategy that meets your needs and then periodically review this strategy to ensure that it satisfies your backup requirements.

TEST YOUR BACKUP/RESTORATION STRATEGY

Many DBAs back up SQL Server on a frequent basis, but only the good DBAs actually test their backup strategy by simulating database recovery. You should frequently test the integrity of your backups by actually performing a database recovery. Try to cover all the scenarios: dead server, lost drives, corrupt database, and so on. Do not put yourself in the position of having to be the guy that has to tell the CEO that your backup strategy didn't work!

RUN ESSENTIAL DBCC COMMANDS

It is important to frequently run key DBCC commands, and if possible, run the DBCC commands before you run your backup. These essential DBCC commands alert you to logical and/or physical errors. The reason that you want to run these commands before you back up your database is that you may be unable to restore a database if it is corrupt, thus making your backup useless.

Tip

Do not forget to include the master database in your list of databases that are inspected by DBCC.

The following is a list of DBCC commands that should be run on a frequent basis. (Refer to Appendix D for a complete explanation of these commands.)

- ◆ DBCC CHECKDB checks all tables and indexes in a database for pointer and data page errors.
- ◆ DBCC NEWALLOC checks data and index pages for extent structure errors.
- ◆ DBCC CHECKCATALOG ensures consistency among system tables in a database.

Tip

Use the @@error global variable to help automate nightly DBCC routines. The following is an example.

```
dbcc checkdb(pubs)
if @@error <> o
    run some error reporting routine (such as e-mail notification)
```

AUDIT DATABASE ACCESS

You should periodically perform a review of who has access to your production databases and what type of rights they possess. This can help prevent unauthorized access to production data.

TABLE/OBJECT MAINTENANCE

The following list summarizes the types of maintenance that should be performed at the table/object level.

- ◆ UPDATE STATISTICS
- ◆ Monitor Record Count
- ◆ Audit Object Permissions

UPDATE STATISTICS

Keeping the statistics of an index up-to-date is crucial for maintaining performance. Frequently issue the UPDATE STATISTICS command on tables that contain indexes that are subject to frequent data medications.

Tip

Automate UPDATE STATISTICS by using SQL Server's scheduling feature. See Chapter 24 for more information.

MONITOR RECORD COUNT

In a transaction-oriented environment, it may be necessary to establish a limit on the number of records that should exist in your tables. Once the limit is exceeded, the records should be deleted from the table. This helps to ensure a consistent performance level.

AUDIT OBJECT PERMISSIONS

Periodically review the types of permissions (SELECT, INSERT, UPDATE, DELETE, and EXECUTE) that each user has to your production data. This can help prevent security violations.

WINDOWS NT MAINTENANCE

The following list summarizes the types of maintenance that should be performed at the Windows NT level:

- ◆ Monitor Windows NT event log
- ◆ Back up the registry
- ◆ Keep the emergency repair disk current

♦ Run disk fragmentation utilities

♦ Monitor available disk space

♦ Monitor CPU and memory usage

MONITORING WINDOWS NT EVENT LOG

When it comes to monitoring the Event Log, you should be looking for two types of errors: system errors and application errors.

System errors are hardware and operating system specific. Examples include network errors, hardware problems, and driver errors.

Application errors are where certain types of SQL Server errors will be logged. Examples include connection errors, abnormal termination errors, and database failure errors.

BACKING UP THE REGISTRY

The registry is vital to the Windows NT operating system. It stores operating system details, hardware information, software information, and user account information. If the registry is damaged, you may be able to restore it from a backup.

To back up the registry, use the tape backup software provided with Windows NT or use REGBACK.EXE (REGBACK.EXE is part of the Windows NT resource kit).

KEEPING THE EMERGENCY REPAIR DISK CURRENT

Whenever hardware and software configurations change, you should update the Emergency Repair disk. Use RDISK.EXE to keep your Emergency Repair disk current.

RUNNING DISK FRAGMENTATION UTILITIES

You should periodically run disk fragmentation utilities on your server's hard disks. A high degree of hard disk fragmentation can lead to decreased hard disk performance. An NTFS drive must be checked with a third-party product. A FAT drive can be checked with SCANDISK.EXE.

MONITORING AVAILABLE DISK SPACE

It's a good idea to have at least 25 percent of the server's hard disk not in use. This leaves enough free space for temporary files, such as database dumps, BCP imports/exports, script generation, and so on.

MONITORING CPU AND MEMORY USAGE

The easiest way to monitor CPU and memory usage is to use the Performance Monitor (for more information on using the Performance Monitor, refer to Chapter 17). If you see sustained spikes in CPU usage, it may be time to upgrade your CPU or redistribute the workload. Also keep an eye on memory usage and the number of free bytes. Insufficient memory will lead to a high number of page faults, which degrades performance.

CHECKLIST	
MAINTENANCE CHECKLIST	
Frequency	**Task of Execution**
Daily	Monitor error logs
☐	Back up database and transaction log
☐	Run essential DBCC commands
☐	UPDATE STATISTICS
☐	Monitor Windows NT Event Log
☐	Monitor CPU and memory usage
Weekly	Monitor available disk space
Monthly	Test your backup strategy
☐	Monitor record count
☐	Review the number of concurrent users
☐	Manage logins
☐	Audit database access
☐	Audit object permissions
As Needed	Record configuration information
(SQL Server configuration* and device allocation**)	
☐	Back up the registry
☐	Keep the Emergency Repair disk current
☐	Run disk fragmentation utilities

*Information should be recorded whenever SQL Server configuration information is changed.

**Information should be recorded whenever a database is modified or created.

SUMMARY

Several types of tasks are required to maintain SQL Server. Many of these tasks can be automated through SQL Server's scheduler and alert manager. The next chapter "Automating Database Administration Tasks" will discuss in detail how to automate common DBA tasks.

- Task Scheduler

- Alert Manager

- Between the Lines

CHAPTER 24

Automating Database
Administration Tasks

Virtually every organization can reduce administration effort by automating common DBA tasks. SQL Server 6.0 provides two new tools that can help automate common tasks: Task Scheduler and Alert Manager.

TASK SCHEDULER

The *Task Scheduler* is robust and easy to use. In addition to being a scheduler, it includes other useful features, such as a history log and the capability to e-mail or page an operator when an event occurs.

Following are just a few of the types of tasks that can be automated with the Task Scheduler:

Automate Backups: Automatic database backups should be an integral part of everyone's production systems. The scheduler can be used to automatically back up a database at preset interval. See Chapter 13 for more information on automatically backing up the database.

Automate UPDATE STATISTICS: It is important to keep index distribution statistics up-to-date. Otherwise, the optimizer may ignore existing indexes. To automatically keep statistics fresh, use the scheduler to call a stored procedure that issues the UPDATE STATISTICS command.

Schedule DBCC commands: DBCC commands should be run frequently to check for corrupt databases and tables. Depending on the size of your databases, try to schedule the DBCC commands before you back up your database. It is important to do this because if you back up a corrupt database, you may be unable to restore it.

Automate Data Imports and Exports: Many companies that use SQL Server also must import and export data to other non-SQL Server systems within the organization. An easy way to facilitate the transfer of information is to schedule a task that directly calls BCP or by creating a stored procedure that in turn calls BCP. The advantage of using a stored procedure to call BCP is that you can chain additional tasks to the procedure, such as validating data, summarizing data, and so on.

Tip

To call BCP from a stored procedure, use the extended stored procedure xp_cmdshell.

USING THE TASK SCHEDULER

Now that you know the types of tasks that can be automated, go through a simple example of actually scheduling a task. For this example, assume that you want to schedule a stored procedure that removes any sales data that is greater than seven days old. Also assume that you want the procedure to run on a nightly basis at 3:00 a.m. and you want to be notified by e-mail that the procedure successfully ran.

The following is a sample procedure:

```
CREATE PROCEDURE usp_remove_old_data AS
/* remove transactions that are 7 or more days old */
DELETE
FROM sales
WHERE DATEDIFF(dd,sales_date,getdate()) > = 7
```

Note

SQLExecutive must be running for the Task Scheduler to work. To determine whether SQLExecutive is running, open the SQL Service Manager (to open the SQL Service Manager, go to Program Manager, and click on the SQL Service Manager icon in the Microsoft SQL Server 6.0 (Common) group). Select SQLExecutive from the Services list box. The color of the stop light indicates the status of the service.

To schedule the `usp_remove_old_data` stored procedure, follow these steps:

1. Click on the Task Scheduling toolbar button in the Enterprise Manager (see Figure 24.1). The Task Scheduling dialog box appears (see Figure 24.2).

Figure 24.1.
Task Scheduling
toolbar button.

2. Click on the New Task toolbar button to add a task (see Figure 24.3). The New Task dialog box appears.

3. Enter the following task information: task name, task type, database, and command to execute (see Figure 24.4). From the New Task dialog box, you can execute the following types of commands:

TSQL	Executes Transact SQL statements. Examples include `TRUNCATE TABLE authors`, `UPDATE authors SET au_id = 100`, `EXEC usp_my_proc`, and so on.
CmdExec	Execute a .BAT, .EXE, or .CMD file. Examples include BCP.EXE, ISQL.EXE, CUSTOM.BAT files, and so on.

Distribution	Used in conjunction with replication. Enables you to define replication distribution commands.
LogReader	Used in conjunction with replication. Enables you to define replication log reader commands.
Sync	Used in conjunction with replication. Enables you to define replication synchronization commands.

Figure 24.2.
Task Scheduling
dialog box.

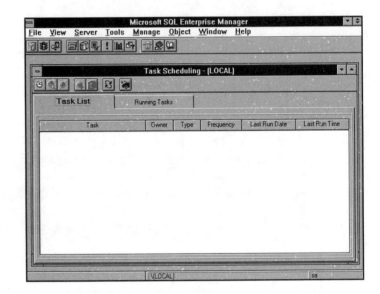

Figure 24.3.
New Task toolbar
button.

Figure 24.4.
New Task dialog box.

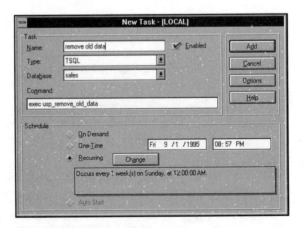

> **Note**
>
> Be sure to select the appropriate database when running TSQL
> commands; otherwise, the command may fail.

4. For this example, you want the stored procedure to run every night at 3:00
   p.m. To do this, click on the Change button. The Task Schedule dialog box
   appears.

5. From the Task Schedule dialog box, enter the corresponding scheduling
   information and click on the OK button (see Figure 24.5).

Figure 24.5.
Task Schedule
dialog box.

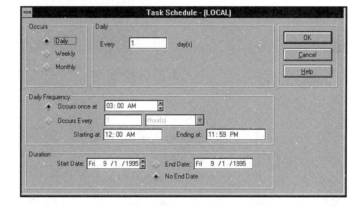

6. As mentioned earlier, you want to be notified by e-mail when the task is
   successfully executed. To add the notification click on the Options button in
   the Edit Task dialog box. The Task Options dialog box appears.

7. For this example, specify an e-mail operator (at this point you can define a
   new e-mail operator by selecting the <New Operator> option from the
   e-mail Operator list box). Select the On Success Write To Windows NT
   Event Log checkbox (see Figure 24.6). Click on OK to save the notification
   information.

> **Note**
>
> To notify an operator by e-mail, the e-mail service must be running on
> the same server as SQL Server. Consult your e-mail documentation
> for more information.

Tip

Use the extended stored procedure xp_sendmail to test whether your e-mail service is properly configured, as in the following example:

```
xp_sendmail 'ots', 'this is a test'
```

Figure 24.6.
Task Options
dialog box.

8. To save the task, click on the Add button in New Task dialog box.

After a task has been created, it is a good idea to test it by manually executing the task. Follow these steps to manually execute a task:

1. From the Task Scheduling dialog box, click on the Run Task toolbar button (see Figure 24.7). This executes the task immediately.

Figure 24.7.
Run Task toolbar
button.

2. To update the task history dialog boxes, click on the Refresh toolbar button (see Figure 24.8). This should always be done *before* clicking on the Task History toolbar button. SQL Server's task dialog boxes are *not* automatically refreshed!

Figure 24.8.
Refresh toolbar button.

3. To determine whether the task ran successfully, click on the Task History toolbar button (see Figure 24.9). The Task History dialog box appears (see Figure 24.10). From this dialog box, you can see that the task was successfully executed.

Figure 24.9.
Task History toolbar
button.

Figure 24.10.
Task History
dialog box.

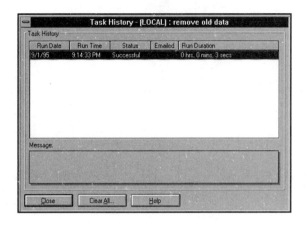

You also can see that the task was successfully executed by looking at your
e-mail and NT's Event Log (see Figures 24.11 and 24.12).

Figure 24.11.
E-mail notification.

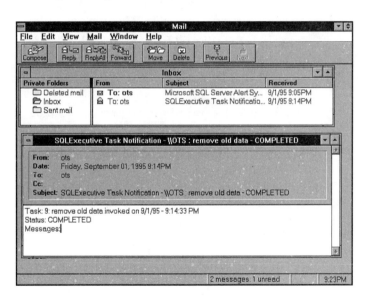

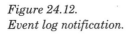

Figure 24.12.
Event log notification.

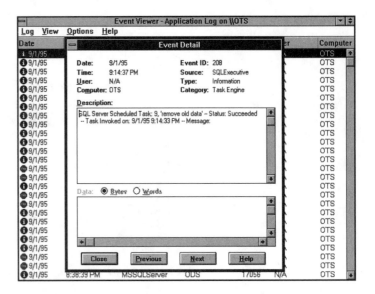

EXTENDING THE TASK SCHEDULER

In the previous section, you learned how to schedule a task and how to e-mail an operator when a task is complete. This section builds on what you learned in the previous section. For this example, assume that you want to schedule the same task, but you need to be e-mailed the number of rows deleted by the stored procedure.

No problem! However, you do have to shift the e-mail notification logic to the stored procedure rather than the Task Scheduler. This is because the Task Scheduler can only e-mail a success or failure message. It cannot return the number of rows deleted, updated, and so on.

To e-mail the number of rows deleted, you need to make a couple of modifications to the usp_remove_old_data stored procedure. The biggest modification is the additional call to the xp_sendmail extended stored procedure. The xp_sendmail command enables you to e-mail a message that contains the number of rows deleted.

The following stored procedure contains the necessary modifications:

```
CREATE PROCEDURE usp_remove_old_data AS
declare @rows_deleted int
declare @e-mail_message varchar(255)

/* remove transactions that are 7 or more days old */
DELETE
FROM transaction_control
WHERE DATEDIFF(dd,transaction_date,getdate()) > = 7

/* store number of rows deleted to a variable */
SELECT @rows_deleted = @@rowcount
```

```
/* build message */
SELECT @e-mail_message = 'Numbers of rows removed by usp_remove_old_data = ' +
  CONVERT(varchar(20),@rows_deleted)

/* e-mail the results back to the operator */
EXEC master..xp_sendmail 'OTS', @e-mail_message
```

Note

Whenever you call an extended stored procedure, you should include the master database in the statement (as in master..xp_sendmail). Otherwise, you must be in the master database to run an extended stored procedure.

Now when the Task Scheduler executes the usp_remove_old_data stored procedure, the number of rows deleted will be e-mailed to the operator (see Figure 24.13).

Figure 24.13.
E-mail stating the
number of rows deleted.

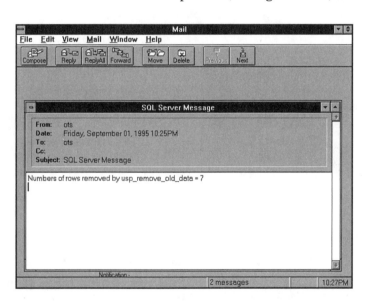

Tip

SQL Server 6.0 enables Transact SQL commands to be resolved at runtime through the use of the EXEC command. This opens up an entire list of DBA functions that can be automated through the use of stored procedures. For example, the following stored procedure will UPDATE STATISTICS for all tables that contain indexes.

```
CREATE PROCEDURE usp_update_statistics AS
        /* declare variables */
        declare @table_name varchar(30)
```

24

```
/* declare a cursor that will contain a list of table */
/* names to be updated */
declare idx_cursor cursor
 for select distinct a.name
   from sysobjects a,sysindexes b
   where a.type = 'U'
   and a.id = b.id
   and b.indid > 0

/* open the cursor */
open idx_cursor

/* get the first row from the cursor */
fetch next from idx_cursor into @table_name

/* loop through the rows in the cursor */
while @@fetch_status = 0
  begin
    /* issue UPDATE STATISTICS */
    EXEC ("UPDATE STATISTICS " + @table_name)

    /* get next table name */
    fetch next from idx_cursor into @table_name
  end

/* close the cursor */
deallocate idx_cursor
```

After you create this stored procedure, you can schedule it to execute automatically on a recurring basis. This helps to ensure that your index statistics are up-to-date.

Stranger than Fiction!

The SQL Server 6.0 documentation incorrectly shows how to use the EXEC statement to execute a command at runtime. The documentation example does not include the concatenation symbol (+) between the command and the variable. The following is the incorrect syntax:

```
EXEC ("DROP TABLE "  @tablename)
```

The following is the correct syntax:

```
EXEC ("DROP TABLE "  + @tablename)
```

ALERT MANAGER

The *Alert Manager* enables you to define alerts that are executed automatically upon the occurrence of an event. When the alert is executed, an operator can be notified by e-mail and/or pager. An alert also can execute additional tasks, such as calling another Transact SQL command or by calling an external program in the form of a .BAT, .EXE, or .CMD file. These features enable a DBA to be more proactive to conditions that require attention.

Through the Alert Manager you can create three types of alerts: standard alerts, Performance Monitor alerts, and business alerts.

The following are examples of standard alerts:

- ◆ Database out of space
- ◆ SQL Server was abnormally terminated
- ◆ Database is corrupt
- ◆ Table is corrupt

The following are examples of Performance Monitor alerts:

- ◆ High CPU Utilization
- ◆ Transaction log almost full
- ◆ Blocking

The following are examples of business alerts:

- ◆ Low inventory
- ◆ Aborted download

STANDARD ALERTS

Now that you have an understanding of the different types of alerts that can be managed, this section will run through a simple example of how to configure the Alert Manager for a standard alert. For this example, assume that you want to define an alert that notifies an operator by e-mail when the pubs database is out of space.

Note

SQLExecutive must be running for the Alert Manager to work.

To create a sample alert, follow these steps:

1. From the Enterprise Manager, click on the Manage Alerts toolbar button (see Figure 24.14). The Manage Alerts dialog box appears (see Figure 24.15). From the Manage Alerts dialog box, you can add, delete, and edit alerts and manage operators.

24

Figure 24.14.
Manage Alerts toolbar
button.

Figure 24.15.
Manage Alerts
dialog box.

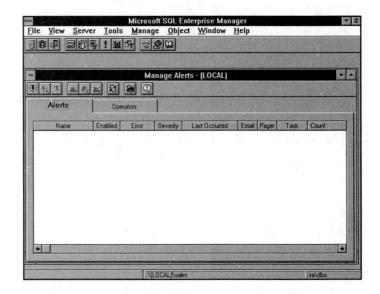

2. From the Operators tab, click on the New Operator toolbar button (see Figure 24.16). The New Operator dialog box appears.

Figure 24.16.
New Operator toolbar
button.

3. In the New Operator dialog box, enter the id and e-mail name (see Figure 24.17). You also can enter pager information at this point. Click OK to save the operator information.

4. Now that you have defined an operator to handle the alert, you need to define the alert. From the Alerts tab in the Manage Alerts dialog box, click on the New Alert toolbar button (see Figure 24.18). The New Alert dialog box appears (see Figure 24.19).

5. For this example, assume that you don't remember which error number is generated when the database is out of space. Just click on the Manage Error Messages button (see Figure 24.20). The Manage SQL Server Messages dialog box appears.

Figure 24.17.
New Operator
dialog box.

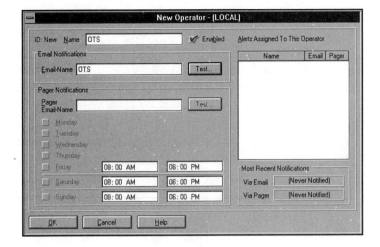

Figure 24.18.
New Alert toolbar
button.

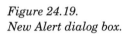

Figure 24.19.
New Alert dialog box.

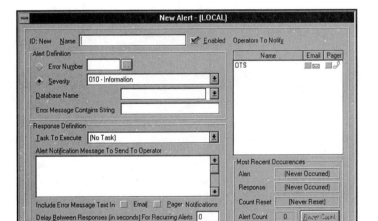

Figure 24.20.
Manage Error
Messages button.

6. From the Manage SQL Server Messages dialog box you can find, add, delete, and edit error messages. To help you find the corresponding error message, enter the following message text:

`out of space`

Click on the Find button to list all matching error messages (see Figure 24.21).

Figure 24.21.
Finding an error
message.

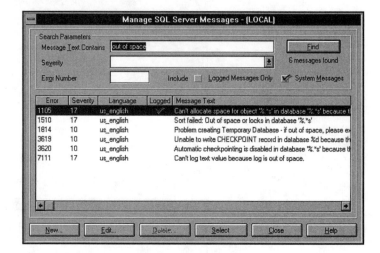

7. You want to base your alert on error number 1105. Highlight the row that contains error number 1105 and click on the Select button.

8. After you select an error number, enter the remaining alert information: alert name, alert definition, response definition, and operators to notify (see Figure 24.22).

9. Click on the OK button to save the new alert.

Congratulations! You just created an alert that will notify an operator when the pubs database is out of space. Figure 24.23 shows the e-mail message the operator will receive when the pubs database is out of space.

Figure 24.22.
Alert information.

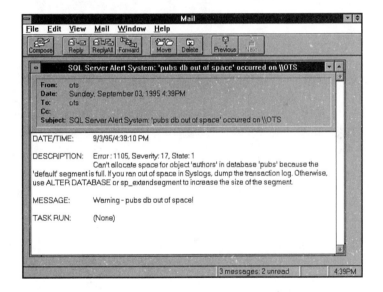

Figure 24.23.
E-mail notification.

PERFORMANCE MONITOR ALERTS

Some types of alerts, such as high CPU utilization, transaction log almost full, and blocking, require the use of the Performance Monitor, SQLALRTR.EXE, and the Alert Manager. Any type of alert that can be created in the Performance Monitor can be passed to the SQL Server Alert Manager. In turn, the Alert Manager can e-mail or page an operator.

To illustrate how the Performance Monitor interacts with the Alert Manager, build an alert that notifies an operator when CPU utilization is greater than 80 percent by following these steps:

1. From the Alert Manager dialog box, click on the New Alert toolbar button. The New Alert dialog box appears (see Figure 24.24). For this example, you need to create a custom error. This error will be used by SQLALRTR.EXE.

Figure 24.24.
New Alert dialog box.

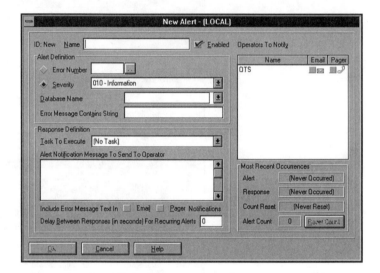

2. To create a custom alert, click on the Manage Error Messages button (refer to Figure 24.20). The Manage SQL Server Messages dialog box appears.

3. From the Manage SQL Server Messages dialog box, click on the New button. The New Message dialog box appears.

4. In the New Message dialog box, enter the error number, severity level, and message text. For this example, use error number 50001 (see Figure 24.25). Be sure to select the Always Write To Windows NT Eventlog option; otherwise, the event will not be recognized by the Alert Manager. Click on the OK button to save the alert.

Note

User-defined error messages must use an error number greater than 50000.

Figure 24.25.
Creating a new error
number message.

New Message	
Error Number	50001	Severity	010 - Information
Message Text	CPU utilization > 80%
Language	us_english	☑ Always Write To Windows NT Eventlog

OK   Cancel   Help

5. Now that you have created a new error number and message, go back and fill in the remainder of the alert notification (see Figure 24.26). Click on the OK button to save the alert.

Figure 24.26.
Alert for CPU utiliza-
tion > 80 percent.

New Alert - [LOCAL]

ID: New   Name CPU utilization > 80%   ☑ Enabled   Operators To Notify

Alert Definition
- ◆ Error Number 50001 [...]
- ◇ Severity
- Database Name
- Error Message Contains String

Name	Email	Pager
OTS	☑	☐

Response Definition
Task To Execute [No Task]
Alert Notification Message To Send To Operator
Warning: CPU utilization > 80%.

Most Recent Occurrences
Alert   (Never Occurred)
Response   (Never Occurred)
Count Reset   (Never Reset)
Alert Count   0   Reset Count

Include Error Message Text In ☑ Email ☐ Pager Notifications
Delay Between Responses (in seconds) For Recurring Alerts 0

OK   Cancel   Help

6. To define the alert in the Performance Monitor, click on the Performance Monitor icon in the Microsoft SQL Server 6.0 (Common) group (see Figure 24.27). The Performance Monitor dialog box appears.

Figure 24.27.
Performance Monitor
icon.

24

7. From the Performance Monitor dialog box, click on the View Alerts toolbar button (see Figure 24.28). This will take you to the View Alerts dialog box.

Figure 24.28.
View Alerts toolbar
button.

8. From this dialog box, click on the Add an Alert Entry toolbar button (see Figure 24.29). The Add To Alert dialog box appears.

Figure 24.29.
Add an Alert Entry
toolbar button.

9. For this example, select the Processor object and % Processor Time counter.

10. From the Alert If box, click on the Over button and enter **80** for the alert threshold level. This means that when CPU utilization is greater than 80 percent, an alert will be issued.

11. From the Run Program on Alert box, enter the SQLALRTR.EXE command. For this example you want to trigger error number 50001. To trigger error 50001, use the following syntax:

```
c:\sql60\binn\SQLALRTR /E50001
```

The following is the SQLALRTR.EXE syntax.

```
sqlalrtr -E error_number [-S server_name] [-P password]
  [-D database_name] [-V severity] [-T ]
```

Note

The -P and -T parameters of SQLALRTR.EXE are mutually exclusive—using them together will cause an error.

12. Click on the Add button to save the alert (see Figure 24.30).

Note

Current alert settings will be discarded when the Performance Monitor is closed unless the settings are manually saved (choose Save Workspace from the File menu).

Figure 24.30.
Performance Monitor
alert.

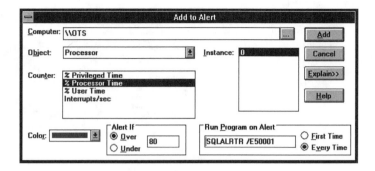

Tip

The Performance Monitor must be running for the Alert Manager to detect that a threshold has been exceeded. The proper way to automatically load the Performance Monitor during the startup of Windows NT is to run the Performance Monitor as a Windows NT Service (see the Windows NT 3.51 Resource Kit for more information).

This completes the CPU > 80% example. Figure 24.31 contains the e-mail message that an operator will receive when this alert is triggered. Figure 24.32 contains the alert that is generated by the Performance Monitor.

Figure 24.31.
CPU > 80% e-mail
message.

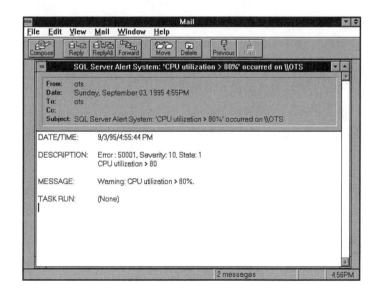

24

AUTOMATING ADMINISTRATION TASKS

Figure 24.32.
CPU > 80% alert in the
Performance Monitor.

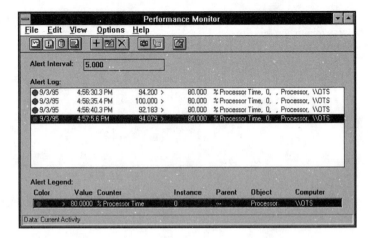

BUSINESS ALERTS

In addition to handling SQL Server errors and thresholds, the Alert Manager can be used to alert operators to business conditions. Suppose that you own a used car dealership and you want to be alerted by e-mail whenever the number of cars on the lot is below 20.

Assume that the number of cars on your lot can be determined by counting the number of records in a table named cars. Also assume that each time a car is sold, it is deleted from the cars table.

The creation of this type of alert consists of three different steps.

1. The error number and message that will correspond to the alert.
2. The event that will execute the error that corresponds to the alert.
3. Alert notification.

STEP 1: ERROR NUMBER AND MESSAGE

1. To define a custom error number, click on the Manage Messages toolbar button in the Manage Alerts dialog box. The Manage SQL Server Messages dialog box appears.
2. From the Manage SQL Server Messages dialog box, click on the New button. The New Message dialog box appears.
3. In the New Message dialog box enter the error number, severity, and message text you want to associate with the low inventory message (see Figure 24.33). For this example, use error number 50002.
4. To save the error, click the OK button in the New Message dialog box and click the Close button in the Manage SQL Server Messages dialog box.

Figure 24.33.
Adding a new error
message.

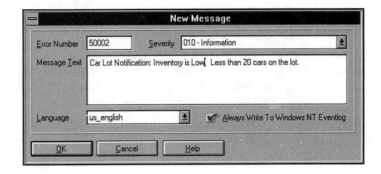

STEP 2: EVENT THAT EXECUTES THE ERROR

For this example, I mentioned that every time a car is sold it is deleted from the cars table. This enables you to use a trigger that checks to see whether the number of cars on hand is below 20. (Remember, triggers are automatically executed when a DELETE, UPDATE, or INSERT occurs.)

The following code illustrates how to create a trigger that will automatically issue error number 50002 when fewer than 20 cars are on the lot. In turn, the Alert Manager will detect error 50002 and will automatically e-mail a message to the operator.

```
DELETE Trigger:
CREATE TRIGGER trg_delete_cars ON dbo.cars
FOR DELETE
AS
/* declare variables */
declare @car_count int

/* count the number of cars on hand */
SELECT @car_count = COUNT(*)
FROM cars

/* If quantity is less than < 20 */
/* issue error 50002 (user defined error message).  This will */
/* fire an alert which will notify an operator */
IF @car_count < 20
  BEGIN
    /* RAISERROR paramater explanation: */
    /* 50002 = low inventory message */
    /* 16 = severity level (miscellaneous user error) */
    /* -1 = error state */
    RAISERROR(50002,16,-1)
  END
```

STEP 3: ALERT NOTIFICATION

Now that you have defined your error number and trigger, you need to build the actual alert notification.

1. In the Manage Alerts dialog box, click on the New Alert toolbar button. The New Alert dialog box appears.

2. In the New Alert dialog box, enter the alert configuration information. Be sure to use the error number defined in Step 1 (50002) for the Alert definition. Also enter the notification message and the operator to notify (see Figure 24.34). Click on the OK button to save the alert.

Now the low inventory alert will be automatically executed whenever the number of cars on hand goes below 20. Figure 24.35 contains the e-mail message that an operator will receive when this alert is triggered.

Figure 24.34.
Low inventory alert.

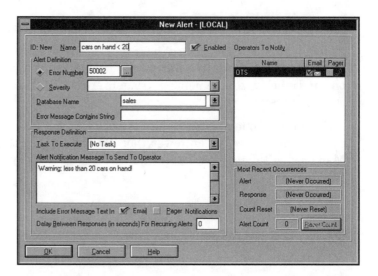

Figure 24.35.
Low inventory e-mail.

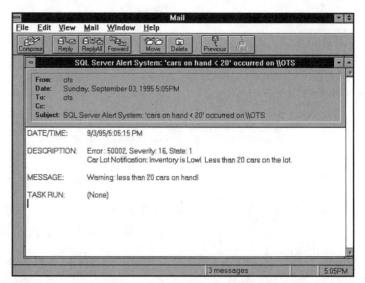

Between the Lines

- ◆ Use the Task Scheduler to automate common DBA tasks, such as backing up a database, updating statistics, and running DBCC commands.
- ◆ Use the Alert Manager to automatically notify an operator of problems, such as a database out of space error, high CPU utilization, or low inventory.
- ◆ Both the Task Scheduler and Alert Manager can notify an operator through e-mail and/or pager.

Summary

The Task Scheduler and Alert Manager are two functions that utilize the SQLExecutive service. In Chapter 25, you will see how the SQLExecutive and OLE technology can further extend the automation of common DBA tasks.

24

AUTOMATING ADMINISTRATION TASKS

CHAPTER 25

SQL OLE Integration

Did you ever feel like Microsoft left out a utility or window of information that you thought would really make your life easier? Well, with SQL Server 6.0, you may be able to write that utility yourself. "How?" you ask. The answer is with an exciting new feature that has been added to SQL Server 6.0—OLE!

OLE stands for Object Linking and Embedding, but in the past few years has come to stand for so much more. A few years ago, Microsoft, along with several integrated system vendors, created an open specification for application intercommunication called OLE. The OLE specifications defined more than applications communicating with one another; it also specified how applications can expose parts of their functionality as objects to be used by other applications.

Application developers could then create applications that use parts of other applications to further enhance their own applications. For example, you could create an application that uses the charting capabilities of another application or include a spell checker into a text editor application.

So what does all this have to do with SQL Server? In SQL Server 6.0, SQL Server is an OLE object application (also called OLE Server). That is, SQL Server exposes several objects, methods, and properties that can be easily controlled programmatically to perform database administrative tasks. Microsoft calls the objects SQL-DMO (SQL Distributed Management Objects). Using SQL-DMO you can easily create applications that perform many DBA tasks for you!

Note

This chapter almost seems out of place in a book on DBA survival; however, it introduces a technology that will truly empower the DBA, enabling you (as the DBA) to create your own powerful database utilities. Even if you think this chapter seems too much like a programming chapter, hang in there! The explanations in this chapter are geared toward DBAs, not programmers. Even if you don't know how to program, you will at least understand what can be done with SQL-DMO and you may be able to have someone program your utility for you!

Before going into more detail, quickly review some OLE terminology.

Container/controller/client application: An application that can create and manage OLE objects. Visual Basic is an example of a container application.

Server/object application: An application that creates OLE objects. SQL Server is an object application.

OLE automation: OLE automation is a standard that enables applications to expose their objects and methods so that other applications can use them.

Object: Defining an object is a bit difficult. If the OLE terminology of an object is used, the discussion gets into many other aspects of OLE that can be found in many other Sams books, but will confuse the topic in this book. So, for this definition of an object, we use a simpler definition and say that an object represents some sort of data with properties and methods. In SQL Server terms, for example, a database is an object and a stored procedure is an object. Using the case of a database object, see the diagram shown in Figure 25.1.

Figure 25.1.
Example of a database
object.

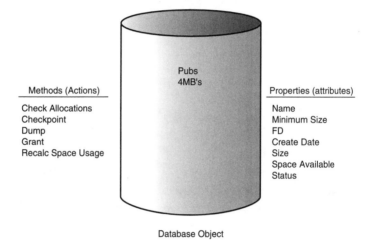

The object has attributes, or in OLE terminology, properties. In Figure 25.1, some of the properties of a database object are listed. Name, CreateDate, Size, and Status are all examples of properties of the database object.

The name property for the database shown in Figure 25.1 is *Pubs*. A property tells you something about the object. You can read properties, and in some cases, you can also set properties.

Objects also have methods. A method is an action the object takes on the data it represents. Examples of the database objects methods are shown in Figure 25.1. The dump method, for example, can be used on the database object. If you invoked the dump method of the database object named pubs, what do you think would happen? If you said, "A database backup," then you are correct!

Collections: A collection is an object that consists of items that can be referred to as a group (see Figure 25.2).

Figure 25.2.
Example of a collection
object.

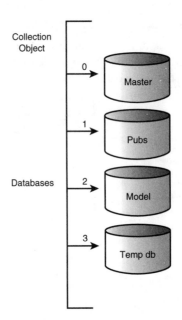

In Figure 25.2, there are several standard SQL Server databases: master, pubs, model, and tempdb. If you group all the databases shown into one large group called *databases*, then you have a collection.

Collections enable you to easily perform tasks on each item in the collection. To perform a DBCC CHECKDB command on every database on your SQL Server, for example, you can use the collection object to get each database on the server and invoke a method to perform a DBA task.

SQL SERVER'S OBJECT MODEL

In order to use SQL-DMO, you must understand the SQL Server object model. The *object model* is the hierarchy of exposed SQL Server objects that you can use programatically. SQL Server's object model, taken from the Distributed Management Help File, is shown in Figure 25.3.

Follow the object model just like you would a file directory tree. The top level of the object model, for example, is the Application object.

Figure 25.3.
SQL Server distributed
management object
model.

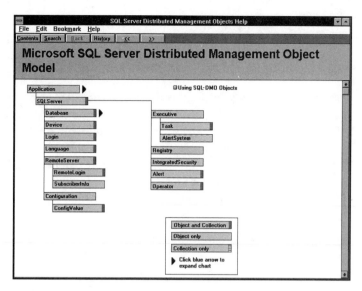

Note

It is standard practice when creating OLE object models from a stand-alone application to include an Application object.

Follow the tree to the next level and you will find the primary object you will use: the SQL Server object. If you look at Figure 25.3, you will see that the database, device, login, language, remoteserver, and configuration objects are all below the SQL Server object. These objects are said to be dependent upon the SQL Server object; that is, you must have a SQL Server object before you can "get to" (i.e. use) any of the dependent objects.

WHY USE SQL-DMO?

What benefits can you get from learning how to use SQL-DMO? The real gain to you is that you can easily create custom solutions for your database administration environment, allowing you more free time to perform other tasks. For example, you could create a user wizard that performs a series of tasks, such as adding the user to every database based on the user's group.

Using SQL-DMO, you can create applications that you would normally have to perform manually! Currently, you can automate many tasks you perform regularly using stored procedures. Stored procedures are very useful for automating and performing many different tasks for you. The advantage SQL-DMO has over stored procedures for performing administrative tasks is simplicity. By using collection objects, you can easily perform DBCC commands on every database on the server, using only a few lines of code. Many Transact SQL commands have been simplified. The DBCC command and the many different DBCC options become methods of different objects.

Another advantage over stored procedures is that you can take advantage of true programming languages that have more powerful programming features than Transact SQL. Not to mention, you can easily integrate your applications into other desktop applications, such as word processors or spreadsheets, to enhance your customized database administration applications. The following is a brief list of some of the many different administrative tasks you can perform. (Remember, this is a very brief list; SQL-DMO enables you to perform almost any system administrative task):

◆ Backup/restore a database
◆ Generate scripts for stored procedures
◆ Perform the UPDATE STATISTICS command
◆ Perform DBCC commands, such as CheckTable, CheckCatalog, and so on
◆ Grant and revoke privileges
◆ Add Alerts
◆ Manage Users

CREATING APPLICATIONS WITH SQL-DMO

Using SQL-DMO requires a 32-bit programming language that can create OLE controller applications. Such tools as Microsoft Visual C++ or Excel for Windows NT with 32-bit VBA (Visual Basic for Applications) can easily be used. The following examples and code samples shown in this chapter will be based on Microsoft Visual Basic 4.0. The selection of Visual Basic is an easy one because it is the most popular rapid application development tool available. The core language of Visual Basic 4.0 is VBA (Visual Basic for Applications) and can be found in the Windows 95 releases of Access, PowerPoint, and Excel.

The remainder of the chapter focuses on using SQL-DMO objects to perform a variety of different database administration tasks using Visual Basic.

USING VISUAL BASIC

Tip

If you are not familiar with Visual Basic, pick up a beginner's book and learn the Visual Basic basics. Once you know the basics, you will be able to use the suggestions and examples in this chapter effectively to create your own applications. The following discussion of Visual Basic is very brief and primarily given for those of you who do not know Visual Basic well, so that you can understand SQL-DMO.

The following is a very brief introduction to Visual Basic to help you understand the terminology used later when creating an application that takes advantage of SQL-DMO. Visual Basic 4.0 is shown in Figure 25.4.

Figure 25.4.
Visual Basic 4.0.

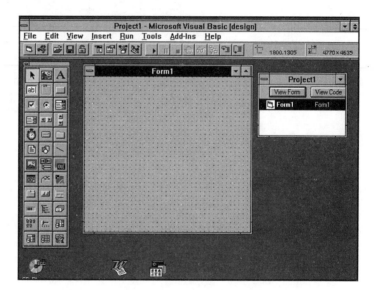

Creating Visual Basic applications consists of creating forms, adding controls to the forms using the toolbar, and adding code to modules and forms that make up the application. The forms and code modules that make up a Visual Basic application are called *projects* and can be found in the project window shown in Figure 25.4. Next, you'll step through some Visual Basic basics you will need to later create your own SQL-DMO applications or to enhance the application provided with this book (the DBA Assistant) and created in the next few pages.

ADDING A CONTROL TO A FORM AND SETTING PROPERTIES

A Visual Basic control is similar to a SQL-DMO object in that they both have properties and methods. Understanding the properties and methods used for a Visual Basic control will help you better understand the concept of SQL-DMO objects and properties. To add a control to a form, perform the following steps:

1. Click once on the icon on the toolbar of the control you want to add to the form. Common controls used on the toolbar are shown in Figure 25.5.

Figure 25.5.
Visual Basic toolbar.

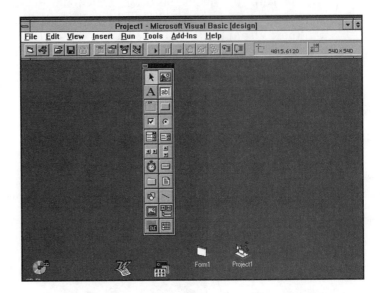

2. Place the mouse cursor on the form and while holding down the left mouse button, drag the mouse down. Visual Basic will begin to draw a control on the form.

3. Release the left mouse button. You now have added a control to the form.

4. To set properties, such as color, name, height, width and so on, for the control or the form, click on the form or control to make it the active object and then press F4. The properties window for the object appears (see Figure 25.6).

5. To change a property, select the property field and enter a new value.

DECLARING A SQL-DMO OBJECT IN VISUAL BASIC

In order to use a SQL-DMO object, you must first declare the object in your code. With Visual Basic, you can use the generic object type that can hold any type of OLE object, or you can declare an object of a specific SQL-DMO object type using the type library. To create a variable using a generic object, use the following syntax:

```
Dim Variable_Name As Object
```

To create a specific SQL-DMO, use the following syntax:

```
Dim Variable_Name As SQLOLE.SQL_DMO_OBJECT
```

Figure 25.6.
Visual Basic Form
Properties window.

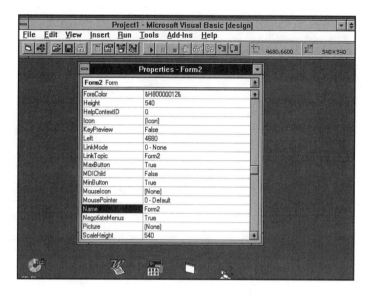

25

Where SQL_DMO_OBJECT is the specific SQL-DMO object such as SQLServer, Database, Table, and so on. For example, to define a SQL-DMO SQL Server object using the type library, enter the following:

```
Dim MySqlServer As SQLOLE.SQLServer
```

Tip

Declare SQL-DMO variables using the type library and declaring specific SQL Server objects rather than the generic object. Using specific objects is faster and enables Visual Basic to perform "early binding" and check that you are using proper object and methods during compilation rather than at runtime.

CREATING A SQL-DMO OBJECT WITH VISUAL BASIC

After you declare a variable to be a SQL-DMO object, you must create the object in order to use the methods and properties of the object.

Note

Creating an object also is referred to as getting an instance of the object.

You can create the object with either the keyword New or the function CreateObject. The following is an example of using the New keyword when declaring a variable:

```
Dim MySqlServer As New SQLOLE.SQLServer
```

You also can use the New keyword in code, as follows:

```
Set MySQLServer = New SQLOLE.SQLServer
```

The CreateObject function has the following syntax:

```
CreateObject("application_name.object_type")
```

The following code creates a new SQL Server SQL-DMO object with CreateObject:

```
Set MySqlServer = CreateObject("SQLOLE.SQLServer")
```

After you create an object, you can use the objects, properties, and methods to perform DBA tasks.

RELEASING OBJECTS

Just as important as creating an object is releasing the object when you are finished. Objects in Visual Basic will be released when they go out of scope. If the object is declared in a procedure, then the object is released when the procedure completes. If the object is declared in a form, then the object is released when the form unloads. Global objects are not released until the application is closed.

It is always good Visual Basic coding practice to release your objects in code when you are finished with them using the keyword Nothing. The following code, for example, releases a SQL-DMO table object called MyTable:

```
Set MyTable = Nothing
```

REQUIRED SQL-DMO FILES

In order to create SQL-DMO objects using Visual Basic, you must have the following files that are included with the 32-bit versions of SQL Server client utilities for Windows NT and Windows 95.

You can find the following files from the SQL Server 6.0 home directory (C:\SQL60) in the directory \DLL:

- ◆ SQLOLE.HLP SQL-DMO help files, including object hierarchy
- ◆ SQLOLE.REG registry file for SQL-DMO
- ◆ SQLOLE32.DLL in process SQL-DMO server
- ◆ SQLOLE32.TLB type library for OLE Automation Controllers

CHECKLIST

YOU CAN USE THE FOLLOWING CHECKLISTS WHEN CREATING SQL-DMO APPLICATIONS. USING THIS CHECKLIST ENSURES THAT YOU HAVE THE PROPER FILES AND UTILITIES REQUIRED TO USE SQL-DMO:

- ☐ Windows NT or Windows 95

- ☐ Have installed a 32-bit OLE automation controller (Visual Basic)

- ☐ Install the proper SQL-DMO files from the 32-bit SQL Server Client utilities

THE FOLLOWING CHECKLIST INCLUDES THE STEPS REQUIRED TO CREATE SQL-DMO OBJECTS FROM VISUAL BASIC:

- ☐ Include the SQL-DMO type library in the Visual Basic environment by adding "Microsoft SQLOLE Object Library" to the Visual Basic references.

- ☐ Declare a SQL-DMO SQLServer object.

- ☐ Create the SQLServer object.

- ☐ Connect the SQLServer object to SQL Server.

- ☐ Use the SQLServer objects, properties, and methods, and declare and create any other required SQL-DMO objects to accomplish your required DBA task.

- ☐ Release using the keyword Nothing SQL-DMO objects when you are done using them.

- ☐ Disconnect the SQLServer object.

- ☐ Release the SQLServer object.

Note

SQL-DMO is only available in 32-bit Windows environments (Windows NT and Windows 95).

CREATING SQL SERVER DBA ASSISTANT

Now comes the real value-added part of the chapter. As you probably know by now, examples of using SQL-DMO are hard to find. SQL Server ships with a few SQL-DMO samples that are not well-documented, and the overall SQL-DMO documentation contains very few descriptive examples, concentrating instead on describing the objects and methods.

On the disc included with this book is a Visual Basic project titled samsdb.vbp. The project contains all the source code to the application included on the disc and is called the SQL Server DBA Assistant. The source code is included as a foundation for you to modify and enhance to meet your own needs. The following sections discuss the most important parts of the SQL Server DBA Assistant.

Note

The source code for the application is included with the book. The following sections concentrate on the code that uses SQL-DMO, not the Visual Basic code that does not deal with SQL-DMO. The Visual Basic code is well-documented so that you can use the code and form to easily add your own functionality to the project.

WHAT'S IN THE SQL SERVER DBA ASSISTANT?

Before getting started on developing the SQL Server DBA, you must decide what type of functionality you are going to put in the application. First, because the purpose of the utility is for actual DBA work and learning, you should create an application that uses several different SQL-DMO objects.

What do I think is missing from Microsoft SQL Server 6.0? Memory configuration for SQL Server is very important, and yet there is no screen that graphically illustrates how much memory is currently allocated to SQL Server, the procedure cache, data cache, or SQL Server overhead. You could always do a DBCC MEMUSAGE command, but again, it's not very graphical.

Because of this, the first task your SQL Server DBA Assistant will accomplish is to perform SQL Server memory estimates and breakouts using the formulas published in Chapter 20 and in the SQL Server documentation.

To perform this task requires using the SQL Server object and the Configuration object. You will concentrate on setting up a program that enables you to perform table maintenance on several different databases. To perform these tasks requires using the SQL-DMO database object and the table object. Following is a list of the functionalities of the SQL Server DBA Assistant:

◆ Estimate and graph SQL Server memory break out
◆ List all the databases in a combo box for selection
◆ Perform table maintenance on selected tables

CONNECTING TO SQL SERVER

Note

We are skipping a few steps here that are Visual Basic–related, such as creating a new project called samsdba and adding controls to the logon form.

Assuming that you have all the proper files and have added the Microsoft SQLOLE Object Library references to Visual Basic, it now is time to declare a SQL Server object and connect to SQL Server. For logon purposes, use the form that is shown in Figure 25.7 (frmLogon).

Figure 25.7.
SQL Server DBA
Assistant Logon form.

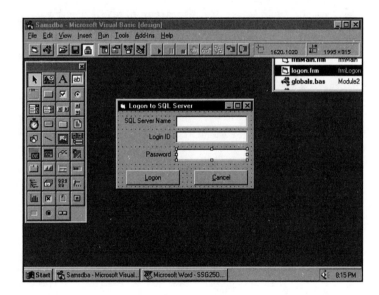

Using your checklist for creating a SQL-DMO application, perform Step 2: Declaring a SQL-DMO object, as follows in the Visual Basic module globals.bas:

```
Public MySqlServer As SQLOLE.SQLServer 'Global SQL Server Object
```

The next step is to create a SQL Server Object. The code to create a SQL Server object is located in the Visual Basic module sqlserv.bas in the procedure main. The code for the main procedure is shown in Listing 25.1.

LISTING 25.1. PROCEDURE main: CREATING A SQL SERVER OBJECT.

```
Public Sub main()
'SAMS -Microsoft SQL Server DBA Survival Guide
'
'Main - The procedure main creates an OLE SQL Server Object
'        and then prompts the user to enter the correct SQL Server
'        name.  If the user properly connects to the SQL Server
'        the main form of the application is shown.
'
'Set up Error handling

On Error GoTo Err_Main

    '
'Check if the application is already running
'
If App.PrevInstance > 0 Then
    MsgBox "SQL Server DBA Assistant already running on this machine.", _
            vbCritical, "Already Running"
    End
End If

    '
'Create a New SQL Server OLE Object
'
Set MySqlServer = CreateObject("SQLOLE.SQLServer")

Connected = False 'Set Global to Not Connected
'
'Set SQL Server Connection Timeout Value
'
MySqlServer.LoginTimeout = 15 'Set for 15 seconds
'
'Display the Logon Screen
'
frmLogon.Show 1
Set frmLogon = Nothing   'Reclaim Object Memory

'If We established a Connection Display the Main form
' Otherwise exit the application
If Connected = True Then
    frmSplash.Show    'Display Splash Screen
    DoEvents          'Allow time to Paint the Splash Screen
    Load frmMain      'Load the Main Form
    frmMain.Show      'Make it Appear
    Unload frmSplash  'Make it disappear
    Set frmSplash = Nothing 'Reclaim Memory
    Exit Sub
End If
'
'Exit - If not Connected
Quit_App:

    If Not (MySqlServer Is Nothing) Then
        'Release SQL Server Object
        Set MySqlServer = Nothing
    End If
```

```
        End 'End the program
'
'Error Handler
'
Err_Main:
        '
        'Display Error Message
        MsgBox Err.Description, vbCritical, "Connection Error"
        Resume Next

End Sub
```

The following line creates a SQL-DMO SQL Server object using the function `CreateObject` (Step 3 of your SQL-DMO list):

```
Set MySqlServer = CreateObject("SQLOLE.SQLServer")
```

When this line of code executes, the variable `MySqlServer` will contain a SQL Server object.

Before you try to connect to a SQL Server by logging on, you set the login timeout value by setting the SQL Server object property `LoginTimeout`, as follows:

```
MySqlServer.LoginTimeout = 15 'Set for 15 seconds
```

You now are ready to perform Step 4 of your checklist to establish a connection to SQL Server. The login form appears (refer to Figure 25.7). A user then enters the SQL Server, user name, and password and clicks the Logon button on the form. The code shown in Listing 25.2 then is executed to establish a connection to the SQL Server.

LISTING 25.2. SQL SERVER CONNECTION.

```
Private Sub cmdLogon_Click()

    'Set up the Error Handler
    '
    On Error GoTo Err_Logon
    '
    'Connect to the SQL Server
    '
    If txtServer <> "" Then
        Me.MousePointer = vbHourglass 'Turn Cursor to HourGlass
        '
        'Invoke Connect Method of the SQL Server Object
        '
        MySqlServer.Connect ServerName:=txtServer.TEXT, _
                            Login:=txtLogon.TEXT, _
                            Password:=txtPassword.TEXT
        '
        'Sql Server Connected Correctly - Unload the form
        '
        Connected = True             'Set Global Connection Variable
```

continues

LISTING 25.2. CONTINUED

```
        Me.MousePointer = vbDefault 'Turn Mousepointer back to default
        Unload Me                    'Unload the Logon form
    Else
        MsgBox "You must enter a SQL Server Name to Connect", _
            vbCritical, "Invalid Entry"
    End If
    '
    'Exit the routine - If Not Logged In Try Again
    '
Exit_Logon:

    Exit Sub
    '
' Error handler
    '
Err_Logon:
    Me.MousePointer = vbDefault
    MsgBox "Error Connection to Server. Error: " & Err.Description, _
        vbCritical, "Error Connection"
    Resume Exit_Logon
End Sub
```

The following lines of code establish a connection with SQL Server using the Connection method of the SQL Server object:

```
    'Invoke Connect Method of the SQL Server Object
    '
    MySqlServer.Connect ServerName:=txtServer.TEXT, _
                    Login:=txtLogon.TEXT, _
                    Password:=txtPassword.TEXT
```

After you establish a successful connection to SQL Server, you now are ready to perform Steps 5 and 6 of the SQL-DMO application checklist and perform various tasks by creating objects, invoking methods, and setting properties.

ESTIMATING MEMORY

To configure the memory breakout for SQL Server, you need to read the memory configuration parameter to get the total amount of memory. You also need to get the configuration value for the procedure cache and subtract that value from 100 to get the percentage of memory used for the data cache. Before the procedure and data cache values can be computed, you must compute the SQL Server overhead.

Computing SQL Server overhead again requires reading configuration values and computing the total amount of memory used by each configuration object and adding the value to SQL Server static memory requirements. Using the SQL-DMO object model that was shown in Figure 25.3, you can see the SQL Server configuration object. Using the configuration object, you can easily obtain the configuration values. To create the configuration object, you first declare the configuration object, as follows:

```
Dim MyConfig As SQLOLE.Configuration, ConfigV As SQLOLE.ConfigValue
```

To create the configuration object, you use your SQL Server object by executing the following code because the configuration object is dependent upon the SQL Server object:

```
'Get a configuration object
Set MyConfig = MySqlServer.Configuration
```

The variable MyConfig now contains a SQL-DMO configuration object. Using the ConfigValues collection of the configuration object, the configuration values can easily be obtained. To get the running configuration value for the memory configuration parameter, for example, execute the following code:

```
TotalMemory = CInt((DATA_PAGE * MyConfig.ConfigValues("memory").RunningValue) /
MEGA_BYTE)
```

The memory configuration value is in 2K data pages. For the memory estimation graph, all the values will be converted to megabytes. Rather than using the ConfigValues collection, you could also create an instance of a specific ConfigValue object and then retrieve the values. The following example creates a ConfigValue object for locks and then retrieves the value:

```
'Locks
    Set ConfigV = MyConfig.ConfigValues("locks")
    TempValue = ConfigV.RunningValue * MEM_LOCKS
```

Note

To compute the memory requirements for configuration objects to estimate SQL Server overhead, constants were used so that if Microsoft publishes more accurate object memory requirements, you can easily modify the constants located in the module global.bas.

To estimate SQL Server memory breakdown, the various configuration values will be read using the configuration object and ConfigValues collection. The SQL Server overhead, procedure, and data cache will then be computed and graphed. The breakout of SQL Server memory is computed during the loading process of the main form (frmMain) of the SQL Server DBA Assistant. The SQL Server DBA Assistant Memory Estimate dialog box is shown in Figure 25.8.

Figure 25.8.
SQL Server DBA
Assistant Memory
Estimate dialog box.

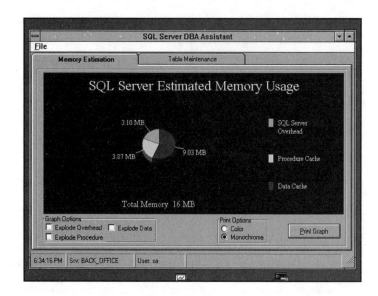

The code to perform the memory estimate and build the graph shown in Figure 25.8 is shown in Listing 25.3.

LISTING 25.3. MEMORY ESTIMATE CODE.

```
Public Sub EstimateMemory()
'
'Define Values to Compute Memory Allocation
'
Dim MyConfig As SQLOLE.Configuration, ConfigV As SQLOLE.ConfigValue
Dim MemoryOverhead As Single, DataCache As Single, ProcCache As Single
Dim TempValue As Single, TotalMemory As Integer

    On Error GoTo Memory_Estimate_Error
    '
    'Use the standard formula to compute Memory usage estimates
    Set MyConfig = MySqlServer.Configuration
    '
    'Get Memory
    '
    '    Note: We will use two different methods to get at the configuration
    '          values (for learning purposes).
    '                    Method 1 uses the Configuration Configvalues collection
    '                    Method 2 creates a ConfigValue Object
    ' Method 1
    TotalMemory = CInt((DATA_PAGE * MyConfig.ConfigValues("memory").RunningValue) /
MEGA_BYTE)
    '
    'Get Procedure Cache and Data Cache Values
    '
    ProcCache = MyConfig.ConfigValues("procedure cache").RunningValue
    DataCache = 100 - ProcCache
    '
```

```
'Do SQL Server Overhead
'
MemoryOverhead = MEM_DEVICES + MEM_STATIC_OVERHEAD
'
'Method 2
'
'Locks
Set ConfigV = MyConfig.ConfigValues("locks")
TempValue = ConfigV.RunningValue * MEM_LOCKS
MemoryOverhead = MemoryOverhead + TempValue
'
'Users
Set ConfigV = MyConfig.ConfigValues("user connections")
TempValue = ConfigV.RunningValue * MEM_USER
MemoryOverhead = MemoryOverhead + TempValue
'
'Databases
Set ConfigV = MyConfig.ConfigValues("open databases")
TempValue = ConfigV.RunningValue * MEM_DATABASE
MemoryOverhead = MemoryOverhead + TempValue
'
'Objects
'
Set ConfigV = MyConfig.ConfigValues("open objects")
TempValue = ConfigV.RunningValue * MEM_OBJECTS
MemoryOverhead = (MemoryOverhead + TempValue) / (MEGA_BYTE)
'
'Compute Values
'
TempValue = TotalMemory - MemoryOverhead
ProcCache = TempValue * (ProcCache / 100)
DataCache = TempValue * (DataCache / 100)

'
'Release the Objects
'
Set ConfigV = Nothing
Set MyConfig = Nothing

'
'Setup the Graph With Information
'   Setup Data Points
With grphMemory
    .AutoInc = 1     'Turn Auto Increment On
    .DrawMode = 0    'Disable drawing until the end
    .NumPoints = 3   'Set total number of points
    .ThisPoint = 1   'Start with Point 1
    'OverHead
    .GraphData = CInt(MemoryOverhead) 'Set graph point - Using Integer
    'Procedure Cache
    .GraphData = CInt(ProcCache)
    'Data Cache
    .GraphData = CInt(DataCache)
End With

' Setup Colors for the Graph
With grphMemory
```

continues

LISTING 25.3. CONTINUED

```
            .ColorData = 7      'Red
            .ColorData = 14
            .ColorData = 12
        End With

        'Setup labels for each graph
        With grphMemory
            .LabelText = Format(MemoryOverhead, "######.00 MB")
            .LabelText = Format(ProcCache, "######.00 MB")
            .LabelText = Format(DataCache, "######.00 MB")
        End With

        'Setup The legend and the title on the bottom
         With grphMemory
            .BottomTitle = "Total Memory " & Str$(TotalMemory) & " MB"
            .LegendText = "SQL Server Overhead"
            .LegendText = "Procedure Cache"
            .LegendText = "Data Cache"
            .DrawMode = 2    'Draw the graph
        End With
    '
Memory_Estimate_Exit:
    Exit Sub
    '
' Error handler
    '
Memory_Estimate_Error:
    Me.MousePointer = vbDefault
    MsgBox "Error estimating memory configuration." _
        & "Error: " & Err.Description, _
        vbCritical, "Memory Configuration Error"
    Resume Memory_Estimate_Exit
End Sub
```

FILLING A COMBO BOX WITH DATABASES

In order to make the SQL Server DBA Assistant a useful tool during database table maintenance, you will add the capability to select a database from a combo box and then read all the non-system tables associated with the database into a Visual Basic list box control.

To read all the databases on the selected server into a combo box, you will use the SQL Server SQL-DMO object and the databases collection. The code shown in Listing 25.4 populates a Visual Basic combo box with all the database names in your SQL Server object collection.

LISTING 25.4. POPULATING A COMBO BOX WITH DATABASE NAMES.

```
Dim Db As SQLOLE.DATABASE

    CenterForm frmMain
    '
    'Fill the Combo Box on the form with the
    'available databases by using the SQL Server databases collection
    '
    For Each Db In MySqlServer.Databases
        '   Make sure the database is not currently being loaded
        '
        If Db.Status <> SQLOLEDBStat_Inaccessible Then
            cmbDatabase.AddItem Db.Name
        Else
            MsgBox "Database: """ + Db.Name _
                + " "" can not be accessed at this time.", _
                vbCritical, "Database Loading"
        End If
    Next
    Set Db = Nothing
```

To populate a list box with the tables in the database, you will read the tables collection of the selected database. The code to populate the list box using the selected database is shown in Listing 25.5.

LISTING 25.5. POPULATING A LIST BOX WITH TABLE NAMES USING A DATABASE OBJECT AND TABLES COLLECTION.

```
Private Sub cmbDatabase_Click()
Dim WorkTable As SQLOLE.TABLE 'SQL-DMO Table Object

    On Error GoTo Get_Tables_Error
    '
    'Database changed - Modify Database Object
    '
    Set WorkDb = Nothing       'Clear the Work Database object
    lstTables.Clear            'Clear tables list box
    lstOperateTables.Clear     'Clear the operate tables list Box

    'Get the currently selected database object
    '
    Set WorkDb = MySqlServer.Databases(cmbDatabase.TEXT)


    '
    'Fill The list box with the table names using the database
    'tables collection exclude any system tables.
    '
    For Each WorkTable In WorkDb.Tables 'Do For Each table in the database
        If Not (WorkTable.SystemObject) Then
            lstTables.AddItem WorkTable.Name 'Add to the list Box
        End If
    Next WorkTable
```

continues

LISTING 25.5. CONTINUED

```
Exit_Get_Tables:
    Set WorkTable = Nothing
    Exit Sub   'Leave the Procedure

    '
    ' Error handler
    '
Get_Tables_Error:
    Me.MousePointer = vbDefault
    MsgBox "Error reading tables collection " & Err.Description, _
        vbCritical, "Filling Combo Box Error"
    Resume Exit_Get_Tables

End Sub
```

Tip

You can begin to see that using SQL-DMO is quite simple once you become familiar with the SQL-DMO object model. Study the model and become familiar with the collections, objects, and the hierarchy.

Getting a list of objects is simple using the Visual Basic FOR EACH - NEXT statement. For Each - Next is used to read through all items of an array or collection. Examples of the For Each - Next statement can be found in Listings 25.4 and 25.5.

PERFORMING TABLE MAINTENANCE

Once a database has been selected, a database object can easily be created using the selected database name and the SQL Server object, as follows:

```
'Get the currently selected database object
    '
    Set WorkDb = MySqlServer.Databases(cmbDatabase.TEXT)
```

Once the line of code executes, you have a SQL-DMO database object for the selected database. If you remember the object model for SQL-DMO, you can easily create a table object using the database object. Once the table object has been created, you then can perform a variety of table maintenance tasks using the different table methods. Following are some examples of the table object methods and the tasks they perform:

CheckTable	Performs the DBCC CheckTable command.
Grant	Grants table privileges to a list of SQL Server users or groups.

RecalcSpaceUsage	Recalculates the space information for the table.
Script	Generates the Transact SQL statements to create the table.
Update Statistics	Updates the data distribution pages used by the Query Optimizer to make proper index selection.

With the SQL Server DBA Assistant, you will be able to select the tables you want to perform a table maintenance operation on and then click a button to perform the appropriate action. The code that scans through the list of selected tables and invokes the method is as follows:

```
'Execute Update Statistics command on selected tables
    '
    For X = 0 To lstOperateTables.ListCount - 1
        ProgressBar1.VALUE = X
        Set WorkTable = WorkDb.Tables(lstOperateTables.List(X))
        '
        'Update Statistics on the Table - using the UpdateStatistics Method
        '
        WorkTable.UpdateStatistics
        'Release the Work Table object
        Set WorkTable = Nothing
    Next X
```

The SQL Server DBA Assistant Table maintenance dialog box is shown in Figure 25.9.

Figure 25.9.
SQL Server DBA
Assistant Table
Maintenance
dialog box.

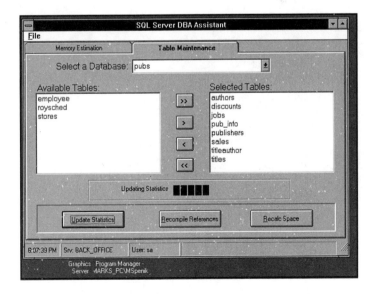

Listing 25.5 shows the code used behind the Update Statistics button (shown in Figure 25.9).

LISTING 25.5. PERFORMING UPDATE STATISTICS ON SELECTED TABLES.

```
Private Sub cmdUpdate_Click()
Dim WorkTable As SQLOLE.TABLE 'SQL-DMO Table Object
Dim X As Integer

    On Error GoTo Up_Stats_Error
    SSPanel1.Enabled = False
    frmMain.MousePointer = vbHourglass
    '
    'Setup The Progress Bar
    ProgressBar1.MAX = lstOperateTables.ListCount - 1
    ProgressBar1.VALUE = 0
    lblStatus.Caption = "Updating Statistics"
    frmStatus.Visible = True   'Turn On Progress Bar
    DoEvents 'Allow Screen to repaint
    '
    StatusBar1.Panels("status").TEXT = "Updating Statistics - Please Wait..."

    'Execute Update Statistics command on selected tables
    '
    For X = 0 To lstOperateTables.ListCount - 1
        ProgressBar1.VALUE = X
        Set WorkTable = WorkDb.Tables(lstOperateTables.List(X))
        '
        'Update Statistics on the Table - using the UpdateStatistics Method
        '
        WorkTable.UpdateStatistics
        'Release the Work Table object
        Set WorkTable = Nothing
    Next X
    'Cleanup and Exit
Up_Stats_Exit:
    '
    frmStatus.Visible = False
    StatusBar1.Panels("status").TEXT = ""
    SSPanel1.Enabled = True
    frmMain.MousePointer = vbDefault
    Exit Sub
'
' Error handler
'
Up_Stats_Error:
    Me.MousePointer = vbDefault
    MsgBox "Error Updating statistics on table " & lstOperateTables.List(X) _
        & "Error: " & Err.Description, _
        vbCritical, "Update Statistics Error"
    Resume Up_Stats_Exit
End Sub
```

Tip

We have provided you with the following three table maintenance functions already programmed and ready to use!

◆ Update Statistics

◆ Recompile References

◆ Recalculate Space Usage

As stated earlier, the purpose of the SQL Server DBA Assistant is to provide you with a foundation to create your own application. If you look behind each of the buttons, you will notice that the code is almost identical, except for the methods added. You can easily add more functionality by cutting and pasting the code into new buttons and adding new methods. You also can optimize the application by reducing the code behind the buttons using a shared function or procedure. The list is endless, so what are you waiting for?

SUMMARY

For the non-Visual Basic DBAs in the crowd, I hope my explanations and code examples were easy for you to follow and that they motivated you to learn Visual Basic.

Using SQL-DMO, you can easily create powerful DBA tools that can even be integrated in applications, such as Microsoft Word and Excel. Study the various Visual Basic examples that ship with SQL Server and review the code that ships with this book, and soon you will have the power and capability to write your own tools and simplify your job!

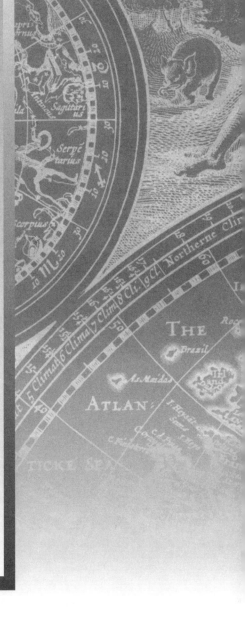

P A R T VII

Appendixes

Naming Conventions

The following are recommended naming conventions for SQL Server.

SUGGESTED NAMING CONVENTIONS

Object	Naming Convention	Example
database	(business name)	sales
device		
data device	(business name) + _data	sales_data
log device	(business name) + _log	sales_log
dump device	(business name) + _dump	sales_dump
table	(business name)	customer
constraint		
foreign key constraint	(table name) + _fk	customer_fk
primary key constraint	(table name) + _pk	customer_pk
unique key constraint	(table name) + _uniq	customer_uniq
index		
clustered	(column_name) + _cdx	customer_id_cdx
nonclustered	(column name) + _idx	customer_id_idx
trigger		
delete	(table name) + _dtr	customer_dtr
insert	(table name) + _itr	customer_itr
update	(table name) + _utr	customer_utr
insert & update	(table name) + _iutr	customer_iutr
stored procedure (naming convention 1)	usp + (_business name) (usp stands for User-defined Stored Procedure)	usp_customer_inquiry

stored procedure
(naming convention 2)

This naming convention combines the action being performed in the stored procedure with a business name. For example, a stored procedure that deletes the customer profile would be named del_customer. If the stored procedure performs multiple business functions, use oth + (_business name).

DELETE	del + (_business name)	del_customer
INSERT	ins + (_business name)	ins_customer
SELECT	sel + (_business name)	sel_customer

UPDATE	upd + (_business name)	upd_customer
Other types of actions	oth + (_business name)	oth_customer
view	(business name_) + view	customer_view

> **Note**
>
> SQL Server is case-sensitive. I generally make everything lowercase to avoid confusion.

Using Extended Stored
Procedures

Extended stored procedures were first introduced with Microsoft SQL Server Version 4.21 for Windows NT. An extended stored procedure is not really a stored procedure, but a function in a dynamic link library, DLL, that can be executed like a stored procedure from SQL Server and can return status codes to the calling process like normal stored procedures. Extended stored procedures can be created by developers and then called from SQL Server; however, only the SA can add an extended stored procedure to the system. The following is a reference to the extended stored procedures that come with SQL Server and the stored procedures used to manage extended stored procedures.

Tip

Microsoft extended stored procedures start with xp_, unlike the standard system stored procedures that start with sp_.

SP_ADDEXTENDEDPROC

sp_addextendedproc is a SQL Server stored procedure used to register an extended stored procedure with SQL Server. The command must be executed by the SA in the master database. The syntax for the command is as follows:

```
sp_addextendedproc function, dll
```

Where function is the extended stored procedure function name and dll is the name of the dll containing the function.

SP_DROPEXTENDEDPROC

sp_dropextendedproc is a SQL Server stored procedure used to remove (drop) an extended stored procedure from SQL Server. The syntax for the command is as follows:

```
sp_dropextendedproc function
```

Where function is the name of the extended stored procedure to remove.

SP_HELPEXTENDEDPROC

sp_helpextendedproc displays the extended stored procedures on a SQL Server. The syntax is as follows:

```
sp_helpextendedproc
```

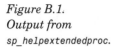

Figure B.1.
Output from
sp_helpextendedproc.

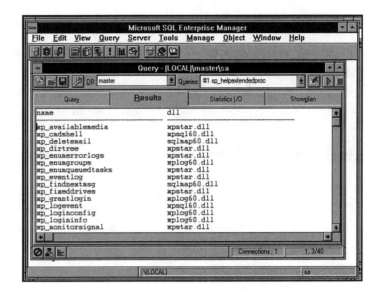

Figure B.1 shows the output from sp_helpextendedproc. Note the function and dll name are displayed.

XP_CMDSHELL

The xp_cmdshell extended stored procedure executes a command string as a system command shell and returns any output.

> ### Tip
>
> xp_cmdshell is extremely useful for executing commands from stored procedures or triggers. If you need to execute several commands or a single command with a long command string, place the commands in a batch file (.bat extension) and execute the batch file.

The syntax for xp_cmdshell is as follows:

```
xp_cmdshell command[, no_output]
```

Where *command* is the command to execute and *no_output* is an optional parameter that tells the server to execute the command but don't return any output.

Note

If you use xp_cmdshell to start an application or batch file that does not return immediately, the connection that issued the extended stored procedure will block and wait until the application exits or the batch file completes (even with the *no_output* flag).

Warning

xp_cmdshell can execute any Windows NT command that SQL Server has permission to execute. If users are given permission to xp_cmdshell, they will be able to execute commands SQL Server has permission to execute.

XP_LOGEVENT

xp_logevent logs user messages to the Windows NT event log and/or the SQL Server error log. The syntax is as follows:

```
xp_logevent error_number, User_Message, [Event_Log_Severity]
```

Where *error_number* is a number between 50,001 and 2,147,483,647. *User_Message* is a user-defined message up to 255 characters. *Event_Log_Severity* is an optional parameter that can have the value informational, warning, or error. The default is Informational.

Tip

xp_logevent can be used in triggers to audit table changes. Use xp_logevent for error reporting in stored procedures.

XP_MSVER

New for SQL Server Version 6.0, xp_msver returns information about SQL Server. The syntax for xp_msver is as follows:

```
xp_msver [option]
```

Where *option* can be any of the parameters listed in the Name column shown in Figure B.2.

Figure B.2.
Output of xp_msver
command.

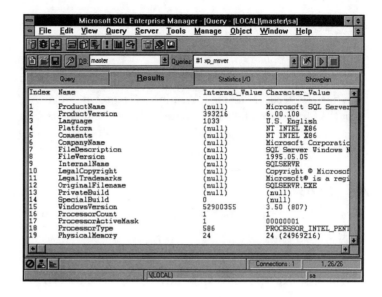

SQL INTEGRATED SECURITY EXTENDED STORED PROCEDURES

The following extended stored procedures are used to set up integrated or mixed security. It is recommended that you use the SQL Security Manager instead of the extended stored procedures.

XP_GRANTLOGIN

xp_grantlogin adds a Windows NT user group or user to SQL Server. The syntax is as follows:

```
xp_grantlogin 'NT_Account_Name' [, {'admin' ¦ 'repl' ¦ 'user'}]
```

Where *NT_Account_Name* is a Windows NT group or user. The optional parameter determines the type of SQL Server privileges assigned the login—admin = SA, repl=repl_publisher, and user.

XP_REVOKELOGIN

xp_revokelogin drops the user account or group from the SQL Server. The syntax is as follows:

```
xp_revokelogin 'NT_Account_Name'
```

Where *NT_Account_Name* is a Windows NT group or user.

XP_LOGININFO

xp_logininfo provides SQL Server account access information.

xp_logininfo ['*NT_Account_Name*'] [, '*all*' ¦ '*members*'] [, *variable_name*]

Where *NT_Account_Name* is a Windows NT group or user, '*all*' reports all permission paths for the account and '*members*' reports information on all members of the group. *variable_name* is an optional output parameter that returns the permission level of the account (such as admin, repl, user).

XP_LOGINCONFIG

xp_loginconfig reports SQL Server login security information. The syntax is as follows:

xp_loginconfig ['*Config_Name_Parm*']

Where *Config Name Parm* can be any of the parameters listed in the name column shown in Figure B.3.

Figure B.3.
Output from
xp_loginconfig
command.

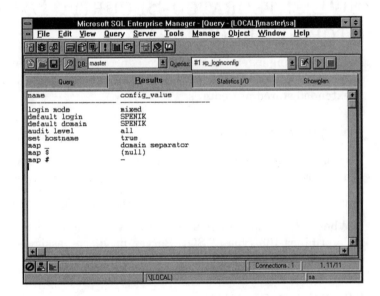

XP_SPRINTF

xp_sprintf is new for SQL Server Version 6.0 and is similar to the C function sprintf. Use xp_sprintf to build an output string from a format list and a list of strings. The syntax is as follows:

xp_sprintf *Build_String output*, *Build_String_Format* [, *string arguments*]..

Where *Build_String* is the output string for the formatted string. *Build_String_Format* currently can only be %s (strings) and *string_arguments* is the list of arguments to build the output string based on the format string.

XP_STARTMAIL

xp_startmail starts a SQL Server mail client session. xp_startmail has the following syntax:

```
xp_startmail ['mail_user_name'] [, 'password']
```

Where *mail_user_name* is a valid mail user name and *password* is the password for the user.

XP_STOPMAIL

xp_stopmail halts a SQL Server mail session. xp_stopmail has the following format:

```
xp_stopmail
```

XP_SENDMAIL

xp_sendmail can be used to send a mail message or query from SQL Server to several users via e-mail. xp_sendmail has the following syntax:

```
xp_sendmail recipient, [...recipientn,]]
{@message ¦ @query ¦ @attachments}
[, copy_recipients] [, blind_copy_recipients] [, subject] [, type]
[, attach_results] [, no_output] [, no_header] [, width]
[, separator] [, echo_error] [, set_user]
```

Where *recipient* is the user or list of users to receive the mail.

@message or *@query* or *@attachment* is the body of the mail message. If a query is specified, the results of the query will be sent.

copy_receipients and *blind_copy_recipients* are other users to include on the mail list to receive the message.

subject is the subject of the message.

type is used to set a custom message.

attach_results specifies that the results of query should be included as an attached file instead of appended on the end of the mail message.

no_output specifies not to return results to the mail client.

no_header specifies not to include the column header information for a query.

width sets the line width for the message.

Tip

Use the extended stored procedure mail functions for error reporting and to send the results of nightly batch runs.

System Stored Procedures

SQL Server comes with many different stored procedures that enable you to view and modify the system tables called *system procedures*. This appendix is a listing of the different system stored procedures that ship with Microsoft SQL Server.

SP_ADDALIAS

Creates an alias for one user to another in a database.

```
sp_addalias login_id, user_name
login_id = Login Id of user to assign alias
user_name = Database user to alias the login id
```

SP_ADDEXTENDEDPROC

Registers the new extended stored procedure name with SQL Server.

```
sp_addextendedproc function, dll
function = Function name
dll = Name of the DLL containing the function
```

SP_ADDGROUP

Creates a group in the database from which the command is executed.

```
sp_addgroup group_name
group_name = Name of the group to add to the database
```

SP_ADDLOGIN

Adds a new login id to SQL Server and modifies the system syslogins table.

```
sp_addlogin login_id [, password [, default_db [, default_language]]]
login_id = User login id to add
password = Password for the new login id
default_db = default database for the login_id
default_language = default language for the login id
```

SP_ADDMESSAGE

Enables you to add a custom information or error message to the sysmessages system table.

```
sp_addmessage message id, severity, 'message text'
        [, language [, {true ¦ false} [, REPLACE]]]
message id = Integer message number must be greater then 50001
severity = Severity level of the message (valid levels 1 to 25)
message text = Message description
language = Language of message, US English is the default
{true ¦ false} = If True, message automatically written to NT event log
REPLACE - Used to overwrite an existing message
```

SP_ADDREMOTELOGIN

Adds a login id for a remote user.

```
sp_addremotelogin remote_server [, login_ID [, remote_name]]
remote_server = Remote server for which the login_id applies
login_ID = Login id of user on the local server
remote_name = Login Id used by the remote serve when logging on to the local server
```

SP_ADDSEGMENT

Creates a segment on a device in the current database.

```
sp_addsegment seg_name, logicalname
seg_name = Name of the new segment
logicalname = database device where the segment will be located
```

SP_ADDSERVER

Adds a remote SQL Server.

```
sp_addserver servername [, LOCAL]
servername = Name of the remote server to add
[, LOCAL] = Identifies server being added as a local server
```

SP_ADDTYPE

Adds a new user-defined datatype.

```
sp_addtype type_name, physical_type [, null_type]
type_name = Name of the data type
physical_type = SQL Server supplied data type on which new type is based
null_type = Defines how user data type treats NULLS
```

SP_ADDUMPDEVICE

Adds a new dump device to SQL Server.

```
sp_addumpdevice {'disk' ¦ 'diskette' ¦ 'tape'}, 'logicalname','physicalname'
[, [, noskip ¦ skip [, mediacapacity]] ]
disk,diskette,tape = Valid types of dump devices
logicalname = Name of the dump device
physicalname = Physical location of the dump device
noskip,skip = Read or skip ANSI labels
```

SP_ADDUSER

Adds a new user to the current database.

```
sp_adduser login_id [, user_name [, group_name]]
login_id = Login id of the new user
user_name = User name in the database
group_name = User group name
```

C

SYSTEM STORED PROCEDURES

SP_ALTERMESSAGE

Changes the state of a system error message located in sysmessages.

```
sp_altermessage messageid, WITH_LOG, {true ¦ false}
messageid = Id of the message to alter
WITH_LOG = If set to true the message is written to the Window NT event log.
```

SP_BINDEFAULT

Binds a default to a table column or user-defined object.

```
sp_bindefault default_name, object_name [, future_only]
default_name = Name of the default
object_name = Name of object having default bound
future_only = Used for user defined data types only, prevents existing data from
inheriting the new default
```

SP_BINDRULE

Binds a rule to a table column or user-defined object.

```
sp_bindrule rule_name, object_name [, future_only]
rule_name = Name of the new rule
object_name = Name of the object having the rule bound
future_only = Used for user defined data types only, prevents existing data from
inheriting the new rule
```

SP_CERTIFY_REMOVABLE

Verifies that a database is properly configured for removable media distribution.

```
sp_certify_removable database_name[, AUTO]
database_name = Name of database
AUTO = Gives ownership of the databases and objects to sa and removes user created
database users and non-default permissions.
```

SP_CHANGEDBOWNER

Changes the database owner.

```
sp_changedbowner login_id [, true]
login_id = Login id of the new database owner
true = Transfers to the new owner aliases and permissions
```

SP_CHANGEGROUP

Changes the group of a user.

```
sp_changegroup group_name, user_name
group_name = Group name
user_name = User name to add to the group
```

SP_CONFIGURE

Sets or displays SQL Server configuration parameters.

```
sp_configure [configuration_name [, configuration_value]]
configuration_name = Name of the parameter to modify
configuration_value = New Value
```

SP_DBOPTION

Turns on or off a specified database option. If called with no parameters, displays the current option settings of the default database.

```
sp_dboption [database_name, option_name, {true ¦ false}]
database_name = Name of the database to set the option
option_name = Option Name
{true ¦ false}] = Value of option, true = ON, false = OFF
```

SP_DBREMOVE

Used to drop a database and, optionally, any device(s) of which the database has exclusive ownership.

```
sp_dbremove database[, drop_device]
database = Database to remove
drop_device = Device(s) to remove
```

SP_DEFAULTDB

Sets the login_id user's default database.

```
sp_defaultdb login_id, default_database
login_id = login_id of the user
default_database = Default database name
```

SP_DEFAULTLANGUAGE

Changes the default language of a user.

```
sp_defaultlanguage login_id [, language]
login_id = Login Id of the user
language = New default language
```

SP_DEPENDS

Displays object dependencies.

```
sp_depends object_name
object_name = Database object to view dependencies (view, table, trigger, or stored
procedure).
```

C

SYSTEM STORED PROCEDURES

SP_DEVOPTION

Displays or sets the status of a device.

```
sp_devoption [device_name [, option_name {, true ¦ false} [, override]]]
device_name = Name of the device to display or set
option_name = Name of the Option (True = ON, False = OFF)
override = Only for "read only" option, allows you set read/write database to read
only
```

SP_DISKDEFAULT

Determines whether the device can be used as part of the default device pool used
for CREATE DATABASE statements without specifying a device.

```
sp_diskdefault database_device, {defaulton ¦ defaultoff}
database_device = Device name
defaulton ¦ defaultoff = Adds or removes the device from the default pool
```

SP_DROPALIAS

Drops the alias login_id.

```
sp_dropalias login_id
login_id = Login id of user with alias to drop
```

SP_DROPDEVICE

Drops a device.

```
sp_dropdevice logical_name [, DELFILE]
logical_name = Logical name of the device to drop
DELFILE = Delete physical file after the device is dropped
```

SP_DROPEXTENDEDPROC

Removes an extended stored procedure from SQL Server.

```
sp_dropextendedproc function_name
function_name = Name of extended stored procedure to remove
```

SP_DROPGROUP

Drops a group from a database.

```
sp_dropgroup group_name
group_name = Name of the group to remove
```

SP_DROPLANGUAGE

Removes an alternate language from SQL Server.

```
sp_droplanguage language [, drop_messages]
language = Language to drop
drop_messages = Drops all associated system messages
```

SP_DROPLOGIN

Removes the login_id from SQL Server.

```
sp_droplogin login_id
login_id = Login Id to remove
```

SP_DROPMESSAGE

Removes a message from the sysmessages table.

```
sp_dropmessage [msgid [, language ¦ 'all']]
msgid = Message id of the message to drop
language = Language of message to drop
all = Drop message from all languages
```

SP_DROPREMOTELOGIN

Drops a remote login id from the SQL Server.

```
sp_dropremotelogin remote_server [, login_name [, remote_name]]
remote_server = Server with remote login to drop
login_name = Local Server's login name to drop
remote_name = Remote user named mapped to the local login name
```

SP_DROPSEGMENT

Drops a segment from a database.

```
sp_dropsegment segment_name [, logical_name]
segment_name = Segment name to drop
logical_name = Database device you no longer want the segment to use
```

SP_DROPSERVER

Drops a server from SQL Server's known list of servers.

```
sp_dropserver server_name [, drop_logins]
server_name = Server name to drop
drop_logins = Indicates any remote logins to remove
```

C

SYSTEM STORED PROCEDURES

SP_DROPTYPE

Removes a user-defined datatype.

```
sp_droptype type_name
type_name = Name of the data type to remove.
```

SP_DROPUSER

Removes a user from the current database.

```
sp_dropuser user_name
user_name = User name to remove
```

SP_EXTENDSEGMENT

Expands a segment to another database device.

```
sp_extendsegment segment_name, logical_name
segment_name = Segment name to expand
logical_name = Database device to add
```

SP_HELP

Displays information on a specific database object, or if no parameter is given, displays the objects in the current database.

```
sp_help [object_name]
object_name = Name of the object to display information
```

SP_HELPCONSTRAINT

Displays information on the constraints associated with the table.

```
sp_helpconstraint table_name
table_name = Table name you want constraint information on
```

SP_HELPDB

Displays information on the specified database. If no database is specified, displays help on all the databases.

```
sp_helpdb [database_name]
database_name = Database name to display information
```

SP_HELPDEVICE

Displays information on a specified device or all system devices when called without a parameter.

```
sp_helpdevice [logical_name]
logical_name = Device name
```

SP_HELPEXTENDEDPROC

Displays information on a specified extended stored procedure or all extended stored procedures when called without a parameter.

```
sp_helpextendedproc [function_name]
function_name = Name of extended stored procedure
```

SP_HELPGROUP

Displays information about the group in the current database or all the groups in the current database if called with no parameters.

```
sp_helpgroup [group_name]
group_name = Group name to display information
```

SP_HELPINDEX

Displays index information on the specified table.

```
sp_helpindex table_name
table_name = Name of the table to obtain index information
```

SP_HELPLANGUAGE

Displays information on the specified language or all the languages if called with no parameters.

```
sp_helplanguage [language]
language = Language to obtain information
```

SP_HELPLOG

```
sp_helplog
```

Displays information on the device that contains the first page of the log in the current database. There are no parameters for this.

SP_HELPREMOTELOGIN

Displays information on a remote servers specified login or all remote logins when called with no parameters.

```
sp_helpremotelogin [remote_server [, remote_name]]
remote_server = Server to obtain login information
remote_name = Remote user name to obtain information
```

SP_HELPROTECT

Displays permissions for a database object and, optionally, a specific user of the object.

```
sp_helprotect Object [, user_name]
object = Database object to display permissions
user_name = User name
```

SP_HELPSEGMENT

Displays information on the specified segment or all segments in the current database when called with no parameters.

```
sp_helpsegment [segment_name]
segment_name = Name of the segment to obtain information.
```

SP_HELPSERVER

Displays information on a specified remote server or replication server or all servers if called with no parameters.

```
sp_helpserver [server_name]
server_name = Name of server to display specific information
```

SP_HELPSORT

Displays the default sort order and character set. There are no parameters for this.

```
sp_helpsort
```

SP_HELPSQL

Displays syntax for Transact SQL statements.

```
sp_helpsql ['topic']
topic = Topic or statement to display help
```

SP_HELPSTARTUP

Displays the stored procedures that are executed automatically when SQL Server starts. There are no parameters for this.

```
sp_helpstartup
```

SP_HELPTEXT

Displays the text for the following objects: stored procedures, views, triggers, or default.

```
sp_helptext object_name
object_name = Name of object
```

SP_HELPUSER

Displays information about a specific user in a database or displays all users if called with no parameters.

```
sp_helpuser [user_name]
user_name = User name
```

SP_LOCK

Displays information about current locks on SQL Server for a specific system process id(s) (spid) or all the locks if called with no parameters.

```
sp_lock [spid1 [, spid2]]
spid1 = System Process Id to obtain lock information
spid2 = System Process Id to obtain lock information
```

SP_LOGDEVICE

Places the syslogs table (that is, the transaction log) on a separate device.

```
sp_logdevice database_name, database_device
database_name = Database with the transaction log to move
database_device = Name of the database device to move syslogs
```

SP_MAKESTARTUP

Makes the stored procedure an auto procedure that runs when the system is restarted.

```
sp_makestartup procedure_name
procedure_name = Name of the procedure to execute at startup
```

SP_MONITOR

Displays statistical information on SQL Server. There are no parameters for this.

```
sp_monitor
```

SP_PASSWORD

Changes the login_id password.

```
sp_password old_password, new_password [, login_id]
old_password = Old login id password
new_password = New login id password
login_id = login_id to modify
```

SP_PLACEOBJECT

Places future allocation for a table or index on the specified segment.

```
sp_placeobject segment_name, object_name
segment_name = Name of the segment for future allocation
object_name = Table or index name to place on segment
```

SP_PROCESSMAIL

Uses extended stored procedures to process an incoming mail message.

```
sp_processmail [@subject = subject] [[,] @file_type = file_type]
    [[,] @separator = separator] [[,] @set_user = user] [[,] @dbuse =
database_name
subject = Subject line of the mail message
file_type = File extension to use to send back query results
separator = Column separator
user = Security context in which command is run
database_name = database context in which command is run
```

SP_RECOMPILE

Recompiles all stored procedures and triggers that use the specified table name.

```
sp_recompile table_name
table_name = Table name
```

SP_REMOTEOPTION

Changes or displays remote login option.

```
sp_remoteoption [remote_server, login_name, remote_name, option_name, {true ¦
false}]
remote_server = Remote server name
login_name = Login name
remote_name = Remote user name
option_name = Option name (True = On, False = OFF)
```

SP_RENAME

Renames a database object.

```
sp_rename object_name, new_name [, COLUMN ¦ INDEX ]
object_name = Old object name
new_name = New Object name
COLUMN = specifies object being renamed is a column
INDEX = specifies object being renamed is an index
```

SP_RENAMEDB

Renames a database.

```
sp_renamedb old_db_name, new_db_name
old_db_name = Name of old database
new_db_name = Name of the new database
```

SP_SERVEROPTION

Sets the specified server option.

```
sp_serveroption [server_name, option_name, {true ¦ false}]
server_name = Name of server to set option
option_name = Name of the option to set (True = ON, False = OFF)
```

SP_SETLANGALIAS

Sets an alias or changes an alias for an alternate language.

```
sp_setlangalias language, alias
language = language to alias
alias = alias name
```

SP_SPACEUSED

Displays the number or rows and the overall space usage of the specified object or database.

```
sp_spaceused [object_name] [[,] @updateusage = {true ¦ false}]
object_name = Name of the object to display information
@updateusage = When set to true, issues a DBCC UPDATEUSAGE command before display-
ing information
```

SP_UNBINDEFAULT

Removes a default from the specified object.

```
sp_unbindefault object_name [, futureonly]
object_name = Name of the object to unbind the default.
futureonly = Used only for user data types, leaves default value with existing data
```

SP_UNBINDRULE

Removes the rule from the specified object.

```
sp_unbindrule object_name [, futureonly]
object_name = Object to remove the rule
futureonly = Used only for user data types, leaves rule with existing data
```

SP_UNMAKESTARTUP

Stops procedure previously marked to auto start from executing when SQL Server is first started.

```
sp_unmakestartup procedure_name
procedure_name = Name of stored procedure
```

SP_WHO

Displays information for a specified *login_id* or specified process or all users and processes when called with no parameters.

```
sp_who [login_id ¦ 'spid']
login_id = Login Id to display information
spid = System Process Id to display information
```

Function Reference

SQL Server contains several built-in functions that can be used with the Transact-SQL language. The following list categorizes the built-in functions.

AGGREGATE FUNCTIONS

The following section covers aggregate functions.

AVG([ALL | DISTINCT] EXPRESSION)

Sum of values in a column. Nulls are ignored.

COUNT([ALL | DISTINCT] EXPRESSION)

Count number of non-null values in a column. Nulls are ignored.

COUNT(*)

Count number of rows. Nulls are counted.

MAX(EXPRESSION)

Maximum value for a column. Nulls are ignored.

MIN(EXPRESSION)

Minimum value for a column. Nulls are ignored.

SUM([ALL | DISTINCT] EXPRESSION)

Sum of values for a column. Nulls are ignored.

> PARAMETER EXPLANATION
>
> ALL applies the function to all values. ALL is the default.
>
> DISTINCT applies the function to only distinct values.
>
> expression is a column name.

DATE FUNCTIONS

The following section covers date functions.

DATEADD(DATEPART,NUMBER,DATE)

Returns a date incremented by value specified.

DATEDIFF(DATEPART,NUMBER,DATE)

Returns a date decremented by value specified.

DATENAME(DATEPART,DATE)

Returns the date part of a specified date as a string.

DATEPART(DATEPART,DATE)

Returns the date part of a specified date as an integer.

GETDATE()

Returns the current date and time.

PARAMETER EXPLANATION

date is a valid date.

datepart is a date part or abbreviation. (See Table D.1 for valid datepart abbreviations.)

number is a valid number.

TABLE D.1. VALID datepart ABBREVIATIONS.

Date part	Abbreviation	Values
year	yy	1753-9999
quarter	qq	1-4
month	mm	1-12
day of year	dy	1-366
day	dd	1-31
week	wk	1-53
weekday	dw	1-7 (Sun.-Sat.)
hour	hh	0-23

continues

TABLE D.1. CONTINUED

Date part	Abbreviation	Values
minute	mi	0-59
second	ss	0-59
millisecond	ms	0-999

MATHEMATICAL FUNCTIONS

The following section covers mathematical functions.

ABS(NUMERIC_EXPR)

Returns the absolute value of a specified expression.

ACOS(FLOAT_EXPR)

Returns the angle in radians of a cosine expression.

ASIN(FLOAT_EXPR)

Returns the angle in radians of a sin expression.

ATAN(FLOAT_EXPR)

Returns the angle in radians of a tangent expression.

ATN2(FLOAT_EXPR1,FLOAT_EXPR2)

Returns the angle in radians of a tangent expression where `float_expr1/float_expr2`.

CEILING(NUMERIC_EXPR)

Returns a rounded up integer based on the specified expression.

COS(FLOAT_EXPR)

Returns the cosine of a specified expression.

COT(FLOAT_EXPR)

Returns the cotangent of a specified expression.

DEGREES(NUMERIC_EXPR)

Returns the degrees of a specified expression.

EXP(FLOAT_EXPR)

Returns the exponential value of a specified expression.

FLOOR(NUMERIC_EXPR)

Returns a rounded down integer based on the specified expression.

LOG(FLOAT_EXPR)

Returns the natural logarithm of a specified expression.

LOG10(FLOAT_EXPR)

Returns the base-10 logarithm of a specified expression.

PI()

Returns pi.

POWER(NUMERIC_EXPR,Y)

Returns the value of numeric_expr to the y.

RADIANS(NUMERIC_EXPR)

Returns the radians of a specified expression.

RAND([INTEGER_EXPR])

Returns a random float number between 0 and 1. Use optional integer_expr as seed value.

ROUND(NUMERIC_EXPR,INTEGER_EXPR)

Returns a number rounded to the precision specified by integer_expr.

SIGN(NUMERIC_EXPR)

Returns +1, 0, or -1 based on sign of expression.

SIN(*FLOAT_EXPR*)

Returns the sine of an angle specified in radians.

SQRT(*FLOAT_EXPR*)

Returns the square root of a specified expression.

TAN(*FLOAT_EXPR*)

Returns the tangent of an angle specified in radians.

NILADIC FUNCTIONS

Niladic functions are new to SQL Server 6.0. These functions allow default values to be inserted into a table. Prior to Version 6.0, you had to use triggers to insert these types of default values. For more information on these functions, see the CREATE TABLE statement in your SQL Server manual.

CURRENT_TIMESTAMP

Current date and time.

CURRENT_USER

Name of person doing the insert.

SESSION_USER

Name of person doing the insert.

SYSTEM_USER

Login id of person doing the insert.

USER

Name of person doing the insert.

STRING FUNCTIONS

The following section covers string functions.

+

Concatenates two or more non-numeric expressions.

ASCII(CHAR_EXPR)

Returns the corresponding ASCII code value of a specified expression.

CHAR(INTEGER_EXPR)

Returns the corresponding character from ASCII code value. Code must be between 0 and 255.

CHARINDEX('PATTERN', EXPRESSION)

Returns the first position of a pattern within an expression.

DIFFERENCE(CHAR_EXPR1, CHAR_EXPR2)

Determines the similarities between two strings and returns a value from 0 to 4 with 4 being the best match.

LOWER(CHAR_EXPR)

Converts an expression to lowercase.

LTRIM(CHAR_EXPR)

Removes leading spaces.

PATINDEX('%PATTERN%', EXPRESSION)

Returns the first position of a pattern in the specified expression.

REPLICATE(CHAR_EXPR, INTEGER_EXPR)

Replicates a character expression n number of times.

REVERSE(CHAR_EXPR)

Returns a reversed expression.

RIGHT(CHAR_EXPR, INTEGER_EXPR)

Returns number of specified characters from the right.

RTRIM(*CHAR_EXPR*)

Removes trailing spaces.

SOUNDEX(*CHAR_EXPR*)

Returns a four-digit SOUNDEX code.

SPACE(*INTEGER_EXPR*)

Returns *n* number of spaces.

STR(*FLOAT_EXPR* [, *LENGTH* [, *DECIMAL*]])

Returns a character string converted from numeric data.

STUFF(*CHAR_EXPR1*, *START*, *LENGTH*, *CHAR_EXPR2*)

Stuffs `char_expr1` into `char_expr2`.

SUBSTRING(*EXPRESSION*, *START*, *LENGTH*)

Returns a portion a string.

UPPER(*CHAR_EXPR*)

Converts an expression to uppercase.

SYSTEM FUNCTIONS

The following section covers system functions.

COL_LENGTH('*TABLE_NAME*', '*COLUMN_NAME*')

Returns the length of a column in a table.

COL_NAME(*TABLE_ID*, *COLUMN_ID*)

Returns the name of a column based on id.

DATALENGTH('*EXPRESSION*')

Returns the length of a specified expression.

DB_ID(['*DATABASE_NAME*'])

Returns the database identification number a specified database name.

DB_NAME([*DATABASE_ID*])

Returns the database name for a specified database id.

HOST_ID()

Returns the workstation identification number.

HOST_NAME()

Returns the workstation name.

IDENT_INCR('*TABLE_NAME*')

Returns the increment value used for the creation of an identity column.

IDENT_SEED('*TABLE_NAME*')

Returns the seed value used for the creation of an identity column.

INDEX_COL('*TABLE_NAME*', *INDEX_ID*, *KEY_ID*)

Returns the index name for an indexed column.

ISNULL(*EXPRESSION*, *VALUE*)

Replaces NULL expression with a specified value.

OBJECT_ID('*OBJECT_NAME*')

Returns the id for a specified object name.

OBJECT_NAME(*OBJECT_ID*)

Returns the name for a specified object id.

STATS_DATE(*TABLE_ID*, *INDEX_ID*)

Returns the date statistics where last updated for an index.

SUSER_ID([‘LOGIN_NAME’])

Returns the login id for a specified login name.

SUSER_NAME([SERVER_USER_ID])

Returns the login name for a specified login id.

USER_ID([‘USER_NAME’])

Returns the user's database id for a specified user name.

USER_NAME([USER_ID])

Returns the user's database name for a specified user id.

TEXT/IMAGE FUNCTIONS

The following section covers text/image functions.

DATALENGTH(‘EXPRESSION’)

Returns the length of a specified expression.

PATINDEX(‘%PATTERN%’, EXPRESSION)

Returns the first position of a pattern in the specified expression.

TEXTPTR(COLUMN_NAME)

Returns the text-pointer value.

TEXTVALID(‘TABLE_NAME.COLUMN_NAME’, TEXT_PTR)

Returns 1 if text pointer is valid, 0 if the pointer is invalid.

TYPE-CONVERSION FUNCTION

The following section covers the CONVERT function.

CONVERT(DATATYPE[(LENGTH)], EXPRESSION [, STYLE])

> ## PARAMETER EXPLANATION
>
> *datatype* is any valid SQL Server datatype.
>
> *length* is used with char, varchar, binary, and varbinary datatypes.
>
> *expression* is the value to convert.
>
> *style* is the date format to use with datetime or smalldatetime data conversion. (See Table D.2 for valid styles.)

TABLE D.2. VALID STYLES.

Without century (yy)	With century (yyyy)	Standard	Output
-	0 or 100 (*)	Default	mon dd yyyy hh:miAM (or PM)
1	101	USA	mm/dd/yy
2	102	ANSI	yy.mm.dd
3	103	British/French	dd/mm/yy
4	104	German	dd.mm.yy
5	105	Italian	dd-mm-yy
6	106	-	dd mon yy
7	107	-	mon dd, yy
8	108	-	hh:mm:ss
-	9 or 109 (*)	Default + milliseconds	mon dd yyyy (hh:mi:ss:mmmAM (or PM))
10	110	USA	mm-dd-yy
11	111	JAPAN	yy/mm/dd
12	112	ISO	yymmdd
-	13 or 113 (*)	Europe default+ milliseconds	dd mon yyyy hh:mi:ss:mmm(24h)
14	114	-	hh:mi:ss:mmm(24h)

D

DBCC Purpose

DBCC stands for *Database Consistency Checker*. Version 6.0 of SQL Server has extended the scope of DBCC by introducing several new commands that can help a DBA probe into the inner workings SQL Server. This appendix discusses the traditional DBCC commands along with the enhancements included in Version 6.0.

DBCC commands are commonly used to perform the following tasks.

◆ **Routine Maintenance**: It is good idea to periodically run the essential DBCC commands listed in Table E.2. These commands will help detect database and table problems before they manifest themselves into larger issues.

◆ **Investigate Errors**: Use DBCC to pinpoint the source of errors such as `Table Corrupt` or `Extent not with segment`.

◆ **Perform Before a Backup**: Run the essential DBCC commands before backing up the database. This will ensure that the backup data does not contain errors. Backups that contain errors may be unrestorable.

Note

The commands discussed in this section do not resolve errors—they only report that error exists.

QUICK REFERENCE

Table E.1 provides a quick syntax reference for DBCC commands.

TABLE E.1. DBCC QUICK REFERENCE.

Command	Notes	
DBCC CHECKALLOC [(*database_name* [, NOINDEX])]	*B*	Use NEWALLOC instead
DBCC CHECKCATALOG [(*database_name*)]		
DBCC CHECKTABLE (*table_name* [, NOINDEX ¦ *index_id*]	*I*	Performance improved with Version 6.0
DBCC CHECKDB [(*database_name* [, NOINDEX])]	*I*	Performance improved with Version 6.0
DBCC CHECKIDENT [(*table_name*)]	*N*	
DBCC DBREPAIR (*database_name*, DROPDB [, NOINIT])		

Command	Notes	
DBCC dllname (FREE)		
DBCC INPUTBUFFER (*spid*)	*N*	
DBCC MEMUSAGE		
DBCC NEWALLOC	*N*	Replaces CHECKALLOC
[(*database_name* [, NOINDEX])]		
DBCC OPENTRAN	*N*	
({*database_name*} ¦ {*database_id*})		
[WITH TABLERESULTS]		
DBCC OUTPUTBUFFER (*spid*)	*N*	
DBCC PERFMON	*N*	
DBCC PINTABLE	*N*	
(*database_id*, *table_id*)		
DBCC SHOW_STATISTICS	*N*	
(*table_name*, *index_name*)		
DBCC SHOWCONTIG	*N*	
(*table_id*, [*index_id*])		
DBCC SHRINKDB (*database_name* [, *new_size*	*N*	
[, 'MASTEROVERRIDE']])		
DBCC SQLPERF	*I*	New counters with
({IOSTATS ¦ LRUSTATS ¦ NETSTATS		Version 6.0
¦ RASTATS [, CLEAR]} {THREADS} ¦ {LOGSPACE})		
DBCC TEXTALL [({*database_name* ¦ *database_id*}		
[, FULL ¦ FAST])]		
DBCC TEXTALLOC [({*table_name* ¦ *table_id*}		
[, FULL ¦ FAST])]		
DBCC TRACEOFF (*trace#*)	*N*	
DBCC TRACEON (*trace#*)	*N*	
DBCC TRACESTATUS (*trace#* [, *trace#*...])	*N*	
DBCC UNPINTABLE (*database_id*, *table_id*)	*N*	
DBCC UPDATEUSAGE ({0 ¦ *database_name*}	*N*	
[, *table_name* [, *index_id*]])		
DBCC USEROPTIONS	*N*	

E

DBCC PURPOSE

The following abbreviations are used in the preceding table:

(N)ew in Version 6.0

(I)mproved in Version 6.0

Use for (B)ackwards compatibility

Tip

When DBCC performance is a primary concern (especially when working with very large databases), use the NOINDEX argument with the following commands: CHECKALLOC, CHECKTABLE, CHECKDB, NEWALLOC. When the NOINDEX argument is specified, only clustered indexes will be inspected for errors. All nonclustered indexes will be ignored. This option is generally safe to use because damaged indexes can be dropped and re-created without affecting the data within a table

READING THE OUTPUT FROM DBCC COMMANDS

DBCC commands often generate an extraneous amount of output. The problem is determining what is relevant within the output. Use the following list as a guide of what to look for in the DBCC output.

◆ Any message that contains the string corrupt (for example, Table Corrupt)

◆ Error messages that range from 2500 to 2599 or 7900 to 7999. DBCC error messages usually contain these error numbers.

◆ Messages that contain the string error :.

Tip

To help automate the process of detecting error messages in DBCC output, use the FINDSTR.EXE utility provided with Windows NT. Look for key words such as corrupt, error :, and so on.

RESOLVING ERRORS REPORTED BY DBCC

When an error is reported by DBCC, you should immediately investigate it. Unresolved errors can propagate throughout a database, consequently increasing the likelihood of permanent data corruption.

The following items provide a general guideline for investigating and resolving errors reported by DBCC:

◆ Save and print DBCC output. On large databases DBCC can sometimes take hours to run. Do not take a chance on forgetting an error message and having to rerun the DBCC command!

◆ With CHECKDB, NEWALLOC, and CHECKALLOC, you may receive erroneous messages if the database is not in single-user mode. If the command was run when the database was not in single-user mode, set the database to single-user mode and rerun the command. This may resolve the problem.

◆ Look up the specific error code in the chapter titled "Handling Error Messages" in the Microsoft *SQL Server Administrator's Companion* book. The chapters offers error specific solutions may resolve the problem.

◆ Shutdown and restart the SQL Server. This will flush out the data cache and may resolve the problem.

◆ Contact Microsoft Support for additional assistance.

ESSENTIAL DBCC COMMANDS

The commands listed in Table E.2 should be run on a frequent basis. These commands will detect database and table corruption, along with structure inconsistencies.

TABLE E.2. ESSENTIAL DBCC COMMANDS.

Command
DBCC CHECKDB
DBCC CHECKTABLE
DBCC NEWALLOC
DBCC CHECKCATALOG

COMPARISON OF ESSENTIAL DBCC COMMANDS

Table E.3 details the scope of several DBCC commands, along with their performance and effectiveness.

TABLE E.3. COMPARISON OF ESSENTIAL DBCC COMMANDS.

Command	Coverage	Locks Generated	Performance	Effectiveness
CHECKTABLE CHECKDB	page chains, sort order, data rows for ALL indexes	generates shared table lock that is released table has been checked	slow	high
CHECKTABLE CHECKDB with NOINDEX	page chains, sort order, data row for CLUSTERED INDEXES	generates shared table lock that is released table has been checked	significantly faster than equivalent command without NOINDEX option	medium/high
NEWALLOC CHECKALLOC	page chains	none	slow	high
NEWALLOC CHECKALLOC with NOINDEX	page chains	none	significantly faster than equivalent command without NOINDEX option	high
CHECKCATALOG	system table rows	shared page locks	fast	high

DBCC COMMANDS FOR TABLES AND DATABASES

The following DBCC commands are used for tables and databases.

CHECKALLOC

CHECKCATALOG

CHECKTABLE

CHECKDB

CHECKIDENT

NEWALLOC

TEXTALL

TEXTALLOC

SHOWCONTIG

UPDATEUSAGE

CHECKALLOC

Syntax:

```
DBCC CHECKALLOC [(database_name [, NOINDEX])]
```

CHECKALLOC is designed for compatibility with previous versions of SQL Server. In Version 6.0, use NEWALLOC instead of CHECKALLOC. NEWALLOC provides greater detail and continues to process the remainder of the database after an error has been detected.

CHECKALLOC scans the database to insure that page allocation is correct.

CHECKCATALOG

Syntax:

```
DBCC CHECKCATALOG [(database_name)]
```

CHECKCATALOG checks the system tables for consistency by ensuring that each type in the syscolumns table has a matching entry in the systypes table, that each table and view in the sysobjects database has one or more matching records in the syscolumns table, and that the last checkpoint in the syslogs table is correct. Segment information will also be displayed.

Use this command prior to dumping the database or when you suspect corruption within the system tables.

Example:

```
DBCC CHECKCATALOG (pubs)
```

Sample Output:

```
The following segments have been defined for database 4 (database name pubs).
virtual start addr     size     segments
-------------------     ------   --------------------------
              2052      512
                                 0
                                 1
                                 2
             10756      1024
                                 0
                                 1
                                 2
```

CHECKTABLE

Syntax:

```
DBCC CHECKTABLE (table_name [, NOINDEX ¦ index_id])
```

CHECKTABLE checks that all pointers are consistent, data and index pages are properly linked, indexes match the proper sort order, and that page offsets and page information is correct. Run this command when you suspect a table is corrupt or as part of your periodic maintenance plan.

> *Note*
>
> When CHECKTABLE is used in conjunction with the syslogs table, the amount of free and remaining log space will also be reported.

Example:

```
DBCC CHECKTABLE(titles)
```

Sample Output:

```
The total number of data pages in this table is 3.
Table has 18 data rows.
```

Example:

```
DBCC CHECKTABLE(syslogs)
```

Sample Output:

```
The total number of data pages in this table is 4389.
The number of rows in Sysindexes for this table was 198216. It has been corrected
to 198217.
*** NOTICE: Space used on the log segment is 8.78 Mbytes, 95.25.
```

```
*** NOTICE: Space free on the log segment is 0.44 Mbytes, 4.75.
Table has 198217 data rows.
```

CHECKDB

Syntax:

```
DBCC CHECKDB [(database_name [, NOINDEX])]
```

Checks all tables and indexes in a database for pointer and data page errors. This command may generate the following message:

```
The number of data pages in Sysindexes for this table was 9. It has been corrected
to 1.
The number of rows in Sysindexes for this table was 273. It has been corrected to
16.
```

Do not be alarmed when you see this message. It means that SQL Server is performing some internal housekeeping in order to keep row counts accurate for the sp_spaceused command.

In terms of error checking, CHECKDB is the same as CHECKTABLE, except that it inspects every table in the database as opposed to only checking a single table in the database.

Warning

Do *not* run DBCC CHECKDB while other users are in the database! This command should be run when the database is in single-user mode. This ensures that the information reported by CHECKDB is accurate. Also, the number of locks generated by CHECKDB could lead to severe blocking and contention for resources if other users are in the database.

Example:

```
/* set database to single user */
sp_dboption pubs,'single user',TRUE
go

DBCC CHECKDB(pubs)
go

/* reset database option */
sp_dboption pubs,'single user',FALSE
go
```

Sample Output:

```
Checking 1
The total number of data pages in this table is 4.
```

```
Table has 69 data rows.
Checking 2
The total number of data pages in this table is 4.
Table has 49 data rows.
Checking 3
The total number of data pages in this table is 1.
The number of data pages in Sysindexes for this table was 9. It has been corrected
to 1.
The number of rows in Sysindexes for this table was 273. It has been corrected to
16.
```

CHECKIDENT

Syntax:

```
DBCC CHECKIDENT [(table_name)]
```

The CHECKIDENT command checks the IDENTITY datatype in a table. It returns the current identity value and the maximum identity value.

Example:

```
DBCC CHECKIDENT(jobs)
```

Sample Output:

```
Checking identity information: current identity value '14', maximum column value
'14'.
```

NEWALLOC

Syntax:

```
DBCC NEWALLOC [(database_name [, NOINDEX])]
```

Introduced in SQL Server 6.0, NEWALLOC is the improved version of the CHECKALLOC command. NEWALLOC provides greater detail than CHECKALLOC and continues to process the remainder of the database after an error has been detected, unlike CHECKALLOC, which will stop processing when an error has been detected.

NEWALLOC scans the data and index pages for extent structure errors. It ensures that page allocation is correct and all allocated pages are in use.

Warning

Do *not* run DBCC NEWALLOC while other users are in the database! This command should be run when the database is in single-user mode. This ensures that the information reported by NEWALLOC is accurate.

Example:

```
/* set database to single user */
sp_dboption pubs,'single user',TRUE
go

DBCC NEWALLOC(pubs)
go

/* reset database option */
sp_dboption pubs,'single user',FALSE
go
```

Sample Output:

```
Checking pubs
****************************************************************
TABLE: sysobjects          OBJID = 1
INDID=1    FIRST=1     ROOT=8      DPAGES=4    SORT=0
    Data level: 1.  4 Data  Pages in 1 extents.
    Indid     : 1.  1 Index Pages in 1 extents.
INDID=2    FIRST=40    ROOT=41     DPAGES=1    SORT=1
    Indid     : 2.  3 Index Pages in 1 extents.
TOTAL # of extents = 3
****************************************************************
TABLE: sysindexes          OBJID = 2
INDID=1    FIRST=24    ROOT=32     DPAGES=4    SORT=0
    Data level: 1.  4 Data  Pages in 1 extents.
    Indid     : 1.  1 Index Pages in 1 extents.
TOTAL # of extents = 2
****************************************************************
TABLE: jobs        OBJID = 592005140
INDID=1    FIRST=496   ROOT=520    DPAGES=1    SORT=0
    Data level: 1.  1 Data  Pages in 1 extents.
    Indid     : 1.  2 Index Pages in 1 extents.
TOTAL # of extents = 2
****************************************************************
TABLE: employee        OBJID = 688005482
INDID=1    FIRST=648   ROOT=656    DPAGES=2    SORT=1
    Data level: 1.  2 Data  Pages in 1 extents.
    Indid     : 1.  2 Index Pages in 1 extents.
INDID=2    FIRST=664   ROOT=664    DPAGES=1    SORT=1
    Indid     : 2.  2 Index Pages in 1 extents.
TOTAL # of extents = 3
****************************************************************
TABLE: pub_info        OBJID = 864006109
INDID=1    FIRST=568   ROOT=584    DPAGES=1    SORT=0
    Data level: 1.  1 Data  Pages in 1 extents.
    Indid     : 1.  2 Index Pages in 1 extents.
INDID=255  FIRST=560   ROOT=608    DPAGES=0    SORT=0
TOTAL # of extents = 2
****************************************************************
Processed 49 entries in the Sysindexes for dbid 4.
Alloc page 0 (# of extent=32 used pages=57 ref pages=57)
Alloc page 256 (# of extent=26 used pages=35 ref pages=35)
Alloc page 512 (# of extent=15 used pages=38 ref pages=38)
Alloc page 768 (# of extent=1 used pages=1 ref pages=1)
Alloc page 1024 (# of extent=2 used pages=9 ref pages=2)
```

```
Alloc page 1280 (# of extent=1 used pages=1 ref pages=1)
Total (# of extent=77 used pages=141 ref pages=134) in this database
DBCC execution completed. If DBCC printed error messages, see your System Adminis-
trator.
```

TEXTALL

Syntax:

```
DBCC TEXTALL [({database_name ¦ database_id}[, FULL ¦ FAST])]
```

TEXTALL checks the allocation of TEXT and IMAGE columns for all tables in a database that contain TEXT or IMAGE columns. The FULL option generates a complete allocation report while the FAST option does not generate an allocation report. FULL is the default report option.

Example:

```
DBCC TEXTALL (pubs, FULL)
```

Sample Output:

```
*******************************************************************
TABLE: sysarticles        OBJID = 16
INDID=255    FIRST=328    ROOT=328    DPAGES=0    SORT=0
    Data level: 1.  1 Data  Pages in 0 extents.
    Indid     : 255.  0 Index Pages in 0 extents.
*******************************************************************
TABLE: pub_info       OBJID = 864006109
INDID=255    FIRST=560    ROOT=608    DPAGES=0    SORT=0
    Data level: 1.  1 Data  Pages in 0 extents.
    Indid     : 255.  73 Index Pages in 0 extents.
```

TEXTALLOC

Syntax:

```
DBCC TEXTALLOC [({table_name ¦ table_id}[, FULL ¦ FAST])]
```

TEXTALLOC checks a specified table for TEXT or IMAGE allocation errors. The FULL option generates a complete allocation report while the FAST option does not generate an allocation report. FULL is the default report option.

Sample:

```
DBCC TEXTALLOC (pub_info, FULL)
```

Output:

```
*******************************************************************
TABLE: pub_info       OBJID = 864006109
INDID=255    FIRST=560    ROOT=608    DPAGES=0    SORT=0
    Data level: 1.  1 Data  Pages in 0 extents.
    Indid     : 255.  73 Index Pages in 0 extents.
```

SHOWCONTIG

Syntax:

```
DBCC SHOWCONTIG (table_id, [index_id])
```

SHOWCONTIG determines the amount of table fragmentation. A high degree of fragmentation can lead to poor query performance. This is because more data pages must read by SQL Server to process a query, thus resulting in sub-optimal performance.

Fragmentation occurs when modification statements (DELETE, INSERT, and UPDATE) are performed on a table. A table that is subject to a high degree of modification statements is more likely to become fragmented than a table that is seldom modified.

In order to determine the degree of fragmentation, inspect the Scan Density, Avg. Page density, and Avg. Overflow Page density values generated by the SHOWCONTIG command. A Scan Density value less than 100% indicates that some fragmentation exists.

To defragment a table, drop and re-create the table's clustered index or BCP out the data, drop the table, re-create the table, and BCP in the data.

Tip

> Use the object_id() function to determine a table's id.

Example:

```
/* get table id */

SELECT object_id('sample_table')

-----------

96003373

/* run DBCC command */

DBCC SHOWCONTIG(96003373)
```

Sample Output:

```
Table: 'sample_table' (96003373)  Indid: 0  dbid:6
TABLE level scan performed.
- Pages Scanned...............................: 4096
- Extent Switches............................: 514
- Avg. Pages per Extent.......................: 8.0
- Scan Density [Best Count:Actual Count].......: 99.42% [512:515]
- Avg. Bytes free per page....................: 89.0
- Avg. Page density (full)....................: 95.58%
```

```
- Overflow Pages...............................: 4095
- Avg. Bytes free per Overflow page...........: 89.0
- Avg. Overflow Page density..................: 95.6%
- Disconnected Overflow Pages.................: 0
```

UPDATEUSAGE

Syntax:

```
DBCC UPDATEUSAGE ({0 ¦ database_name} [, table_name [, index_id]])
```

Whenever an index is dropped from a table, sp_spaceused will inaccurately report space utilization. Use the UPDATEUSAGE command to correct the inaccuracy.

Warning

> The output from the system procedure sp_spaceused should only be used as estimate for space utilization. When an index is dropped, the information returned from sp_spaceused will be inaccurate until the UDPATEUSAGE command is executed or the table is dropped and re-created.

Example:

```
DBCC UPDATEUSAGE('sales','sample_table')
```

Sample Output:

```
DBCC UPDATEUSAGE: Sysindexes row for Table 'sample_table' (IndexId=0) updated:
RSVD Pages: Changed from (4103) to (4120) pages
```

DROP A DAMAGED DATABASE

The following command is used to drop a damaged database.

Syntax:

```
DBCC DBREPAIR (database_name, DROPDB [, NOINIT])
```

Warning

> DBREPAIR does *not* repair a corrupt database! Instead, it drops a corrupt database.

In Version 6.0, a corrupt database can be dropped with the DROP DATABASE command. Previous versions of SQL Server required that the DBREPAIR command be used to drop a damaged database. If you are unable to drop a database with the DROP DATABASE command, use the system procedure sp_dbremove to drop a damaged database.

RETURN PROCESS INFORMATION

The following two DBCC commands return process information.

Syntax:

```
DBCC INPUTBUFFER (spid)

DBCC OUTPUTBUFFER (spid)
```

The INPUTBUFFER and OUTPUTBUFFER commands allow a DBA to monitor process activity. The INPUTBUFFER command displays the command last executed by a process and the OUTPUTBUFFER command displays the corresponding result. Unfortunately, the information returned from the OUTPUTBUFFER command can be difficult to understand because it is displayed in hexadecimal and ASCII text.

Tip

Use the system procedure sp_who to determine the spid of a process.

Tip

Use the INPUTBUFFER command to diagnose blocking and resource utilization problems. When performance begins to suffer, look for data modification queries that do not contain WHERE clauses or SELECT queries that perform table scans on large tables.

Example:

```
DBCC INPUTBUFFER(11)
```

Sample Output:

```
Input Buffer
------------
select *
from authors
```

RETURN PERFORMANCE MONITOR STATISTICS

The following DBCC commands return Performance Monitor statistics.

Syntax:

```
DBCC PERFMON

DBCC SQLPERF ({IOSTATS ¦ LRUSTATS ¦ NETSTATS ¦ RASTATS [, CLEAR]}
        {THREADS} ¦ {LOGSPACE})
```

The PERFMON combines the different components of the SQLPERF command (IOSTATS, LRUSTATS, and NETSTATS) into a single DBCC statement.

Example:

```
DBCC PERFMON
```

Sample Output:

```
Statistic                      Value
----------------------------------------------
Log Flush Requests             110.0
Log Logical Page IO            112.0
Log Physical IO                94.0
Log Flush Average              1.17021
Log Logical IO Average         1.19149
Batch Writes                   68.0
Batch Average Size             2.72
Batch Max Size                 8.0
Page Reads                     643.0
Single Page Writes             132.0
Reads Outstanding              0.0
Writes Outstanding             0.0
Transactions                   92.0
Transactions/Log Write         0.978723
```

TRACE FLAG COMMANDS

The following commands are used to turn on and off trace flags and to check the status of a trace flag.

Syntax:

```
DBCC TRACEOFF (trace#)

DBCC TRACEON (trace#)

DBCC TRACESTATUS (trace# [, trace#...])
```

> *Tip*
>
> The trace flag 1200 can be useful for tracking locking behavior. You must also turn on trace flag 3604 to echo trace information to the client workstation.

Example:

```
DBCC traceon(3604)
DBCC traceon(1200)
UPDATE t_1
SET c_1 = 0
```

Sample output from DBCC trace flag 1200:

```
Process 11 requesting page lock of type SH_PAGE on 7 25
Process 11 releasing page lock of type SH_PAGE on 7 25
...
Process 11 releasing page lock of type SH_PAGE on 7 26
Process 11 requesting table lock of type EX_TAB on 7 80003316
...
Process 11 clearing all pss locks
```

MEMORY AND DATA CACHE COMMANDS

The MEMUSAGE command displays memory usage, buffer cache, and procedure cache information.

Syntax:

```
DBCC MEMUSAGE
```

The PINTABLE command forces a table to remain in cache until it is removed from the cache with the UNPINTABLE command. Pinning a table in cache should be used with prudence. By keeping a table constantly in the cache, you can improve data access performance. However, a large table can dominate the data cache. This could reduce the amount of data held in cache for other tables, thus hindering performance.

Syntax:

```
DBCC PINTABLE (database_id, table_id)

DBCC UNPINTABLE (database_id, table_id)
```

OPENTRAN

OPENTRAN reports the oldest open transaction. Long running or open transactions can be a result of an aborted transaction that was not properly terminated by the server, a runaway transaction, or poor transaction management. If necessary, you can terminate the offending transaction by issuing the KILL command with the process id returned from the DBCC OPENTRAN command.

Tip

Long-running transactions can lead to contention for resources, which can lead to blocking. Use DBCC OPENTRAN to detect open transactions. If necessary, use the KILL command to cancel the transaction.

Tip

Before dumping the transaction log, use DBCC OPENTRAN to determine whether any open transactions exist. Any pending transactions will prevent the transaction log from being completely truncated.

Syntax:

```
DBCC OPENTRAN ({database_name} ¦ {database_id}) [WITH TABLERESULTS]
```

Example:

```
DBCC OPENTRAN(pubs)
```

Sample Output:

```
Transaction Information for database: pubs
Oldest active transaction:
        SPID          : 12
        UID           : 1
        SUID          : 1
        Name          : del
        RID           : (14653 , 30)
        Time Stamp    : 0001 0003CB68
        Start Time    : Sep 20 1995  9:30:41:690PM
```

OTHER DBCC COMMANDS

This section covers some of the other types of DBCC commands.

SHOW_STATISTICS

Syntax:

```
DBCC SHOW_STATISTICS (table_name, index_name)
```

SHOW_STATISTICS displays index distribution information.

SHRINKDB

Syntax:

```
DBCC SHRINKDB (database_name [, new_size [, 'MASTEROVERRIDE']])
```

Note

Size is specified in 2K pages.

SHRINKDB has two purposes:

◆ When a size is not specified, the command will return the minimum size to which a database can be shrunk.

◆ When size is specified, the command will shrink the database to the specified size. The MASTEROVERRIDE command is required when the master database is shrunk.

DBCC USEROPTIONS

Syntax:

DBCC USEROPTIONS

Displays the status of SET commands for the current session.

DBCC DLLNAME (FREE)

Syntax:

DBCC dllname (FREE)

This command removes a DLL (dynamic link library) from memory.

Cursors

Cursors allow you to perform row-oriented operations on a set of data. This means that you can process data row by row. With SQL Server's cursors, you can navigate forward and backward through the result set. The power of cursors can really be exploited when combined with the EXEC command and a string variable substitution.

> *Note*
>
> ANSI standard cursors are new with Version 6.0. Prior versions of SQL Server required cursors to be processed at the client through DB Library function calls or through ODBC.

Cursors can be used in the following locations:

◆ In a batch

◆ Within a stored procedure

◆ Within a trigger

CREATING A CURSOR

Every cursor must have at least four components. The four key components *must* follow the order in the following list:

1. DECLARE the cursor.

2. OPEN the cursor.

3. FETCH from the cursor.

4. CLOSE or DEALLOCATE the cursor.

STEP 1: *DECLARE* THE CURSOR

The DECLARE statement contains the user-defined name that will be used to reference the result set, as well as the SQL SELECT statement that generates the result set. You can think of the DECLARE statement as a temporary table that contains a pointer to your actual data source.

SYNTAX

```
DECLARE cursor_name [INSENSITIVE] [SCROLL] CURSOR
FOR select_statement
[FOR {READ ONLY ¦ UPDATE [OF column_list]}]
```

cursor_name is the cursor name.

INSENSITIVE specifies that changes in your data source will not be reflected in the cursor. Updates are not allowed to a cursor when this option is specified.

SCROLL allows the following FETCH commands to be used: PRIOR, FIRST, LAST, ABSOLUTE *n*, and RELATIVE *n*.

select_statement is a SQL SELECT statement. The following SQL commands will force a cursor to be declared as INSENSITIVE: DISTINCT, UNION, GROUP BY, and/or HAVING.

READ ONLY prohibits updates from occurring against the cursor.

UPDATE [OF *column_list*] allows updates to be performed against the cursor. The optional clause [OF *column_list*] specifies which columns in the cursor can be updated.

EXAMPLE 1: STANDARD CURSOR

```
declare pub_crsr cursor
for
select pub_id,pub_name
from publishers
```

EXAMPLE 2: READ-ONLY CURSOR

```
declare pub_crsr cursor
for
select pub_id,pub_name
from publishers
FOR·READ ONLY
```

EXAMPLE 3: CURSOR THAT ALLOWS UPDATES

```
declare pub_crsr cursor
for
select pub_id,pub_name
from publishers
FOR UPDATE
```

STEP 2: *OPEN* THE CURSOR

Now that you have declared a cursor, you need to open it. This statement should immediately follow the DECLARE statement.

SYNTAX

```
OPEN cursor_name
```

cursor_name is the name of cursor to open.

EXAMPLE

```
OPEN pub_crsr
```

F

CURSORS

STEP 3: *FETCH* FROM THE CURSOR

After the cursor has been opened, you can now retrieve information from the result set on a row-by-row basis. SQL Server 6.0 is one of the few RDBMS products that provides forward scrolling cursors *and* backward scrolling cursors.

SYNTAX

```
FETCH [[NEXT ¦ PRIOR ¦ FIRST ¦ LAST ¦ ABSOLUTE n ¦ RELATIVE n] FROM] cursor_name
[INTO @variable_name1, @variable_name2, ...]
```

NEXT retrieves the next row.

PRIOR retrieves the prior row.

FIRST retrieves the first row.

LAST retrieves the last row.

ABSOLUTE *n* retrieves a row based on the absolute position within the result set.

RELATIVE *n* retrieves a row based on the relative position within the result set.

Tip

Use negative numbers to move backward within a result set when using the ABSOLUTE and RELATIVE arguments.

cursor_name is the name of cursor.

INTO @*variable_name1*, @*variable_name2*, and so on copies the contents of a column into a variable.

EXAMPLE 1: RETURN THE NEXT ROW IN THE RESULT SET

```
fetch next from pub_crsr
```

EXAMPLE 2: RETURN THE FIFTH ROW IN THE RESULT SET

```
fetch absolute 5 from pub_crsr
```

EXAMPLE 3: COPY THE CONTENTS OF THE NEXT ROW INTO HOST VARIABLES

```
fetch next from pub_crsr into @pub_id,@pub_name
```

STEP 4: *CLOSE* OR *DEALLOCATE* THE CURSOR

After you finish processing your cursor, you need to CLOSE or DEALLOCATE the cursor. The CLOSE statement closes the cursor but does not release the data structures used by the cursor. Use this option if you plan on reopening the cursor for subsequent use. The DEALLOCATE statement closes the cursor and releases the data structures used by the cursor.

Tip

Always CLOSE or DEALLOCATE a cursor as soon as processing is complete. Cursors consume resources, such as locks, memory, and so on. If these resources are not released, performance and multi-user problems may arise.

SYNTAX

```
CLOSE cursor_name

DEALLOCATE cursor_name
```

cursor_name is the cursor name.

EXAMPLE 1: CLOSE A CURSOR

```
CLOSE pub_crsr
```

EXAMPLE 2: DEALLOCATE A CURSOR

```
DEALLOCATE pub_crsr
```

POSITIONAL *UPDATE* AND *DELETE*

In addition to being able to retrieve data from a cursor, you can perform positional updates and deletes against the data contained in the cursor. When a modification is made to a cursor, it will automatically cascade to the cursor's data source.

POSITIONAL *UPDATE* SYNTAX:

```
UPDATE table_name
SET column_name1 = {expression1 ¦ NULL ¦ (select_statement)}
[, column_name2 = {expression2 ¦ NULL ¦ (select_statement)}...]
WHERE CURRENT OF cursor_name
```

POSITIONAL *DELETE* SYNTAX

```
DELETE FROM table_name
WHERE CURRENT OF cursor_name
```

table_name is the name of table to UPDATE or DELETE.

column_name is the name of column to UPDATE.

cursor_name is the cursor name.

EXAMPLE 1: *UPDATE* THE *PUB_NAME* COLUMN IN THE *PUBLISHERS* TABLE

This update is based on the current row position in the cursor.

```
UPDATE publishers
SET pub_name = 'XYZ publisher
WHERE CURRENT OF pub_crsr
```

EXAMPLE 2: *DELETE* A ROW IN THE *PUBLISHERS* TABLE

This delete is based on the current row position in the cursor.

```
DELETE FROM publishers
WHERE CURRENT OF pub_crsr
```

GLOBAL VARIABLES

The following two global variables can be used to monitor the status of a cursor.

SYNTAX

```
@@fetch_status
```

```
@@cursor_rows
```

@@fetch_status displays the status of a last FETCH command. Following are the possible values are

0	Successful fetch
-1	Fetch failed or the fetch caused the cursor to go beyond the result set.
-2	Fetch row is missing from the data set.

The following is an example of @@fetch_status:

```
while @@fetch_status = 0
    ...do some processing
```

@@cursor_rows displays the number of rows in the cursor set. Use this variable *after* the cursor has been opened. Following are the possible values:

-n   Cursor is currently being loaded with data. The number returned will indicate the number of rows currently in the key result set; however, the number will continue to increase as SQL Server processes the SELECT statement (this is known as *asynchronous processing*).

n   Number rows in the result set.

0   No matching rows in the result set.

PUTTING IT ALL TOGETHER

Now that you know something about cursor statements, positional updates, and global variables, the following cursor examples will illustrate how all these components fit together.

EXAMPLE 1: LOOP THROUGH A TABLE

This example shows how the different components of a cursor (DECLARE, OPEN, FETCH, and DEALLOCATE) are used to loop through the publishers table. The @@fetch_status global variable is referenced each time a FETCH is performed. Once the record pointer reaches the end of the result set, the @@fetch_status variable will be equal to -1. This prevents the code inside the while @@fetch_status = 0 section from being executed.

```
/* suppress counts from being displayed */
SET NOCOUNT ON

/* declare a cursor that will contain the pub_id, pub_name columns */
/* from the publishers table */
declare pub_crsr cursor
for
select pub_id,pub_name
from publishers

/* open the cursor */
open pub_crsr

/* get the first row from the cursor */
fetch next from pub_crsr

/* loop through the rows in the cursor */
while @@fetch_status = 0
begin

  /* get next row */
  fetch next from pub_crsr
end

/* close the cursor */
deallocate pub_crsr
```

OUTPUT

```
0736    New Moon Books
0877    Binnet & Hardley
1389    Algodata Infosystems
1622    Five Lakes Publishing
1756    Ramona Publishers
9901    GGG&G
9952    Scootney Books
9999    Lucerne Publishing
```

EXAMPLE 2: DISPLAY OBJECT NAMES AND OBJECT TYPES

This example displays object names and types for all user-defined objects in the pubs database. It uses two variables (@name and @type) and conditional logic to determine object type.

```
/* suppress counts from being displayed */
SET NOCOUNT ON

/* declare variables */
declare @name varchar(30)
declare @type char(2)

/* declare a cursor that will contain a list of object */
/* names and object types */
declare object_list cursor
for
select name, type
from sysobjects
where type <> 'S'
order by type

/* open the cursor */
open object_list

/* get the first row from the cursor */
fetch next from object_list into @name,@type

/* loop through the rows in the cursor */
while @@fetch_status = 0
begin
  /* determine object type */
  if @type = 'C'
    select '(CHECK constraint) ' + @name
  if @type = 'D'
    select '(Default or DEFAULT constraint) ' + @name
  if @type = 'F'
    select '(FOREIGN KEY constraint) ' + @name
  if @type = 'K'
    select '(PRIMARY KEY or UNIQUE constraint) ' + @name
  if @type = 'L'
    select '(Log) ' + @name
  if @type = 'P'
    select '(Stored procedure) ' + @name
  if @type = 'R'
```

```
        select '(Rule) ' + @name
    if @type = 'RF'
        select '(Stored procedure for replication) ' + @name
    if @type = 'TR'
        select '(Trigger) ' + @name
    if @type = 'U'
        select '(User table) ' + @name
    if @type = 'V'
        select '(View) ' + @name
    if @type = 'X'
        select '(Extended stored procedure) ' + @name

    /* get next tablename */
    fetch next from object_list into @name,@type
end

/* close the cursor */
deallocate object_list
```

OUTPUT

```
(CHECK constraint) CK__authors__au_id__02DC7882
(CHECK constraint) CK__authors__zip__04C4C0F4
(CHECK constraint) CK__jobs__max_lvl__2719D8F8
(CHECK constraint) CK__jobs__min_lvl__2625B4BF
(CHECK constraint) CK__publisher__pub_i__089551D8
(CHECK constraint) CK_emp_id
(Default or DEFAULT constraint) DF__authors__phone__03D09CBB
(Default or DEFAULT constraint) DF__employee__hire_d__30A34332
(Default or DEFAULT constraint) DF__employee__job_id__2BDE8E15
(Default or DEFAULT constraint) DF__employee__job_lv__2DC6D687
(Default or DEFAULT constraint) DF__employee__pub_id__2EBAFAC0
(Default or DEFAULT constraint) DF__jobs__job_desc__25319086
(Default or DEFAULT constraint) DF__publisher__count__09897611
(Default or DEFAULT constraint) DF__titles__pubdate__0F424F67
(Default or DEFAULT constraint) DF__titles__type__0D5A06F5
(FOREIGN KEY constraint) FK__discounts__stor__2160FFA2
(FOREIGN KEY constraint) FK__employee__job_id__2CD2B24E
(FOREIGN KEY constraint) FK__employee__pub_id__2FAF1EF9
(FOREIGN KEY constraint) FK__pub_info__pub_id__3567F84F
(FOREIGN KEY constraint) FK__roysched__title__1E8492F7
(FOREIGN KEY constraint) FK__sales__stor_id__1AB40213
(FOREIGN KEY constraint) FK__sales__title_id__1BA8264C
(FOREIGN KEY constraint) FK__titleauth__au_id__1312E04B
(FOREIGN KEY constraint) FK__titleauth__title__14070484
(FOREIGN KEY constraint) FK__titles__pub_id__0E4E2B2E
(PRIMARY KEY or UNIQUE constraint) PK__jobs__job_id__243D6C4D
(PRIMARY KEY or UNIQUE constraint) PK_emp_id
(PRIMARY KEY or UNIQUE constraint) UPK_storeid
(PRIMARY KEY or UNIQUE constraint) UPKCL_auidind
(PRIMARY KEY or UNIQUE constraint) UPKCL_pubind
(PRIMARY KEY or UNIQUE constraint) UPKCL_pubinfo
(PRIMARY KEY or UNIQUE constraint) UPKCL_sales
(PRIMARY KEY or UNIQUE constraint) UPKCL_taind
(PRIMARY KEY or UNIQUE constraint) UPKCL_titleidind
(Stored procedure) byroyalty
(Stored procedure) reptq1
```

F

CURSORS

```
(Stored procedure) reptq2
(Stored procedure) reptq3
(Trigger) employee_insupd
(User table) authors
(User table) discounts
(User table) employee
(User table) jobs
(User table) pub_info
(User table) publishers
(User table) roysched
(User table) sales
(User table) stores
(User table) titleauthor
(User table) titles
(View) titleview
```

EXAMPLE 3: UPDATE STATISTICS FOR ALL TABLES IN A DATABASE

This example combines the EXEC command with a cursor to automatically update the statistics for all tables within a database.

```
/* declare variables */
declare @table_name varchar(30)

/* declare a cursor that will contain a list of table */
/* names to be updated */
declare idx_cursor cursor
for select distinct a.name
from sysobjects a,sysindexes b
where a.type = 'U'
and a.id = b.id
and b.indid > 0

/* open the cursor */
open idx_cursor

/* get the first row from the cursor */
fetch next from idx_cursor into @table_name

/* loop through the rows in the cursor */
while @@fetch_status = 0
  begin
    /* issue UPDATE STATISTICS */
    EXEC ("UPDATE STATISTICS " + @table_name)

    /* get next table name */
    fetch next from idx_cursor into @table_name
  end

/* close the cursor */
deallocate idx_cursor
```

> ## STRANGER THAN FICTION!
>
> The SQL Server 6.0 documentation incorrectly shows how to use the
> EXEC statement to execute a command at runtime. In their example,
> they forgot to include the concatenation symbol (+) between the
> command and the variable.
>
> **Incorrect Syntax**:
>
> ```
> EXEC ("DROP TABLE "  @tablename)
> ```
>
> **Correct Syntax:**
>
> ```
> EXEC ("DROP TABLE "  + @tablename)
> ```

EXAMPLE 4: POSITIONAL UPDATE

This example looks at each row in the publishers id table. If the pub_id column =
'1389', then the pub_name column will be updated to 'XYZ publisher'.

```
/* suppress counts from being displayed */
SET NOCOUNT ON

/* declare variables */
declare @pub_id char(4),@pub_name varchar(40)

/* declare a cursor that will contain the pub_id, pub_name columns */
/* from the publishers table */
/* NOTE: for UPDATE clause allows position updates */
declare pub_crsr cursor
for
select pub_id,pub_name
from publishers
for UPDATE OF pub_id,pub_name

/* open the cursor */
open pub_crsr

/* get the first row from the cursor */
fetch next from pub_crsr into @pub_id, @pub_name

/* loop through the rows in the cursor */
while @@fetch_status = 0
begin
  if @pub_id = '1389'
    update publishers
    set pub_name = 'XYZ publisher'
    where current of pub_crsr

  /* get next row */
  fetch next from pub_crsr into @pub_id, @pub_name
end

/* close the cursor */
deallocate pub_crsr
```

Appendix G

System Tables

System tables are the tables installed with SQL Server that are used by SQL Server to manage the users, devices, and all the other SQL Server objects. System tables are found in every database. The following is a brief description of each of the system tables and their physical layout. This section is broken into two parts: system tables found only in the master database and system tables found in all databases.

MASTER DATABASE SYSTEM TABLES

The following system tables (in alphabetical order) are found in the master database and are used by SQL Server to manage and maintain the server.

SYSCHARSETS

syscharsets contains a single row for each valid character set and sort order available.

TABLE STRUCTURE

Column	Datatype
type	smallint
id	tinyint
csid	tinyint
status	smallint
name	varchar(30)
description	varchar(255)
definition	image

INDEX

Unique clustered index on id.

Unique nonclustered index on name.

SYSCONFIGURES

sysconfigures contains one row for each user-configurable configuration parameter.

TABLE STRUCTURE

Column	Datatype
config	smallint
value	int

| comment | varchar(255) |
| status | smallint |

INDEX

Unique clustered index on config.

SYSCURCONFIGS

syscurconfigs contains the current system configuration values—one for each user-configurable parameter and an additional four entries that describe the configuration structure. syscurconfigs is built dynamically when queried by a user.

TABLE STRUCTURE

Column	Datatype
config	smallint
value	int
comment	varchar(255)
status	smallint

INDEX

Unique clustered index on config.

SYSDATABASES

sysdatabases contains an entry for each database on SQL Server.

TABLE STRUCTURE

Column	Datatype
name	varchar(30)
dbid	smallint
suid	smallint
mode	smallint
status	smallint
version	smallint
logptr	int
crdate	datetime
dumptrdate	datetime
category	int

G

Note

The `column` category is new for SQL Server Version 6.0 and is used for publication and constraints.

INDEX

Unique clustered index on `name`.

Unique nonclustered index on `dbid`.

SYSDEVICES

`sysdevices` contains a row for every device on the SQL Server.

TABLE STRUCTURE

Column	Datatype
low	int
high	int
status	smallint
cntrltype	smallint
name	varchar(30)
phyname	varchar(127)
mirrorname	varchar(127)
stripeset	varchar(30)

INDEX

Unique clustered index on `name`.

SYSLANGUAGES

`syslanguages` contains a single row for each language installed on SQL Server.

Note

U.S. English is not in `syslanguages` but is always available to SQL Server.

TABLE STRUCTURE

Column	Datatype
angid	smallint
dateformat	char(3)
datefirst	tinyint
upgrade	int
name	varchar(30)
alias	varchar(30)
months	varchar(251)
shortmonths	varchar(119)
days	varchar(216)

INDEX

Unique clustered index on langid.

Unique nonclustered index on name.

Unique nonclustered index on alias.

SYSLOCKS

syslocks is dynamically built when queried by a user and contains information about active locks.

TABLE STRUCTURE

Column	Datatype
id	int
dbid	smallint
page	int
type	smallint
spid	smallint

INDEX

None

SYSLOGINS

syslogins contains a single row for each valid SQL Server login account.

TABLE STRUCTURE

Column	Datatype
suid	smallint
status	smallint
accdate	datetime
totcpu	int
totio	int
spacelimit	int
timelimit	int
resultlimit	int
dbname	varchar(30)
name	varchar(30)
password	varchar(30)
language	varchar(30)

INDEX

Unique clustered index on suid.

Unique nonclustered index on name.

SYSMESSAGES

sysmessages contains the system errors and warning messages returned by SQL Server.

TABLE STRUCTURE

Column	Datatype
error	int
severity	smallint
dlevel	smallint
description	varchar(255)
langid	smallint

INDEX

Clustered index on error, dlevel.

Unique nonclustered index on error, dlevel, langid.

SYSPROCESSES

sysprocesses is built dynamically when queried by a user and contains information about SQL Server processes.

TABLE STRUCTURE

Column	Datatype
pid	smallint
kpid	smallint
status	char(10)
suid	smallint
hostname	char(10)
program_name	char(16)
hostprocess	char(8)
cmd	char(16)
cpu	int
physical_io	int
memusage	int
blocked	smallint
waittype	binary
dbid	smallint
uid	smallint
gid	smallint

INDEX

None

SYSREMOTELOGINS

sysremotelogins contains a single row for each remote user allowed to execute remote procedure calls.

TABLE STRUCTURE

Column	Datatype
remoteserverid	smallint
remoteusername	varchar(30)
suidsmall	int
status	smallint

INDEX

Unique clustered index on `remoteserverid`, `remoteusername`.

SYSSERVERS

`sysservers` contains a single row for each remote SQL Server. This enables SQL Server to execute remote procedures.

TABLE STRUCTURE

Column	Datatype
srvid	smallint
srvstatus	smallint
srvname	varchar(30)
srvnetname	varchar(32)
topologyx	int
topologyy	int

INDEX

Unique clustered index on `srvid`.

Unique nonclustered index on `srvname`.

SYSUSAGES

`sysusages` contains a single row for each disk allocation piece assigned to a database.

TABLE STRUCTURE

Column	Datatype
dbid	smallint
segmap	int
lstart	int
size	int
vstart	int

INDEX

Unique clustered index on `dbid`, `lstart`.

Unique nonclustered index on `vstart`.

DATABASE SYSTEM TABLES

The following tables are the system tables found in each database, including the master database, on SQL Server.

SYSALTERNATES

sysalternates contains a single row for each aliased user in the database.

TABLE STRUCTURE

Column	Datatype
suid	smallint
altsuid	smallint

INDEX

Unique clustered index on suid.

SYSARTICLES

sysarticles contains a single row for each article posted by the publishing server.

Note

sysarticles is new for SQL Server 6.0.

TABLE STRUCTURE

Column	Datatype
artid	int
columns	varbinary(32)
creation_script	varchar(127)
del_cmd	varchar(255)
description	varchar(255)
dest_table	varchar(30
filter	int
filter_clause	text
ins_cmd	varchar(255)
name	varchar(30)
objid	int

continues

Column	Datatype
pubid	int
pre_creation_cmd	tinyint
status	tinyint
sync_objid	int
type	tinyint
upd_cmd	varchar(255)

INDEX

Unique nonclustered index on artid, pubid.

SYSCOLUMNS

syscolumns contains a single row for each parameter in a stored procedure and each column in a table and view.

TABLE STRUCTURE

Column	Datatype
id	int
number	smallint
colid	tinyint
status	tinyint
type	tinyint
length	tinyint
offset	smallint
usertype	smallint
cdefault	int
domain	int
name	varchar(30)
printfmt	varchar(255)
prec	tinyint
scale	tinyint

INDEX

Unique clustered index on id, number, colid.

SYSCOMMENTS

syscomments contains entries for database objects such as views, rules, defaults, triggers, and procedures.

TABLE STRUCTURE

Column	Datatype
id	int
number	smallint
colid	tinyint
language	smallint
text	varchar(255)

INDEX

Unique clustered index on id, number, colid, texttype.

SYSCONSTRAINTS

sysconstraints contains constraint mappings to owning objects.

> **Note**
>
> sysconstraints is new for SQL Server 6.0.

G

TABLE STRUCTURE

Column	Datatype
constid	int
id	int
colid	tinyint
spare1	tinyint
status	int
actions	int
error	int

INDEX

Clustered index on id, colid.

Unique nonclustered index on constid.

SYSDEPENDS

sysdepends contains rows for object dependencies.

TABLE STRUCTURE

Column	Datatype
id	int
number	smallint
depid	int
depnumber	smallint
depdbid	smallint
depsiteid	smallint
status	smallint
selall	bit
resultobj	bit
readobj	bit

INDEX

Unique clustered index (ignore duplicate key) on id, number, depid, depnumber, depdbid, depsiteid.

SYSINDEXES

sysindexes contains a single row for each of the following:

◆ Clustered index

◆ Nonclustered index

◆ Tables with no clustered indexes

◆ Table with text or image columns

TABLE STRUCTURE

Column	Datatype
name	varchar(30)
id	int
indid	smallint
dpages	int
reserved	int
used	int
rows	int
first	int
root	int
distribution	int
OrigFillFactor	tinyint
segment	smallint

status	smallint
rowpage	smallint
minlen	smallint
maxlen	smallint
maxirow	smallint
keycnt	smallint
keys1	varbinary(255)
keys2	varbinary(255)
soid	tinyint
csid	tinyint

INDEX

Unique clustered index on id, indid.

SYSKEYS

syskeys contains information on primary, foreign, and common keys.

> **Note**
>
> syskeys is not used to maintain referential integrity.

TABLE STRUCTURE

Column	Datatype
id	int
type	smallint
depid	int
keycnt	int
size	int
key1	tinyint
key2	tinyint
key3	tinyint
key4	tinyint
key5	tinyint
key6	tinyint
key7	tinyint
key8	tinyint
depkey1	tinyint
depkey2	tinyint
depkey3	tinyint

continues

Column	Datatype
depkey4	tinyint
depkey5	tinyint
depkey6	tinyint
depkey7	tinyint
depkey8	tinyint

INDEX

Clustered index on id.

SYSLOGS

syslogs is used for the transaction log and is used by SQL Server for rollforward and recovery.

Warning

Do not try to modify syslogs! Doing so will result in an infinite loop until the database fills up.

TABLE STRUCTURE

Column	Datatype
xactid	binary(6)
op	tinyint

INDEX

None

SYSOBJECTS

sysobjects contains a single entry for each database object, such as tables, views, stored procedures, constraints, rules and so on.

TABLE STRUCTURE

Column	Datatype
name	varchar(30)
id	int
uid	smallint

type	char(2)
userstat	smallint
sysstat	smallint
indexdel	smallint
schema	smallint
refdate	datetime
crdate	datetime
version	datetime
deltrig	int
instrig	int
updtrig	int
seltrig	int
category	int
cache	smallint

INDEX

Unique clustered index on id.

Unique nonclustered index on name, uid.

Note

The following values are the valid values for the column type and can be used to query for specific database objects (and sometimes appear on the certification test):

- c Check constraint
- D Default
- F Foreign key reference constraint
- K Primary or unique constraint
- L Log
- P Stored procedure
- R Rule
- S System table
- TR Trigger
- U User table
- V View
- X Extended stored procedure

SYSPROCEDURES

sysprocedures contains entries for defaults, rules, views, triggers, and stored procedures.

TABLE STRUCTURE

Column	Datatype
type	smallint
id	int
sequence	smallint
status	smallint
number	smallint

INDEX

Unique clustered index on id, number, type, and sequence.

SYSPROTECTS

sysprotects contains user GRANT and REVOKE permissions information.

TABLE STRUCTURE

Column	Datatype
id	int
uid	smallint
action	tinyint
protecttype	tinyint
columns	varbinary(32)

INDEX

Clustered index on id, uid, and action.

SYSPUBLICATIONS

syspublications contains a single entry for each publication posted by the publishing server.

> **Note**
>
> syspublications is new for SQL Server 6.0.

TABLE STRUCTURE

Column	Datatype
description	varchar(255)
name	varchar(30)
repl_freq	tinyint
restricted	bit
status	tinyint
sync_method	tinyint
taskid	int

INDEX

Unique nonclustered index on pubid.

Unique nonclustered index on name.

SYSREFERENCES

sysreferences contains foreign key table mappings to their reference tables.

> **Note**
>
> sysreferences is new for SQL Server 6.0.

TABLE STRUCTURE

Column	Datatype
constid	int
fkeydbid	smallint
rkeyid	int
rkeydbid	smallint
rkeyindid	smallint
keycnt	smallint
fkey1	tinyint
fkey2	tinyint
fkey3	tinyint
fkey4	tinyint
fkey5	tinyint
fkey6	tinyint
fkey7	tinyint
fkey8	tinyint

continues

Column	Datatype
fkey9	tinyint
fkey10	tinyint
fkey11	tinyint
fkey12	tinyint
fkey13	tinyint
fkey14	tinyint
fkey15	tinyint
fkey16	tinyint
rkey1	tinyint
rkey2	tinyint
rkey3	tinyint
rkey4	tinyint
rkey5	tinyint
rkey6	tinyint
rkey7	tinyint
rkey8	tinyint
rkey9	tinyint
rkey10	tinyint
rkey11	tinyint
rkey12	tinyint
rkey13	tinyint
rkey14	tinyint
rkey15	tinyint
rkey16	tinyint

INDEX

Unique clustered index on constid.

Nonclustered index on fkeyid.

Nonclustered index on rkeyid.

SYSSEGMENTS

syssegments contains a single entry for each segment defined.

TABLE STRUCTURE

Column	Datatype
segment	smallint
name	varchar(30)
status	smallint

INDEX

None

SYSSUBSCRIPTIONS

`syssubscriptions` is used to associate published articles with receiving subscription servers.

> **Note**
>
> `syssubscriptions` is new for SQL Server 6.0.

TABLE STRUCTURE

Column	Datatype
artid	int
srvid	smallint
dest_db	varchar(30)
status	tinyint
sync_type	tinyint
timestamp	timestamp

INDEX

Unique nonclustered index on `artid` and `srvid`.

SYSTYPES

`systypes` contains a single entry for all user and system defined data types.

TABLE STRUCTURE

Column	Datatype
uid	smallint
usertype	smallint
variable	bit
allownulls	bit
type	tinyint
length	tinyint
tdefault	int
domain	int

continues

G

Column	Datatype
name	varchar(30)
printfmt	varchar(255)
prec	tinyint
scale	tinyint

Note

The columns prec and scale are new in Version 6.0.

INDEX

Unique clustered index on name.

Unique nonclustered index on usertype.

SYSUSERS

Contains a single row for each user and group allowed to use the database.

TABLE STRUCTURE

Column	Datatype
suid	smallint
uid	smallint
gid	smallint
name	varchar(30)
environ	varchar(255)

INDEX

Unique clustered index on suid.

Unique nonclustered index on name.

Unique nonclustered index on uid.

Object Manager

The Object Manager is graphical object administration tool provided with Version 4.*x* of SQL Server. This tool allows you to manage tables, indexes, stored procedures, and other SQL Server objects.

Note

This appendix is intended to be a point of reference for users who are running a version of SQL Server prior to 6.0. The Object Manager is *not* included with SQL Server 6.0. Use the Enterprise Manager included with SQL Server 6.0 to perform the functions discussed in this appendix.

However, those sites that run SQL Server 4.*x* and SQL Server 6.0 can use the Object Manager to administer a SQL Server 6.0 database. To administer SQL Server 6.0 with the Object Manager, you must run the following script.

```
\SQL60\INSTALL\OBJECT60.SQL
```

STARTING OBJECT MANAGER

To start Object Manager, double-click on the SQL Object Manager icon in the SQL Server for Windows NT (Common) group (see Figure H.1).

Figure H.1.
SQL Object Manager icon.

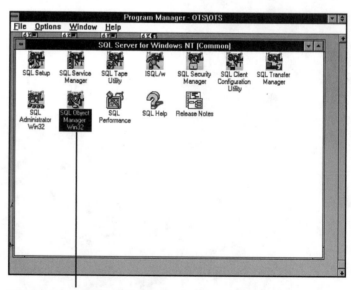

Click here to start Object Manager

CONNECTING TO THE SERVER

Perform the following steps to connect to the server:

1. Double-click on the SQL Object Manager icon in the SQL Server for Windows NT (Common) group. The Microsoft SQL Object Manager and the Connect Server dialog box will appear (see Figure H.2).

*Figure H.2.
Connecting to
SQL Server.*

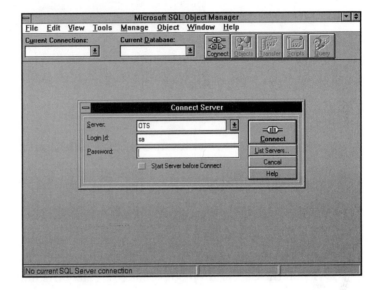

2. To connect to SQL Server, you must enter the server name, login id, and password.

3. Click on the Connect button to connect to the server. The Microsoft SQL Object Manager window appears.

Figure H.3.
Microsoft SQL Object
Manager window.

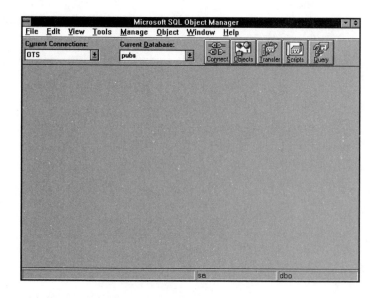

DISCONNECTING FROM SQL SERVER

Perform the following steps to disconnect from SQL Server:

1. From the Microsoft SQL Object Manager window, click on the Connect toolbar button. The Connect Server dialog box appears.
2. From the Server drop-down list box, select the name of the server from which you want to disconnect.
3. Click the Disconnect button (see Figure H.4).

Figure H.4.
Disconnecting from
SQL Server.

BROWSING DATABASE OBJECTS

From the Microsoft SQL Object Manager window, click on the Objects toolbar button. The Database Objects dialog box appears. From here, you can browse all objects that are contained within a database. From this dialog box you can directly edit an object by double-clicking on the object (see Figure H.5).

Figure H.5.
Browsing database
objects.

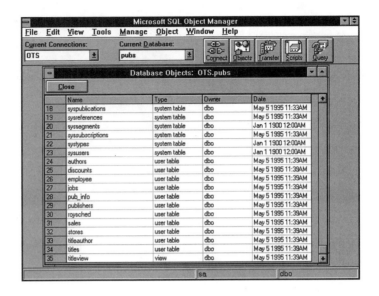

MANAGING TABLES

From the Microsoft SQL Object Manager window, choose Tables from the Manage menu. The Manage Tables dialog box appears (see Figure H.6). From this dialog box, you can create, alter, rename, and drop a table.

Figure H.6.
Managing tables.

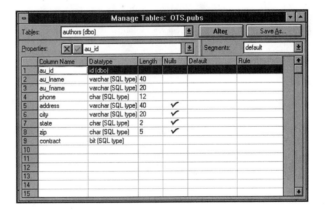

MANAGING INDEXES

From the Microsoft SQL Object Manager window, choose Indexes from the Manage menu. The Manage Indexes dialog box appears (see Figure H.7). From this dialog box, you can create, modify, rename, and drop an index.

Figure H.7.
Managing indexes.

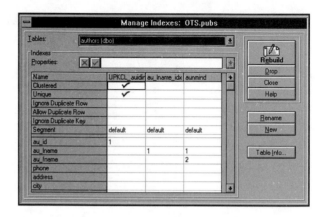

MANAGING STORED PROCEDURES

From the Microsoft SQL Object Manager window, choose Stored Procedures from the Manage menu. The Manage Stored Procedures dialog box appears (see Figure H.8). From this dialog box, you can create and edit stored procedures.

Figure H.8.
Managing stored
procedures.

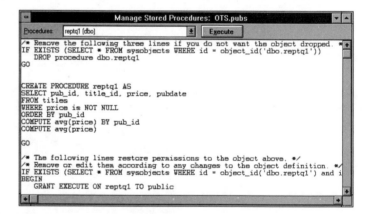

MANAGING OBJECT PERMISSIONS

From the Microsoft SQL Object Manager window, choose Object Permissions from the Object menu. The Object Permissions dialog box appears (see Figure H.9). From this dialog box, you can grant and revoke object permissions.

Figure H.9.
Managing object
permissions.

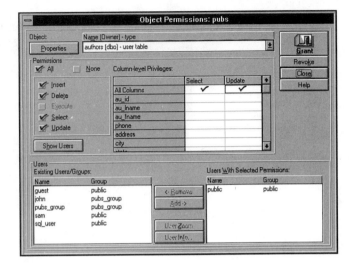

TRANSFERRING DATA

From the Microsoft SQL Object Manager window, click on the Transfer toolbar button. The Transfer Data dialog box appears (see Figure H.10). From this dialog box, you can graphically import and export data.

Figure H.10.
Transferring data.

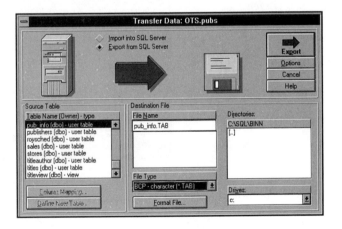

GENERATING SQL SCRIPTS

From the Microsoft SQL Object Manager window, click on the Generate Scripts toolbar button. The Generate SQL Scripts dialog box appears (see Figure H.11). From this dialog box, you can export object definition SQL.

Figure H.11.
The Generate SQL
Scripts dialog box.

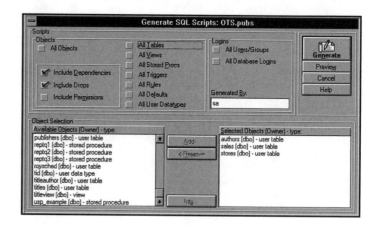

RUNNING QUERIES

From the Microsoft SQL Object Manager window, click on the Query toolbar button.
The Query window appears (see Figure H.12). From this window, you can build and
execute SQL queries.

Figure H.12.
The Generate SQL
Scripts window.

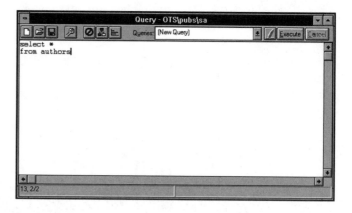

SQL Administrator

The SQL Administrator is a graphical object administration tool provided with Version 4.*x* of SQL Server. This tool allows you to manage devices, databases, logins, remote servers, and server configuration.

Note

This appendix is intended to be a point of reference for users who are running a version of SQL Server prior to 6.0. The SQL Administrator is *not* included with SQL Server 6.0. Use the Enterprise Manager included with SQL Server 6.0 to perform the functions discussed in this appendix.

However, those sites that run SQL Server 4.*x* and SQL Server 6.0 can use the SQL Administrator to administer a SQL Server 6.0 database. To administer SQL Server 6.0 from the SQL Administrator, you must run the following script.

```
\SQL60\INSTALL\ADMIN60.SQL
```

STARTING SQL ADMINISTRATOR

Perform the following steps to start SQL Administrator:

1. Double-click on the SQL Administrator icon in the SQL Server for Windows NT (Common) group (see Figure I.1). The Connect Server dialog box appears. From the Connect dialog box, you must enter the server name, login id, and password.

2. Click on the Connect button in the Connect dialog box to connect to the server (see Figure I.2). The Microsoft SQL Administrator dialog box appears (see Figure I.3).

I

Figure I.1.
SQL Admin-
istrator icon.

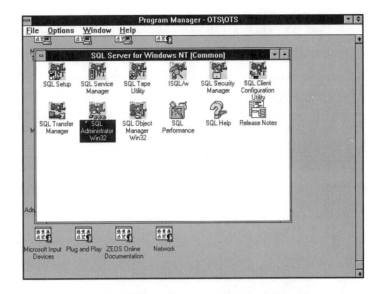

Figure I.2.
Connecting to
SQL Server.

Figure I.3.
Microsoft SQL Admin-
istrator window.

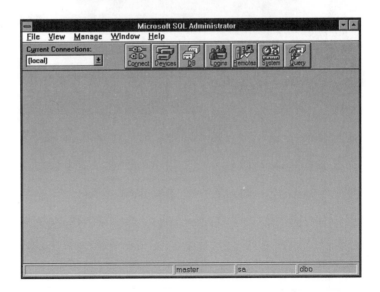

DISCONNECTING FROM SQL SERVER

Perform the following steps to disconnect from SQL Server:

1. From the Microsoft SQL Administrator window, click on the Connect toolbar button. The Connect Server dialog box appears.

2. From the Server drop-down list box, select the name of the server from which you want to disconnect.

3. Click the Disconnect button (see Figure I.4).

Figure I.4.
Disconnecting from
SQL Server.

MANAGING DEVICES

From the Microsoft SQL Administrator window, click on the Devices toolbar button. The Device Management dialog box appears (see Figure I.5). From the Manage menu bar, you can create, drop, and edit devices. Double-clicking on an existing device will display the properties of the selected device.

Figure I.5.
Managing devices.

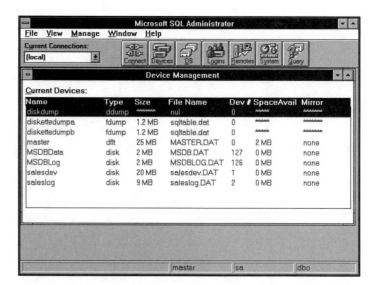

MANAGING DATABASES

From the Microsoft SQL Administrator window, click on the DB toolbar button. The Database Management dialog box appears (see Figure I.6). From the Manage menu bar, you can create, alter, drop, and edit a database.

Figure I.6.
Managing databases.

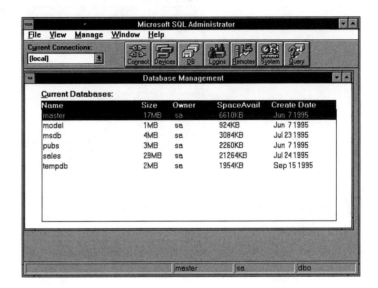

MANAGING LOGINS

From the Microsoft SQL Administrator window, click on the Logins toolbar button. The System Logins Management dialog box appears (see Figure I.7). From the Manage menu bar, you can create, edit, and drop a system login.

Figure I.7.
Managing logins.

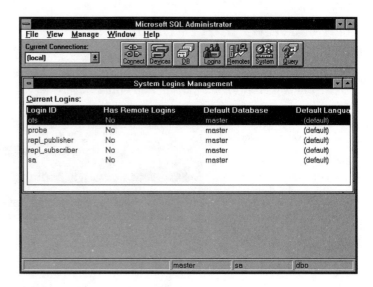

Managing Remote Servers

From the Microsoft SQL Administrator window, click on the Remotes toolbar button. The Remote Server Management dialog box appears (see Figure I.8). From the Manage menu bar, you can create, edit, and drop remote server information.

Figure I.8.
Managing remote servers.

MANAGING SQL SERVER

From the Microsoft SQL Administrator window, click on the System toolbar button. The Sys Options/Active Resources dialog box appears (see Figure I.9). From this dialog box, you can view system processes. The information in this dialog box can also be obtained by using the sp_who system procedure. From the Manage menu bar, you can configure SQL Server and issue DBCC commands.

Figure I.9.
Managing SQL Server.

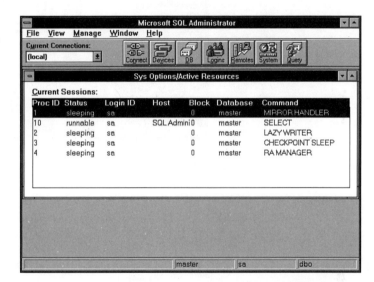

RUNNING QUERIES

From the Microsoft SQL Administrator window, click on the Query toolbar button. The Query window appears (see Figure I.10). From this window, you can create and execute SQL queries.

Figure I.10.
Query window.

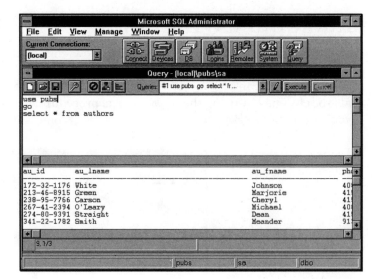

APPENDIX J

What's on the Disc

The following two applications have been included with this book to help you with your database administration tasks:

◆ The SQL Server DBA Assistant
◆ The Database Estimator

THE SQL SERVER DBA ASSISTANT

The SQL Server DBA Assistant is an application written in 32-bit Visual Basic 4.0. Using the SQL Server Assistant you can perform the following tasks:

◆ Estimate the size of memory
◆ Populate a combo box with database names
◆ Perform table maintenance functions, including recalculating space usage, updating statistics, and recompiling references

The SQL Server DBA Assistant source code is included so that you can make your own modifications and enhancements to the application.

Note

The code in the application is discussed in detail in Chapter 25.

Following are the prerequisites for using the SQL Server DBA Assistant:

◆ You must be running Windows NT 3.51 or Windows 95
◆ You must have the following files (included with the SQL Server Client Utilities Installation):

SQLOLE.HLP	SQL-DMO help files, including object hierarchy
SQLOLE.REG	Registry file for SQL-DMO
SQLOLE32.DLL	In-process SQL-DMO server
SQLOLE32.TLB	Type Library for OLE Automation Controllers

INSTALLING SQL SERVER DBA ASSISTANT

To install the SQL Server DBA Assistant, run the executable SETUP.EXE included on the disk.

USING SQL SERVER DBA ASSISTANT

The following steps explain how to use the SQL Server DBA Assistant.

1. To start the SQL Server DBA Assistant, click on the icon installed during setup or run the executable (SAMSDBA.EXE). The Logon dialog box appears (see Figure J.1).

Figure J.1.
Logon dialog box.

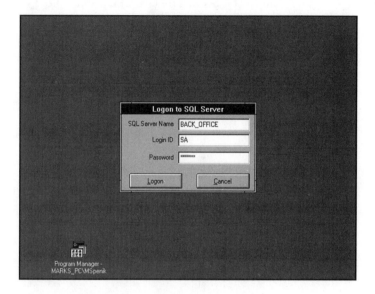

2. Enter the name of the SQL Server to which you want to log on.
3. Enter the Login Id and the password and then click on the Logon button. An attempt will be made to connect to SQL Server. If the logon is successful, a splash screen will appear onscreen, followed by the SQL Server DBA dialog box (see Figure J.2).

Figure J.2.
The Memory Estima-
tion tab in the SQL
Server DBA Assistant
dialog box.

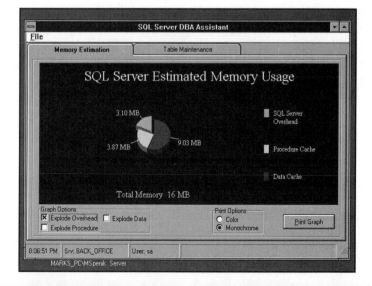

The Memory Estimation Tab displays the estimated memory amounts for SQL Server overhead, procedure cache, and the data cache. The values graphed are only an estimate and are based on memory calculation formulas found in the book. The Graph Options allow you to explode any of the specified memory breakouts from the pie chart. The print options determine how the graph will be printed when the Print Graph button is clicked.

4. To perform table maintenance, click the Table Maintenance tab (see Figure J.3).

Figure J.3.
The Table Mainten-
ance tab in the SQL
Server DBA Assistant
dialog box.

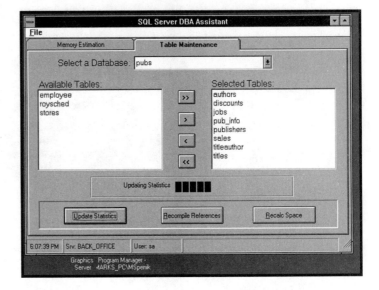

5. You can select a database from the combo box. To select a table, click on the table. To move a table from the Available Tables list box to the Selected Tables list box, click the > button. The < button moves the selected table from the Selected Tables list box to the Available Tables list box. The >> and << buttons move all the tables.

6. To perform table maintenance, click on the appropriate button. The selected function will be performed on all selected databases. Any error messages or results returned from SQL Server will be displayed.

ESTIMATOR

by Paul Galaspie

Tired of manually calculating space requirements? (See Figure J.4.)

Figure J.4.
Manual Calculation.

```
.          Calculate the data row size:
4          (Overhead)
+100       Sum of bytes in all fixed-length columns
+50        Sum of bytes in all variable-length columns
___
154        Subtotal
154        Subtotal
+1         (Subtotal / 256) 1 (Overhead)
+3         Number of variable-length columns 1
+2         (Overhead)
___
160        Data row size
2.         Calculate the number of data pages:
2016 / 160 = 12 Data rows per page
9,00,000 / 12 = 750,000 Data pages
3.         Calculate the size of clustered index rows:
5          Overhead
+4         Sum of bytes in the fixed-length index keys
___
9          Clustered index row size
4.         Calculate the number of clustered index pages:
(2016 / 9) - 2 = 222 Clustered index rows per page
750,000 / 222 = 3378 Index pages (Level 0)
3378 / 222 = 15 Index pages (level 1)
15 / 222 = 1 Index page (Level 2)
5.         Calculate the total number of pages:
Totals:  Pages      Rows
Level 2  (root)     1          15
Level 1  15         3,378
Level 0  3,378      750,000
Data     750,000    9,000,000
3/4----
Total number of 2K pages 753,394
```

Let the Estimator automatically calculate database space requirements!

The following sections discuss some of the features of the Estimator product.

AUTOMATIC SPACE CALCULATION

Are you creating a new database and you need to determine how much space is needed to store the data? Do you have an existing database and you need to predict future space requirements?

The Estimator is designed to help a DBA determine the amount of storage space required for a new or existing table (and associated indexes). The Estimator enables you to perform this type of analysis without have to resort to complicated formulas (see Figure J.5).

Figure J.5.
Automatic space
calculation.

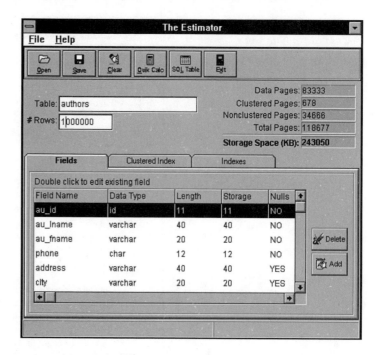

SQL SERVER CONNECTIVITY

Have you already created a table and you need to determine future table size? The Estimator can connect to SQL Server (through ODBC) and load table definitions into the Estimator (see Figure J.6). Loading existing table definitions is useful for determining the impact on storage requirements prior to making modifications, such as adding new fields and/or indexes.

Figure J.6.
Reading a table
in SQL Server.

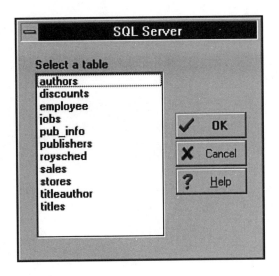

QUICK CALCULATOR

Use the Quick Calculator to get a rough estimate of storage space requirements without having to resort to field level definitions (see Figure J.7). Just enter overall column size, overall index size, and number of rows. Click on the Calculate button and you will have your answer.

Figure J.7.
The Quick Calculator.

SAVES ESTIMATES

Do you need to save an estimate for future use? No problem! Just click on the Save
button (see Figure J.8).

Figure J.8.
Saving an estimate.

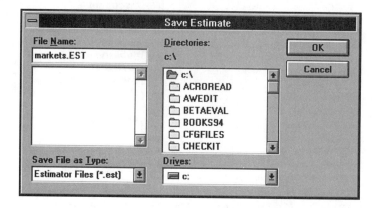

Index

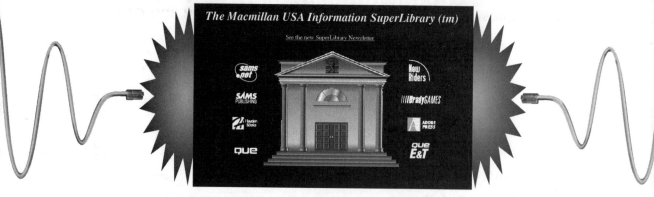

Add to Your Sams Library Today with the Best Books for Programming, Operating Systems, and New Technologies

The easiest way to order is to pick up the phone and call

1-800-428-5331

between 9:00 a.m. and 5:00 p.m. EST.
For faster service please have your credit card available.

ISBN	Quantity	Description of Item	Unit Cost	Total Cost
0-672-30860-6		Windows NT Server Survival Guide (Book/CD-ROM)	$49.99	
0-672-30685-9		Windows NT Unleashed, 2E	$39.99	
0-672-30840-1		Understanding Local Area Networks	$29.99	
0-672-30717-0		Tricks of the Doom Programming Gurus (Book/CD-ROM)	$39.99	
0-672-30714-6		The Internet Unleashed, 2E	$35.00	
0-672-30737-5		The World Wide Web Unleashed, 2E	$39.99	
0-672-30706-5		Programming Microsoft Office (Book/CD-ROM)	$49.99	
0-672-30474-0		Windows 95 Unleashed (Book/CD-ROM)	$39.99	
0-672-30602-6		Programming Windows 95 Unleashed (Book/CD-ROM)	$49.99	
0-672-30791-X		Peter Norton's Complete Guide to Windows 95	$29.99	
1-57521-014-2		Teach Yourself Web Publishing with HTML in 14 Days	$39.99	
1-57521-005-3		Teach Yourself More Web Publishing with HTML in a Week	$29.99	
0-672-30745-6		HTML & CGI Unleashed	$49.99	
		Shipping and Handling: See information below.		
		TOTAL		

❏ 3 ½" Disk

❏ 5 ¼" Disk

Shipping and Handling: $4.00 for the first book, and $1.75 for each additional book. Floppy disk: add $1.75 for shipping and handling. If you need to have it NOW, we can ship product to you in 24 hours for an additional charge of approximately $18.00, and you will receive your item overnight or in two days. Overseas shipping and handling adds $2.00 per book and $8.00 for up to three disks. Prices subject to change. Call for availability and pricing information on latest editions.

201 W. 103rd Street, Indianapolis, Indiana 46290

1-800-428-5331 — Orders   1-800-835-3202 — FAX   1-800-858-7674 — Customer Service

Book ISBN 0-672-30797-9

CD-ROM Installation

What's on the Disc

The companion CD-ROM contains software developed by the authors and an assortment of third-party tools and product demos. The disc is designed to be explored with a browser program. Using the Sams Publishing Guide to the CD-ROM browser, you can view information concerning products and companies, and you can install programs with a single click of the mouse. To install the browser, follow the instructions described below.

WINDOWS 95 INSTALLATION INSTRUCTIONS

1. Insert the CD-ROM disc into your CD-ROM drive. If the AutoPlay feature of your Windows 95 system is enabled, the setup program will start automatically.
2. If the setup program does not start automatically, double-click the My Computer icon.
3. Double-click the icon representing your CD-ROM drive.
4. Double-click the icon titled Setup.exe to run the installation program. Follow the onscreen instructions that appear. When Setup ends, the Guide to the CD-ROM program starts up, so that you can begin browsing immediately.

WINDOWS 3.1 INSTALLATION INSTRUCTIONS

1. Insert the disc into your CD-ROM drive.
2. From File Manager or Program Manager, choose Run from the File menu.
3. Type `<drive>\setup` and press Enter, where `<drive>` corresponds to the drive letter of your CD-ROM. For example, if your CD-ROM is drive D:, type `D:\setup` and press Enter.
4. Installation creates a Program Manager group named "SQL Server DBA." To browse the CD-ROM, double-click the Guide to the CD-ROM icon inside this Program Manager group.

Following installation, you can restart the Guide to the CD-ROM program by clicking the Start button and selecting Programs, then SQL Server DBA and Guide to the CD-ROM.

Note

The Guide to the CD-ROM program requires at least 256 colors. For best results, set your monitor to display between 256 and 64,000 colors. A screen resolution of 640 × 480 pixels is also recommended. If necessary, adjust your monitor settings before you use the CD-ROM.